WITHDRAWN
UTSA LIBRARIES

HISTORY
OF THE
CATHOLIC CHURCH
FROM
THE RENAISSANCE TO THE
FRENCH REVOLUTION

HISTORY

OF THE

CATHOLIC CHURCH

FROM THE RENAISSANCE TO
THE FRENCH REVOLUTION

BY

REV. JAMES MacCAFFREY

VOLUME I

 BOOKS FOR LIBRARIES PRESS
FREEPORT, NEW YORK

First Published 1915
Reprinted 1970

Nihil Obstat:
THOMAS O'DONNELL, C.M.
CENSOR THEOL. DEPUT.

Imprimi Potest:
✠ GULIELMUS,
ARCHIEP. DUBLINEN.,
HIBERNIÆ PRIMAS.

DUBLINI, 16 *Decembris*, 1914

INTERNATIONAL STANDARD BOOK NUMBER:
0-8369-5531-5

LIBRARY OF CONGRESS CATALOG CARD NUMBER:
75-130558

PRINTED IN THE UNITED STATES OF AMERICA

PREFACE

THE fifteenth century may be regarded as a period of transition from the ideals of the Middle Ages to those of modern times. The world was fast becoming more secular in its tendencies, and, as a necessary result, theories and principles that had met till then with almost universal acceptance in literature, in art, in education, and in government, were challenged by many as untenable.

Scholasticism, which had monopolised the attention of both schools and scholars since the days of St. Anselm and Abelard, was called upon to defend its claims against the advocates of classical culture; the theocratico-imperial conception of Christian society as expounded by the canonists and lawyers of an earlier period was forced into the background by the appearance of nationalism and individualism, which by this time had become factors to be reckoned with by the ecclesiastical and civil rulers; the Feudal System, which had received a mortal blow by the intermingling of the classes and the masses in the era of the Crusades, was threatened, from above, by the movement towards centralisation and absolutism, and from below, by the growing discontent of the peasantry and artisans, who had begun to realise, but as yet only in a vague way, their own strength. In every department the battle for supremacy was being waged between the old and the new, and the printing-press was at hand to enable the patrons of both to mould the thoughts and opinions of the Christian world.

It was, therefore, an age of unrest and of great intellectual activity, and at all such times the claims of the Church as the guardian and expounder of Divine Revelation are sure to be questioned. Not that the Church has need to fear inquiry, or that the claims of faith and reason are incompatible, but because some daring spirits are always to be reckoned with, who, by mistaking hypotheses for facts, succeed in convincing themselves and their followers that those in authority are unprogressive, and as such, to be despised.

This was particularly true of some of the Humanists. At first sight, indeed, it is difficult to understand why the revival of classical learning should lead to the danger of the rejection of Christian Revelation, seeing that the Catholic Church has shown at all times such a practical appreciation of the great literary products of Greece and Rome, and that, even in the days of the Renaissance, the Popes and the bishops were reckoned amongst the most generous patrons of the classical movement. Yet the violence of extreme partisans on both sides rendered a conflict almost unavoidable.

On the one hand, many of the classical enthusiasts, not content with winning for their favourite studies a most important place on the programmes of the schools, were determined to force on the Christian body the ideals, the culture, and the outlook on the world, which found their best expression in the masterpieces of pagan literature; while, on the other, not a few of the champions of Scholastic Philosophy seemed to have convinced themselves that Scholasticism and Christianity were identified so closely that rejection or criticism of the former must imply disloyalty to the latter. The Humanists mocked at the Scholastics and dubbed them obscurantists on account of their barbarous Latinity, their uncritical methods, and their pointless wranglings; the Scholastics retorted by denouncing their opponents as pagans, or, at least, heretics. In this way the claims of religion were drawn into the arena, and, as neither the extreme Scholastics nor the extreme Humanists had learned to distinguish between dogmas and systems, between what was essential and what was tentative, there was grave danger that religion would suffer in the eyes of educated men on account of the crude methods of those who claimed to be its authorised exponents.

Undoubtedly, at such a period of unrest, the Church could hardly expect to escape attack. Never since the days when she was called upon to defend her position against the combined forces of the Pagan world had she been confronted with such a serious crisis, and seldom, if ever, was she so badly prepared to withstand the onslaughts of her enemies. The residence at Avignon, the Great Western Schism, and the conciliar theories to which the Schism gave rise, had weakened the power of the Papacy at the very time when the bonds of religious unity were being strained almost to the snapping point by the growth of national jealousy. Partly owing to the general downward tendency of the age, but mainly on account of the interference of the secular authorities with ecclesiastical appointments, the gravest abuses had manifested themselves in nearly every department of clerical life, and the cry for reform rose unbidden to the lips of thousands who entertained no thought of revolution. But the distinction between the divine and the human element in the Church was not appreciated by all, with the result that a great body of Christians, disgusted with the unworthiness of some of their pastors, were quite ready to rise in revolt whenever a leader should appear to sound the trumpet-call of war.

Nor had they long to wait till a man arose, in Germany, to marshal the forces of discontent and to lead them against the Church of Rome. Though in his personal conduct Luther fell far short of what people might reasonably look for in a self-constituted reformer, yet in many respects he had exceptional qualifications for the part that he was called upon to play. Endowed with great physical strength, gifted with a marvellous memory and a complete mastery of the German language, as inspiring in the pulpit or on the platform as he was with his pen, regardless of nice limitations or even of truth when he wished to strike down an opponent or to arouse the enthusiasm of a mob equally at home with princes in the drawing-room as with peasants in a tavern—Luther was an ideal demagogue to head a semi-religious, semi-social revolt. He had a keen appreciation of the tendencies of the age, and of the thoughts that were coursing through men's minds, and he had sufficient powers of organisation to know how to direct the different forces at work into the same channel. Though fundamentally the issue raised by him was a religious one, yet it is remarkable what a small part religion played in deciding the result of the struggle. The world-wide jealousy of the House of Habsburg, the danger of a Turkish invasion, the long-drawn-out struggle between France and the Empire for supremacy in Europe and for the provinces on the left bank of the Rhine, and the selfish policy of the German princes, contributed much more to his success than the question of justification or the principle of private judgment. Without doubt, in Germany, in Switzerland, in England, in the Netherlands, and in the Scandinavian countries, the Reformation was much more a political than a religious movement.

The fundamental principle of the new religion was the principle of private judgment, and yet such a principle found no place in the issues raised by Luther in the beginning. It was only when he was confronted with the decrees of previous councils, with the tradition of the Church as contained in the writings of the Fathers, and with the authoritative pronouncements of the Holy See, all of which were in direct contradiction to his theories, that he felt himself obliged, reluctantly, to abandon the principle of authority in favour of the principle of private judgment. In truth it was the only possible way in which he could hope to defend his novelties, and besides, it had the additional advantage of catering for the rising spirit of individualism, which was so characteristic of the age.

His second great innovation, so far as the divine constitution of the Church was concerned, and the one which secured ultimately whatever degree of success his revolution attained, was the theory of royal supremacy, or the recognition of the temporal ruler as the source of spiritual jurisdiction. But even this was more or less of an after-thought. Keen student of contemporary politics that Luther was, he perceived two great influences at work, one, patronised by the sovereigns in favour of absolute rule, the other, supported by the masses in favour of unrestricted liberty. He realised from the beginning that it was only by combining his religious programme with one or other of these two movements that he could have any hope of success. At first, impressed by the strength of the popular party as manifested in the net-work of secret societies then spread throughout Germany, and by the revolutionary attitude of the landless nobles, who were prepared to lead the peasants, he determined to raise the cry of civil and religious liberty, and to rouse the masses against the princes and kings, as well as against the bishops and the Pope. But soon the success of the German princes in the Peasants' War made it clear to him that an alliance between the religious and the social revolution was fraught with dangerous consequences; and, at once, he went to the other extreme.

The gradual weakening of the Feudal System, which acted as a check upon the authority of the rulers, and the awakening of the national consciousness prepared the way for the policy of centralisation. France, which consisted formerly of a collection of almost independent provinces, was welded together into one united kingdom; a similar change took place in Spain after the union of Castile and Aragon and the fall of the Moorish power at Granada. In England the disappearance of the nobles in the Wars of the Roses led to the establishment of the Tudor domination. As a result of this centralisation the Kings of France, Spain, and England, and the sovereign princes of Germany received a great increase of power, and resolved to make themselves absolute masters in their own dominions.

Having abandoned the unfortunate peasants who had been led to slaughter by his writings, Luther determined to make it clear that his religious policy was in complete harmony with the political absolutism aimed at by the temporal rulers. With this object in view he put forward the principle of royal supremacy, according to which the king or prince was to be recognised as the head of the church in his own territories, and the source of all spiritual jurisdiction. By doing so he achieved two very important results. He had at hand in the machinery of civil government the nucleus of a new ecclesiastical organisation, the shaping of which had been his greatest worry; and, besides, he won for his new movement the sympathy and active support of the civil rulers, to whom the thought of becoming complete masters of ecclesiastical patronage and of the wealth of the Church opened up the most rosy prospects. In Germany, in England, and in the northern countries of Europe, it was the principle of royal supremacy that turned the scales eventually in favour of the new religion, while, at the same time, it led to the establishment of absolutism both in theory and practice. From the recognition of the sovereign as supreme master both in Church and State the theory of the divine rights of kings as understood in modern times followed as a necessary corollary. There was no longer any possibility of suggesting limitations or of countenancing rebellion. The king, in his own territories, had succeeded to all the rights and privileges which, according to the divine constitution of the Church, belonged to the Pope.

Such a development in the Protestant countries could not fail to produce its effects even on Catholic rulers

PREFACE   xiii

who had remained loyal to the Church. They began to aim at combining, as far as possible, the Protestant theory of ecclesiastical government with obedience to the Pope, by taking into their own hands the administration of ecclesiastical affairs, by making the bishops and clergy state-officials, and by leaving to the Pope only a primacy of honour. This policy, known under the different names of Gallicanism in France, and of Febronianism and Josephism in the Empire, led of necessity to conflicts between Rome and the Catholic sovereigns of Europe, conflicts in which, unfortunately, many of the bishops, influenced by mistaken notions of loyalty and patriotism, took the side of their own sovereigns. As a result, absolute rule was established throughout Europe; the rights of the people to any voice in the government were trampled upon, and the rulers became more despotic than the old Roman Emperors had been even in their two-fold capacity of civil ruler and high priest.

Meanwhile, the principle of private judgment had produced its logical effects. Many of Luther's followers, even in his own life-time, had been induced to reject doctrines accepted by their master, but, after his death, when the influence of Tradition and of authority had become weaker, Lutheranism was reduced to a dogmatic chaos. By the application of the principle of private judgment, certain leaders began to call in question, not merely individual doctrines, but even the very foundations of Christianity, and, in a short time, Atheism and

Naturalism were recognised as the hall-mark of education and of good breeding.

The civil rulers even in Catholic countries took no very active steps to curb the activity of the anti-Christian writers and philosophers, partly because they themselves were not unaffected by the spirit of irreligion, and partly also because they were not sorry to see popular resentment diverted from their own excesses by being directed against the Church. But, in a short time, they realised, when it was too late, that the overthrow of religious authority carries with it as a rule the overthrow of civil authority also, and that the attempt to combine the two principles of private judgment and of royal supremacy must lead of necessity to revolution.

. . . .

I wish to express my sincere thanks to the many friends who have assisted me, and particularly to the Very Rev. Thomas O'Donnell, C.M., President, All Hallows College. My special thanks are due also to the Rev. Patrick O'Neill (Limerick), who relieved me of much anxiety by undertaking the difficult task of compiling the Index.

JAMES MacCAFFREY.

St. Patrick's College, Maynooth,
   Feast of the Immaculate Conception.

CONTENTS OF VOL. I

CHAPTER I

CAUSES OF THE REFORMATION

(a) The Renaissance
PAGE

Scholasticism—Revival of Classical Studies in Italy—Dante—Petrarch—Boccaccio—Extreme and moderate Humanists—Attitude of the Popes to the Humanist movement—Nicholas V and Leo X—The Renaissance in Germany—Ulrich von Hutten—Reuchlin—*Epistolæ virorum obscurorum*—Erasmus—Humanism in France—Paris University—The Humanist movement in England—In Spain—General effects of Humanism in Europe 1–29

(b) Political and Social Condition of Europe

The decay of Feudalism and the tendency towards centralisation—Discontent of the lower classes—Effects of the new political movement on the Church 29–34

(c) The Religious Condition of Europe.

Evil effects of the Great Western Schism—The authority of General Councils—Humanist and Political Popes—The Concordat of 1516—Papal taxation—Abuses in regard to Benefices—The religious condition of the Secular and Regular Clergy—General clamour for reform in the Church—Councils of Constance and Basle—Inactivity of the Popes—The Fifth Lateran Council 34–53

CHAPTER II

THE RELIGIOUS REVOLUTION
LUTHERANISM AND ZWINGLIANISM

(a) In Germany

PAGE

Martin Luther — Education and theological studies—Becomes Professor at Wittenberg—His views about Faith and Justification—His *Theses* against Indulgences — Eck's *Obelisks* — Disputation at Leipzig—Attitude of Leo X—The Augsburg inquiry—The Bull, *Cum postquam*—Mission of Miltitz — Election of Charles V—Luther's final rupture with Rome—The Bull, *Exsurge Domine*—The Diet of Worms—Imperial decree against Luther—Theological system of Luther—Faith and Justification—The Anabaptists—Luther's appeal to the lower classes—Peasant Rebellions—Organisation of Lutheran Church—The Diet of Nürenberg—Efforts of the Popes for peace—Political alliances in Germany—Strife between Emperor and Pope—The *Augsburg Confession*—Efforts for reunion—The Peace of Nürenberg—Progress of Lutheranism—Holy League formed—The *Ratisbon Interim*—Moral state of princes and people—Luther's character and ability — War between Emperor and Protestant Princes—The *Augsburg Interim*—War—Peace of Augsburg—Charles V 54–110

(b) Zwingli in Switzerland : His attitude towards Lutheranism

Political and Religious condition of Switzerland—Zwingli—His influence in Zurich—His rupture with the Church—His doctrine — Oecolampadius — Religious revolt in Basle—Opposition between urban and rural cantons—Peace of Kappel—Lutheran and Zwinglian doctrine on the Eucharist 110–24

(c) Northern Europe

Political state of Denmark—Lutheranism favoured by Kings—Reformation introduced by force—The Reformation in Norway and Iceland—Political and religious condition of Sweden—Gustavus Vasa introduces Lutheranism—Calvinism introduced—Efforts of John III for Catholic revival—Reaction in favour of Lutheranism—Deposition of Sigismund 124–39

CONTENTS

CHAPTER III

PROGRESS OF CALVINISM

(a) *In Switzerland*

PAGE

Calvin—His career in Geneva—Theodore Beza—Doctrine of Calvinism 140–49

(b) *Calvinism in France*

Religious condition of France before the Reformation—Alliance of Francis I with German Protestant Princes—Heretical sects in South of France—Catharine de' Medici—Huguenot conspiracies—Spread of Calvinism in the South—Civil Wars—Charles IX favours Huguenots—Massacre of St. Bartholomew—New Civil Wars—Struggle for the French throne—Edict of Nantes—Policy of Louis XIV 150–69

(c) *Calvinism in the Netherlands*

Policy of Charles V in the Netherlands—Discontent under Philip II—*Les Gueux*—Calvinism gaining ground—Regency of Duke of Alva—Calvinism in the Northern Provinces—Southern Provinces remain loyal to Spain—Universities founded 169–77

CHAPTER IV

THE COUNTER-REFORMATION

The success of Protestantism due mainly to political causes—Reaction in favour of Catholicism . . 178–80

(a) *The Council of Trent*

The desire for reform—Reasons for its delay—Policy of Clement VII—Convocation of Council of Trent—Preliminary Sessions—Doctrine regarding Tradition, Scripture, Original Sin, Justification—Removal of Council to Bologna—Reconvocation by Julius III—Decrees about the Eucharist—Suspension of the Council—Policy of Paul IV—Reconvocation of Council by Pius IV—Remaining Sessions—Controversies—Further decrees—Importance of the Council of Trent—Disciplinary reforms—Education of the clergy—Decrees enforced by Pius IV—Catechism of the Council 180–202

CONTENTS

(b) The Reforming Activity of the Popes

Foundations of religious revival laid—Efforts of Pius IV and Pius V—Battle of Lepanto—Many Colleges founded—Gregorian Calendar—Administrative ability of Sixtus V—Roman Curia organised—Clement VIII—Paul V—Missionary activity of Gregory XV—Urban VIII—Innocent X 202-18

(c) The Religious Orders and the Counter-Reformation

Religious Orders—The Benedictines—Dominicans—Franciscans—Theatines—Barnabites—Oblates of St. Charles Borromeo—Oratorians—Brothers of Charity—Piarists—Brothers of the Christian Schools—Vincentians—Sulpicians—Society of Jesus—Sisters of Charity—Institute of Mary 218-42

(d) The Thirty Years' War

The *Ecclesiasticum Reservatum*—Cologne and Aachen—Indifference of Emperors—Catholic Revival—The *Union* and the *League*—Trouble in Bohemia—Peace of Lübeck—*Edict of Restitution*—Gustavus Adolphus—Peace of Westphalia—Its religious and historical importance 242-57

CHAPTER V

CATHOLIC MISSIONS

New fields for missionaries—Work of St. Francis Xavier in India and Japan—Father de' Nobili—The *Malabar Rites*—Jesuit Missionaries—Controversy about the *Chinese Rites* — Persecutions in Japan — African Missions—Missions in West Indies, Central and South America—Missions in North America . . . 258-75

CHAPTER VI

THEOLOGICAL CONTROVERSIES AND STUDIES

(a) Baianism

Doctrinal views of Baius—Papal condemnation of these views 276-80

(b) The Molinist Controversy

The controversy in Louvain and in Spain—Molina and Bañez—The points of dispute—*Congregatio de Auxiliis* 280-84

(c) Jansenism

Jansen's education—*Augustinus*—Jansenist views on Grace, and on the Eucharist—Papal Condemnations—Pascal's *Lettres Provinciales*—The *Clementine Peace* . . 284-91

CONTENTS

(d) The Immaculate Conception

Repeated confirmations of the doctrine—Declared to be the common belief of the Church 291–93

(e) Tyrannicide

The question of its lawfulness—Views of Petit and Falkenberg—Luther's teaching—Mariana's book . . 293–95

(f) The Copernican System. Galileo Galilei

View of Copernicus about solar system—*De Revolutionibus Orbium Coelestium*—Galileo's teaching condemned—Trial of Galileo 295–99

(g) Progress of Theological Studies

Impetus given to study of Theology—Many able scholars and theological authors—Ascetical writings—Scriptural Studies—Ecclesiastical History . . . 299–308

CHAPTER VII

THE AGE OF ABSOLUTISM AND UNBELIEF
NEW CONTROVERSIES AND ERRORS

Political and intellectual results of the Reformation . 309–11

(a) Gallicanism

The beginnings of Gallicanism—Concordat of 1516—Richer's views on the Church—Louis XIV—Defence of Papacy by Sorbonne—*Regalia*—Conflicts between King and Pope—Gallican Liberties—Schism threatened—Reconciliation of Louis XIV with Pope—Gallicanism lingering until 1869 311–22

(b) Febronianism and Josephism

Gallicanism in the Empire—Views of Febronius adopted by Emperors—Failure of policy of Joseph II—The *Punctuation of Ems*—Submission of Prince-Bishops—Febronianism in Tuscany—Scipio Ricci . . . 323–31

(c) Jansenism

Jansenism after the *Clementine Peace*—Quesnel's *Réflexions Morales*—The Bulls, *Vineam Domini* and *Unigenitus*—The *Appellants*—Jansenists protected by the Parliament of Paris—Decline of Jansenism—Jansenism in Holland 331–39

(d) Quietism

Quietism of Molinos—Madame Guyon's Semi-Quietism—Controversy between Bossuet and Fénelon . . 339–44

CHAPTER VIII

RATIONALISM AND ITS EFFECTS

(a) *Anti-Christian Philosophy of the Eighteenth Century*

The Principles of the Reformation—Rationalism in England and in France—Voltaire and Rousseau—The Encyclopædists 345–51

(b) *The Aufklärung Movement in Germany*

The Philosophy of Leibniz—Christian Wolf—Kant's influence on religious thought—The new rationalist Theology in Germany 351–57

(c) *Freemasonry*

The rise of Freemasonry—Its aims—Papal condemnations of the society of Freemasons 357–60

(d) *The Suppression of the Society of Jesus*

The success of the Jesuits against the Reformation—Opponents of the Society—Persecution of the Jesuits in Portugal and in France—The Jesuits in Spain—Suppression of the Society by Clement XIV . 360–71

(e) *Failure of Attempts at Re-Union. Protestant Sects*

Formation of new Protestant Sects—Attempts at re-union in Germany—Opposition between Lutherans and Calvinists—Domestic controversies of the Lutherans—Calvinist controversies—*Anabaptists—Schwenkfeldians—Socinianism — Pietism — Herrnhuters — Swedenborgians* 371–88

CHAPTER IX

THE PAPACY

Position of the Papacy after 1648—Attacks on Papal Supremacy—Alexander VII—Innocent XII—Clement XI—Benedict XIV—Clement XIV—Pius VI . 389–403

CHAPTER X

THEOLOGICAL STUDIES. RELIGIOUS LIFE

Decline of theological studies—Theological Writers—Theory of Probabilism — St. Alphonsus — Biblical studies—Historical Theology—Canon Law—Preaching—New systems of Philosophy—The Redemptorists and Passionists 404–19

History of the Catholic Church

FROM THE RENAISSANCE TO THE FRENCH REVOLUTION

CHAPTER I

CAUSES OF THE REFORMATION.

(a) THE RENAISSANCE.

Baudrillart, *The Catholic Church, The Renaissance, and Protestantism* (*Tr.*), 1908 (chap. i.-iii.). Guiraud, *L'Église et les Origines de la Renaissance*, 1902. Burckhardt, *Die Cultur der Renaissance in Italien*, 11 auf., 1913 (*Eng. Trans.* by Middlemore, 1878). A Baumgartner, S.J., *Geschichte der Weltliteratur*, vol. iv., 1900. *The Cambridge Modern History*, vol. i. (*The Renaissance*, 1902). Stone, *The Reformation and Renaissance*, 1904. Janssen, *Geschichte des deutschen Volkes*, 1887 (*Eng. Trans.* by Mitchell and Christie, London, 1896 *sqq.*). Pastor, *Geschichte der Päpste im Zeitalter der Renaissance*, Freiburg, 1886 *sqq.* (*Eng. Trans.* by Antrobus, London, 1891 *sqq.*). Müntz, *La Renaissance en Italie et en France à l'époque de Charles VIII.*, 1885. Gasquet, *The Eve of the Reformation*. Mourret, *La Renaissance et la Réforme*, 1912.

THE great intellectual revival, that followed upon the successful issue of the struggle for freedom waged by Gregory VII. and his successors, reached the zenith of its glory in the thirteenth century. Scholasticism, as expounded by men like Alexander of Hales, Albert the Great, Roger Bacon, St. Bonaventure, and St. Thomas, and illustrated by a wealth of material drawn alike from the Scriptures, the writings of the Fathers, the wisdom of Pagan philosophers, and the conclusions of natural science, was alone deemed worthy of serious attention. Classical studies either were neglected entirely even in the centres of learning, or were followed merely for the assistance they might render in the solution of the philosophical and theological problems, that engaged men's minds in an age when Christian faith reigned supreme.

The Catholic Church, indeed, had never been hostile to classical studies, nor unmindful of their value, as a means of developing the powers of the human mind, and of securing both breadth of view and beauty of expression. Some few teachers here and there, alarmed by the danger of corrupting Christian youth by bringing it into contact with Pagan ideals, raised their voices in protest, but the majority of the early Fathers disregarded these warnings as harmful and unnecessary. Origen, St. Clement of Alexandria, St. Gregory of Nazianzen, St. Basil, and St. Jerome, while not ignoring the dangers of such studies, recommended them warmly to their students, and in the spirit of these great leaders the Catholic Church strove always to combine classical culture and Christian education.

With the fall of the Empire, consequent upon its invasion by the barbarian hordes, classical studies were banished to some extent to the Western Isles, Ireland and Britain, from which they were transplanted to the Continent principally during the Carlovingian revival.* In the cathedral, collegiate, and monastic schools the classics were still cultivated, though beyond doubt compilations were used more frequently than were the original works; and even in the darkest days of the dark ages some prominent ecclesiastics could be found well versed at least in the language and literature of Rome. It looked, too, for a time, as if the intellectual revival of the twelfth century were to be turned towards the classics; but the example of men like John of Salisbury was not followed generally, and the movement developed

---

* Sandys, *History of Classical Scholarship*, 2nd edition, 1906. Rogers, *L'Enseignement des lettres classiques d'Ausone à Alcuin*, 1905. Gougaud, *Les Chrétientés Celtiques*, 1911, chap. viii. (An excellent bibliography.) Esposito, *Greek in Ireland during the Middle Ages* (*Studies*, i., 4, 665-683).

rapidly in the direction of philosophy. As a consequence, the study of Latin was neglected or relegated to a secondary place in the schools, while Greek scholarship disappeared practically from Western Europe. The Scholastics, more anxious about the logical sequence of their arguments than about the beauties of literary expression, invented for themselves a new dialect, which, however forcible in itself, must have sounded barbarous to any one acquainted with the productions of the golden age of Roman literature or even with the writings of the early Fathers of the Latin Church. Nor was it the language merely that was neglected. The monuments and memorials of an earlier civilisation were disregarded, and even in Rome itself, the City of the Popes, the vandalism of the ignorant wrought dreadful havoc.

So complete a turning away from forces that had played such a part in the civilisation of the world was certain to provoke a reaction. Scholasticism could not hold the field for ever to the exclusion of other branches of study, especially, since in the less competent hands of its later expounders it had degenerated into an empty formalism. The successors of St. Thomas and St. Bonaventure had little of their originality, their almost universal knowledge, and their powers of exposition, and, as a result, students grew tired of the endless wranglings of the schools, and turned their attention to other intellectual pursuits.

Besides, men's ideas of politics, of social order, and of religion were changing rapidly, and, in a word, the whole outlook of the world was undergoing a speedy transformation. In the Middle Ages religion held the dominant position and was the guiding principle in morals, in education, in literature, and in art; but as the faith of many began to grow cold, and as the rights of Church and State began to be distinguished, secularist tendencies soon made themselves felt. Philosophy and theology were no longer to occupy the entire intellectual field, and other subjects for investigation must be found. In these circumstances what was more natural than that some should advocate a return to the classics and all that the classics enshrined? Again, the example set by the tyrants who had grasped the reins of power in the Italian States, by men like Agnello of Pisa, the Viscontis and Francesco Sforza of Milan, Ferrante of Naples, and the de' Medici of Florence, was calculated to lower the moral standard of the period, and to promote an abandonment of Christian principles of truth, and justice, and purity of life. Everywhere men became more addicted to the pursuit of sensual pleasure, of vain glory, and material comfort; and could ill brook the dominant ideas of the Middle Ages concerning the supernatural end of man, self-denial, humility, patience, and contempt for the things that minister only to man's temporal happiness. With views of this kind in the air it was not difficult to persuade them to turn to the great literary masterpieces of Pagan Rome, where they were likely to find principles and ideals more in harmony with their tastes than those set before them by the Catholic Church.

The thirteenth, fourteenth, and fifteenth centuries, then, mark a period of transition from the Middle Ages to modern times. They saw a sharp struggle being waged between two ideals in politics, in education, in literature, in religion, and in morality. In this great upheaval that was characterised by a demand for unrestricted liberty of investigation, a return to the study of nature and of the natural sciences, the rise and development of national literatures, and the appearance of a new school of art, the Humanist movement or the revival of the study of the classics, the *literae humaniores*, played the fundamental part. In more senses than one it may be called the Age of the Renaissance.

Nor was it a matter of chance that this revival of interest in classical studies should have made itself felt first in Italy, where the downfall of the Empire, and the subsequent development of petty states seem to have exercised a magical influence upon the intellectual development of the people. The Italians were the direct heirs to the glory of ancient Rome. Even in the days of their degradation, when the capital deserted by the Popes was fast going to ruin, and when foreigners and native tyrants were struggling for the possession of their fairest territories, the memory of the imperial authority of their country, and the crumbling monuments that bore witness to it still standing in their midst, served to turn their patriotic ardour towards the great literary treasures bequeathed to them by Pagan Rome. Greek literature, too, was not forgotten, though in the thirteenth century few western scholars possessed any acquaintance with the language. Many causes, however, combined to prepare the way for a revival of Greek. The commercial cities of Italy were in close touch with the Eastern Empire, especially since the Crusades; ambassadors, sent by the Emperors to seek the assistance of the Pope and of the Western rulers in the struggle against the Turks, were passing from court to court; the negotiations for a reunion of the Churches, which had been going on since the days of the first Council of Lyons, rendered a knowledge of Greek and of the writings of the Greek Fathers necessary for some of the leading ecclesiastics of the West; while, finally, the fall of Constantinople in 1453 forced many Greek scholars to seek a refuge in Italy or France, and provided the agents sent by the Popes and Italian rulers with a splendid opportunity of securing priceless treasures for the Western libraries.

Though Dante (1265-1321) is sometimes regarded as the earliest of the Humanist school* on account of his professed admiration for some of the Pagan masters and of the blending in his *Divina Comedia* of the beauties of Roman literature with the teaching of the Fathers and Scholastics, still, the spirit that inspired him was the spirit of Christianity, and his outlook on life was frankly

* Monnier, *La Renaissance de Dante à Luther*, 1884.

the outlook of the Middle Ages. To Petrarch (1304-74) rather belongs the honour of having been the most prominent, if not the very first writer, whose works were influenced largely by Humanist ideals. Born in Arezzo in 1304, he accompanied his father to Avignon when the latter was exiled from Florence. His friends wished him to study law; but, his poetic tendencies proving too strong for him, he abandoned his professional pursuits to devote his energies to literature. The patronage and help afforded him willingly by the Avignonese Popes* and other ecclesiastics provided him with the means of pursuing his favourite studies, and helped him considerably in his searches for manuscripts of the classics. Though only a cleric in minor orders, he was appointed Canon of Lombez (1335), papal ambassador to Naples (1343), prothonotary apostolic (1346), and archdeacon of Parma (1348). These positions secured to him a competent income, and, at the same time, brought him into touch with libraries and influential men.

The ruin of Italy and Rome, caused in great measure by the absence of the Popes during their residence at Avignon, roused all the patriotic instincts of Petrarch, and urged him to strive with all his might for the restoration of the ancient glory of his country. Hence in his politics he was strongly nationalist, and hence, too, he threw the whole weight of his influence on the side of Cola di Rienzi, when in 1347 the latter proclaimed from the Capitol the establishment of the Roman Republic. Nor did he hesitate to attack the Popes, to whom he was indebted so deeply, for their neglect of Rome and the Papal States, as well as for the evils which he thought had fallen upon Italy owing to the withdrawal of the Popes to Avignon. He himself strove to awaken in the minds of his countrymen memories of the past by forming collections of old Roman coins, by restoring or protecting wherever possible the Pagan monuments, and by searching after and copying manuscripts of the classical

---

* Guiraud, *L'Église et la Renaissance*, chap. iii.

writers. In poetry, Virgil was his favourite guide. As a rule he wrote in Italian, but his writings were saturated with the spirit of the early Pagan authors; while in his pursuit of glory and his love for natural, sensible beauty, he manifested tendencies opposed directly to the self-restraint, symbolism, and purity of the Middle Ages. His longest poem is *Africa,* devoted to a rehearsal of the glories of ancient Rome and breathing a spirit of patriotism and zeal for a long lost culture, but it is rather for his love songs, the *canzoni,* that he is best remembered.

Petrarch, though a Humanist,* was no enemy of the Christian religion, nor did he imagine for a moment that the study of the Pagan classics could prove dangerous in the least degree to revealed religion. It is true that his private life did not always correspond to Christian principles of morality, and it is equally true that at times his patriotism led him to speak harshly of the rule of the Popes in Italy and Rome; but he never wavered in his religious convictions, and never recognised that Pagan literature and ideals should be judged by other than current Christian standards.

The example of Petrarch was not followed, however, by several of the later Humanists. His friend and disciple, Boccaccio (1313-75), imitated his master in his love for the classics and in his zeal for classical culture, and excelled him by acquiring, what Petrarch had failed utterly to acquire, a good knowledge of Greek. Like Petrarch, he was assisted largely by the Popes, and took service at the papal court. But his views of life and morality were coloured by Paganism rather than by Christianity. Many of his minor poems are steeped in indecency and immorality, and reflect only too clearly the tendency to treachery and deceit so characteristic of the Italian rulers of his day; while the *Decameron,* his greatest work, is more like the production of a Pagan writer than of one acquainted with Christian ethics and

* Nolhac, *Pétrarque et l'Humanisme,* 1892.

ideals. He delighted in lampooning the clergy, particularly the monks, charging them with ignorance, immorality and hypocrisy. Such a line of conduct was not likely to recommend the apostles of the new learning to the admirers of Scholasticism, nor to create and foster a friendly alliance between the two camps. Yet, personally, Boccaccio was not an enemy of Christianity, and never aimed, as did some of the later Humanists, at reviving Paganism under the guise of promoting literature. He was unshaken in his acceptance of the Christian revelation, and, as the years advanced, he began to realise the evil of his ways and the dangerous character of his writings. Strange to say, it was to a body of the monks, whom he delighted in attacking, that he bequeathed the valuable library which he had brought together with such labour.

Had the Humanists contented themselves with advocating merely a return to classical studies, and had the Scholastics recognised that philosophy was not the only path to culture, it might have been possible to avoid a conflict. But, unfortunately for religion, there were extremists on both sides. On the one hand, some of the later Humanists, influenced largely by the low moral tone of the age, aimed at nothing less than the revival of Paganism, pure and simple; while, on the other, not a few of the Scholastics insisted strongly that Pagan literature, however perfect, should have no place in Christian education. Between these two conflicting parties stood a large body of educated men, both lay and cleric, who could see no irreconcilable opposition between Christianity and the study of the classics, and who aimed at establishing harmony by assigning to the classics the place in education willingly accorded to them by many of the Fathers of the Church.

But the influence of this latter body could not effect a reconciliation. A large section of the Humanists openly vindicated for themselves freedom from the intellectual and moral restraints imposed by Christianity.

Laurentius Valla * (1405-57) in his work, *De Voluptate*, championed free indulgence in all kinds of sensual pleasures, attacked virginity as a crime against the human race, and ridiculed the idea of continence and self-denial, while in his own life he showed himself a faithful disciple of the Epicurianism that he propounded in his writings. His denunciations, too, of the Popes as the usurping tyrants of Rome in his work on the Constantine Donation were likely to do serious injury to the head of the Church in his spiritual as well as in his temporal capacity. But bad as were the compositions of Valla, they were harmless when compared with the books and pamphlets of Beccadelli, the Panormite, who devoted himself almost exclusively to what was indecent and repulsive. Poggio Bracciolini in his work, *Facetiae*, and Filelfo, though not equally bad, belong to the same category. In the hands of these men the Renaissance had become, to a great extent, a glorification of Pagan immorality. Their books were condemned by many of the religious orders, but without avail. They were read and enjoyed by thousands, in whom the wholesale corruption prevalent in Florence, Siena, and Venice, had deadened all sense of morality.

A large number of the later Renaissance school were Christians only in name. If the great body of them were judged by the heathen figures and phraseology with which their works abound, they could hardly be acquitted of Pagan tendencies; but in case of many of them these excesses are to be attributed to pedantry rather than to defection from the faith. In case of others, however, although they were wary in their expressions lest they might forfeit their positions, Christian teaching seems to have lost its hold upon their minds and hearts. Carlo Marsuppini, Chancellor of Florence, Gemistos Plethon, the well-known exponent of Platonic philosophy, Marsilio Ficino, Rinaldo degli Albizzi, and the members of the Roman Academy (1460), under the

* Mancini, *Vita di Lorenzo Valla*, 1891.

leadership of Pomponius Laetus, were openly Pagan in their lives and writings. Had the men in authority in Italy been less depraved such teaching and example would have been suppressed with firmness; or had the vast body of the people been less sound in their attachment to Christianity, Neo-Paganism would have arisen triumphant from the religious chaos.*

But not all the Humanists belonged to the school of Valla, Beccadelli, Poggio, and Marsuppini. The Camaldolese monk, Ambrogio Traversari, his pupil Giannozzo Manetti (1431-59), a layman thoroughly devoted to the Church, and the first of the Humanists to turn his attention to the Oriental languages, Lionardo Bruni, so long Apostolic Secretary at the papal court and afterwards Chancellor of Florence, Maffeo Vegio (1407-58), the Roman archæologist, who in his work on education endeavoured to combine classical culture with Christian revelation, Vittorino da Feltre, a model in his life and methods for Christian teachers, Pico della Mirandola, Sadoleto, and Bida, were all prominent in the classical revival, but at the same time thoroughly loyal to the Church. They were the moderate men between the Pagan Humanists and the extreme Scholastics. Their aim was to promote learning and education, and to widen the field of knowledge by the introduction of the ancient literary masterpieces, not at the expense of an abandonment of Christianity, but under the auspices and in support of the Catholic Church. Following in the footsteps of Origen, St. Gregory, St. Basil, and St. Augustine, they knew how to admire the beauties of Pagan literature without accepting its spirit or ideals, and hence they have been called the Christian Humanists.

The revival of Greek in Italy, where Greek literature was practically unknown, is due in great measure to the arrival of Greek scholars, who were induced to come by promises of a salary and position, or who travelled

---

* Pastor, *History of the Popes*, i., pp. 12-33.

thither on political or ecclesiastical missions. Of these
the principal were Manuel Chrysoloras engaged at work
in Florence from 1396, Cardinal Bessarion (1403 ?-72)
who came westward for the Council of Florence and
ended his days in Venice to which he bequeathed his
library, Gemistos Plethon (1355-1450) the principal
agent in the establishment of the Platonic academy at
Florence, George of Trebizond, Theodore Gaza, Lascaris, Andronicus Callistus, and others who fled from
Greece to escape the domination of the Turks. With the
help of these men and their pupils a knowledge of Greek
and of Greek literature was diffused through Italy, and
in a short time throughout the Continent. Everywhere
collections of Greek manuscripts began to be formed;
agents were sent to the East to buy them wherever they
could be discovered, and copyists and translators were
busy at work in all the leading centres of Italy. The
fall of Constantinople in 1453 tended to help the Greek
revival in the West by the dispersion of both scholars
and manuscripts through Italy, France, and Germany.

Humanism owes its rapid development in Italy not
indeed to the universities, for the universities, committed
entirely to the Scholastic principles of education, were
generally hostile, but rather to the exertions of wandering teachers and to the generous support of powerful
patrons. In Rome it was the Popes who provided funds
for the support of Humanist scholars, for the collection
and copying of manuscripts, and for the erection of
libraries where the great literary treasures of Greece and
Rome might be available for the general public; in
Florence it was the de' Medici, notably Cosimo (1429-64)
and Lorenzo the Magnificent (1449-92), by whose exertions Florence became the greatest centre of literary
activity in Europe; in Milan it was the Viscontis and
the Sforzas; in Urbino Duke Federigo and his friends;
and in Ferrara and Mantua the families of d'Este and
Gonzaga. Academies took the place of universities.
Of these the academy of Florence, supported by the de'

Medici and patronised by the leading Greek and Italian scholars, was by far the most influential and most widely known. The academy of Rome, founded (1460) by Pomponius Laetus, was frankly Pagan in its tone and as such was suppressed by Paul II. It was revived, however, and patronised by Sixtus IV., Julius II., and Leo X. Similar institutions were to be found in most of the Italian States, notably at Venice and Naples. In nearly all these cities valuable manuscript libraries were being amassed, and were placed generously at the disposal of scholars.

Another important aid to the popularisation of the works of the Greek and Latin writers was the invention of printing and its introduction into Italy. The first printing press in Italy was established at the Benedictine monastery of Subiaco, whence it was transferred to Rome. From this press were issued editions of the Latin classics, such as the works of Lactantius, Caesar, Livy, Aulus Gellius, Virgil, Lucan, Cicero, and Ovid. Aldo Manuzio, himself an enthusiastic student of Greek literature, settled at Venice in 1490, and established a printing press with the intention of bringing out editions of the principal Greek authors. His house was the great centre for Greek scholars from all parts of Italy, and from the Aldine Press were issued cheap and accurate editions of the Greek classics. Later on when Florence and Milan were disturbed by the invasion of Charles VIII. of France (1483-98), and when Naples was captured by the Spaniards the Humanist movement found a generous patron in Leo X., a scion of de' Medici family. From the press founded by Leo X. many classical texts were issued till the pillaging of the city by the imperial troops in 1527 dealt a death blow to the revival in Italy.

That there was no opposition between the study of the classics and the teaching of Christianity is evidenced by the friendly attitude adopted by the Papacy towards the Humanist movement. The Avignon Popes, Benedict XII. (1334-42) and Clement VI. (1342-52), heaped honours and emoluments upon Petrarch and provided him with the means of acquiring manuscripts and of meeting scholars likely to assist him. A similar attitude towards the movement was adopted by Urban V. (1362-70). The leading classical scholars such as Coluccio, Salutati, Francesco Bruni, Lionardo d'Aretino, etc., were employed at the Papal court, and the apostolic college of secretaries became one of the greatest centres for the propagation of Humanism. The troubles that fell upon the Church during the Great Western Schism diverted the attention of the rival Popes from literary pursuits; but as soon as peace had been restored by the Council of Constance Martin V. (1417-31) assembled around him in Rome many of the ablest classical scholars, and vied with his cardinals in his protection of the Humanist movement. Eugene IV. (1431-47) was, if anything, more favourable, but yet his sympathies did not blind him to the dangerous tendencies of the revival as manifested in the books of men like Beccadelli.*

With the election of Nicholas V. (1447-55) † the triumph of Humanism at Rome seemed secure. The new Pope was himself one of the party. As a tutor in Florence he had been brought into contact with the great literary men of the time and had become an ardent student of the classics, nor did his enthusiasm lose any of its ardour when he ascended the Papal throne. His aim was to make Rome the intellectual as well as the religious capital of the world, and with this object in view he invited to his court the most distinguished scholars of the age, and bestowed upon not a few of them, such as Albergati, Capranica, and Caesarini the rank of cardinal. That he fully recognised the advantages which religion might derive from the revival of letters, and that he aimed at employing the services of the Humanists in defence of Christianity is evident from

* Pastor, *op. cit., p.* 24.
† Müntz, *Les arts à la cour des Papes pendant le XVe. et le XVIe. siècle,* 1878-9.

the works to which he directed the attention of scholars. The texts of the Scripture, the translations of the Greek Fathers, and the preparation of critical studies on the Lives of the Saints were amongst the works recommended to his literary friends. At the same time he did not proclaim war upon the less orthodox of the Humanist school. Men like Valla, Poggio, Filelfo, and Marsuppini were treated with friendliness and even with favour. Whether such a line of conduct was dictated by prudence and by the hope of winning over these scholars to a better understanding, or whether his anxiety for the success of his own literary schemes blinded him to the serious excesses of such leaders it is difficult to say; but, at any rate, it serves to show the great liberty enjoyed by literary men at this period even in the very city of the Popes.

As a means of ensuring to Rome the most prominent place in the revival, agents were dispatched to Greece, Turkey, Germany, France, and even to Sweden and Norway, to hunt for manuscripts. No expense was spared to secure everything that could be purchased or to have copies made where purchase was impossible. In order to preserve these treasures and make them available for scholars the Vatican Library was undertaken by orders of the Pope. Though long before this time the library of the Popes was of considerable importance, yet on account of the immense number of volumes procured by Nicholas V. he is generally regarded as the founder of the Vatican Library. The number of volumes which it contained at the time of his death is variously estimated at from one to nine thousand. The works of the Fathers of the Church, and the Scholastics and Canonists were well represented.*

After the death of Nicholas V. the Pagan side of the Humanist movement became more and more apparent. Pius II. (1458-64), who, as Aeneas Sylvius, was well known as a clever writer of the Humanist school, seems

---

* Müntz-Fabre, *La Bibliothèque du Vatican au XVe. siècle*, 1887.

as Pope to have been decidedly suspicious of his former friends. His own private library was filled with Christian authors, and care was taken to show favour only to those classical scholars whose writings were above reproach. Yet the cares of his office and the promotion of the crusade on which he had set his heart prevented him from taking the necessary steps for the purification of his court, and, as a result, many of the members of the College of Abbreviators were allowed to remain in office though they were really Pagan at heart. Paul II. could not tolerate such a state of affairs. He promptly abolished the College of Abbreviators, suppressed the Roman Academy, and arrested its two prominent leaders, Pomponius Laetus and Platina.

If Paul II. erred on the side of severity some of his successors went to the other extreme of laxity. The period of the political Popes, from Sixtus IV. to Julius II. (1471-1513), was marked by a serious decline in the religious spirit, nor can it be said that the policy of the Popes was calculated to check the downward tendency. Their attention was occupied too much by the politics of the petty Italian States to permit them to fulfil the duties of their high office; and, as a consequence, the interests of religion were neglected. Sixtus IV. adopted the friendly attitude of Nicholas V. towards the Renaissance. The College of Abbreviators was restored, the Roman Academy was recognised, and Platina was appointed librarian. The manuscripts in the Vatican Library were increased, more ample accommodation was provided, and every facility was given to scholars to consult the papal collection. Hence it is that Sixtus IV. is regarded generally as the second founder of the Vatican Library.

The revolutions and wars, caused by the invasion of Italy by the French and the Spaniards during the closing years of the fifteenth century and the early portion of the sixteenth, dealt a serious blow to Humanism in Florence, Milan, Venice, and other Italian centres. But the misfortunes of these cities served to strengthen the movement at Rome. Julius II. (1503-13) proved himself a generous patron of literature and in a special manner of art. Men like Giuliano da Sangallo, Sansovino, Bramante, Michael Angelo, and Raphael were invited to Rome and induced to devote their genius to the service of religion and the glory of the Papacy. On the death of Julius II. in 1513 the complete triumph of the Humanist movement in Rome was assured by the election of Giovanni de' Medici who took the name of Leo X. (1513-21).* As the son of Lorenzo the Magnificent, to whom Florence owes its literary renown, and as the pupil of the celebrated Humanists, Poliziano and Marsilio Ficino, he was committed almost of necessity to the Humanist movement. Scholars and artists flocked to Rome from all sides to greet the new Pope and to assure themselves of his favour and protection. Under the new régime literary merit was the principal qualification sought for in candidates aspiring to the highest ecclesiastical honours. The Roman University was reorganised; the search for manuscripts was renewed with vigour; a new college for the promotion of Greek studies in Rome was founded, and the services of Lascaris and Musuro were secured; and artists like Raphael and Bramante received every encouragement. Humanism was at last triumphant in Rome, but, unfortunately, its triumph was secured at the expense of religion. Nor was Humanism destined to enjoy the fruits of the victory for a lengthened period. The outbreak of the Reformation and the capture of Rome by the soldiers of Charles V. turned the attention of the Popes to more pressing concerns.

The Renaissance movement in Germany is due largely to the influence of Italian scholars and to the teaching of the Brothers of the Common Life in their school at Deventer.† The close political relations existing be-

* Pastor, *op. cit.*, vol. vii. Conforti, *Leone X. ed il suo secolo*, 1896. Roscoe, *Life and Pontificate of Leo X.*, 1883.

† Delprat, *Die Brüderschaft des gemeinsamen Lebens*, 1840.

CAUSES OF THE REFORMATION

tween the German States and the cities of Northern Italy, the mission of Petrarch to the court of Charles IV., the intermingling of German and Italian scholars at the councils of Constance, Florence, and Basle, and the exertions of Aeneas Sylvius, afterwards Pius II., during his term of office as Chancellor of Frederick III., helped largely to promote the study of the classics in Germany, especially when the invention and development of the art of printing had solved the difficulty of procuring manuscripts. As in Italy, Humanism owes much of its success to the generosity of powerful patrons such as the Emperor Maximilian I., Frederick Elector of Saxony and his kinsman, Duke George, Joachim I. of Brandenburg, and Philip of the Palatinate, Bishop John von Dalberg of Worms, and Archbishop Albrecht of Mainz; and as in Italy the academies were the most powerful means of disseminating classical culture, so also in Germany learned societies like the *Rhenana*, founded by Bishop Dalberg, and the *Danubiana* in Vienna, were most successful in promoting the literary propaganda.

But, unlike the Italian, the German revival was assisted largely by the universities. Basle, Erfurt, Heidelberg and Leipzig showed unmistakably their sympathy towards the movement, and in a short time the programmes of university studies in nearly all the leading centres were modified in accordance with the new ideas of education. Scholasticism was obliged to make way for the classics and natural science. Cologne, alone in Germany, refused to abandon its old system, and, though not unfriendly to the classics, as is evident by the presence of Ortwin Gratius on its list of professors, still it showed itself highly distrustful of the tendencies of some of the Humanist leaders. Yet German Humanism had little, if anything, in common with the flagrant irreligion and immorality of the Italian school. With one or two exceptions German Humanists never assailed revealed religion as such, but attacked instead the prevailing educational system, which they held to be responsible for the widespread ignorance and general decline of the religious spirit. Many of the leading German scholars were exemplary in their moral character and in their loyalty to the Church, and few, even of those who were regarded as hostile, showed any sympathy with Luther once they understood that he aimed at revolt rather than reform.

Some of the greatest of the German Humanists differed from their Italian contemporaries also in the fact that they turned the intellectual revival into scientific channels, and made the study of the classics subservient to mathematical and astronomical research. Cardinal Nicholas of Cusa (1400-64), George Peurbach of Vienna (d. 1461), John Müller of Königsberg (1436-76), better known by his Latin name Regiomontanus, and the great churchman and astronomer Copernicus (1473-1543) belonged to this section, which prepared the way for modern scientific developments. With these men religion and science went hand in hand.

On the purely literary side the most famous of the German Humanists were Conrad Celtes (1459-1508) the most active of the promoters of the classical revival beyond the Alps and one of the earliest of the German poets; Pirkheimer (1470-1528), who hoped for great things from the Lutheran movement at first, but having realised its real nature remained loyal to the Church; Mutianus Rufus (1471-1526), a canon of Gotha and at the same time a well-known free-thinker; Grotus Rubeanus (1480-1504), who at first favoured Luther; Jakob Wimpheling (1450-1528), and Johannes Trithemius (1462-1516), the learned historian and abbot of Sponheim; Ulrich von Hutten (1488-1523), and Johann Reuchlin (1455-1522).

Of these the most important from the point of view of ecclesiastical history are von Hutten * and Reuchlin. The former was born in the year 1488 and was sent for

* Strauss, *Ulrich von Hutten*, 2 auf., 1871 (*Eng. Trans.*, 1874).

CAUSES OF THE REFORMATION 19

his education to the monastery of Fulda, from which he fled with very little mental equipment except a lasting hatred and distrust of all monks and ecclesiastics. As a wandering student he visited the leading centres of learning in Germany and Northern Italy, where he was particularly remarkable for his dissolute life, his ungovernable temper, and his biting sarcasm. Taking advantage of the rising spirit of unfriendliness between the Teuton and the Latin countries, he posed as a patriot burning with love for Germany and the Germans, and despising the French, the Italians, and in particular the Pope. Against the monks and the theologians he directed his bitterest satires, to the delight of many, who did not foresee the dangers of such attacks at a time when the German nation generally was growing less friendly to the Papacy.

A dispute, which broke out about the destruction or suppression of Jewish books, afforded him a splendid opportunity of venting his spleen against the Church. A converted Jew of Cologne named Pfefferkorn advocated the suppression of all Jewish religious books except the Old Testament, as the best means of converting his former co-religionists. The Emperor, Maximilian, was not unwilling to listen to such advice supported as it was by the universities of Cologne, Mainz, and Erfurt. Reuchlin, a professor of Heidelberg and himself a well-known Hebrew scholar, opposed such a policy as bad in itself and as injurious to the proper understanding of the Old Testament. A warm controversy thereupon ensued. The Dominicans of Cologne espoused the cause of Pfefferkorn, while the Humanists, scenting in the attack upon Jewish literature an onslaught directed against the entire literary revival, supported the contentions of Reuchlin. It was a war between two opposing schools—the Theologians and the Humanists; and, unfortunately for the Theologians, they had selected their ground badly, and were but poorly equipped for a battle in which victory was to be decided by popular opinion.

Reuchlin was summoned to appear before the Inquisitor to answer for the views put forward in his *Augenspiegel* (1511), and was condemned. He appealed to Rome, and the Bishop of Speier was ordered to investigate the case. The result was the acquittal of Reuchlin (1514), but his adversaries, having objected to the mode of trial, the case was transferred once more to the Roman courts. Meanwhile the controversy was carried on in Germany with great bitterness. Reuchlin published a volume of sympathetic letters* received by him from the leading scholars of Germany, and Erasmus issued a new edition (1515) of his *Praise of Folly* (*Encomium Moriæ*) in which he ridiculed especially the monks and theologians.

But the book which was most damaging to the opponents of Humanism was beyond doubt the *Epistolae virorum obscurorum*. It was a work consisting of two volumes, the first brought out by Grotus Rubeanus in 1514, and the second mostly from the pen of Urich von Hutten (1517). Like Reuchlin's work it purported to be a collection of letters addressed by the theologians to Ortwin Gratius, the champion of Cologne university and, indeed, of the whole Scholastic party. It was full of bitterness and vulgarity, but, as a humorous caricature of the theologians, their arguments and modes of expression, it was calculated to make them ridiculous especially in the eyes of the university students. Against an attack of this kind serious arguments were unavailing, and, unfortunately, there was no apologist of theology capable of producing a reply couched in a strain similar to that of the *Epistolae*. Gratius himself did undertake the task in his *Lamentationes obscurorum virorum,* but without success, and undoubtedly in the eyes of the general public the victory rested with the Humanists. The whole controversy was extremely unfortunate, because it helped to

---

* *Clarorum virorum Epistolae latinae graecae et hebraicae,* 1514.

CAUSES OF THE REFORMATION

blind many to the real issues at stake when the Lutheran movement began. By it the Theologians and Humanists were divided into two hostile camps, with the result that the latter were inclined to support Luther against their own former opponents and in vindication of the liberal policy which they had advocated; while the Theologians, having been discredited as narrow-minded obscurantists in the eyes of a large body of university men, were handicapped seriously in a struggle with Luther even though their struggle was for fundamental religious principles.*

The most remarkable of the men, who, though not Germans, were closely identified with German Humanists, was Desiderius Erasmus (1466-1535).† He was born at Rotterdam, was sent to school with the Brothers of the Common Life at Deventer, entered a monastery of the Canons Regular attracted by its library rather than by its rule, and left it after two years to become secretary to the Bishop of Cambrai. He studied classics at the University of Paris, and after his ordination as priest by the Bishop of Utrecht he became tutor to an English nobleman. Later on he paid a visit to England, where he received a warm welcome from scholars like Fisher, Bishop of Rochester, Colet, Dean of St. Paul's, and Sir Thomas More, and where he was honoured by an appointment as Professor of Greek in Oxford. But the fever of travel was upon him. He returned to Paris, made a brief stay at Louvain, and started out to visit the leading literary centres of Italy, notably Bologna, Venice, and Rome, in the latter of which he was well received by Julius II.

On the accession of Henry VIII. he returned to England and lectured for some time at Cambridge. Later on he removed to Basle and settled down to the work of preparing editions of the New Testament and of the Fathers. The triumph of the Reformation party in

---

* Janssen, *History of the German People*, iii., pp. 44-79.
† Capey, *Erasmus*, 1901.

Basle drove him for a time to seek a refuge in Freiburg, but he returned to die at Basle in 1536.

In his wanderings Erasmus was brought into contact with the leading scholars of France, England, Germany, and Italy, and was thoroughly acquainted with the lights and shadows of the Renaissance movement. In his knowledge of Greek he was surpassed by few of his contemporaries, and in the purity and ease of his Latin style he stood without a serious rival. Like many others of the Humanist school he delighted in attacking the ignorance of the monks and Scholastics, and in denouncing the abuses of the age, though, as was the case with most of the literary reformers of the time, his own life as an ecclesiastic was far from exemplary.

Yet Erasmus himself was never an enemy of Christianity, nor did he desire the overthrow of ecclesiastical authority. He did, indeed, advocate reform, and in his advocacy of reform he may have been carried too far at times, but in his heart Erasmus had little sympathy with doctrinal changes. Ignorance he believed to be at the root of the decline of religion, and hence he would have welcomed a complete change in the educational system of the Church. Instead of Scholasticism he advocated study of the Scriptures and of the early Fathers, and in order to prepare the way for such a policy he devoted himself at Basle to the task of preparing an edition of the New Testament and of the Greek Fathers. He was on terms of the closest intimacy with the leading Humanists of Germany, and shared all their contempt for scholastic theologians and much of their distrust of the Pope and the Roman Curia. Hence the sympathy and encouragement of Erasmus were not wanting to Luther during the early days of his revolt and before the true object of the movement was rightly understood; but once Erasmus realised that union with Luther meant separation from the Church he became more reserved in his approval, and finally took the field against him. In his work, *De Libero Arbitrio,* he opposed the teach-

CAUSES OF THE REFORMATION 23

ing of Luther on free will, and before his death he received a benefice from Paul III. which he accepted, and an offer of a cardinal's hat which he declined. His life as an ecclesiastic was certainly not edifying, and his hatred of ignorance, antiquated educational methods, and abuses may have led him into excesses, but his theology was still the theology of the Middle Ages rather than that of the German Reformers.

In France the earliest of the Humanists were Nicholas of Clemanges and Gerson, both rectors of Paris University, and both well-known theologians. They were specially active in putting an end to the Great Western Schism, but in doing so they laid down certain principles that led almost inevitably to Gallicanism. The influence of these two men did not, however, change the policy of Paris University. For years France lagged behind in the classical movement, and it was only in the early portion of the sixteenth century that French Humanism made itself felt.

The movement gained ground by the exertions of individuals and of literary societies, by the results of the activity of the printing press, and the protection of influential patrons at the Court of Francis I. (1515-47). Paris University became more friendly to the classics, and eminent scholars like Lascaris and Aleandro were invited to lecture on Greek. The College of St. Barbe became a great classical stronghold within the university, and the movement began to develop so rapidly as to excite the jealousy and suspicions of the theologians. This unfortunate division was rendered more acute by the foundation of the Collège de France in 1529. It was handed over entirely to the Humanist party in spite of the opposition of the more conservative school, and served as a centre for all kinds of literary, philological, and antiquarian researches.

The most eminent of the French Humanists were Budaeus (1467-1540), regarded in his own time as but slightly inferior to Erasmus, Germanus Brixius (Germain de Brie), Canon of Notre Dame and translator of portion of the works of St. John Chrysostom, Stephen Poncher, Bishop of Paris and advocate of the Humanist party at the Court of Francis I., the Dominican, William Petit, Robert (1503-59) and Henri (1528-98) Estienne (Stephanus) to whom we are indebted for the two monumental works, *Thesaurus Linguae Latinae* and *Linguae Graecae,* Scaliger (1540-1609) the well-known authority on chronology and epigraphy, and the philologist and classicist Isaac Casaubon (1559-1614).

In France there was a sharp rivalry from the beginning between the Scholastics and the Humanists. The university was divided into separate camps. The college of St. Barbe was opposed by the Montaigue College, the rector of which was the leader of the Scholastic party. The Humanists regarded the Theologians as antiquated, while the Theologians looked upon their opponents as supporters of the Reformation movement. In case of a few of these, as for example Lefèvre d'Étaples,* Gérard Roussel, and others, these suspicions were fully justified; but in case of many others their faith was sound, and however much they may have wavered in life they preferred to die at peace with the Church. To this latter section belongs Marguerite of Valois,† sister of Francis I. She was a patroness of the Humanists and Reformers in Paris and was opposed undoubtedly to many Catholic practices; but it is not so clear that she wished for a religious revolution, and at any rate it is certain that she died a Catholic. This rivalry between the Theologians and Humanists and the misunderstandings to which it gave rise are largely responsible for the rapid development of Calvinism amongst certain classes of French society.

The classical movement in England is due largely to Italian influences, though the visit of the Greek Emperor Manuel in 1400, and the subsequent visits of Greek

* *Lefèvre d'Étaples son influence sur les origines de la réforme Franc.*, 1900.
† Lalanne, *Mémoires de Mᵉ de Valois*, etc., 1858.

CAUSES OF THE REFORMATION

envoys and scholars must have contributed not a little to awaken an interest among English students in Greek studies. Individual Englishmen began to turn towards the great centres of Italian Humanism, and to return to their own country imbued with something of the literary zeal of their Italian masters. Of these the two who, more than others, contributed to give Greek and Latin a good standing in the schools of the country were William Selling and William Hadley, both Benedictine monks of Canterbury. They studied at Bologna, Padua and Rome, and were brought into contact with Politian and other distinguished Humanists. Selling was recognised as an accomplished Greek scholar, and on his return he set himself to remodel the course of studies at Canterbury so as to ensure for the classics their proper place. The influence of Canterbury and of Prior Selling helped very much to spread the classical revival in England.

Selling's most remarkable pupil was Thomas Linacre (1460-1524), who went to Oxford after having completed his early education at Canterbury, and was chosen Fellow of All Soul's College. Later on he accompanied his old master to Italy, where he had an opportunity of mastering the intricacies of Latin style from Politian, the tutor of the children of Lorenzo de'Medici, and of Greek from Demetrius Chalcondylas. He turned his attention to medicine and received a degree both at Padua and Oxford. His position at the courts of Henry VII. and Henry VIII. gave him an opportunity of enlisting the sympathies of the leading ecclesiastical and lay scholars of his day in favour of the literary revival. In his later years he was ordained priest and held some important ecclesiastical offices. Other distinguished scholars and patrons of the revival in England were Grocyn, a companion of Linacre at Oxford and in Italy and afterwards lecturer on Greek at Exeter College, Oxford; John Colet (1467-1519), Dean of St. Paul's, the friend of Budaeus, Erasmus, Linacre, and Grocyn, and founder of St. Paul's School; William Lilly, appointed by Dean Colet as first master in this school; Fisher (1459-1535) Bishop of Rochester; and Sir Thomas More (1480-1535).

The Humanist movement in England, unlike the corresponding movement in Italy, was in no sense hostile to religion or to the Catholic Church. Many of its leaders desired reform, but not a single one of the prominent scholars of the period showed any sympathy with Luther's revolt. The very founders of the revival in England, Selling, Hadley, Linacre and Grocyn, were ecclesiastics whose faith was beyond suspicion; Colet died as he had lived, thoroughly devoted to the Church; while Fisher and Sir Thomas More sealed their loyalty to the ancient faith with their blood.*

The revival in Spain owes much to the patronage of Queen Isabella and the exertions of Cardinal Ximenez (1436-1517). The leading universities, Seville, Alcalá, and Salamanca, were not unfriendly, and the whole educational system was remodelled in favour of the classics. Cardinal Ximenez devoted himself to the preparation of the Polyglot edition of the Bible, the New Testament portion of which was printed so early as 1514, and the whole work was published in 1522. The leading Humanist scholars were Lebrixa, or as he is called in Latin Lebrissensis, Nunĕz, and Ludovico Vives (1492-1540), the latter of whom was deemed by his contemporaries not unworthy of being compared with Erasmus and Budaeus.

The Humanist movement and the general revival of literary, scientific, philological and historical studies to which it gave birth were not in themselves anti-religious, nor did they find in the Catholic Church a determined opponent. Such studies, on the contrary, might have contributed much to promote a more enlightened understanding of theology, and more especially of the Scrip-

* On the Humanist movement in England, *cf.* Gasquet, *Eve of the Reformation*, 1900, chap. ii. Seebohm, *Oxford Reformers* (Colet, Erasmus, More), 1867. Einstein, *The Italian Renaissance in England*, 1902.

tures, a fact which was understood thoroughly by the ablest ecclesiastics of the time. In Italy, Germany, France, and England, bishops and abbots vied with secular princes in their patronage of scholars, while the influence of the Popes, notably Nicholas V., Sixtus IV., Julius II., and Leo X. was entirely in favour of the Humanist party.

Yet, while all this is true, the Humanist movement did much, undoubtedly, to prepare men's minds for the great religious revolt of the sixteenth century. Springing into life as it did at a time when the faith of the Middle Ages was on the wane, and when many educated men were growing tired of the cold formalism and antiquated methods of the Schoolmen, it tended to develop a spirit of restless inquiry that could ill brook any restriction. The return to the classics recalled memories of an earlier civilisation and culture opposed in many particulars to the genius of Christianity, and the return to nature tended to push into the background the supernatural idea upon which the Christian religion is based. But the revival did more. The study of the classics brought into prominence serious problems regarding the authenticity, age, and value of certain writings and manuscripts, and by so doing it created a spirit of criticism and of doubt for which the Theologians of the day were but poorly prepared. In a word, it was a period of transition and of intellectual unrest, when new ideals in education were endeavouring to supplant the old ones, and when neither the friends of the old nor of the new had distinguished clearly between what was essential in Christianity and what was purely accidental.

In such a time it was to be expected that ardent Humanists, filled with their new-born zeal for classical studies, should advance too rapidly, and by confounding religion with the crude methods of some of its defenders should jump to the conclusion that a reconciliation between the revival and religion was impossible. Nor should it be a matter of surprise that the Theologians, confident in the strength of their own position and naturally suspicious of intellectual novelties, were not inclined to look with favour on a movement which owed its inspiration largely to Pagan sources. Moderate men, on the contrary, whether Humanists or Scholastics, aimed at a complete reconciliation. They realised that the great literary and scientific revival could do much for the defence of religion, and that the Pagan classics must be appraised according to Christian standards.

But this work of reconciliation was rendered very difficult by the attitude of extremists on both sides. Many of the Italian Humanists, as has been shown, were Christians only in name. In their writings and in their lives they showed clearly that they were thoroughly imbued with the spirit of Paganism. Such men merited severe condemnation, and it is to be regretted that the Popes, particularly Sixtus IV. and Leo X., did not adopt a firmer attitude towards this section of the Italian school. But before judging too harshly the friendly relations maintained by Sixtus IV. and Leo X. with the Italian Humanists, it is well to remember that the age in which they lived was noted for its general laxity and for the decline of a proper religious spirit, that the Pagan tone and Pagan forms of expression used by these writers were regarded as exhibitions of harmless pedantry rather than as clear proofs of opposition to Christianity, that most of these writers were always ready to explain away whatever might appear objectionable in their works, and that, finally, mildness in the circumstances may have been deemed the best policy. The attitude of the Popes at any rate prevented an open conflict between the representatives of the two schools in Italy until the outbreak of the Reformation and the invasion of Rome put an end to the danger by destroying the Humanist movement.

In Germany and France there were few traces of an anti-Christian tendency amongst the supporters of the new learning. But in both countries, more especially in the former, the supporters of the new learning criticised

CAUSES OF THE REFORMATION

severely the ignorance of the monks and Theologians, and took little pains to conceal their contempt for the Scholastic methods of education. They blamed the Popes for their neglect of the true interests of the Church, and held them responsible in a large measure for the general decline of religion. According to them the study of theology must be reformed so as to give a more prominent place to the Scriptures and the writings of the early Fathers; the development of the internal spirit of religion as distinct from mere external formalism was to be encouraged, and many of the existing practices might be discarded as superstitious. Such views tended naturally to excite the opposition of the Theologians and to unsettle the religious convictions of educated men who watched the struggle with indifference.

In this way the ground was prepared for a complete religious revolt. Luther's movement was regarded by many as merely the logical sequence of Humanism, but that the Humanists themselves were not willing to accept this view is clear from the fact that once the early misunderstandings had been removed, and once the real issues were apparent, most of the Humanists in Germany and France remained true to the Church. Instead of regarding Luther as a friend they looked upon him as the worst enemy of their cause, and on the Reformation as the death-knell of the Renaissance.

(b) POLITICAL AND SOCIAL CONDITION OF EUROPE.

See the works of Pastor, Janssen and Gasquet cited in section (a.) *The Cambridge Modern History*, vol. i. (gives an excellent bibliography). Hergenröther-Kirsch, *Handbuch der Allgemeinen Kirchengeschichte*, Bd. 2 (pp. 996-1002). Ranke, *Deutsche Geschichte im Zeitalter der Reformation*, 1844 (Eng. Trans. by Austin, 1845-7). Idem., *Geschichte der Romanischen und Germanischen Völker* (1419-1514). Kaser, *Deutsche Geschichte zur Zeit Maximilians I.* (1486-1519), 1912. Cherrier, *Histoire de Charles VIII.*, 1868. Prescott, *Ferdinand and Isabella*, 1887. Busch-Todd, *England under the Tudors*, 1892-5. Hunt-Poole, *The Political History of England*. vol. v., 1910 (chap. v.).

The struggle between the Papacy and the Empire, ending, as it did, in the downfall of the House of Hohenstaufen, put an end to the old conception of a universal monarchy presided over by the Emperor and the Pope. A new tendency began to make itself felt in European politics. Hitherto the feudal system, on which society was based, had served as a barrier against the development of royal power or the formation of united states. Under this system the king was sometimes less powerful than some of his nominal subjects, and was entirely dependent upon the good-will of the barons for the success of any action he might take outside his own hereditary dominions. This was the real weakness of the system, and so long as it remained the growth of Nationalism was impossible.

Gradually, however, by the exertions of powerful sovereigns the power of the barons was broken, the smaller states were swallowed up in the larger ones, and the way was prepared for the rise of the nations of modern Europe. In France the policy of centralisation begun in the thirteenth century, was carried to a successful conclusion in the days of Louis XI. (1461-83). The English provinces, Aquitane, Burgundy and Brittany, were all united to form one state, knowing only one supreme ruler. In Spain the old divisions disappeared almost completely with the union of Castile and Aragon under Ferdinand (1479-1516) and Isabella the Catholic (1474-1504), and with the complete destruction of the Moorish power by the conquest of Granada (1492). In England the slaughter of the nobility in the Wars of the Roses left the way ready for the establishment of the Tudor domination. As part of the same movement towards unification Henry VIII. was declared to be King of Ireland instead of Feudal Lord, and serious attempts were made to include Scotland within his dominions. Inside the Empire similar tendencies were at work, but with exactly opposite results. The interregnum in the Empire and a succession of weak rulers left the territorial princes free to imitate the rulers of Europe by strengthening their own power at the expense of the

CAUSES OF THE REFORMATION

lower nobility, the cities and the peasantry; but, having secured themselves, they used their increased strength to arrest the progress of centralisation and to prevent the development of a strong imperial power.

As a direct result of this centralisation tendency and of the increase of royal authority that it involved, the rulers of Europe initiated a campaign against all constitutional restrictions on the exercise of their authority. The feudal system with all its faults was in some senses wonderfully democratic. The sovereign was dependent upon the decisions of the various representative assemblies; and though the lower classes had little voice except in purely local affairs, yet the rights and privileges of all classes were hedged round so securely by written charters or immemorial usage that any infringement of them might be attended with serious results. In England the Parliament, in Spain the Cortes, in France the States General, and in Germany the Diet, should have proved a strong barrier against the establishment of absolute rule. But the authority of such assemblies was soon weakened or destroyed. Under the Tudors the English Parliament became a mere machine for registering the wishes of the sovereign; the Cortes and States General were rarely consulted in Spain and France; and, though the Diet retained its position in the Empire, it was used rather to increase the influence of the princes than to afford any guarantee of liberty to the subject.

In bringing about such a complete revolution the rulers were assisted largely by the introduction of the Roman Code of Justinian.* According to the principles of the Roman Code the power of the sovereign was unlimited, and against his wishes no traditional customs or privileges could avail. Such a system was detested especially by the Germans, who clung with great pertinacity to their own national laws and customs; but the princes, supported by the universities, carried through

* *Cambridge Modern History*, ii., p. 176. Janssen, *op. cit.*, Eng. Trans., ii., chap. ii.

the reform on which they had set their heart. They succeeded in strengthening their own power and in trampling down the rights guaranteed to their subjects by the old Germanic Code, while at the same time they were untiring in their resistance to imperial reforms, and were unwilling to do anything to increase the power of the Emperor.

As a result of the development of arbitrary rule the lower classes had great reason to complain of the increase of taxation and of the difficulties of obtaining justice in the ordinary courts of law. They were ready to listen to the advice of interested leaders, who urged them to band together in defence of their rights against the usurpations of land owners and kings. As a result nearly every country in Europe found itself involved in a great struggle. The Peasants' War in Hungary (1514), the revolt against Charles V. in Spain (1520), the resistance of the Flemish Communes, led by Ghent, to the ordinances of the Dukes of Burgundy, the discontent of the lower classes in France with the excessive taxes levied by Louis XI., and the secret associations, which prepared the way for the great uprising of the lower classes in Germany (1524), were clear indications that oppression and discontent were not confined to any particular country in Europe.

With all these political developments the interests of religion and of the Church were closely connected. Even though it be admitted that in themselves there is no real opposition between Nationalism and Catholicism, yet in the circumstances of the time, when national rivalry was acute, the dependence of the Holy See upon any particular nation was certain to excite serious jealousy. From that time nations began to regard the Pope as an ally or an enemy according to the side he favoured instead of looking to him as a common father, and consequently the danger of a conflict between national patriotism and loyalty to the Head of the Church was rendered less improbable. This feeling was

CAUSES OF THE REFORMATION

increased by the residence of the Popes at Avignon, when the Holy See was so completely associated with the interests of France, and by the policy pursued by Sixtus IV. and his successors in regard to the Italian States. Nowhere, however, was this opposition to the Papacy manifested more clearly than in Germany. This was due partly to the growing feeling of antipathy between the Teutonic and the Latin races, partly to the tradition of the great struggle of the thirteenth century in which the Emperors were worsted by the Popes, and partly also to the discontent excited amongst all classes of the German people, lay and cleric, by the taxations of the Curia. The attitude of the three ecclesiastical electors in 1455, the complaints of the clergy in 1479, and the list of *Gravamina* presented to Maximilian in 1510 were harbingers of the revolution that was to come.

Besides, the growth of absolutism in Europe was likely to prove dangerous to the liberties of the Church. Rulers, who aimed at securing for themselves unlimited authority, were not blind to the importance of being able to control the ecclesiastical organisation, and to attain this result their legal advisers quoted for them the maxims of the old Roman Code, according to which the king was the source of all spiritual as well as temporal power. Their predecessors had usurped already a strong voice in the appointments to benefices, but now civil rulers claimed as a right what those who had gone before were glad to accept as a privilege. Hence they demanded that the Holy See should hand over to them the nomination of bishops, that it should modify the old laws regarding exemption of ecclesiastical property from taxation, trial of clerics, and right of sanctuary, and that it should submit its pronouncements for the royal *Exequatur* before they could have the force of law in any particular state. The Pragmatic Sanction of Bourges (1438) and the Concordat wrung from Leo X. by Francis I. of France in 1516, the Concordat of Princes in 1447, and the new demands formulated by the Diet of the

Empire, the Statutes of *Provisors* and *Præmunire* in England (1453), and the concessions insisted upon by Ferdinand and Isabella in Spain (1482), were clear proofs that absolutism was destined to prove fatal to the liberty of the Church and the authority of the Holy See.

Finally, the universal discontent of the masses, and the great social revolutions of the first quarter of the sixteenth century were likely to prove dangerous to ecclesiastical authority. In all revolutions the most extreme men are certain to assume control at least in the earlier stages of the movement, and their wildest onslaughts on Church and State are sure to receive the applause of the crowd. But there was special danger that these popular outbreaks might be turned into antireligious channels at a time when so many of the bishops were secular princes, and when the Church appeared to be so closely identified with the very interests against which the peasants took up arms. In these circumstances it was not difficult for designing men to push forward their plans of a religious reform under guise of a campaign for liberty and equality.*

(c) THE RELIGIOUS CONDITION OF EUROPE.

<small>Pastor, *op. cit.* Janssen, *op. cit.* Creighton, *History of the Papacy from the Great Western Schism to the Sack of Rome*, 2nd edition, 1897. Ranke, *Die Römische Päpste im 16 und 17 jahrhunderten* (xxxvii-xxxix), 1900 (Eng. Trans., 3 vols., 1866). Haller, *Papsttum und Kirchenreform*, 1904. Mansi, *Sacrorum Conciliorum Collectio*, 1900. Hefele, *Conciliengeschichte* 2 auf. 1873-90 (Eng. Trans. in part, French Trans.). Imbart de la Tour, *Les origines de la Réforme*, ii., 1909. Thomas, *Le Concordat de 1516*, 1910. Ullman, *Reformatoren vor der Reformation*, 1866 (Eng. Trans. by Menzies, 1855).</small>

The withdrawal of the Popes from the capital of Christendom and the unfortunate schism, for which their residence at Avignon is mainly responsible, proved dis-

---

* Janssen, *op. cit.* Eng. Trans., vols. i.-iii. Pastor, *op. cit.*, Eng. Trans., vols. i.-iii.

CAUSES OF THE REFORMATION

astrous to the authority of the Holy See. The Avignon Popes were Frenchmen themselves. Their cardinals and officials belonged for the most part to the same favoured nation. They were dependent upon the King of France for protection, and in return, their revenues were at times placed at his disposal in order to ensure victory for the French banners. Such a state of affairs was certain to alienate the rulers and people of other nations, especially of Germany and England, and to prepare the way for a possible conflict in the days that were to come.

The Great Western Schism that followed upon the residence at Avignon divided Christian Europe into hostile camps, and snapped the bond of unity which was already strained to the utmost by political and national rivalries. Sincere believers were scandalised at the spectacle of two or three rival Popes, each claiming to be the successor of St. Peter, and hurling at his opponents and their supporters the severest censures of the Church. While the various claimants to the Papacy were contending for supreme power in the Church, they were obliged to make concession after concession to the rulers who supported them and to permit them to interfere in religious affairs, so that even when peace was restored and when Martin V. was universally recognised as the lawful Pope, he found himself deprived of many of the rights and prerogatives, for which his predecessors from Gregory VII. to Boniface VIII. had struggled so bravely.

Nor was this all. In their efforts to bring about a reunion, and despairing of arriving at this happy result by an agreement among the contending Popes, many honest theologians put forward principles, which, however suitable to the circumstances of the schism, were utterly subversive of the monarchical constitution of the Church. They maintained that in case of doubtful Popes the cardinals had the right to summon a General Council to decide the issue, and that all Christians were bound to submit to its decrees. In accordance with these principles the Council of Constance was convoked, and, elated with the success of this experiment, many of the more ardent spirits seemed determined to replace, or at least, to limit the authority of the Popes by the authority of General Councils summoned at regular intervals. The Pope was to be no longer supreme spiritual ruler. His position in the Church was to be rather the position of a constitutional sovereign in a state, the General Council being for the Pope what modern Parliaments are for the king.

Fortunately for the Popes such a theory was completely discredited by the excesses of its supporters at the Council of Basle, but it served to weaken the authority of the Holy See, and to put into the hands of its opponents a weapon which they were not slow to wield whenever their personal interests were affected. Henceforth appeals from the Pope to a General Council, although prohibited, were by no means unfrequent.

Yet in spite of all these reverses, had the Church been blessed with a succession of worthy Popes burning with zeal for religion, free to devote themselves to a thorough reform, and capable of understanding the altered political and social conditions of the world, the Papacy might have been restored to its old position. But unfortunately the Popes from Nicholas V. to Leo X. were not the men to repair the damage that was done, or to ward off impending danger. The calamities that threatened Europe from the advance of the Turks, and the necessity of rousing its rulers to a sense of their responsibilities occupied a large share of their attention; while the anxiety which they displayed in the miserable squabbles of the Italian kingdoms, sometimes out of disinterested regard for the temporal States of the Church, as in case of Julius II., more frequently from a desire of providing territories for their unworthy relations, left them little time to safeguard the general well-being of the Church. In case of some of them, too, if one may judge them by their actions, the progress of Humanism seemed to be nearer to their hearts than the progress of religion.

In his personal life Nicholas V. (1447-55) was not unworthy of his exalted position, but the necessity of repairing the damage that had been done by the unruly assembly at Basle, which arrogated to itself the authority of an independent General Council, the removal of the last obstacle to the Turkish invasion of Europe in the fall of Constantinople, and the importance of securing for Rome a pre-eminent position in the great classical revival, engaged all his energies to the exclusion of necessary reforms. Calixtus III. (1455-58) was too old to do much, yet, notwithstanding his advancing years and the indifference of the European rulers, he threw himself into the struggle against the Turks, aiding and encouraging Hungary and Albania in their resistance, and it is due largely to his efforts that the victorious advance of Mahomet II. was checked by the overthrow of his forces at Belgrade (1456). Pius II.* (1458-64), though in his youth not the most exemplary of the Humanist school, devoted himself with earnestness and zeal to the duties of his sacred office. He published a Bull retracting all the attacks which he had made against the Papacy in his capacity as secretary to the *Conciliabulum* at Basle. He set himself to the study of the Scriptures and the early Fathers in place of the Pagan classics, and he showed his approbation of the Christian Humanists. But he was unable to undertake the work of reform. In view of the danger that still threatened Europe he convoked an assembly of the princes at Mantua to organise a crusade against the Turks, but they turned a deaf ear to his appeals, and, at last weary of their refusals and indifference, he determined to place himself at the head of the Christian forces for the defence of Europe and Christianity. He reached Ancona broken down in spirits and bodily health, and died before anything effective could

---

* Weiss, *Aeneas Silvius als Papst Pius II.*, 1897. Boulting, *Aeneas Silvius, Orator, Man of Letters, Statesman, and Pope*, 1908.

be done. Paul II. (1464-71), who succeeded, made some efforts to purify the Roman Court. He suppressed promptly the College of Abbreviators who were noted for their greed for gold and their zeal for Paganism, and closed the Roman Academy. On account of his severity in dealing with the half Christian Humanists of the Curia he has been attacked with savage bitterness by Platina, one of the dismissed officials, in his *Lives of the Popes*,* but nobody is likely to be deceived by scurrilous libels, the motives of which are only too apparent. The worst that can be said against Paul II. is that he was too fond of appointing his relatives to high positions in the Church; but in mitigation of that it is well to remember that his reforms had raised up so many enemies against him in Rome, and disaffection was so rife amongst even the highest officials of his court, that he may have deemed it prudent to have relatives around him on whom he could rely.

Sixtus IV. (1471-84) was the first of the political Popes, Leo X. being the last. They are so called on account of the excessive interest they displayed in Italian politics of the period, to the neglect of the higher interests with which they were entrused. Most of them, with the exception of Alexander VI., were not positively unworthy men, but they were too much concerned with secular pursuits to undertake a reform of the gross abuses that flourished at the very gates of their palace. The papal court was no worse and very little better than the courts of contemporary rulers, and the greed for money, which was the predominant weakness of the curial officials, alienated the sympathy of all foreigners, both lay and cleric.

Julius II. (1503-13) did, indeed, undertake the difficult task of restoring the States of the Church that had been parcelled out into petty kingdoms by his predecessors, but his policy soon brought him into conflict with Louis XII. of France. Louis demanded that a General

* *Vitae Pontificum Romanorum*, etc., 1479.

Council should be convoked, not so much out of zeal for reform as from a desire to embarrass the Pope, and when Julius II. refused to comply with his request the king induced some of the rebellious cardinals to issue invitations for a council to meet at Pisa (Sept. 1511). Most of the bishops who met at Pisa at the appointed time were from France. The Emperor Maximilian held aloof, and the people of Pisa regarded the conventicle with no friendly feelings. The sessions were transferred from Pisa to Milan, and finally to Lyons. As a set off to this Julius II. convoked a council to meet at Rome, the fifth Lateran Council (May 1512), for the threefold purpose of healing the French schism, of proscribing certain doctrinal errors, and of undertaking the work of reform. The earlier sessions were taken up almost entirely with the schism, and before the work of reform was begun Julius II. passed away.

He was succeeded by the young and learned John de' Medici, son of Lorenzo the Magnificent of Florence, who took the name of Leo X. (1513-21). Like his father, the new Pope was a generous patron of art and literature, and bestowed upon his literary friends, some of whom were exceedingly unworthy, the highest dignities in the Church. Humanism was triumphant at the Papal Court, but, unfortunately, religion was neglected. Though in his personal life Leo X. could not be described as a deeply religious man, yet he was mindful of his vows of celibacy, attentive to the recitation of the divine office, abstemious, and observant of the fasts of the Church. As a secular ruler he would have stood incomparably higher than any of the contemporary sovereigns of Europe, but he was out of place considerably as the head of a great religious organisation. Worldliness and indifference to the dangers that threatened the Church are the most serious charges that can be made against him, but especially in the circumstances of the time, when the Holy See should have set itself to combat the vicious tendencies of society, these faults were serious enough.

The defeat of the French forces at Novara (1513), and the loyalty of the other rulers of Europe to the Holy See induced Louis XII. of France to make peace with the new Pope, and to recognise the Lateran Council. But on the accession of Francis I. (1515-47) a fresh expedition into Italy was undertaken; the Swiss troops were overthrown at Marignano (1515) and Leo X. was obliged to conclude a Concordat* with the French King. By the terms of this agreement France agreed to abandon the Pragmatic Sanction of Bourges, while the Pope bestowed upon Francis I. and his successors the right of presentation to the bishoprics and abbacies in his dominions. The work of reform, which should have claimed special attention at the Lateran Council, was never undertaken seriously. Some decrees were passed prohibiting plurality of benefices, forbidding officials of the Curia to demand more than the regulation fees, recommending preaching and religious instruction of children, regulating the appointment to benefices, etc., but these decrees, apart from the fact that they left the root of the evils untouched, were never enforced. The close of the Lateran Council synchronises with the opening of Luther's campaign in Germany, for the success of which the Council's failure to respond to the repeated demands for reform is to a great extent responsible.

In any scheme for the reform of the abuses that afflicted the Church the reformation of the Papal Court itself should have occupied the foremost place. At all times a large proportion of the cardinals and higher officials were men of blameless lives, but, unfortunately, many others were utterly unworthy of their position, and their conduct was highly prejudicial to religion and to the position of the Holy See. Much of the scandalous gossip retailed by Platina in his *Lives of the Popes,* and by Burcard † and Infessura ‡ in their *Diaries* may be

* Thomas, *Le Concordat de* 1516, 1910.
† Burcardus, *Diarium Innocen. VIII. et Alex. VI.*, Florence, 1884. *Diarium sive rerum urbanarum Commentarii* (1483-1506), 1883-5.
‡ Infessura, *Diario d. Città di Roma*, 1890.

CAUSES OF THE REFORMATION 41

attributed to personal disappointment and diseased imaginations, but even when due allowance has been made for the frailty of human testimony, enough remains to prove that the Papal Court in the fourteenth and fifteenth centuries was not calculated to inspire strangers to Rome with confidence or respect. Such corrupt and greedy officials reflected discredit on the Holy See, and afforded some justification for the charges levelled against them of using religion merely as a means of raising money.

The various taxations,* direct and indirect, levied by the Popes during the fourteenth and fifteenth centuries helped to give colour to these accusations. It ought to be remembered, however, that the Popes could not carry on the government of the Church, and support the large body of officials whose services were absolutely necessary, without requiring help from their subjects in all parts of the world. During the residence of the Popes at Avignon additional expenses were incurred owing to the necessity of providing residences for themselves and their court, and, at the same time, the rebellions and disorders in the Papal States put an end to any hope of deriving any revenue from their own temporal dominions. On their return to Rome money was required to repair the palaces that had gone to ruin, and to enable the Popes to maintain their position as patrons of art and literature, and as the leaders of Europe in its struggle against the forces of Islam.

For this last purpose, namely, to organise the Christian forces against the Turks, the Popes claimed the right of levying a fixed tax on all ecclesiastical property. The amount of this varied from one-thirtieth to one-tenth of the annual revenue, and as a rule it was raised only for some definite period of years. Even in the days when the crusading fever was universal, such a tax

* Tangl, *Das Taxwesen der päpstlichen Kanzlei*, 1892. Samaran et Mollat, *La fiscalité pontificale en France du XVe siècle*, 1905. Kirsch, *Die päpstlichen Kollektorien in Deutschland während des 14 Jahr*, 1894.

excited a great deal of opposition; but when Europe had grown weary of the struggle, and when the Popes could do little owing to the failure of the temporal rulers to respond to their appeals, this form of taxation was resented bitterly, and the right of the Popes to raise taxes in this way off ecclesiastical property was questioned by the ecclesiastics affected as well as by the temporal rulers. England and France took measures to protect themselves; but in Germany the absence of any strong central authority, and the want of unity among the princes made it difficult to offer any effective resistance to these demands. In 1354, 1372, 1459, 1487, and in 1500, the German bishops protested strongly against the attempts of the Pope to levy taxes on ecclesiastical property.

But in addition to these extraordinary levies there were many permanent sources of revenue for the support of the Papal Court. In the first place from the time of Boniface IX. annats, which consisted of a certain proportion of the first year's revenue, were to be paid by all clerics on whom a minor benefice was conferred by the Holy See. In case of the major benefices, bishoprics and abbacies, the *servitia communia* and the *servitia minuta* took the place of annats. The *servitia communia* was a fixed sum the amount of which depended upon the annual revenue of the See or abbey, and was divided between the Pope and the cardinals of the Curia. The *servitia minuta,* amounting to about 3½ per cent. of the *servitia communia,* was given to the lower officials, who prepared the letters of appointment. The revenues of vacant Sees and the property of deceased bishops were also claimed by the Holy See. From England the Pope received yearly the Peter's Pence, and from all countries that acknowledged his feudal jurisdiction he was entitled to a definite annual tribute.

Furthermore, the reservations[*] of benefices were another fruitful source of revenue. The policy of re-

[*] Lux, *Constitutionum Apostolicarum de generali beneficiorum reservatione ab anno* 1265 *ad an.* 1378, etc., 1904.

CAUSES OF THE REFORMATION 43

serving benefices to the Holy See might be defended, on the ground that it was often necessary in order to counterbalance the interference of secular rulers in regard to ecclesiastical appointments, and that it afforded the Pope a convenient means of rewarding officials whose services were required for the government of the Church. But the right of the Pope to reserve benefices was abused during the fourteenth and fifteenth centuries, and gave rise to constant friction with the civil and ecclesiastical authorities in different countries of Europe. Reservations, instead of being the exception, became very general, and, as a result, the eyes of all ambitious clerics were turned towards Rome from which they hoped to receive promotion, whether their immediate superiors deemed them worthy or unworthy. Such a state of affairs opened the way to the most serious abuses, and not unfrequently to disedifying wrangles between rival candidates, all of whom claimed to have received their appointments from Roman officials.

Intimately connected with papal reservations were expectancies or promises given to certain persons that they should be appointed to certain benefices as soon as a vacancy would occur. Such promises of appointment were unknown in the Church before the twelfth century, but later on they became very general, and led to most serious abuses during the residence of the Popes at Avignon and during the disturbances caused by the Great Western Schism. Expectancies were adopted by Clement V. and his successors as a means of raising money or of securing support. Various attempts were made to put an end to such a disastrous practice, as for example at the Councils of Constance and Basle, but it was reserved for the Council of Trent to effect this much needed reform.

Again the custom of handing over benefices *in commendam,* that is of giving some person the right of drawing the revenues of a vacant benefice for a certain specified time, was highly prejudicial to the best interests

of religion. Such a practice, however justifiable in case
of benefices to which the care of souls was not attached,
was entirely indefensible when adopted in regard to
bishopric, abbacies, and minor benefices, where so much
depended upon personal activity and example. The
person who held the benefice in *commendam* did nothing
except to draw the revenue attached to his office, while
the whole work was committed to an underpaid vicar
or representative, who was obliged often to resort to all
kinds of devices to secure sufficient means of support.
Again though plurality of benefices was prohibited by
several decrees, yet during the fourteenth and fifteenth
centuries nothing was more common than to find one
individual holding, by virtue of a papal dispensation,
two, three, six, ten, and possibly more benefices to most
of which the care of souls was attached. Such a state of
affairs was regarded as an intolerable scandal by right
minded Christians, whether lay or cleric, and was
condemned by decrees of Popes and councils; but as
exceptions were made in favour of cardinals or princes,
and as even outside these cases dispensations were given
frequently, the evils of plurality continued unabated.

Again, the frequent applications for and concessions
of dispensations in canonical irregularities by the
Roman congregations were likely to make a bad impression, and to arouse the suspicion that wholesome
regulations were being abandoned for the sake of the
dispensation fees paid to the officials. Similarly, too,
complaints were made about the dispensations given in
the marriage impediments, and the abuses alleged
against preachers to whose charge the duty of preaching
indulgences was committed. Furthermore, the custom
of accepting appeals in the Roman Courts, even when
the matters in dispute were of the most trivial kind, was
prejudicial to the local authorities, while the undue prolongation of such suits left the Roman lawyers exposed
to the charge of making fees rather than justice the
motive of their exertions.

The disturbances produced by the schism, and the interference of the state in episcopal elections helped to secure the appointment of many unworthy bishops. Even in the worst days of the fifteenth and sixteenth centuries a large proportion of the bishops in the different countries of Europe were excellent men, but a large percentage also, especially in Germany, were thoroughly worldly. They were more anxious about their position as secular princes or proprietors than about the due fulfilment of their sacred duties. Very often they were sprung from the nobility, and were appointed on account of their family influence without any regard to their qualifications, and, as a rule, the duties of visitation, of holding synods, and even of residing in their dioceses were neglected. Besides, even when they were anxious to do their best, the claims of the lay patrons and the papal reservation of benefices made it difficult for them to exercise proper disciplinary control over their clergy. In many cases, too, the cathedral chapters were utterly demoralised, mainly owing to outside influence in the appointment of the canons. The clergy as a body were very far from being as bad as they have been painted by fanatical reformers or by the followers of Luther. The collections of sermons that have come down to us, the prayer books for the instruction of the faithful, the catechisms, the compilations from the Holy Scriptures, the hymns, theological works, and especially the compendums prepared for the use of those engaged in hearing confessions give the lie to the charge of wholesale neglect*; but, at the same time the want of sufficient control, the interference of lay patrons in the appointments to benefices, the absence of seminaries, and the failure of the universities to give a proper ecclesiastical training, produced their natural effect on a large body of the clergy. Grave charges of ignorance, indifference, concubinage, and

---

* *Cf.* Gasquet, *Eve of the Reformation,* chap. ix.. Janssen, *op. cit.,* Eng. Trans., vol. i., pp. 9-86. Leclerc, *Mémoire sur la prédication au XIV. siècle* (*Hist. Littér. de France,* tom. xxiv.).

simony were not wholly groundless, as the decrees of various councils sufficiently testify.

Many causes contributed to bring about a relaxation of discipline in many of the religious orders. The uncanonical appointment of abbots, the union of various abbacies in the hands of a single individual, the custom of holding abbacies *in commendam,* and the wholesale exemption from episcopal authority for which many of the religious orders contended, are sufficient to account for this general relaxation. The state of the various houses and provinces even belonging to the same order depended largely on the character of the superiors, and hence it is not fair to judge one country or one province, or even one house, by what happened in other countries, provinces, or houses. Hence arises the difficulty of arriving at any general conclusion about the religious houses. It is safe, however, to say that with the exception of the Carthusians all the older orders required reform. From the beginning of the fifteenth century various attempts were made to restore the old discipline in the Benedictine communities and with considerable success. The Carmelites were divided into two main branches, the Calced and the Discalced; the Franciscans were divided into three main bodies, the Conventuals, the Observants, and the Capuchins; the Dominicans made various efforts to restore the ancient discipline especially from about the beginning of the fifteenth century; while many of the Augustinians who were determined on reform established new congregations, as for example, the Discalced Augustinian Hermits, who spread themselves over France, Spain, and Portugal. In addition, various new congregations, amongst them the Oblates founded in 1433 by St. Francisca Romana, and the Hermit Brothers in 1435 by St. Francis of Paula, were established to meet the necessities of the age.*

* Hélyot, *Hist. des ordres monastiques,* 8 vols., 1714-19 Henrion, *Allgem. Geschichte der Mönchsorden,* 1855.

CAUSES OF THE REFORMATION

Unfortunately the endless disputes between the religious and secular clergy* at this period tended to distract the attention of both from their spiritual work, and to give rise to considerable disorder and discontent. On the one side, men like the Paris professor, John Poilly and Richard Fitzralph, Archbishop of Armagh, were too extreme, and seemed inclined to leave to the religious orders no place in the ministration of the Church, while on the other, some of the religious, such as the Franciscan, John von Gorrel, wished to assert for themselves complete independence of episcopal control. Various attempts were made by Boniface VIII., Benedict XI., Alexander V., John XXII., Calixtus III., Sixtus IV., and by the Councils of Constance and Basle to settle these disputes, but without much permanent result. It was only in the eleventh session of the Fifth Lateran Council (1516) that Leo X. promulgated the decrees, which in substance hold good at the present time, fixing the relation between the bishops and the regular clergy.†

Many of the fanatical preachers anxious for reform were guilty of undoubted exaggeration in the pictures which they paint of clerical life at the time, as were also not a few of the Humanists, anxious to cast ridicule on their opponents. But even when all due allowance has been made for these exaggerations in such works as the *Onus Ecclesiae* ‡ of Bishop Berthold, the rhymed sermons of one of the great Franciscan opponents of Luther, Thomas Murner (1475-1537), which became popular in Germany under the titles of the *Narrenbeschwörung* and the *Schelmenzunft,* Faber's *Tractatus de Ruinae Ecclesiae Planctu,* the *Encomium Moriae* of Erasmus, the Dialogues of St. German in England, the *Narrenschiff* of Sebastian Brant, and the petitions of the

---

* Paulus, *Welt und Ordensklerus beim Ausgange des* 13 *Jahrh,* etc., 1901.

† Raynaldus, *Annal. an.* 1515, 1516.

‡ Published in 1524.

Spanish Cortes, enough remains to convince any reasonable man that a reform of the clergy was an urgent necessity.

For many years the cry of reform of the Church in its head and members had been heard in nearly every country of Europe. The justice of such a demand was admitted universally, but the difficulties in the way were so great that no Pope cared to risk a generous scheme of reform. Most of the abuses of the fifteenth and sixteenth centuries might be traced back to the decline of the papal power during the Avignon exile and the Great Western Schism. When peace was restored to the Church, and when the Popes might have done something for the revival of ecclesiastical discipline, the advocates of the conciliar theory blocked the way by their extravagant attacks on the Papacy, and by their attempts to destroy the supremacy of the Holy See under the guise of reforming the Roman Curia. Besides, it was impossible to carry through any effective measures for the removal of abuses without attacking what were regarded as vested interests, and the holders of these interests were determined not to yield without a struggle. The cardinals wished to restrict the rights of the Pope; the bishops wished to reform the cardinals and the Papal Court; the Paris doctors wished to reform the bishops and the regular clergy; while the regular clergy traced all the evils in the Church to the indifference and neglect of the secular priests. Unfortunately there was no man endowed with the foresight and the courage of Gregory VII. to put his finger upon the real cause of the downfall, namely, the slavery of the Church, and to lead a campaign for the independence of the spiritual power, particularly for the restoration of free canonical elections.

At the Council of Constance everybody recognised the necessity of reform, but the jealousies of the various nations, the opposition of the interests concerned, and the fear of provoking a new schism, made it impossible to do more than to adopt temporary expedients, which, it was hoped, might give some relief. Decrees concerning exemption from episcopal authority, the union of benefices, simony, tithes, and the duties of the clerical state were promulgated in the fourteenth session, and the other questions, upon which the different nations could not agree, were to be regulated by Concordats with the Holy See. The Concordat with the German nation dealt with canonical election, appeals to Rome, annats, indulgences, dispensations, and the limitation of excommunication; the English Concordat insisted on the right of England to be represented in the college of cardinals and contained clauses dealing with indulgences and dispensations; the Concordat with Castile regarded the number of cardinals, the reservation and collation of benefices, annats, *commendams,* appeals, and indulgences; by the Concordat with France it was arranged that owing to the wars in which France was engaged the annats and other taxes payable to the Holy See should be reduced considerably. Measures such as these were utterly inadequate even had they been observed to the letter, but in reality complaints were made frequently, especially in Germany, that they were disregarded.

The Council which met in Siena (1524) was entirely unrepresentative, and was dissolved without having accomplished anything. But great hopes were expressed that the Council of Basle would formulate and carry out a thorough scheme of reform. Unfortunately, however, these hopes were doomed to disappointment. An extreme section, hostile to the Papacy and determined to weaken its position, dominated the Council, and made it impossible to do the work for which the assembly had been convoked. Though the Council held its first session in 1431, nearly four years passed before any reform decrees were issued. They dealt with concubinage, excommunication, the abuse of interdicts, and the abolition of annats and other taxes payable to the Holy See. The violence with which the Council assailed Eugene IV., and the fear of a new schism alienated many who were anxious for reform, but who were not willing to attack the essential prerogatives of the Pope. The clergy of France met at Bourges in 1432, and with their consent the Pragmatic Sanction of Bourges was published by the king in 1438. According to this edict annats were retained, but were reduced to one-fifth of the amount formerly paid, and most of the reformatory decrees of Basle were adopted for use in France. Germany was desirous of reform, but at the same time unwilling to break with the Holy See, and hence the German nation remained neutral in the disputes between Eugene IV. and the Council. Finally Germany returned to its allegiance, and the Concordat of Vienna was signed in 1448, according to which the right of the Pope to make appointments to benefices in the Empire and the amount of the fees to be paid to the Curia were regulated. This agreement was not regarded with favour in some parts of Germany, and complaints were made frequently by the princes that the terms of the agreement were not observed by the Roman officials. England also took steps to protect itself by the Statutes of *Provisors* and *Praemunire* (1453). These statutes rendered null and void all collations, reservations or provisions of benefices made by the Holy See in England, and forbade all appeals to the Roman tribunal on questions which could be settled before English tribunals.

During the pontificate of Nicholas V., Calixtus III., and Pius II., very little was done for reform. The fear that if another General Council were convoked the disgraceful scenes of Basle might be repeated, and the dangers which threatened Europe from a Turkish invasion, seem to have paralysed the Popes, and to have prevented them from taking effective measures to abolish evident abuses. Paul II. did, indeed, take action against the Pagan Humanists who barely concealed their antipathy to Christianity even in the city of the Popes, but he took no steps to remove the influences which had made such a state of affairs possible. As a rule at each

CAUSES OF THE REFORMATION

successive conclave the cardinal electors pledged themselves that whichever of them should be elected would undertake certain measures, some of which might have redounded to the good of the universal Church, others of them merely to the advantage of the sacred college itself; but these election agreements were always quashed, and the evil was allowed to increase without check. From the election of Sixtus IV. the tendency was steadily downwards, till in the days of Alexander VI. the Papacy reached its lowest point. At a time when even people indifferent to religion were shocked by the state of affairs at the Roman Court, it is no wonder that a zealous and holy ecclesiastic like the great Dominican Savonarola * should have denounced these abuses in no uncertain language, and should have warned Alexander VI. of the terrible judgment in store for the Church unless some steps were taken to avert the indignation of an offended Almighty. The threats and warnings of Savonarola were, however, scoffed at as the unbridled outbursts of a disappointed fanatic, and the cry for reform was put aside as unworthy of attention.

Julius II. (1503-1513) was personally above reproach, but the circumstances of his time allowed him very little opportunity to undertake a generous plan of reform. The recovery of the Papal States that had been frittered away by his predecessors in providing territories for their family connections, the wars in Italy, and the schemes of Louis XII. forced the Pope to play the part of a soldier rather than that of an ecclesiastic, and delayed the convocation of the General Council to which right-minded Christians looked for some relief. Louis XII., taking advantage of this general desire, forestalled the Pope by inducing some of the cardinals to summon a General Council to meet at Pisa (September 1511). The assembly met at Pisa and adjourned to Lyons, but the feeling of loyalty to the Pope was too strong for Louis

* Lucas, *Fra Girolamo Savonarola*, 1906. O'Neill, *Jerome Savonarola*, 1898.

XII., and the assembly at Lyons could count on very little support outside France. Julius II. determined to summon a General Council to meet in Rome for the reformation of the Church. This, the Fifth Lateran Council, as it is called, was opened in May 1512, but the earlier sessions were devoted almost entirely to the condemnation of the French schism, the decrees of the *Conciliabulum* at Lyons, and the Pragmatic Sanction. Before the work of reform could be taken in hand Julius II. died (1513), and the young cardinal deacon, John de' Medici, ascended the papal throne under the title of Leo X.

From the new Pope, if one were to judge him by his antecedents, a development of classical learning and art might be expected rather than a renewal of religion. Personally Leo X. was not a wicked man. On the contrary in his private life he was attentive to his religious duties, but he was indifferent and inclined to let things shape their own course. The Lateran Council did, indeed, undertake the restoration of ecclesiastical discipline. It condemned abuses in connexion with the bestowal of benefices, decreed the reformation of the Curia, especially in regard to taxes, defined the position of the regulars in regard to the bishops of the dioceses in which their houses were situated, ordered the bishops to enforce their censorship over books published within their jurisdiction, and approved of the Concordat that had been arranged between Leo and Francis I. (1516).

Such reforms as these were so completely inadequate that they failed to give satisfaction to the hosts of clerics and laymen who desired a thorough reform. The news that the Council was dissolved in March 1517 without having grappled with the urgent reform of the Church in its head and members, sent a thrill of dismay throughout the Christian world, and secured for Luther the sympathy of many when a few months later he opened his campaign at Wittenberg. It was thought at first that he aimed merely at the removal of abuses, and in this work he could have counted upon the active co-operation of some of the leading German ecclesiastics, who showed themselves his strongest opponents once they realised that he aimed not so much at reform as at the destruction of the Church and of all religious authority.

CHAPTER II

THE RELIGIOUS REVOLUTION.

LUTHERANISM AND ZWINGLIANISM.

(a) IN GERMANY.

Janssen, *op. cit.* (i., *a*). Pastor, *op. cit.* (i., *a*). Döllinger, *Die Reformation*, 1846-8. Hergenröther-Kirsch, *op. cit.* (i., *b*). Grisar, S.J., *Luther*, 3 Bde, 1911-12 (Eng. Trans., 1913-14). Denifle-Weiss, O.P., *Luther und Luthertum in der ersten Entwicklung*, 1906-9. Weiss, *Lutherpsychologie als Schlüssel zur Lutherlegende*, 2 auf., 1906. Hausrath, *Luthers Leben*, 2 Bde. 1904. Köstlin-Kawerau, *Martin Luther, Sein Leben und seine schriften*, 1903. Cardauns, *Zur Geschichte der Kirchlichen Unions—und Reformsbestrebungen von 1538-42*, 1910. Laemmer, *Monumenta Vaticana historiam ecclesiasticam saeculi XVI. illustrantia*, 1861. Raynaldus, *Annales Ecclesiastici*, 1755 (tom. xx.-xxi.). Armstrong, *The Emperor Charles V.*, 1902. *Cambridge Modern History*, vol. ii. (The Reformation), 1903. Kidd, *Documents Illustrative of the Continental Reformation*, 1911. For a fairly complete bibliography on this period of history, *cf.* Grisar's *Luther* (Eng. Trans., vol. i., xv.-xxv.; Cambridge Modern History, ii., pp. 728-64; Hergenröther-Kirsch, Bd. iii., pp. 4-8).

THE religious revolt that had been foretold by many earnest ecclesiastics began in Germany in 1517. Its leader was Martin Luther, the son of a miner, born at Eisleben in 1483. As a boy he attended school at Eisenach and Magdeburg, supporting himself by singing in the streets until a kind benefactress came to his assistance in the person of Ursula Cotta. His father, having improved his position in the world, determined to send the youth to study law at the University of Erfurt, which was then one of the leading centres of Humanism on the northern side of the Alps. But though Luther was in close touch with some of the principal classical scholars of Germany and was by no means an indifferent classical scholar himself, there is no evidence of his having been influenced largely in his religious views by the Humanist movement. He turned his attention principally to the study of philosophy, and having received his degree in 1505, he began to lecture on the physics and ethics of Aristotle.

Suddenly, to the surprise of his friends, and the no small vexation of his father the young Luther, who had not been particularly remarkable for his religious fervour, abandoned his career at the university and entered the novitiate of the Augustinian monastery at Erfurt (July 1505). The motives which induced him to take this unexpected step are not clear. Some say he was led to do so by the sudden death of a student friend, others that it was in fulfilment of a vow which he had made during a frightful thunderstorm that overtook him on a journey from his father's house to Erfurt, while he himself tells us that he became a monk because he had lost confidence in himself.* Of his life as a student very little is known for certain. Probably he was no worse and no better than his companions in a university city, which was described by himself in later life as a "beerhouse" and a "nest of immorality."†

The sudden change from the freedom and excitement of the university to the silence and monotony of the cloister had a depressing influence on a man like Luther, who, being of a nervous, highly-strung temperament, was inclined to pass quickly from one extreme to another. He began to be gloomy and scrupulous, and was driven at times almost to despair of his salvation; but Staupitz, the superior of the province, endeavoured to console him by impressing on him the necessity of putting his trust entirely in the merits of Christ. Yet in spite of his scruples Luther's life as a novice was a happy one. He

* Grisar, *Luther* (Eng. Trans.), i., p. 4.
† *Id.* p. 8.

was assiduous in the performance of his duties, attentive to the instruction of his superiors, and especially anxious to acquire a close acquaintance with the Sacred Scriptures, the reading and study of which were strongly recommended to all novices in the Augustinian order at this period.* In 1506 he was allowed to make his vows, and in the following year he was ordained priest. During the celebration of his first Mass he was so overcome by a sense of his own unworthiness to offer up such a pure sacrifice that he would have fled from the altar before beginning the canon had it not been for his assistants, and throughout the ceremony he was troubled lest he should commit a mortal sin by the slightest neglect of the rubrics. At the breakfast that followed, to which Luther's relatives had been invited, father and son met for the first time since Luther entered the monastery. While the young priest waxed eloquent about the happiness of his vocation and about the storm from heaven that helped him to understand himself, his father, who had kept silent throughout the repast, unable to restrain himself any longer interrupted suddenly with the remark that possibly he was deceived, and that what he took to be from God might have been the work of the devil. "I sit here," he continued, "eating and drinking but I would much prefer to be far from this spot." Luther tried to pacify him by reminding him of the godly character of monasticism, but the interruption was never forgotten by Luther himself or by his friends who heard it.

After his ordination the young monk turned his attention to theology, but, unfortunately, the theological training given to the Augustinian novices at this period was of the poorest and most meagre kind.† He studied little if anything of the works of the early Fathers, and never learned to appreciate Scholasticism as expounded by its greatest masters, St. Thomas or St. Bonaventure.

* Grisar, *Luther* (Eng. Trans.), i., p. 14.
† *Id.* chap. iv.

THE RELIGIOUS REVOLUTION 57

His knowledge of Scholastic Theology was derived mainly from the works of the rebel friar William of Occam, who, in his own time, was at constant war with the Popes, and who, during the greater part of his life, if not at the moment of his death, was under sentence of excommunication from the Church. The writings of such a man, betraying as they did, an almost complete unacquaintance with the Scriptures and exaggerating men's natural powers to the undervaluing or partial exclusion of Grace, exercised a baneful influence on a man of Luther's tastes and temperaments. Accepted by Luther as characteristic of Scholastic Theology, such writings prejudiced him against the entire system. Acting on the advice of the provincial, Staupitz, he gave himself up with great zeal to the study of the Bible, and later on he turned his attention to the works of St. Augustine, particularly the works written in defence of the Catholic doctrine on Grace against the Pelagians. In 1508 he went to the University of Wittenberg, founded recently by Frederick of Saxony, to lecture on Logic and Ethics, and to continue his theological studies; but for some reason, as yet unexplained, he was recalled suddenly to his monastery at Erfurt, where he acquired fame rapidly as a lecturer and preacher.

Thirty foundations of the Augustinians in Saxony had accepted the reform begun by Andrew Proles in the fifteenth century, and had separated themselves definitely from the unreformed houses of the order in Germany. They were subject immediately to the general of the order, whose vicar at this time in Saxony was the well-known Humanist, Staupitz.* The latter was anxious to bring about a reunion between the two parties and to have himself appointed as superior; but the party who stood for the strict observance were opposed bitterly to such a step, and determined to send a representative to Rome to plead their cause. The fact that they selected so young a man as Luther to champion their interests is a

* Keller, *Johann von Staupitz und die Anfänge der Reformation*, 1888.

sufficient proof of the position which he had won for himself amongst his religious brethren. He was looked up to already as an ornament of the order, and his selection for this highly important mission served to increase the over-weening pride and self-confidence that had manifested themselves already as weak spots in his character. Accompanied by a companion of his order he started on his long journey across the Alps. As he reached the heights of Monte Mario and surveyed the city of the Popes he fell on his knees, according to the custom of the pilgrims, and hailed "the city thrice sanctified by the blood of martyrs." He had looked forward with pleasure to a stay in Rome, where he might have an opportunity of setting his scruples to rest by a general confession of his sins, but, unfortunately, his brother Augustinians in Rome and those with whom he came most in contact seemed to have been more anxious to regale him with stories about the real or imaginary scandals of the city than to give him spiritual consolation or advice. Yet in later life, when he had definitely separated from the Church and when he was most anxious to blacken the character of Rome and the Popes, it is remarkable that he could point to very little detrimental to them of which he had personal knowledge, and was forced to rely solely on what had been told him by others. Nor did he leave Rome as a declared enemy of the Papacy, for even so late as 1516 he defended warmly the supremacy of the Pope as the one safeguard for the unity of the Church.* Many of his biographers, indeed, assert that, as he stood by the *Scala Sancta* and witnessed the pilgrims ascending on their bare knees, he turned aside disgusted with the sight and repeated the words of St. Paul, "the just man lives by his faith"; but such a statement, due entirely to the imagination of his relatives and admirers is rejected as a legend by those best qualified to judge.†
The threatened union of the strict and unreformed

* Grisar, *op. cit.* (Eng. Trans.), i., 34, 323.
† *Id.* i., 34, Bd. iii., 957-8.

Augustinians that had occasioned Luther's journey to Rome was abandoned; but it is worthy of note that Staupitz had succeeded in detaching him from his former friends, and that he returned to Germany a convinced and violent opponent of the party of strict observance, who had sent him to Rome as their representative. During his stay in the city there is good reason for believing that on his own behalf he sought for permission to lay aside his monastic habit and to devote himself for ten years to study in Italy, but his request was refused on the ground that it was not supported by the authority of his superiors. This petition was probably the foundation for the rumours that were circulated in Germany by his opponents that while in Rome he endeavoured to have himself " secularised " and to obtain a dispensation to marry.

On his return to Germany he devoted himself once more to the study of theology in preparation for the doctorate which he won at Wittenberg in 1512. Almost immediately he was appointed professor at the university and undertook to lecture on the Psalms. His eloquence and his imagination, his retentive memory enabling him to illustrate his texts by parallel passages drawn from the books of the Old Testament, and in a certain way his exaggerations, his strength of diction, and his asperity of language towards all with whose views he did not find himself in agreement, made his lectures most popular at the university, and filled his hall with an eager and attentive audience. Amongst the students Luther had no rival, and even the few professors who were inclined to resent his methods and his views were captivated by the magic influence of their brilliant young colleague. The Augustinians, mindful of the honour he was achieving for their order, hastened to appoint him to the important position of district vicar (1515), while the Elector Frederick could not conceal his delight at having secured the services of so capable a professor for the new university.

At Wittenberg Luther felt himself completely at home. He was proud of the distinctions conferred upon him by his brethren, and of the influence accorded to him by his companions in the university. Great as were his industry and his powers of application, yet they were put to the most severe tests to enable him to complete the programme he had set himself to accomplish. His lectures at the university, his sermons preached in the Augustinian church, his visitations of the houses of his order in the district over which he was vicar, his correspondence, partly routine and partly entailed by his close relations with some of the leading men in Germany, occupied all his time even to the exclusion of the spiritual exercises enjoined by his rule. Very frequently he neglected to celebrate Mass or even to read the divine office, and then alarmed by his negligence and guilt he had recourse to extraordinary forms of penance. Fits of laxity were followed by fits of scrupulousness until at last he was driven at times almost to despair. It was then that he called to mind the consoling advice given to him by his superior that he should put his trust in the merits of Christ, and the teaching of St. Augustine on the frailty of human nature unless it was aided and supported by divine Grace. He began to develop the idea that justification could not be acquired by good works, that concupiscence could not be overcome, and that consequently man could be justified only by the imputation of the merits of Christ. Years before, views such as these had been passing through his mind, as may be seen in his sermons against the Augustinians of the strict observance, but they found adequate expression only in his commentaries on the Epistles of St. Paul to the Romans and to the Galatians (1515-1516). Still, as yet, he held strongly to the principle of authority in matters of religion, and inveighed against heretics who would dare to set aside the authority of the Pope in order to follow their own judgment. In reality, however, his own teaching on merit and justification was no longer in

THE RELIGIOUS REVOLUTION 61

harmony with Catholic doctrine, and only a slight occasion was required to bring him into open and definite conflict with the authorities of the Church.

This occasion was provided by the preaching in Germany of an Indulgence proclaimed by Leo X. (1513-21). The building of St. Peter's had been begun by Julius II. and was continued by his successor Leo X., the son of Lorenzo de' Medici, and the great patron of the Humanist movement. In order to provide funds to enable him to continue this gigantic undertaking Leo X. proclaimed an Indulgence. In addition to Confession and Holy Communion it was ordered that those of the faithful who wished to share in the spiritual favours granted by the Pope should contribute according to their means for the completion of St. Peter's, or that they should pray for the success of the work in case poverty did not permit them to give alms. The publication of the indulgence in a great part of Germany was entrusted to Albrecht of Brandenburg, who had been elected Archbishop of Mainz though he was already Archbishop of of Magdeburg and Administrator of Halberstadt. The fees to be paid by an archbishop appointed to Mainz were exceptionally high not to speak of the large sum required for the extraordinary favour of being allowed to hold two archbishoprics. As a means of enabling Albrecht to raise the required amount, it was proposed by an official of the Datary that he should be allowed to retain half of the contributions given on the occasion of the publication of the Indulgence in the provinces of Mainz and Magdeburg, and in the lands of the House of Brandenburg.

To publish the Indulgence in the above-mentioned territories Albrecht appointed the Dominican John Tetzel,* who had acquired already considerable renown as a preacher. Tetzel was a man of solid education and of good moral standing, whose reputation as a successful

* Paulus, *Johann Tetzel, der Ablassprediger*, 1899. *Die Deutschen Dominikaner im Kampfe gegen Luther*, 1903.

popular preacher stood high in Germany at this period. Many grave abuses have been alleged against him by his enemies concerning his manner of carrying out the office entrusted to him by the archbishop, and in regard to his own private life serious crimes have been laid to his charge; but as a matter of history it is now admitted that Tetzel was a much maligned man, that his own conduct can bear the fullest scrutiny, and that in his preaching the worst that can be said against him is that he put forward as certainties, especially in regard to gaining indulgences for the souls of the faithful departed, what were merely the opinions of certain schools of theologians. Nor is it true to say that as the result of his activity vast sums of money made their way into the papal treasury. The accounts of the monies received during the greater portion of the time are now available, and it can be seen that when all expenses were paid comparatively little remained for either the Archbishop of Mainz or the building fund of St. Peter's.*

Tetzel preached with considerable success in Halberstadt, Magdeburg and Leipzig, and in May 1517 he found himself in the neighbourhood of Wittenberg, whence many people flocked to hear him, and to gain the Indulgence. This was not calculated to please Luther or his patron the Elector, Frederick of Saxony, and provided Luther with an occasion of giving vent to his own views on good works, Grace, and Justification. Years before, both in his sermons attacking the Augustinians of the strict observance for their over confidence in the merits of good works and penance, and in his commentaries on the Epistles of St. Paul to the Romans and to the Galatians, he had indicated already that his views on man's power to do anything good, and on the means and nature of justification differed widely from those put forward by Catholic theologians. At last, after careful consideration, following the bent of his own inclination and the advice of his friends, he determined to take the

* Grisar, *op. cit.* (Eng. Trans.), i., pp. 341-55.

field openly by publishing, on the eve of the festival of All Saints, 1517, his celebrated seventy theses against Indulgences.* This document was drawn up with great skill and foresight. Some of the theses were perfectly orthodox and professed great reverence for the teaching of the Church and the authority of the Pope; others of them were open to an orthodox as well as to an unorthodox interpretation; others, still, were opposed clearly and definitely to Catholic doctrine, and all them were put forward in a way that was likely to arrest public attention and to win the support of the masses.† They were affixed to the doors of the university church in Wittenberg, and copies of them were spread broadcast through Germany. Before a week had elapsed they were discussed with eagerness in all parts of the country, and the state of feeling became so intense that Tetzel was obliged to discontinue his mission, and to retire to Frankfurt, where under the direction of Wimpina, he set himself to draw up a number of counter theses which he offered to defend.

The circumstances of the time were very favourable to a campaign such as Luther had initiated. The princes of Germany and even some of the bishops made no secret of their opinion that indulgences had been abused, and many of them were anything but displeased at the step that had been taken by the Wittenberg professor. The old opposition between the Teuton and the Latin was growing daily more marked owing to the violent and abusive language of men like Ulrich von Hutten, who posed as German patriots; while the Humanist party, roused by the attacks made upon Reuchlin by the Dominicans of Cologne, backed by the Scholastic Theologians, were not sorry to see their opponents challenged in their own special department, and obliged to act on the defensive. The knights or lower nobles, too, who had been deprived of many of their privileges by the

* Kidd, *Documents of the Continental Reformation,* pp. 20-6.
† Specially, Nos. 43, 45, 59, 86.

princes, were ready for any scheme of violence in the hope that it might conduce to their advantage; and the lower classes ground down for centuries were beginning to realise their own strength, partly owing to the spread of secret societies, and were willing to lend a ready ear to a leader who had given expression to views that were coursing already through their own minds.

From all parts of Germany letters of congratulation poured in upon Luther. Many of these came from men who had no desire for a religious change, but who thought that Luther's campaign was directed only against abuses in the Church. From the Humanists, from several of the professors and students of Wittenberg, and even from the superiors of his order he received unstinted praise and encouragement. At least one of the bishops, Lorenz von Bibra of Würzburg, hastened to intercede for him with Frederick the Elector of Saxony, while none of the others took up an attitude of unflinching opposition. Tetzel, who had been forced to abandon his work of preaching, defended publicly at Frankfurt on the Maine a number of counter theses formulated by Conrad Wimpina. To this attack Luther replied in a sermon on indulgences in which he aimed at expressing in a popular style the kernel of the doctrine contained in his theses. Sylvester Prierias, the master of the Sacred Palace in Rome, to whom Luther's theses had been forwarded for examination, published a sharp attack upon them,* and was answered in Luther's most abusive style. The most distinguished, however, of the men who took the field against him was John Eck,† Professor of Theology and Vice-Chancellor of the University of Ingolstadt. He was a man well versed in the Scriptures and in the writings of the Fathers, a ready speaker and an incisive writer, in every way qualified to meet such a versatile opponent. While on a visit with the

---

* *Dialogus . . . in presumptuosas M. Lutheri conclusiones de potestate Papae.*

† Greving, *Johann Eck*, etc., 1906.

THE RELIGIOUS REVOLUTION

Bishop of Eichstätt he was consulted about Luther's theses, and gave his opinion in the *Obelisks* on the dangerous character of the teaching they contained. The *Obelisks* was prepared hastily and was not intended for publication, but it was regarded as so important that copies of it were circulated freely even before it was given to the world. Luther replied in the *Asterisks,* a work full of personal invective and abuse. A Dominican of Cologne, Hochstraten, also entered the lists against Luther, but his intervention did more harm than good to the cause of the Church by alienating the Humanist party whom he assailed fiercely as allies and abettors of Luther. These attacks, however, served only to give notoriety to Luther's views and to win for him the sympathy of his friends. His opponents made one great mistake. Their works were intended in great part only for the learned, while Luther aimed principally at appealing to the masses of the people. The Augustinians represented him as the victim of a Dominican conspiracy, and to show their high appreciation of his services they selected him to conduct the theological disputation at a chapter meeting held at Leipzig six months after the publication of his theses (1518). At this same meeting Luther defended the view that free will in man and all power of doing good were destroyed by original sin, and that everything meritorious accomplished by man is really done by God. His old opponent at the university, Bodenstein (surnamed Carlstadt from his place of birth), declared himself openly in favour of Luther's teaching on free will, and published a reply to Eck.

As a result of this controversy between Eck and Carlstadt it was arranged that a public disputation should be held at Leipzig (27 June-15 July, 1519). The Catholic teaching was to be defended by Eck against his two opponents, Luther and Carlstadt. A hall in the castle of Pleissenburg was placed at the disposal of the disputants by Duke George of Saxony, who was a convinced

Catholic himself, and who believed that the disputation might be the means of removing many doubts and misunderstandings. The acts of the disputation were to be drawn up and forwarded to the Universities of Paris and Erfurt for their decision. When it became known throughout Germany that a meeting had been arranged between Eck and his two principal opponents, the excitement, especially in the learned circles, became intense, and so great was the rush of scholars from all parts of the country to witness the encounter, that the immense hall was packed with an eager and attentive audience when Eck and Carlstadt entered the pulpits that had been prepared for them.

Few men in Germany, or outside it, were more fitted to hold their own in such a disputation than the distinguished Vice-Chancellor of Ingolstadt. He was a man of imposing appearance, gifted with a clear and pleasing voice and good memory, even tempered and ready, quick to detect the weak points of his adversaries, and keenly alert to their damaging concessions and admissions. The first point to be debated between him and Carlstadt was the question of Grace and Free Will. Carlstadt was at last obliged to concede that the human will was active at least to the extent of co-operating or of not co-operating with divine Grace, a concession that was opposed entirely to the thesis that he had undertaken to sustain. Luther, alarmed by the discomfiture of his colleague, determined to enter the lists at once on the question of the primacy of the Roman See. He was not, however, more successful than Carlstadt. Eck, taking advantage of Luther's irascible temperament and his exaggerations of speech, forced him step by step to put aside as worthless interpretations given by the early Fathers to certain passages of Scripture, and to reject the authority and infallibility of General Councils. Such a line of arguments, opposed as it was to the teaching and beliefs of the Church, roused the opposition of the audience, and served to open the eyes of Duke George

THE RELIGIOUS REVOLUTION   67

to the real nature of Luther's movement. Annoyed by his own defeat and by the attentions and applause lavished upon his rival by the people of Leipzig, Luther left the city in disgust. The disputation undoubtedly did good in so far as it made clear to all the position of the two parties, and succeeded in holding Duke George of Saxony and the city of Leipzig loyal to the Church; but it also did much harm by giving Luther the notoriety that he was so anxious to obtain, and by winning to his side Philip Melanchthon, who was destined to be in after life his ablest lieutenant. Both sides, as is usual in such contests, claimed the victory. The Universities of Cologne and Louvain condemned Luther immediately, as did also Paris in 1521, but as far as can be known Erfurt pronounced no decision on the questions submitted.

Meanwhile what was the attitude of the authorities in Rome towards Luther's movement. Leo X., having learned something of the turmoil created in Germany by Luther's theses and sermons, requested the vicar-general of the Augustinians to induce his rebellious subject to recall his teaching or, at least, to keep silent. The vicar wrote to the provincial, Staupitz, but, as the latter was one of those who had encouraged Luther to take the steps he had taken, very little was done to secure peace. Luther was, however, induced to write a most submissive letter to the Pope in which he begged for an investigation, pledging himself at the same time to accept the decision of Leo X. as the decision of Christ (30th May, 1518).* Not satisfied with the course of events, and alarmed by the reports forwarded to him from Germany, the Pope appointed a commission to examine the whole question, the result of which commission was that Luther

---

* "Beatissime Pater, prostratum me pedibus tuae beatitudinis offero cum omnibus quae sum et habeo. Vivifica, occide, voca, revoca, approba, reproba, ut placuerit. Vocem tuam vocem Christi in te praesidentis et loquentis agnoscam. Si mortem merui, mori non recusabo."

was summoned to submit at once or to appear at Rome to defend himself within sixty days.

He and his friends were thrown into a state of great alarm by this unexpected step. On the one hand, were he to submit and to acknowledge that he had been in error his reputation would be shattered, the Augustinians would feel themselves disgraced, and the University of Wittenberg would lose caste in the estimation of educated Germans. On the other hand, if he adopted the bold policy of refusing to yield to the papal entreaties he was in danger of being denounced publicly as a heretic. In this difficult situation his friends determined to invoke the protection of the Elector Frederick of Saxony, the founder and patron of Wittenberg University. Alarmed by the danger that threatened this institution from the removal or excommunication of one of its most popular professors, and anxious to gain time, Frederick requested the Pope to refer the matter for decision to some German bishop or to a neutral university. In reply to this request Leo X. appointed Cardinal Cajetan, papal legate in Germany, to hold an inquiry (23 Aug., 1518). Luther, having armed himself with a safe conduct, went to Augsburg to meet the papal representative, who received him very kindly, and exhorted him to withdraw his statements and submit. Luther endeavoured to induce the cardinal to enter into a discussion on the questions in dispute, but the latter did not allow himself to be drawn into a disputation. Finally, Luther refused to submit, though, at the same time, he declared solemnly that he wished unsaid and unwritten what he had said or written against the Roman Church. A few days later he fled from Augsburg after having drawn up a formal appeal "from the Pope ill-informed to the Pope well-informed," while the cardinal, disappointed by the failure of his efforts, turned to the Elector of Saxony for help against the rebellious monk. But the latter, deceived by the recommendations forwarded on Luther's behalf by his own superior, Staupitz, yielded to the

THE RELIGIOUS REVOLUTION 69

entreaties of Spalatin, the court chaplain, and of the professors of Wittenberg, and declined to take any steps to compel Luther to submit. Fearful, however, lest his patron might not be able to shield him from the censures of Rome, Luther determined to anticipate the expected condemnation by issuing an appeal to a future General Council (28 Nov., 1518).

In the meantime Leo X. who had learned from his representative the result of the Augsburg interviews, issued the Bull, *Cum postquam* (9 Nov., 1518), in which he explained authoritatively the Catholic doctrine on Indulgences, and threatened excommunication against all who refused to accept it. This document was deprived of much of its effect owing to the misrepresentations of Luther and his friends, who announced that it owed its origin to the schemes and intrigues of their Dominican opponents at Rome and in Germany. The occasion called for speedy and decisive action. But the impending imperial election, in which Charles I. of Spain (1516-56) and Francis I. of France (1515-47) were to be rival candidates, made it necessary for the Pope to proceed cautiously, and above all, to do nothing that might antagonise the Elector of Saxony, whose influence would be of the greatest importance in deciding the votes of the electoral college, if, indeed, it did not secure his own election. Had the appointment of a successor to Maximilian I. rested with Leo X. it can hardly be doubted that, in the hope of preserving the balance of power and of securing the freedom of the Holy See, he would have favoured the claims of the Elector against either or both the rival monarchs.*

In these circumstances it was decided to send Karl von Miltitz,† who was by birth a Saxon nobleman and at that period a chamberlain at the Papal Court, to present Frederick with the Golden Rose, and to bring about a peaceful settlement of a controversy that had been dis-

* Pastor, *op. cit.* iv., 177-79.
† Creutzberg, *Karl von Miltitz*, 1907.

turbing the whole Empire. The selection of Miltitz for such a delicate mission was most unfortunate. Proud, obstinate, and ill-informed about the real issues at stake, he was anxious to have the glory of putting an end to the controversy at all costs, and hence he was willing to appear before Luther as a humble suitor for peace rather than as a stern judge. All his severity and reproaches were reserved for Luther's opponents, especially for Tetzel, whom he held primarily responsible for the whole mischief, and towards whom he acted both imprudently and unjustly. The Elector showed himself but little inclined to respond to the advances of Leo X. He consented, however, to arrange an interview between Miltitz and Luther at Altenburg (Jan. 1519). During the course of the interviews that took place between them, Luther pledged himself to remain silent if his opponents were forced to do likewise. He promised, too, that if Miltitz wrote advising the Pope to appoint a German bishop to try the case and to convince him of his error he would be willing to retract his theses, to submit to the Church, and to advise all his supporters to remain loyal to the Holy See. At the same time he prepared a letter for transmission to Rome, in which he addressed the Pope in the most respectful terms, declaring as on oath before God and creatures that it never entered into his mind to attack in any way the authority of the Roman Church or of the Pope, that he confessed willingly that in this Church was vested supreme jurisdiction, and that neither in heaven or on earth was there anything he should put before it except Jesus Christ the Lord of all things.*
Throughout these proceedings it is clear that Luther meant only to deceive Miltitz and to lull the suspicions of the Roman authorities, until the seed he had planted

---

* "*Coram Deo et tota creatura sua testor, me neque voluisse neque hodie velle Ecclesiae Romanae ac Beatitudinis Tuae potestatem ullo modo tangere aut quacunque versutia demoliri; quin plenissime confiteor huius ecclesiae potestatem esse super omnia, nec ei praeferendum quidquid sive in coelo sive in terra praeter unum Jesum Christum Dominum omnium*" (3rd March, 1519). Kidd, *op. cit.*, p. 43.

should have taken root. Only a short time before he had written to a friend, hinting that the Pope was the real Anti-Christ mentioned by St. Paul in the Second Epistle to the Thessalonians, and asserting his ability to prove that he who ruled at the Roman Court was worse than the Turk.*

Several months passed and no further steps were taken by Rome to meet the crisis. This delay was due in great measure to the death of Maximilian I. (1519), and to the sharp contest that ensued. The two strongest candidates were Charles I., King of Spain, who as son of Philip the Handsome (son of Maximilian), and of Joanna of Castile (daughter of Ferdinand and Isabella), was ruler of Spain, the Netherlands, Austria, and Naples, and Francis I., King of France. For centuries the Pope had striven to prevent the union of Naples and the Empire, and with good reason, for such a union must prove almost of necessity highly detrimental to the safety of the Papal States and the independence of the Holy See. For this reason, if for no other, Leo X. did not favour the candidature of Charles. Nor could he induce himself to display any enthusiasm for the cause of Francis I., whose intervention in Italian affairs the Pope had good grounds to dread. As against the two the Pope endeavoured to induce the princes to elect one of their own number, preferably the Elector of Saxony. But the Elector showed no anxiety to accept such a responsible office, and in the end Charles succeeded in winning over to his side the majority of the princes. He was elected and proclaimed Emperor under the title of Charles V. (1519).

While Rome remained inactive, and while the opponents of Luther in Germany were handicapped by the crude diplomacy of Miltitz, Luther was gaining ground with marvellous rapidity. His success was due partly to his own great personal gifts as a popular demagogue, and partly also to the fact that no man knew

* Grisar, *op. cit.* (Eng. Trans.), i, 359.

better than he how to make capital out of the ecclesiastical abuses of the time, and to win to his side all who had any reason to be discontented with the existing order. He was strengthened very much by the inactivity of the German bishops, who seemed unwilling to take any severe measures against him, by the help and encouragement of Frederick of Saxony, who, during the interregnum and for some time after the election of Charles V. was the real administrator of Germany, by his union with the leading Humanist scholars and professors, especially Erasmus, all of whom regarded Luther merely as the champion of liberty against the obscurantism of the Scholastics, and by his secret alliances with discontented nobles, such as Ulrich von Hutten and Franz von Sickingen, whose sole hope of improving their fortunes lay in the creation of public disorder.

Johann Eck, Luther's chief opponent, realising that there was no hope of stirring up the German authorities to take action, hastened to Rome to impress upon the Pope and his advisers the extreme gravity of the situation, and to urge them to proceed against the revolt with all possible energy and despatch. Luther himself recognised clearly enough that the crisis he had long foreseen was at hand, and he began to prepare men's minds for complete rupture with the Church by his sermon on excommunication in which he bade defiance to the ecclesiastical authorities. He threw himself with renewed energy into the fray, turning out volume after volume with feverish rapidity, each more violent and abusive than its predecessor, and nearly all couched in language that was as intelligible to the peasant as it was to the professor. In his *Address to the Nobles of Germany,* in his works *On the Mass, On the Improvement of Christian Morality,* and *On the Babylonian Captivity,* he proclaimed himself a political as well as a religious revolutionary. There was no longer any concealment or equivocation. The veil was lifted at last, and Luther stood forth to the world as the declared enemy of the

THE RELIGIOUS REVOLUTION 73

Church and the Pope, the champion of the Bible as the sole rule of faith, and the defender of individual judgment as its only interpreter. In these works he rejected the Mass, Transubstantiation, vows of chastity, pilgrimages, fasts, the Sacraments, the powers of the priesthood, and the jurisdiction and supremacy of the Pope. With such a man there could be no longer any question of leniency or of compromise. The issues at stake, namely, whether the wild and impassioned assertions of a rebel monk should be accepted in preference to the teaching of Christ's Church, ought to have been apparent to every thinking man; and yet so blinded were some of his contemporaries by their sympathy with the Humanists as against the Theologians, that even still they forced themselves to believe Luther sought only for reform.

At Rome the trouble in Germany was one of the main subjects that engaged the attention of the Curia. It was felt that the time had come when decisive measures must be taken. After long and anxious deliberations Leo X. published the Bull, *Exsurge Domine* (June 1520), in which forty propositions taken from Luther's writings were condemned, his works were ordered to be burned, the full penalties of excommunication were proclaimed against him unless he withdrew his errors and made his submission within sixty days, while his aiders and abettors were besought in the most touching terms to abandon the dangerous path into which they had been betrayed. Had such a pronouncement been issued at the beginning of the movement it might have done much to restore peace to the Church, but, coming as it did at a time when Luther's movement, backed by all the revolutionary forces of Germany, had already acquired considerable dimensions, it failed to put an end to the tumult. Besides, the papal decision was deprived of much of its force by the fact that Eck, Caraccioli, and Aleandro were appointed as a commission to superintend its execution. The appointment of Eck was a great tactical blunder, as it afforded Luther and his friends an opportunity of proclaiming that the sentence of excommunication was procured by the intrigues and misrepresentations of their personal enemies; while the fact that the German bishops were disregarded in the execution of the Bull as if they were not above suspicion themselves, was looked upon by many as a studied insult to the entire German hierarchy. Even though Luther had entertained any thoughts of submission, the triumph of Eck would have created very serious obstacles; but, knowing as he did, that even at the worst he could reckon upon the support of a certain number of the discontented nobles who had pledged themselves to put their swords at his disposal, he had no intention of making his submission.

The reception accorded to the papal document varied according to the views of the local authorities and the state of public feeling in the different cities and provinces. Thus, while its publication was welcomed in Cologne, Mainz, Halberstadt, and Freising, it was received with very mixed feelings at Leipzig and at Erfurt. Frederick of Saxony, to whom Leo X. had addressed a personal appeal, refused to abandon Luther's cause unless it were proved from the Scriptures that he was wrong. He did, indeed, suggest that Luther should write a respectful letter to the Pope, but his suggestion passed unheeded. At first Luther pretended that the Bull was a forgery brought forward by Eck to discredit him, but when this line of defence proved useless, he boldly attacked the papal pronouncement in his pamphlet, *Against the Bull of Anti-Christ,* in which he denounced Leo X. as a heretic and apostate, an enemy of the Holy Scriptures, a tyrant, and a calumniator. Lest, however, the courage of his supporters might be overcome by the terrors of excommunication, he issued an appeal from the sentence of the Pope to the judgment of a future General Council. Finally, on the 10th December, 1520, in the presence of an immense concourse of the citizens and students of Wittenberg, he burned publicly the papal

Bull and the writings of his principal opponents. On this occasion he proclaimed his intention of overthrowing the ecclesiastical organisation, and of introducing a new theological system. For the future it was to be war to the knife against the Pope and the Church, and he called upon German patriots and all true friends of personal liberty to take their stand by his side in the conflict that had been begun.

Charles V. was apparently in a very strong position. Not since the days of Charlemagne had any ruler claimed jurisdiction over so wide a territory as his, comprising, as it did, Germany and Austria, the kingdom of the two Sicilies, Spain, and the Netherlands. But in reality the very extent of his dominions made him much less powerful than he might have been as the sovereign of a smaller but more compact region. It served to awaken the suspicions of his subjects, who feared that he might abolish their distinctive national constitutions and weld his scattered territories into one great empire, and to excite the jealousy of the other rulers of Europe, who imagined that he might declare himself dictator of the western world. The German princes, having resisted successfully all the efforts made by his grandfather, Maximilian I., to convert the loose confederation of the German States into a united and centralised nation, were on their guard lest his successor should attempt a similar policy with the aid of Spanish troops and Spanish gold; the Spaniards resented the absence of the king from Spain, where many of the lower classes were in a state bordering on rebellion; Francis I. of France, trembling for the very existence of his country, was willing to do all things, even to agree to an alliance with the sons of Mohammed, if he could only lessen the influence of his powerful rival. The Turks under Soliman I. were determined to realise the dreams of their race by extending their territories from the Bosphorus to the Atlantic; while even the Pope had good reason to suspect that Charles V., unmindful of the example of his great namesake, might seek to become the master rather than the protector of the Church.*

On account of the troubles in Spain it was only late in the year 1520 that Charles V. could come to Germany to meet the electors, and to take over formally the administration of the Empire (23 Oct.). Less than two weeks had elapsed when the papal representative, Aleandro, himself a distinguished Humanist, sought an interview with the new ruler, and besought him to enforce the papal Bull against Luther with the full weight of his imperial authority. But the wavering attitude of many of the princes and the determined opposition of Frederick of Saxony made the Emperor hesitate to condemn Luther without giving him an opportunity for explanation and defence. The Diet was soon to open at Worms, and Charles V. issued an invitation to Luther to attend, guaranteeing at the same time his personal safety on the way to and from Worms and during his sojourn in the city.

The Diet met in January 1521, but despite the efforts of Aleandro the majority of the princes still failed to realise the gravity of the situation. Feeling against Rome was running very high in Germany at the time. Many of the princes insisted on presenting a document embodying the grievances of Germany (*Centum Gravamina*) † to the papal ambassador, while even such an orthodox supporter of the Church as Duke George of Saxony, brought forward very serious complaints against the clergy, accompanied by a demand that a General Council should be summoned to restore peace to the Church. Luther, strengthened by the safe conduct of the Emperor and by a secret understanding with some of the princes and knights, set out from Wittenberg for Worms, where he arrived in April 1521. On presenting himself before the Diet he was invited to state if he were

* *Cambridge Modern History*, ii., chaps. ii., iii.

† *Imperatorum nationis Germanicae gravamina ad Sedem Romanam*, 1725.

really the author of the works published under his name, copies of which were presented to him, and, if so, was he willing to retract the doctrines contained in them. In reply to the former of these questions he admitted the authorship of the volumes, but asked for time to consider what answer he should make in regard to the latter. A day was allowed him for consideration. When he appeared again, all traces of the hesitation and nervousness that marked his attitude at the previous session had disappeared. He refused to retract his opinions, and made it clear that he acknowledged no longer the authority of the Pope or of General Councils as a safe guide in matters religious.

Thereupon the Emperor intimated to the princes that he was determined to take vigorous action against such a heretic and disturber of the public peace, though at the request of some of the princes he allowed time for private conferences between Luther and representative Catholic theologians, notably Eck and Cochlaeus.* These conferences having failed to produce any result the Emperor issued an order (25th April) commanding Luther to depart from Worms without delay, and forbidding him to preach to the people on his journey under pain of forfeiting his safe conduct. A month later Charles V. published a decree placing Luther under the ban of the Empire. He was denounced as a public heretic whom no one should receive or support; he was to be seized by any one who could do so, and delivered to the Emperor; his writings were to be burned, and all persons proved guilty of countenancing himself or his errors were liable to severe punishment. Many hoped that the decree might put an end to the confusion, but in reality Charles V. was powerless to enforce it, especially as the majority of the princes were unwilling to carry out its terms in their territories. Hence, outside the hereditary dominions of the House of Habsburg, the lands of Joachim I. of

---

* De Weldige-Kremer, *De Joannis Cochlaei Vita et Scriptis*, 1865. He was one of the most energetic opponents of the Reformation party.

Brandenburg and of Duke George of Saxony, and in Bavaria, it remained a dead letter.

On the route from Worms Luther was taken prisoner by soldiers of the Elector, Frederick of Saxony, according to arrangements that had been made for his protection, and was brought to the castle at Wartburg where he remained for close on a year (May 1521-March 1522) under the assumed name of Yonker George, safe in spite of the imperial decrees. In the silence of his retreat at Wartburg Luther had an opportunity for reflection on the gravity of the situation that he had created. At times he trembled, as he thought of separating himself definitely from the great world-wide organisation which recognised the jurisdiction of the Bishop of Rome, and of setting up his own judgment against the faith that had been handed down for centuries, and that was supported by the ablest scholars from the days of Clement of Rome to those of St. Thomas and St. Bonaventure.

In his anxiety of mind he was the victim of hallucinations, believing that the spirit of evil appeared to him in visible form, and held commune with him in human speech. He was assailed, too, with violent temptations of the flesh, which reduced him to a state bordering on despair. But these moments of depression passed away, to be succeeded by fits of wild exultation in which he rejoiced at the storm that he had created already, and at the still greater storm he was soon to create. He set to work with tireless energy, believing himself to be inspired from on high as was the apostle, St. John, during his stay in the island of Patmos. At the instigation of his friends, who urged him to attack the celibacy of the monks and nuns, he turned his attention to this question, and issued a work *On Monastic Vows,* in which he declared that such vows of chastity, being opposed to the freedom of the Gospel, were sinful and should be neglected. In his book *On the Mass* he assailed the Mass and the whole theory of the Christian priesthood, declaring that every believer was in a true sense a priest.

THE RELIGIOUS REVOLUTION 79

He poured out a most violent torrent of abuse against Henry VIII. of England, who, in his *Defence of the Seven Sacraments,* had ventured to join issue with the German reformer. At the same time he undertook to prepare a translation of the New Testament as a means of advancing his propaganda. By aid of mis-translations and marginal notes he sought to popularise his views on Faith and Justification, and to win favour with the people by opening to them the word of God, which he asserted falsely had been closed against them for centuries.

All his pamphlets were couched in popular language and were exactly the kind of works likely to appeal to the masses of the people, as well as to the debased instincts of those who had entered into the religious state in response to the wishes of their parents or guardians rather than in obedience to the call of God. But while Luther thus catered for the multitude, Melanchthon sought to gain the support of the more educated classes by throwing Luther's teaching into scientific and systematic form in his work, *Loci Communes* (1521), a book that remained for centuries the standard authority on Lutheran teaching.

It would be wrong to assume that Luther developed his theological system in its entirety before his separation from the Church. On the question of Justification and Free-will he had arrived at views distinctly opposed to Catholic doctrine, but his system as such took shape only gradually in response to the attacks of his opponents or the demands of his friends. On the one hand, imbued with the ideas of German Pantheistic mysticism, Luther started with the fixed principle that man's action is controlled by necessary laws, and that even after justification man is completely devoid of free will at least in religious matters. According to him, human nature became so essentially maimed and corrupted by the sin of Adam that every work which man can do is and must be sinful, because it proceeds in some way from concupiscence. Hence it is, he asserted, that good works are useless in acquiring justification, which can be obtained only by faith; and by faith he understood not the mere intellectual assent to revealed doctrines, but a practical confidence, resulting, no doubt, from this assent, that the merits of Christ will be applied to the soul. Through this faith the sinner seizes upon the righteousness of Christ, and by applying to himself the justice of his Saviour his sins are covered up. For this reason Luther explained that justification did not mean the actual forgiveness of sin by the infusion of some internal habit called sanctifying grace, but only the non-imputation of the guilt on account of the merits of Christ.

Since faith alone is necessary for justification it followed as a logical consequence that there was no place in Luther's system for the Sacraments, though in deference to old traditions he retained three Sacraments, Baptism, Penance, and the Eucharist. These, however, as he took care to explain, do not produce grace in the soul. They are mere outward pledges that the receiver has the faith without which he cannot be justified. Having in this way rejected the sacramental system and the sacrificial character of the Mass, it was only natural that he should disregard the priesthood, and proclaim that all believers were priests. In harmony with his theory on justification, and its dependence on faith, he denounced Purgatory, Prayers for the Dead, Indulgences, and Invocation of the Saints as being in themselves derogatory to the merits of Christ.

On the other hand, he laid it down as a leading principle that the Bible was the sole rule of faith, and that individual judgment was its only interpreter. Consequently he rejected the idea of a visible authority set up by Christ as an infallible guide in religious affairs. In this way he sought to undermine the authority of the Church, to depreciate the value of the decrees of the Popes and General Councils, and to re-assure his less daring followers by stripping ecclesiastical censures of more than half their terrors.*

The results of Luther's literary activity were soon apparent at Wittenberg and other centres in Germany. The Augustinians in Luther's own convent set aside their vows as worthless, and rejected the Mass. Carlstadt made common cause with the most radical element in the city, celebrated Mass on Christmas morning in the German language (1521), and administered Holy Communion to every one who came forward to receive, without any inquiry about their spiritual condition. Putting himself at the head of a body of students and roughs he went round the churches destroying the pictures, statues, confessionals, and altars. To increase the confusion a party of men at Zwickau led by a shoemaker, Nicholas Storch, and a preacher Thomas Münzer, following the principle of private judgment advocated by Luther, insisted on faith as a condition for baptism and rejected infant baptism as worthless. They were called Anabaptists. They claimed to be special messengers of God, gifted with the power of working miracles, and favoured with visions from on high. In vain did Luther attack them as heretics, and exhort his lieutenants to suppress them as being more dangerous than the Papists. Carlstadt, unable to answer their arguments from Scripture, went over to their side, and even Melanchthon felt so shaken in his opposition that he appealed to Wartburg for guidance. The students at the university became so restless and turbulent that Duke George of Saxony began to take the prompt and decisive action necessary for dealing with such a dangerous situation. Luther, alarmed for the future of his work, abandoned his retreat at Wartburg (March 1522) and returned to Wittenberg, where he had recourse to stern measures to put an end to the confusion. He drove Carlstadt from the city, and even followed him to

* Schwane, *Dogmengeschichte der neuren zeit*, 1890, pp. 131-51, 210-40, 251-92.

other places where he tried to find refuge, till at last, after a very disedifying scene between them in a public tavern, he forced him to flee from Saxony. Carlstadt's greatest offence in the eyes of his master was his preaching against the Real Presence of Christ in the Eucharist, though Luther himself admitted that he should have liked to deny the Real Presence if only to annoy the Pope, were it not that the words of Scripture proved too strong. Carlstadt adopted a different interpretation, but Luther was not the man to tolerate individual judgment in the case of one of his own lieutenants. Carlstadt was denounced as a heretic and a blasphemer, for whom no punishment could be sufficiently severe. Münzer, too, was banished, and with the assistance of the Elector, Luther was enabled to overcome all his opponents.

Luther owed his success in the opening years of his campaign mainly to his ability in gauging the feelings of the different classes whose support he wished to obtain, as well as to his complete mastery of the German language. In appealing to the monks and nuns, who were longing to escape from the obligations they had contracted, he offered them complete liberty by denouncing their vows as opposed to the freedom of the Gospel and consequently sinful. Many of the monks and nuns abandoned their cloisters and fled to Wittenberg to seek the pleasures denied them hitherto, and to put in practice Luther's teaching on the necessity of marriage. Though he encouraged bishops and priests to marry, and though he forwarded his warmest congratulations to Carlstadt on his betrothal to a fifteen year old maiden (1522), Luther himself hesitated long before taking the final plunge; but at last, against the advice of his best friends, he took as his wife Catherine Bora, one of the escaped nuns who had sought refuge in Wittenberg. His marriage (1525) was a source of amusement to his opponents as it was of dismay to his supporters. Melanchthon complained bitterly of the step his master had taken, but he consoled himself with the thought that the marriage might put an end to his former frivolity, and might allay the suspicions that his conduct had aroused.* To the princes, the free cities, and the landless knights he appealed by holding out hopes that they might be enriched by a division of the ecclesiastical estates and of the goods of the monasteries and churches. With the overthrow of the Pope and of the bishops the princes were led to expect that they might themselves become spiritual dictators in their own dominions. To the friends of the Humanist movement and the great body of the professors and students he represented himself as the champion of learning and intellectual freedom, anxious to defend them against the obscurantism of the Scholastics and the interference of the Roman congregations.

A large number of the leading Humanists, believing that Luther had undertaken only a campaign against universally recognised abuses, were inclined at first to sympathise with his movement. The friendly attitude they adopted, and the influence employed by Erasmus and others on his behalf during the early years of his revolt contributed not a little to his final success. But as it became evident that his object was the overthrow of the Church and of doctrines accepted as dogmas of faith by the whole Christian world, his former allies fell away one by one. On the question of free-will Erasmus, who had long played a double rôle, found it necessary to take the field openly against him.† Luther's answer, full of personal abuse and invective, drew a sharp reply from Erasmus, and all friendly intercourse between them was broken off for ever.

But it was on the mass of the people, the peasants and the artisans, that Luther relied mainly for support, and it was to these he addressed his most forcible appeals. The peasants of Germany, ground down by heavy taxes and reduced to the position of slaves, were ready to listen to the revolutionary ideas put forward by leaders like

* Grisar, *op. cit.*, Bd. iii., 228.
† *De Libero Arbitrio*, etc., 1524.

Sickingen and von Hutten, and to respond to the call of Luther to rise against their princes whether they were secular or ecclesiastical. In the imagination of the peasants Luther appeared as the friend of human liberty, determined to deliver them from the intolerable yoke that had been laid upon them by their masters. His attacks were confined at first to the prince-bishops and abbots, but soon realising the strength of the weapon he wielded, he attacked the lay princes in the pamphlets entitled *Christian Liberty* and *The Secular Magistracy*, and advocated the complete overthrow of all authority. It is true, undoubtedly, that many of the peasants were already enrolled in the secret societies, and that had there never been a Luther a popular rising might have been anticipated; but his doctrines on evangelical freedom and his frenzied onslaughts on the ecclesiastical and lay rulers, turned the movement into an anti-religious channel, and imparted to the struggle a uniformity and bitterness that otherwise it could never have acquired.

Risings of the peasantry took place in various parts of Germany, notably in Swabia, Thuringia, the Rhine Provinces, and Saxony (1524). Thomas Münzer, the leader of the Anabaptists, encouraged them in their fight for freedom. At first the attack was directed principally against the spiritual princes. Many monasteries and churches were plundered, and several of the nobles were put to death. Soon the lay princes of Germany, alarmed by the course of the revolutionaries and fearing for the safety of their own territories, assembled their forces and marched against the insurgents. The war was carried on mercilessly on both sides, close upon 100,000 peasants being killed in the field, while many of their leaders, amongst them Thomas Münzer, were arrested and condemned to death. In nearly every important engagement the peasants, as might be expected, suffered defeat, so that before the end of 1525 the movement was, practically speaking, at an end. Luther, who had been consulted by both sides, and who had tried to avoid committing himself to either, frightened by the very violence of the storm he had been instrumental in creating, issued an appeal to the princes calling upon them to show no mercy to the forces of disorder,* and even Melanchthon, gentle and moderate as he usually was, did not hesitate to declare that the peasants of Germany had more liberty than should be allowed to such a rude and uncultured people. The Peasants' War, disastrous as it was, did some good by opening men's eyes to the dangerous consequences of Luther's extravagant harangues, and by giving some slight indications as to the real character and methods of the man, who was posing as a heaven-sent reformer and at the same time as a champion of popular liberty.

But though Luther lost ground in many quarters owing to the part he played before and during the Peasants' War, he had no intention of abandoning the struggle in despair. During the early years of his campaign his mind was so engrossed with the overthrow of existing religious institutions, that he had little time to consider how he should rebuild what he had pulled down. At first he thought that no visible organisation was necessary, as the Church, according to his view, consisted of all those who had true faith and charity. But soon he abandoned this idea in favour of district or local churches that should be left completely independent. The disturbances in Germany during the Peasants' War taught him the hopelessness of such a scheme, and showed him that his only chance of permanent success lay in the organisation of state churches to be placed under the protection and authority of the civil rulers. By this bribe he hoped to conciliate the princes, whom he had antagonised by his attacks on their own body as well as by his attitude during the early stages of the civil disturbance. The Elector John of Saxony, who had succeeded his brother Frederick, hesitated at first to assist him in the momentous work of

* Grisar, *op. cit.*, Bd. i., pp. 483-502.

setting up a rival Christian organisation. But, at last, mindful of the advantages that would accrue to him from being recognised as supreme head of the Church in his own dominions, he gave a reluctant consent to the plans formulated by Luther.

A body of visitors consisting of clerics and lawyers was appointed to draw up a new ecclesiastical constitution, the most noteworthy feature of which was the complete dependence of the new church on the secular authority of each state. Episcopal jurisdiction was rejected, and in place of the bishops, superintendents were appointed. The ordinary administration was to be carried out by a synod of clerics and laymen elected by the various parishes, but, in reality, the right of appointment, of taxation, of apportioning the temporal goods, and of deciding legal difficulties passed under the control of the sovereign. Strange to say, though Luther insisted on individual judgment during his campaign against the Catholic Church, he had no difficulty in urging the civil rulers to force all their subjects to join the new religious body. The goods of the Catholic Church were to be appropriated, some of them being set aside for the support of the new religious organisation, while the greater portion of them found their way into the royal treasury. The Mass, shorn of the Elevation and of everything that would imply the idea of sacrifice, was translated into the German language, so that in all solemn religious services the place of the Sacrifice was taken by the hymns, Scriptural lessons, the sermon, and the Lord's Supper. Melanchthon wrote a Visitation Book (1527) for the guidance of Lutheran ministers, and Luther himself published two catechisms for the instruction of the children. The Lutheran church was organised on a similar plan in Hesse and Brandenburg and in many of the free cities such as Nürnberg, Magdeburg, Bremen, Frankfurt, Ulm, etc. By these measures the separation was completed definitely, and a certain amount of unity was ensured for the new religion.

THE RELIGIOUS REVOLUTION 87

Meanwhile, how fared it with the Emperor and the Pope? Shortly after the Diet of Nürnberg (1522) Charles V. left Germany for the Netherlands. Owing to the troubles in Spain and the long drawn out war with France he was unable to give any attention to the progress of affairs in Germany. The administration of the Empire was committed to three representatives, the ablest of whom was the Elector Frederick of Saxony, the friend and patron of Luther. The result was that Luther had a free hand to spread his views notwithstanding the decree of Worms.

Leo X. died in 1521 and was succeeded by Adrian VI. (1522-23), a former tutor of the Emperor. As a Hollander it might be anticipated that his representations to the German princes would prove more effective than those of his Italian predecessor, particularly as not even his worst enemies could discover anything worthy of reproach either in his principles or personal conduct. Convinced that Luther's only chance of winning support lay in his exaggerated denunciations of real or imaginary abuses, he determined to bring about a complete reform, first in Rome itself and then throughout the entire Christian world. Owing to his ill-disguised contempt for all that was dear to the heart of the Humanist Leo X., and to the severe measures taken by him to reduce expenses at the Roman Court, he encountered great opposition in Rome, and incurred the dislike both of officials and people.

When he learned that a Diet was to be held at Nürnberg (1522) to consider plans for the defence of the Empire against the Turks who had conquered Belgrade, he despatched Chieregati as his nuncio to invite the princes to enforce the decree of Worms, and to restore peace to the Church by putting down the Lutheran movement. In his letters to individual members of the Diet and in his instructions to the nuncio, which were read publicly to the assembled representatives, Adrian VI. admitted the existence of grave abuses both in Rome itself and in nearly every part of the Church.* He promised, however, to do everything that in him lay to bring about a complete and thorough reform.

These admissions served only to strengthen the hands of Luther and his supporters, who pointed to them as a justification for the whole movement, and to provide the princes with a plausible explanation of their inactivity in giving effect to the decree of Worms. The princes refused to carry out the decree of Worms, alleging as an excuse the danger of popular commotion. They brought forward once more the grievances of the German nation against Rome (*Centum Gravamina*), insisted on a General Council being called to restore peace to the Church, and held out a vague hope that an effort would be made to prevent the spread of the new doctrine till the Council should be convoked.

The papal nuncio, dissatisfied with the attitude of the representatives, withdrew from the Diet before the formal reply was delivered to him. Adrian VI., cognisant of the failure of his efforts and wearied by the opposition of the Romans to whom his reforms were displeasing, made a last fruitless effort to win over Frederick of Saxony to his side. The news that the island of Rhodes, for the defence of which he had laboured and prayed so strenuously, had fallen into the hands of the Turks, served to complete his affliction and to bring him to a premature grave. He died in September 1523 to the great delight of the Romans, who could barely conceal their rejoicing even when he lay on his bed of death. He was an excellent Pope, though perhaps not sufficiently circumspect for the critical times in which he lived. Had he been elected a century earlier, and had he been given an opportunity of carrying out reforms, as had been given to some of his predecessors, the Lutheran movement would have been an impossibility.

He was succeeded by Clement VII. (1523-34). The

* Raynaldus, *Ann. Eccl.* (ann. 1522).

THE RELIGIOUS REVOLUTION 89

new Pope was a relative of Leo X., and, like him, a patron of literature and art. He was a man of blameless life and liberal views, and endowed with great prudence and tact, but his excessive caution and want of firmness led to the ruin of his best-conceived plans and to the failure of his general policy. He despatched Cardinal Campeggio as his legate to the Diet of Nürnberg (1524). Once again the princes of Germany closed their ears to the appeal of the Pope, refused to take energetic measures to enforce the decree of Worms, and talked of establishing a commission to consider the grievances of their nation against Rome, and to inquire into the religious issues that had been raised. Campeggio, feeling that it was hopeless to expect assistance from the Diet, turned to the individual princes. He succeeded in bringing about an alliance at Ratisbon (1524) between the rulers of Austria, Bavaria, and several of the ecclesiastical princes of Southern Germany for the purpose of opposing the new teaching and safeguarding the interests of the Catholic Church. A similar alliance of the Catholic princes of Northern Germany was concluded at Dessau in 1526. At the same time the princes who were favourable to Lutheran views, notably Philip of Hesse, John, Elector of Saxony, the rulers of Brandenburg, Prussia, Mecklenburg and Mansfeld, together with the representatives of the cities of Brunswick and Mecklenburg, met and pledged themselves to make common cause, were any attempt made by the Emperor or the Catholic princes to suppress Luther's doctrine by force. In this way Germany was being divided gradually into two hostile camps.

Unfortunately Charles V., whose presence in Germany might have exercised a restraining influence, was so engrossed in the life and death struggle with France that he had no time to follow the progress of the religious revolt. To complicate the issue still more, Clement VII., who had been friendly to the Emperor for some time after his election, alarmed lest the freedom of the Papal States and of the Holy See might be endangered were the French driven completely from the peninsula, took sides openly against Charles V. and formed an alliance with his opponent. The good fortune that had smiled on the French arms suddenly deserted them. In 1525 Francis I. was defeated at Pavia and taken as prisoner to Spain, where he was forced to accept the terms dictated to him by his victorious rival. On his release in 1526 he refused to abide by the terms of the Treaty, and a new alliance, consisting of the Pope, France, England, Venice, Florence, Milan, and Switzerland was formed against Charles V. Disturbances, fomented by the Italian supporters of the Emperor, broke out in the Papal States, and a German army led by the Prince of Bourbon marched on Rome without the knowledge of Charles, captured the city, plundered its treasures, and for several days wreaked a terrible vengeance on the citizens. Charles, who was in Spain at the time, was deeply grieved when the news was brought to him of the havoc that had been wrought by his subordinates. A temporary peace was concluded immediately between the Emperor and the Pope, and the peace of Barcelona in 1529 put an end to this unholy strife. About the same time the hostilities between Charles and Francis I. were brought to a conclusion by the Peace of Cambrai, and the Emperor, having been crowned by the Pope at Bologna (1530), was free at last to turn his attention to the religious revolution in Germany.*

During the struggle between Charles V. and the Pope the Lutheran princes had a free hand to do as they pleased, and, indeed, at one time they were not without hope that Charles might be induced to place himself at their head. Besides, owing to the fact that the Turks were advancing on Hungary and were likely to overrun the hereditary dominions of the House of Habsburg, they felt confident that no attempt could be made to

* Pastor, *op. cit.*, Bd. iv., pp. 212-393.

THE RELIGIOUS REVOLUTION 91

suppress Lutheranism by force. At the Diet of Speier, in 1526, John Duke of Saxony, and Philip of Hesse adopted so violent and unconciliatory an attitude that Germany was on the brink of civil war, had not the Archduke Ferdinand, alarmed by the success of the Turks, used all his powers to prevent a division. It was agreed that both sides should unite against the Turks, that a Council should be called within a year to discuss the religious difficulties, and that in the meantime individual rulers were free to enforce or disregard the decree of Worms as they wished.

These concessions, wrung from the Catholic princes owing to the fear of Turkish invasion, did not satisfy either party. False rumours were spread among the Protestant princes that Duke George of Saxony and other Catholic rulers intended to have recourse to arms, and though the Duke was able to clear himself of the charge, the relations between the two parties became gradually more strained. In 1526 the Turks overcame the Hungarians and Bohemians at Mohacz, and advancing into Austria were encamped under the very walls of Vienna. It became necessary to summon another Diet at Speier (1529). The Catholic princes were in the majority, and the knowledge, that the Emperor had concluded peace with France and the Pope and was now ready to support them, rendered them less willing to accept dictation. It was carried by a majority that the Emperor should endeavour to have a Council convoked within a year, that in the meantime the rulers in whose territories the decree of Worms had been in force should continue to enforce it, and that in the states where the new teaching had taken root the rulers were at liberty to allow it to continue, but, in the interval before the Council they should permit no further changes to be introduced. Nobody should be allowed to preach against the Sacrament of the Altar; the Mass should be celebrated if it had not been abolished, and if abolished no one should be punished for celebrating or attending it, and the Scripture should be expounded according to the traditional interpretation of the Church.

The Lutheran party objected strongly to this decree, and as their objections were over-ruled they submitted a formal protest, on account of which they received the distinctive title of Protestants.* The protest, signed by the Elector of Saxony, the Margrave of Brandenburg, the Dukes of Brunswick—Lüneburg, Philip of Hesse, and the representatives of fourteen cities, having failed to produce any effect on the Diet, a deputation was appointed to interview the Emperor and to place their grievances before him. But Charles V., mindful of his imperial oath, refused to allow himself to be intimidated. He warned the deputation that he and the Catholic princes had also their duties to fulfil towards God and the Church, and that until a Council should assemble they must obey the decrees of the Diet. In January 1530 he convened a new Diet to meet at Augsburg at which he himself promised to be present.

The Diet was convened to meet at Augsburg in April 1530, but it was the middle of June before the Emperor, accompanied by the papal legate, made his formal entrance into the city. On the following day the feast of Corpus Christi was celebrated with the customary solemnities, and the Emperor was pained deeply when he learned that the Protestant princes refused to be present or to take any part in the function. At the opening of the Diet it was agreed that the religious question should take precedence, and the Protestant princes were invited to make a clear statement of their doctrines and demands. Luther himself could not be present on account of the decree of Worms, and hence the duty of preparing a complete exposition of the Protestant doctrine devolved upon the ablest of his lieutenants, Philip Melanchthon. He drew up and presented to the Diet the document

---

* "Of such slender dimensions was the original Protestant Church; small as it was, it was only held together by the negative character of its protest."—*Camb. Mod. Hist.*, ii., p. 205

THE RELIGIOUS REVOLUTION 93

known as the *Augsburg Confession* (*Confessio Augustana*), accepted by Luther himself as a masterly though perhaps too moderate statement of the new teaching. The Confession was divided into two parts, the former of which consisted of twenty-one articles or dogmas of faith received by himself and his friends; the latter dealt with what he termed abuses which they rejected, notable amongst these being celibacy of the clergy, monastic vows, auricular confession, private masses, communion under one kind, abstinence, and episcopal government. The Confession was drawn up very skilfully, great prominence being given to the doctrines on which all Christians were agreed, while the distinctive tenets of the Protestant reformers were put forward in their mildest and least offensive form. The document was read to the Diet in German by Bayer, Chancellor of the Elector of Saxony, and undoubtedly it produced a marked impression on the assembly. The Emperor held a conference with the Catholic princes, some of whom advocated prompt recourse to the sternest measures. Others, however, amongst them being several of the ecclesiastical princes, misled by the temperate and, in a certain sense, misleading character of Melanchthon's statement, and believing that a peaceful solution of the religious difficulty was still possible, urged Charles V. to abstain from decisive action. It was agreed that the work of examining and refuting the Augsburg Confession should be entrusted to a certain number of Catholic theologians, the most prominent of whom were Eck, Cochlaeus, and Conrad Wimpina.* Unfortunately these men allowed their natural feelings of irritation to overcome their judgment, and not content with a calm and judicial refutation of the document submitted to them, they attacked warmly the exaggerations, contradictions, and misrepresentations of Catholic doctrine of which Luther had been guilty, and succeeded in imparting to their reply a bitter and ironical tone more likely to widen than

* Negwer, *Wimpina*, 1909.

to heal the division. At the request of the Emperor they modified it very considerably, confining themselves entirely to a brief and dispassionate examination of the individual points raised by Melanchthon, and in its modified form their refutation (*Confutatio Confessionis Augustanae*) was presented to the Diet (3rd Aug.).

When the reply of the Catholic theologians had been read the Emperor called upon the Protestant princes to return to the unity of the Church; but his appeal fell upon deaf ears, and it seemed as if the issue were to be decided immediately by civil war. By way of compromise it was suggested that representatives of both parties should meet in conference, Eck, Cochlaeus, and Wimpina being selected as the Catholic theologians, Melanchthon, Brenz, and Schnep as the champions of Lutheranism. From the very outset it should have been evident to all that, where disagreement was so fundamental, one party maintaining the theory of an infallible Church as the only safe guide in religious matters, the other rejecting entirely the authority of the Church and the Pope in favour of individual judgment, the discussion of particular dogmas could never lead to unity. As a matter of fact Melanchthon was willing to make most important concessions, and on the question of original sin, free-will, justification, faith, penance, and the intercession of the saints, formulas were put forward not displeasing to either party. Even in regard to the Eucharist, the jurisdiction of the bishops, and the supremacy of Rome, Melanchthon was inclined to go far to meet his opponents, much to the disgust of the extremists of his own party and to the no small alarm of Luther.* But in reality the apparent harmony existed only on paper, and the concessions made by Melanchthon depended entirely on the meaning that should be placed on the ambiguous phraseology and qualifications with which they were clothed. On the question of the Mass, the celibacy of the clergy, and the meritorious character of good works,

* Hergenröther-Kirsch, *op. cit.*, Bd. iii., p. 80.

no agreement was arrived at, as Melanchthon, alarmed by the opposition of his own supporters and the reproofs of Luther, was unwilling to modify his position. What the conference of theologians had failed to do was undertaken by a mixed commission consisting of princes, theologians, and lawyers, but without any result. In September the Emperor announced that he was endeavouring to procure the convocation of a General Council and that in the meantime the Protestants should return to the old faith, a certain time being allowed them for consideration, that they should attempt no further innovations or interference with the followers of the old faith, that they should restore the ecclesiastical goods which had been seized, and that they should unite with the Catholics in opposing the Anabaptists and the Sacramentarians.

The Protestant princes refused to submit on the ground that their doctrines were in harmony with the Word of God, and to justify this contention Melanchthon published the *Apologia Confessionis Augustance,* which was in many points more full and explicit than the Confession itself. Some of the German cities that had embraced the Zwinglian doctrine, notably, Strassburg and Constance, repudiated the Augsburg Confession, and presented a document embodying their beliefs, known as the *Confessio Tetrapolitana* which found no favour with Charles V. or with the Diet. Finally, on the 18th November, the Emperor announced to the Diet that until a General Council should meet, everything must be restored to the *status quo,* that he felt it incumbent upon him as protector of the Church to defend the Catholic faith with all his might, and that in this work he could count on the full support of the Catholic princes. Unfortunately, it was by no means correct to state that the Catholic rulers of Germany stood behind their Emperor. Nearly all of them were anxious to avoid civil war at any cost, and not a few of them hesitated to support the Emperor lest the suppression of the Protestant princes might lead to the establishment of a strong central power. Nor were the Protestants alarmed by the threat of force. With the Turks hovering on the flanks of the empire, they were confident that they might expect concessions rather than violence.

The Protestant princes met in December (1530) at Schmalkald to consider their position, and early in the following year (1531) they formed the Schmalkaldic League for the defence of their religious and temporal interests. Negotiations were opened up with France, Denmark, and England, and notification was made to the Emperor that they must withhold their assistance against the Turks until their religious beliefs were secured. They refused, furthermore, to recognise Ferdinand, brother of Charles V., whom Charles had proclaimed King of the Romans. The Emperor, alarmed by the news that Soliman was preparing an immense army for a general attack on Italy and Austria, and well aware that he could not count either on the assistance of the Catholic princes or the neutrality of France, was forced to give way. In July 1532 peace was concluded at Nürnberg. According to the terms of the Peace of Nürnberg it was agreed that until a General Council should assemble no action should be taken against the Protestant princes, and that in the interval everything was to remain unchanged. This agreement, it was stipulated, should apply only to those who accepted the Confession of Augsburg, a stipulation that was meant to exclude the followers of Zwingli.

Charles V. was really anxious that a Council should be called, nor was Clement VII. unwilling to meet his wishes, if only he could have been certain that a Council constituted as such assemblies had been constituted traditionally, could serve any useful purpose. Time and again Luther had expressed his supreme contempt for the authority of General Councils, though he professed to be not unwilling to submit the matters in dispute to a body of men selected by the civil rulers. In 1532-33

THE RELIGIOUS REVOLUTION 97

Pope and Emperor met at Bologna to discuss the situation, and messengers were despatched to see on what terms the Protestants would consent to attend the Council. The members of the Schmalkaldic League refused (1533) to accept the conditions proposed by the Pope, namely, that the Council should be constituted according to the plan hitherto followed in regard to such assemblies, and that all should pledge themselves beforehand to accept its decrees.*

Clement VII. died in September (1534) and was succeeded by Paul III. (1534-49). He convoked a General Council to meet at Mantua in 1537, but the League refused once more to attend (1535). Even had there been no other difficulties in the way, the war that broke out with renewed bitterness between Charles V. and Francis I. would have made it impossible for such a body to meet with any hope of success. The helpless condition of the Emperor, confronted, as he was, on the one side by the French and on the other by the Turks, raised the hopes of the Protestant party, and made them more determined than ever to attend no Council in which the authority of the bishops or the jurisdiction of the Pope should be recognised. Moreover, each year brought new accessions to their ranks. The appearance of organised Christian bodies, completely national in character, accepting the civil rulers as their head, and conceding to them full power to deal as they liked with ecclesiastical property, created a deep impression on several princes and free cities, and made them not averse to giving the new religion a fair trial. In 1530, the Elector of Saxony, Philip of Hesse and the rulers of Ansbach, Anhalt, Brunswick-Lüneburg, Bayreuth, East Friesland, and a few of the larger cities had gone over to Luther. Before ten years had elapsed the greater part of Northern Germany had fallen from the Catholic Church, and even in Southern Germany Protestantism had made serious inroads. Several of the more

* Pastor, *op. cit.*, Bd. iv., 473-5.

important cities such as Wittenberg, Strassburg, Nürnberg, Magdeburg, Frankfurt-on-Main, Hamburg, and Erfurt became leading centres for the spread of the new teaching, while many of the German universities, for example, Erfurt, Basle, Frankfurt, Rostock, and Marburg supported strongly the efforts of Luther.

The Catholic princes, alarmed by the rapid spread of the new doctrines and by the extravagant demands of the Protestants, met together to form the Holy League (1538) as a defence against the Schmalkaldic confederation. Feeling was running so high at the time that the long expected war might have broken out immediately, had not the dread of a Turkish invasion exercised a restraining influence on both parties. In 1539 negotiations were opened up for a temporary armistice, and another fruitless attempt was made to arrive at peace by means of a religious conference. Before any result had been attained the Emperor summoned a Diet to meet at Ratisbon (April 1541). Three theologians were appointed from both sides to discuss the questions at issue. Though some of the Catholic representatives showed clearly enough that their desire for union was much greater than their knowledge of Catholic principles, an understanding was arrived at only in regard to a few points of difference. By the Recess of the Diet (known as the *Ratisbon Interim*) it was ordered that both parties should observe the articles of faith on which they had agreed until a General Council should meet, that in the interval the terms of the Peace of Nürnberg should be carried out strictly, that the religious houses that had escaped destruction hitherto should remain undisturbed, and that the disciplinary decrees promulgated by the cardinal legate (Contarini) should be obeyed by the Catholics.

The Protestant princes were still dissatisfied. In order to procure their assistance Charles was obliged to yield to further demands, notably, to permit them to suppress the monasteries in their dominions. But, fortunately for

THE RELIGIOUS REVOLUTION 99

the Catholic Church, the agreement embodied in the *Ratisbon Interim* was rejected by the more extreme Protestant party led by Luther himself, and the danger of grave misunderstanding was removed.

During the following years the Lutheran movement continued to advance by leaps and bounds. Duke George of Saxony, one of its strongest opponents, died in 1539, and his successor invited the Lutheran preachers to assist him in the work of reform. Henry, Duke of Brunswick, was driven from his kingdom by the League of Schmalkald and forced to seek refuge in Bavaria. The Bishoprics of Hildesheim and Naumburg were captured by force, and it required all the efforts of the Pope and of the Emperor to prevent Cologne from being handed over to Luther's followers by its prince-bishop (Hermann von Wied). Lutheranism provided almost irresistible attractions for the lay rulers, who desired to acquire wealth and power at the expense of the Church, as well as for the unworthy ecclesiastical princes who were anxious to convert the states of which they were merely administrators into hereditary dominions.

But though outwardly the movement prospered beyond expectation all was far from well within. The fundamental principle enunciated by Luther, namely, the rejection of all religious authority, opened the way for new theories and new sects. Quite apart from the controversies between the followers of Luther and Zwingli, which shall be dealt with later, the Anabaptists and others continued to destroy the harmony of the self-styled reformers. The Anabaptists seized the city of Münster, proclaimed a democratic theocracy with John of Leyden, a tailor, at its head, and announced their intention of taking the field for the overthrow of tyrants and impostors. But their success was short-lived. Conrad, bishop and prince of Münster, raised an army, laid siege to the city which he captured after a desperate struggle, and put to death the fanatical leaders who had deceived the people (1535-6). Other writers and preachers questioned the doctrines of the Trinity and Incarnation, and advocated many heresies condemned by the early Church, some of them going so far as to insist on the revival of circumcision and the Jewish ceremonial law.*

Nor did the new teaching exercise an elevating influence on the morals or conduct of its adherents. Luther himself was forced to admit that the condition of affairs had grown worse even than it had been before he undertook his campaign. " Since we have commenced to preach our doctrine," he said in one of his sermons, "the world has grown daily worse, more impious, and more shameless. Men are now beset by legions of devils, and while enjoying the full light of the Gospel are more avaricious, more impure, and repulsive than of old under the Papacy. Peasants, burghers, nobles, men of all degrees, the higher as well as the lowest are all alike slaves to avarice, drunkenness, gluttony, and impurity, and given over to horrible excesses of abominable passions." †

The princes, free from all religious and ecclesiastical restraints, set an example of licentiousness which their subjects were not slow to imitate. Philip of Hesse was the life and soul of the Lutheran movement. He was married already to Christina, daughter of Duke George of Saxony, by whom eight children had been born to him, but finding it impossible to observe his marriage obligations, and wishing to impart to his own sinful conduct an air of decency, he demanded permission from Luther to marry one of the maids of honour in attendance on his sister. This request placed Luther and Melanchthon in a very delicate position. On the one hand, if they acceded to it they would be regarded as patrons and defenders of adultery and would expose themselves to the ridicule of their opponents; on the other, were they to refuse compliance with his wishes, Philip, forgetful of his former zeal for the pure word of God, might carry

* Hergenröther-Kirsch, *op. cit.*, iii., pp. 102-8.
† For Luther's own views on the results of his preaching, *cf.* Döllinger, *Die Reformation*, Bd. ii., pp. 426-52.

out his threats to return to the Catholic Church. After long and anxious deliberation they determined to exercise a dispensing power such as had never been exercised by any Pope. "In order to provide for the welfare of his soul and body and to bring greater glory to God," they allowed him to take to himself a second wife, insisting, however, that the whole affair should be kept a close secret. But hardly had the marriage ceremony been gone through (1540) than the story of the dispensation became public. Luther was at first inclined to deny it entirely as an invention of his enemies, but he changed his mind when he found that the proofs were irrefragable and determined to brazen out the affair.*

Luther's last years were full of anxiety and sorrow. As he looked round his own city of Wittenberg and the cities of Germany where his doctrines had taken root he found little ground for self-congratulation. Religious dissensions, bitterness, war-like preparations, decline of learning, decay of the universities, and immorality, had marked the progress of his gospel. In many districts the power of the Pope had indeed been broken, but only to make way for the authority of the civil rulers upon whom neither religious nor disciplinary canons could exercise any restraint; the monasteries and religious institutions had been suppressed, but their wealth had passed into the treasuries of the princes, whilst the poor for whose benefit it had been held in trust were neglected, and the ministers of religion were obliged to have recourse to different occupations to secure a livelihood. To his followers and his most intimate associates he denied the liberty of thought and speech that he claimed for himself, by insisting on the unconditional acceptance of his doctrines as if in him alone were vested supreme authority and infallibility. For exercising their right of private judgment, Carlstadt was pursued from pulpit to pulpit till at last he was forced to seek safety in flight; Zwingli was denounced as a heretic for whose salvation

* Grisar, *op. cit.*, Bd. ii., 382-436.

it was useless to pray; the Anabaptists were declared to be unworthy of any better fate than the sword or the halter; Agricola, his most zealous fellow-labourer, was banished from his presence and his writings were interdicted; and even Melanchthon was at last driven to complain of the state of slavery to which he had been reduced.*

His failing health and his disappointments served to sour his temper and to render him less approachable. The attacks that he directed against the Papacy such as *The Papacy an Institution of the Devil*, and the verses prepared for the vulgar caricatures that he induced Cranach to design (1545) surpassed even his former productions in violence and abusiveness. Tired of attacking the Papacy, he turned his attention once more to the Jews, upon whom he invoked the vengeance of Heaven in the last sermon that he was destined to preach on earth. He was taken suddenly ill in Eisleben, where he had come to settle some disputes between the Counts of Mansfeld, and on the 18th February 1546, he passed away.†

Luther is a man whose character it is difficult to appreciate exactly. At times he spoke and wrote as if he were endowed with a deeply religious feeling, convinced of the truth of his doctrines, and anxious only for the success of the work for which he professed to believe he had been raised up by God. Some of his sermons sounded like a trumpet call from Heaven, warning the people that the hour for repentance had drawn nigh, while his conversations with his intimate friends breathed at times a spirit of piety and fervour redolent of the apostolic age. This, however, was only one feature of Luther's character, and, unfortunately, it was a feature that manifested itself only too rarely. As a general rule his writings, his sermons and speeches, and, in a word,

* Grisar, *op. cit.*, Bd. iii., 211-30.

† That there can be no question of suicide is admitted (Paulus *Luthers Lebensende*, 1898).

THE RELIGIOUS REVOLUTION

his whole line of conduct were in direct opposition to everything that is associated generally in the popular mind with the true religious reformer. His replies to his opponents, even to those who, avoiding personalities, addressed themselves directly to his doctrines, were couched in the most violent and abusive language. His wild onslaughts and his demands for vengeance on any one who ventured to question his teaching, whether they were Catholics, Zwinglians, Sacramentarians or Anabaptists, were the very antithesis of the spirit of charity and meekness that should characterise a follower, not to say an apostle, of Christ. Nor were his overweening pride and self-confidence in keeping with the spirit of meekness and humility inculcated so frequently in the writings of the New Testament.

In his letters, and more especially in his familiar intercourse with his friends,* his conversation was frequently risky and indecent; his relations with women, at least before his marriage with Catherine Bora, were, to put it mildly, not above suspicion, as is evident from his own letters and the letters of his most devoted supporters; while his references to marriage and vows of chastity in his sermons and pamphlets were filthy and unpardonable even in an age when people were much more outspoken on such subjects than they are at present. Though he insisted strongly on the necessity of preaching the pure Word of God, he had little difficulty in having recourse to falsehood when truth did not serve his purpose, or in justifying his conduct by advocating the principle that not all lies were sinful particularly if they helped to damage the Roman Church. His frequent and enthusiastic references to the pleasures of the table were more like what one should expect to find in the writings of a Pagan epicure than in those of a Christian reformer. He was not, as is sometimes asserted, a habitual drunkard. His tireless activity as a writer and

* *Tischreden* (*Table Talk*), *cf.* Grisar, ii., 178 *sqq.* Smith, *Luther's Table Talk*, 1907. *Am. Ecc. Review* (1906, pp. 1-18).

preacher is in itself a sufficient refutation of such a charge, but he was convinced that a hard drinking bout was at times good for both soul and body, and in this respect at least he certainly lived up to his convictions.*

It would be a mistake to judge him by his Latin writings, which, both in matter and style, seldom rise above the level of mediocrity. It is in his German books and pamphlets that Luther is seen at his best. There, he appears as a man of great ability and learning, gifted with a prodigious memory, a striking literary style, and a happy knack of seizing upon the weak points of his adversaries and of presenting his own side of the case in its most forcible and attractive form. No man knew better than he how to adapt himself to the tastes of his audience or the prejudices of his readers. He could play the rôle of the judge or professor almost as well as that of the impassioned fanatic convinced that behind him were arrayed all the powers of Heaven. In dealing with men of education, who were not likely to be captivated by rhetoric, he could be calm and argumentative; but when he addressed himself to the masses of the people he appeared in his true character as a popular demagogue, hesitating at nothing that was likely to arouse their indignation against the Roman Church and their enthusiasm for the movement to which he had devoted his life. In words of fiery eloquence he recalled to their minds the real and imaginary grievances of their nation against Rome, the over-weening pride and tyranny of the spiritual princes, the scandalous lives of many of the ecclesiastics, and the failure of Pope and councils to carry through a scheme of wholesale reform. He called upon them to throw off the yoke imposed by foreigners on their fathers and themselves, and to support him in his struggle for the liberty of the people, the independence of the German nation, and the original purity of the Gospel, promising them that if only they would range themselves under his banner, all their grievances, both

* *Personal Character of Luther* (*Ir. Theol. Quart.*, viii., pp. 77-85).

spiritual and temporal, must soon be redressed. Had Luther never appeared, or had he been less gifted as an orator, a writer and a popular leader than he was, a crisis must have arisen at the time; but his genius and enthusiasm turned what might have been a trickling stream into a raging torrent, threatening destruction to beliefs and institutions hitherto regarded as inviolable. The time was ripe for a reformer, and Luther's only claim to greatness was his capacity of utilising in a masterly way the materials, political and religious, that lay ready at his hand. Religious abuses, social unrest, politics, personal vanities, and the excesses always attendant upon a great literary revival, were pressed into his service, and were directed against the Roman Church. And yet his success fell far short of his expectations. Beyond doubt he contrived to detach individuals and kingdoms from their obedience to the Pope and their submission to ecclesiastical authority only to subject them to the spiritual yoke of the secular princes, and to expose them to doctrinal anarchy subversive of dogmatic religion; but the Catholic Church and the See of Rome, for the overthrow of which he had laboured so energetically, emerged triumphant from the terrible trial that had been permitted by God only for its purification.

During the period that intervened between the *Ratisbon Interim* and the death of Luther (1541-46) Charles V., hard pressed by the war with France and the unsuccessful expeditions against the Barbary pirates, was obliged to yield to the increasing demands of the Protestant princes; nor could Paul III., however much he desired it, realise his intention of convoking a General Council. But at last the Peace of Crépy (1544) which put an end to the war with France, and the convocation of a General Council to meet at Trent in March 1545, strengthened the hands of the Emperor, and enabled him to deal effectively with the religious revolution. The Protestant princes announced their determination to take no part in a Council convoked and presided over by the Pope. Charles left no stone unturned to induce them to adopt a more conciliatory attitude, but all his efforts having proved unavailing, he let it be known publicly that he would not allow himself to be intimidated by threats of violence, and that if need be he would insist on obedience at the point of the sword. John Frederick of Saxony and Philip of Hesse, alarmed by the threatening aspect of affairs, determined to anticipate the Emperor, and took the field at the head of an army of forty thousand men (1546).

Charles V., relying upon the aid of the Pope and the co-operation of the Catholic princes, issued a proclamation calling upon all loyal subjects to treat them as rebels and outlaws. Maurice of Saxony deserted his co-religionists on promise of succeeding to the Electorship, joined the standard of Charles V., and in conjunction with Ferdinand directed his forces against Saxony. The Elector was defeated and captured at Mühlberg (April 1547). He was condemned to death as a traitor, but he was reprieved and detained as a prisoner in the suite of the Emperor, while his nephew, Maurice of Saxony, succeeded to his dominions. Philip of Hesse, too, was obliged to surrender, and Charles V. found himself everywhere victorious. He insisted on the restoration of the Bishop of Naumburg and of Henry of Brunswick to his kingdom as well as on the resignation of Hermann Prince von Wied, Archbishop of Cologne. He was unwilling, however, to proceed to extremes with the Protestant princes, well knowing that he could not rely on some of his own supporters. Besides, he had become involved in serious difficulties with Pope Paul III., who complained, and not without reason, of the demands made upon him by the Emperor, and of the concessions that the Emperor was willing to make to the Lutherans.

Charles V. summoned a Diet to meet at Augsburg (1547), where he hoped that a permanent understanding might be secured. A document known as the *Augsburg*

THE RELIGIOUS REVOLUTION

Interim, prepared by Catholic theologians in conjunction with the Lutheran, John Agricola, was accepted provisionally by both parties. The doctrines were expressed in a very mild form, though not, however, altogether unacceptable to Catholics. Protestants were permitted to receive communion under both kinds; their married clergy were allowed to retain their wives; and it was understood tacitly that they might keep possession of the ecclesiastical property they had seized. The *Augsburg Interim,* as might have been anticipated, was displeasing to both parties. Maurice of Saxony, unwilling to give it unconditional approval, consulted Melanchthon and others of his school as to how far he might accept its terms. In their reply they distinguished between matters that were essential and those that were only of secondary importance. The latter might be accepted unreservedly in obedience to the orders of the Emperor. In regard to doctrines, they were willing to compromise on the question of justification and good-works, to accept the sacraments, including confirmation and Extreme Unction, the Mass with the addition of some German hymns, and in a certain sense the jurisdiction of the bishops. Such concessions were a distinct departure from Luther's teaching and would have been impossible had he been alive.

The relations between the Pope and the Emperor took a more friendly turn when the General Council was transferred from Bologna to Trent (1551). The Protestant princes, invited to send representatives, declined at first, but in a short time several of them agreed to accept the invitation. Safe conducts were issued for their representatives by the Council in 1551 and again in 1552. Even the Wittenberg theologians were not unfavourably disposed, and Melanchthon was actually on his way to Trent. But suddenly Maurice of Saxony, who had assembled a large army under pretext of reducing Magdeburg, and had strengthened himself by an alliance with several princes as well as by a secret treaty with Henry

II. of France, deserted the Emperor and placed himself at the head of the Protestant forces. When all his plans were completed he advanced suddenly through Thuringia, took Augsburg, and was within an inch of capturing the Emperor who then lay ill at Innsbruck (1552). At the same time the French forces occupied Lorraine. Charles, finding himself unable to carry on the struggle, opened negotiations for peace, and in 1552 the Treaty of Passau was concluded. Philip of Hesse was to be set at liberty; a Diet was to be called within six months to settle the religious differences; in the meantime neither the Emperor nor the princes should interfere with freedom of conscience; and all disputes that might arise were to be referred to a commission consisting of an equal number of Protestant and Catholic members.

Owing to the war with France it was not until the year 1555 that the proposed Diet met at Augsburg. The Protestant party, encouraged by their victories, were in no humour for compromise, and as it was evident that there was no longer any hope of healing the religious division in the Empire, it was agreed that peace could be secured only by mutual toleration. In September 1555 the Peace of Augsburg was concluded. According to the terms of this convention full freedom of conscience was conceded in the Empire to Catholics and to all Protestants who accepted the Augsburg Confession. The latter were permitted to retain the ecclesiastical goods which they had already acquired before the Treaty of Passau (1552). For the future each prince was to be free to determine the religion of his subjects, but in case a subject was not content with the religion imposed on him by his sovereign he could claim the right to migrate into a more friendly territory.

A great difficulty arose in regard to the disposal of the ecclesiastical property in case a Catholic bishop or abbot should apostatise. Notwithstanding the protests of the Protestant party, it was decreed that if such an event should occur the seceder could claim his own per-

THE RELIGIOUS REVOLUTION 109

sonal property, but not the property attached to his office. This clause, known as the *Ecclesiasticum Reservatum,* gave rise to many disputes, and was one of the principal causes of the Thirty Years' War.

By the *Peace of Augsburg* Protestantism was recognised as a distinct and separate form of Christianity, and the first blow was struck at the fundamental principles on which the Holy Roman Empire had been built. Charles V. was blamed at the time, and has been blamed since for having given his consent to such a treaty, but if all the circumstances of the time be duly considered it is difficult to see how he could have acted otherwise than he did. It is not the Emperor who should be held accountable for the unfavourable character of the Augsburg Peace, but "the most Catholic King of France" who allied himself with the forces of German Protestantism, and the Catholic princes who were more anxious to secure their own position than to fight for their sovereign or their religion. Charles V., broken down in health and wearied by his misfortunes and his failure to put down the religious revolt, determined to hand over to a younger man the administration of the territories over which he ruled, and to devote the remainder of his life to preparation for the world to come. In a parting address delivered to the States of the Netherlands he warned them "to be loyal to the Catholic faith which has always been and everywhere the faith of Christendom, for should it disappear the foundations of goodness would crumble away and every sort of mischief now menacing the world would reign supreme." After his resignation he retired to a monastery in Estremadura, where he died in 1558. Spain and the Netherlands passed to his legitimate son, Philip II., while after some delay his brother, Ferdinand, was recognised as his successor in the Empire.

Charles V. was a man of sound judgment and liberal views, of great energy and prudence, as skilful in war as he was in the arts of diplomacy, and immensely superior in nearly every respect to his contemporaries, Francis I. of France and Henry VIII. of England. Yet in spite of all his admitted qualifications, and notwithstanding the fact that he was the ruler of three-fourths of Western Europe, he lived to witness the overthrow of his dearest projects and the complete failure of his general policy. But his want of success was not due to personal imprudence or inactivity. It is to be attributed to the circumstances of the times, the rebellion in Spain, the open revolt of some and the distrust of others in Germany, the rapid advance of the Turks towards the west, and, above all, the struggle with France. Despite his many quarrels with the Holy See, and in face of the many temptations held out to him to arrive at the worldwide dictatorship to which he was suspected of aspiring, by putting himself at the head of the new religious movement, he never wavered for a moment in his allegiance to the Catholic Church.

(b) ZWINGLI IN SWITZERLAND: HIS ATTITUDE TOWARDS LUTHERANISM.

See works mentioned above (II. *a*). Dändliker, *Geschichte der Schweiz*, 3 Bde, 1904. Dändliker-Salisbury, *A Short History of Switzerland*, 1899. De Haller, *Histoire de la révolution religieuse ou de la réforme protestante dans la Suisse occidentale*, 1837. Gelpke, *Kirchengeschichte der Schweiz*, 1856-61. Schuler-Schulthess, *Opera Huldrici Zwinglii*, 8 vols., 1828-42. Jackson, *Huldreich Zwingli*, 1901.

The territory now known as Switzerland formed portion of the Holy Roman Empire. In 1291, however, during the reign of Rudolph of Habsburg, the three states or cantons of Uri, Schweiz, and Unterwalden, formed a confederation to defend their rights and privileges, thus laying the foundation for the existence of Switzerland as an independent nation. Other cantons joined the alliance, more especially after the victory at Morgarten in 1315, when the Austrian forces despatched against the Swiss were almost annihilated. Austria made

THE RELIGIOUS REVOLUTION   111

various attempts to win back the Swiss to their allegiance but without success, and in 1394 the independence of the allied cantons was practically recognised.

About the time of the Reformation in Germany Switzerland consisted of thirteen cantons and several smaller "allied" or "friendly" states not admitted to full cantonal rights. Though bound together by a loose kind of confederation for purposes of defence against aggression, the various states enjoyed a large measure of independence, and each was ruled according to its own peculiar constitution. The Federal Diet or General Assembly was composed of representatives appointed by the cantons, and its decisions were determined by the votes of the states, the largest and most populous possessing no greater powers than the least influential member of the confederation. Some of the states were nominally democratic in their form of government, but, as in most countries during this period, the peasants had many grounds for reasonable complaint, particularly in regard to taxation, treasury pensions, and the enlisting and employment of the Swiss mercenary troops, then the best soldiers in Europe.

As in Germany, many causes were at work to prepare the ground for the new religious teaching. On account of the free character of its institutions refugees of all kinds fled to Switzerland for asylum, and were allowed great liberty in propagating their views. Again, the Swiss mercenaries, returning from their campaigns and service, during which they were brought into contact with various classes and nations, served much the same purpose as does the modern newspaper. In both these ways the peasants of Switzerland were kept in touch with the social, political, and religious condition of the rest of Europe, and with the hopes and plans of their own class in other kingdoms. Humanism had not, indeed, made very striking progress in Switzerland, though the presence of Erasmus at Basle, and the attacks that he directed against the monks and the clergy, could not fail to produce some effect on a people whose minds were already prepared for such methods by their acquaintance with modern developments.

If, however, the Church in Switzerland had been free from abuses not all the wit and eloquence of Erasmus and his followers could have produced a revolt, but unfortunately, the influences that led to the downfall of religion in other countries were also at work in the Swiss cantons. The cathedral chapters were composed for the greater part of men who had no vocation to the priesthood, and who adopted the clerical profession because they wished to enrich themselves from the revenues of the Church, and were ensured of good positions through the influence of their relatives and patrons. Many of the clergy were far from being perfect, nor were all the religious institutions mindful of the spirit or even of the letter of their constitutions. Unfortunately, too, owing to the peculiar political development of the country, the bishops of Switzerland were subject to foreign metropolitans, two of them being under the jurisdiction of the Archbishop of Mainz, two under Besançon, one under Aquileia, and one subject immediately to Rome. Partly for this reason, partly, also, owing to the increasing encroachments of the civil power, disputes and conflicts between the ecclesiastical and temporal jurisdictions were not unfrequent. But it would be a mistake to suppose that there were no good ecclesiastics in Switzerland at this time. There were many excellent priests, both secular and regular, who recognised the sad condition of affairs, and who supported measures such as those undertaken by the Bishop of Basle in 1503 with all their power. The great body of teachers known as the Friends of God were at work in Switzerland as in the Netherlands, and were doing splendid service for education, both secular and religious.

The man, who played in Switzerland the part played so successfully by Luther in Germany, was Ulrich Zwingli. He was the son of rich parents, born at Wildhaus, in the canton of Saint Gall (1484), educated at the Universities of Berne, Basle, and Vienna, and after his ordination to the priesthood, appointed to the parish of Glarus. He was a young man of remarkable ability both as a student and as a preacher, and was fortunate enough to attract the notice of the papal legate, through whose influence a pension was assigned to him to enable him to prosecute his studies. He was a good classical scholar with a more than average knowledge of Hebrew, and well versed in the Scriptures and in the writings of the Fathers. For a time he acted as chaplain to some Swiss regiments fighting in Italy for the Pope against France, and on his return to his native country he was appointed preacher at the famous shrine of Our Lady at Einsiedeln.* Here his oratorical powers stood him in good stead, but his judgment and level-headedness were not on the same high plane as his declamatory powers, nor was his own private life in keeping with the sanctity of the place or with the denunciations that he hurled so recklessly against his clerical brethren. He began to attack pilgrimages and devotions to the Blessed Virgin, but it was not so much for this as for his unlawful relations with a woman of bad character that he was relieved from his office.† He retired to Zurich where he was appointed preacher in the cathedral. Here he denounced the lives of the clergy and the abuses in the Church, relying, as he stated, upon what he had seen himself in Italy during his residence there as chaplain to the Swiss mercenaries. Like Luther, he well knew how to win the attention and sympathy of the mob by his appeals to the national feelings of his countrymen, and like Luther he insisted that the Scriptures were the sole rule of faith. He denounced in the strongest language the immorality and vices of the clergy, celibacy, vows of chastity, pilgrimages and the veneration of the saints, but for so far he had not broken entirely with the Church.

* *Précis Historique de l'Abbaye et du Pélerinage de Notre-Dame-des-Ermites*, 1870.
† *Realencycl. für Protestantische Theol.*, xxi., p. 778.

The preaching of the Indulgences promulgated by Leo X. in Constance was entrusted to the Franciscans. Their work was a difficult one especially as the Grand Council of Zurich forbade them to persist, as, indeed, did also the able and zealous Hugo von Hohenlandenberg, Bishop of Constance, in whose diocese Zurich was situated. Zwingli, confident of the support of the city authorities, attacked the doctrine of Indulgences and was backed by the Grand Council, which ordered, at his instigation, that the Word of God should be preached according to the Scriptures, regardless of tradition or the interpretation of the Church. Later on he directed his attacks against the meritoriousness of good works and the practice of fast and abstinence (1522), and about the same time he addressed a petition to the Bishop of Constance demanding that he should not interfere with the preaching of the pure Word of God nor set any obstacle to the marriage of his priests. He admitted publicly that his relations with women had been disgraceful, that he had learned from his own personal experience how impossible of fulfilment was the vow of chastity, and that marriage was the only remedy that would enable him to overcome the emotions of carnal lust referred to by St. Paul in his epistle to the Corinthians (I. 7, 9). The bishop refused to yield to this demand insisting on the strict observance of celibacy, and appealed to the Grand Council to support him with the full weight of their authority (April 1522).

Incensed by this refusal, Zwingli shook off the yoke of ecclesiastical authority, rejected the primacy of the Pope, and the infallibility of General Councils, denounced celibacy and vows of chastity as inventions of the devil, and called upon the Swiss people to support him in his fight for religious freedom. Once before, in 1520, Leo X. had summoned Zwingli to Rome to answer for his teaching, but the summons had been unheeded. Adrian VI. made another attempt to win him from his dangerous course by a letter full of kindness and sympathy, but his remonstrance produced no effect (1523). The Grand Council of Zurich, hopeful of securing a preponderating influence in Switzerland by taking the lead in the new movement, favoured Zwingli. Instead of responding to the appeal of the Bishop of Constance it announced a great religious disputation to be held in January 1523, to which both Zwingli and his opponents were summoned for the explanation and defence of their views. Zwingli put forward sixty-seven theses, the principal of which were that the Bible is the sole rule of faith, that the Church is not a visible society but only an assembly of the elect, of which body Christ is the only true head, that consequently the jurisdiction of the Pope and of the bishops is a usurpation devoid of scriptural authority, that the Mass, Confession, Purgatory, and Intercession of the Saints are to be rejected as derogatory to the merits of Christ, and finally, that clerical celibacy and monastic vows, instead of being counsels of perfection, are only cloaks for sin and hypocrisy. The Bishop of Constance refused to take part in such a disputation. His vicar-general, Johann Faber of Constance, however attended the meeting, not indeed to take part in the discussion but merely to protest against it as opposed to the authority of the Church and of the councils. As his protests were unheeded, he undertook to defend the doctrines attacked, but in the end the Grand Council declared that the victory rested with Zwingli.

Flushed with his triumph Zwingli now proceeded to put his theories into practice. Supported by a mob he endeavoured to prevent the celebration of Mass, religious processions, the use of pictures and statues, and the solemn ceremonial associated with Extreme Unction and the Viaticum. He compiled an introduction to the New Testament for the use of the clergy, called upon them to abandon their obligations of celibacy, and set them an example by taking as his wife a woman who had been for years his concubine. He and his followers, supported by the majority of the Grand Council, went through the city destroying altars, pictures, statues, organs, and confessionals, and erecting in place of the altars plain tables with a plate for bread and a vessel for wine. The Catholic members of the Grand Council were driven from their position, and Catholic worship was forbidden in Zurich (1523-25).

The system of Zwingli was much more rationalistic and, in a certain sense, much more logical than that of Luther. Imbued with the principles of pantheistic mysticism, he maintained that God is in Himself all being, created as well as uncreated, and all activity. Hence it was as absurd to speak of individual liberty or individual action as to speak of a multiplicity of gods. Whether it was a case of doing good or doing evil man was but a machine like a brush in the hands of a painter. In regard to sin he contended man may be punished for violating the law laid down by God even though the violation is unavoidable, but God, being above all law, is nowise to blame. Concupiscence or self-love is, according to him, at the root of all misdeeds. It is in itself the real original sin, and is not blotted out by Baptism. His teaching on the Scriptures, individual judgment, ecclesiastical authority as represented by the bishops, councils, and Pope, good works, indulgences, purgatory, invocation of the saints, and vows of chastity differed but slightly from what Luther had put forward. On the question of Justification, and particularly on the doctrine of the Eucharist, the two reformers found themselves in hopeless conflict.*

Zwingli's teaching did not at first find much favour in other portions of German Switzerland. Lucerne declared against it in 1524. The city authorities forbade the introduction of the new teaching, and offered an asylum to those Catholics who had been forced to flee from Zurich. Other cantons associated themselves with Lucerne, and a deputation was sent to Zurich to request the city authorities to abandon Zwingli and to take part in a general movement for a real and consti-

* Schwane, *op. cit.*, p. 141.

tutional reform. But the Grand Council, mindful of the political advantages which would accrue to Zurich from its leadership in the new religious revolt, declined to recede from their position.

While Zwingli was at work in Zurich, Oecolampadius (1482-1531) set himself to stir up religious divisions in Basle. He was born at Weinsberg, studied law at Bologna and theology subsequently at Heidelberg, was ordained priest, and appointed to a parish in Basle (1512). With Erasmus he was on terms of the closest intimacy, and, as Basle was then one of the great literary centres of the world, he soon became acquainted with Luther's pamphlets and teaching. Some of the clergy in Basle, notably Wolfgang Capito, a warm friend of Zwingli, were already showing signs of restlessness especially in regard to the Mass, purgatory, and invocation of the saints, and Oecolampadius was not slow to imbibe the new ideas. In 1518 he was appointed preacher in the Cathedral of Augsburg, but, having resigned this office on account of failing health, he withdrew to the convent of Altmünster, where, for some time, he lived a retired life. Subsequently he acted as chaplain to the well-known German knight, Franz von Sickingen, and finally, in 1524, he accepted the parish of St. Martin's in Basle.

He now proclaimed himself openly a supporter of Zwingli, advocated the new teaching on justification and good works, and attacked several Catholic doctrines and practices. For him, as indeed for most of the other reformers, clerical celibacy was the great stumbling block. He encouraged his followers by taking as his wife a young widow, who was subsequently in turn the wife of the two renowned Lutheran preachers, Butzer and Capito. At first the city authorities and a large body of the university professors were against him, but owing to the disturbances created by his partisans full liberty of worship was granted to the new sect (1527). Not content with this concession, they demanded that the Mass should be suppressed. In 1529 the followers of Oecolampadius rose in revolt, seized the arsenal of the city, directed the cannon on the principal squares, and attacked the churches, destroying altars, statues, and pictures. Erasmus, disgusted with such methods of propagating religion, left Basle and sought a home in Freiburg. The Catholics were expelled from the city council, their religion was proscribed, and Basle joined hands with Zurich in its rebellion against the Church.

The revolt soon spread into other cantons of Switzerland. In Berne and Schaffhausen both parties were strong and determined, and for a time the issue of the conflict was uncertain, but in 1528 the party of Zwingli and Oecolampadius secured the upper hand. Similarly in St. Gall, Glarus, etc., victory rested with the new teaching. Other cantons, as for example, Solothurn, wavered as to which side they should take, but the three oldest cantons of Switzerland, Uri, Schweiz and Unterwalden, together with Zug, Freiburg and Lucerne, refused to be separated from the Church.

Apart altogether from the question of religion, there was a natural opposition between populous and manufacturing centres like Berne and Basle, and the rural cantons, devoted almost entirely to agricultural and pastoral pursuits. When religious differences supervened to accentuate the rivalry already in existence, they led almost inevitably to the division of Switzerland into two hostile camps. Zurich, Basle, Berne, Schaffhausen, and St. Gall, though they were the most important cities, soon found themselves unable to force their views on the rest of the country, as they were withstood by the federal council, the majority of which was still Catholic. The latter insisted that a conference should be held to settle the religious disputes. The conference was arranged to take place at Baden in 1526. Eck, assisted by two other Catholic theologians, Faber and Murner, undertook to defend the Catholic position. Zurich refused to send representatives, but the reforming party were represented

THE RELIGIOUS REVOLUTION 119

by Oecolampadius, Haller, and others of their leaders. The conference was attended by delegates from twelve cantons, and was approved of by the Swiss bishops. After a discussion lasting fifteen days during which Eck defended the Catholic doctrine regarding the Mass, Eucharist, Purgatory, and the Intercession of the Saints, the majority of the cantons decided in his favour, and a resolution was passed forbidding religious changes in Switzerland and prohibiting the sale of the works of Luther and Zwingli.

It was soon evident, however, that peace could not be secured by such measures. The rural and Catholic cantons were in the majority, much to the disgust of flourishing cities like Berne and Zurich. These states, believing that they were entitled to a controlling voice in the federal council, determined to use the religious question to bring about a complete change in the constitution of the country by assigning the cantonal representation in the federal council on the basis of population. They formed an alliance with the other Protestant cantons and with Constance to forward their claims (1527-8), but the Catholic cantons imitated their example by organising a Catholic federation to which the Archduke, Ferdinand of Austria, promised his support (1529).

Zwingli was most eager for war, and at his instigation the army of Zurich, backed by Berne, took the field in 1529. The Catholic states, however, made it clear that they were both able and willing to defend the constitution, but the bond of national unity and the dislike of civil war exercised such an influence on both parties that a conflict was averted by the conclusion of the Peace of Kappel (1529). The concessions secured for his party by this Peace did not satisfy Zwingli, who desired nothing less than the complete subjugation of the Catholic cantons. Negotiations were opened up with Philip of Hesse, with the German Lutherans, and with Francis I. of France, and when the news of the formation of the League of Schmalkald reached the Protestants of

Switzerland, it was thought that the time had come when the triumph of Zurich and Berne, which meant also the triumph of the new teaching, should be secured. Zwingli besought his followers to issue a declaration of war, but it was suggested that the reduction of the Catholic cantons could be secured just as effectively by a blockade. In this movement Zurich took the lead. The result, however, did not coincide with the anticipations of Zwingli. The Catholic cantons flew to arms at once, and as their territories formed a compact unit, they were able to put their united army into the field before the forces of Zurich and Berne could effect a junction. The decisive battle took place at Kappel in October 1531, when the Zwinglians suffered a complete defeat, Zwingli himself and five hundred of the best men of Zurich being left dead on the field. The army of Berne advanced too late to save their allies or to change the result of the war. The Catholic cantons used their victory with great moderation. Instead of crushing their opponents, as they might have done, they concluded with them the second Peace of Kappel (Nov. 1531). According to the terms of this treaty no canton was to force another to change its religion, and liberty of worship was granted in the cantonal domains. Several of the districts that had been wavering returned to the Catholic faith, and the abbot of St. Gall was restored to the abbey from which he had been expelled.

Oecolampadius followed Zwingli to the grave in a short time, having been carried off by a fever about a month after the defeat of Kappel, and the leadership of the movement devolved upon their successors, Bullinger and Myconius.

With regard to the Sacraments Luther and Zwingli agreed that they were only signs of grace, though in the explanation of this view Zwingli was much more extreme, because much more logical, than Luther. Believing as he did that justification depended upon faith alone, he contended that the Sacraments were mere ceremonies by which a man became or showed himself to be a follower of Christ. They were devoid of any objective virtue, and were efficacious only in so far as they guaranteed that the individual receiving them possessed the faith necessary for justification. But it was principally in regard to the Eucharist that the two reformers found themselves in hopeless disagreement. Had Luther wished to be consistent he should have thrown over the Real Presence as well as Transubstantiation, but the force of tradition, the fear that any such teaching would arouse the opposition of the people, and the plain meaning of the texts of Scripture forced him to adopt a compromise. "Had Doctor Carlstadt," he wrote, "or any one else been able to persuade me five years ago that the sacrament of the altar is but bread and wine he would, indeed, have done me a great service, and rendered me very material aid in my efforts to make a breach in the Papacy. But it is all in vain. The meaning of the texts is so evident that every artifice of language will be powerless to explain it away." He contended that the words "This is My body and This is My blood" could bear only one meaning, namely, that Christ was really present, but while agreeing with Catholics about the Real Presence of Christ in the Eucharist, he rejected the doctrine of Transubstantiation, maintaining in its place Consubstantiation or Impanation.

Though Luther insisted so strongly on the Real Presence, it is not clear that in the beginning he had any very fixed views on the subject, or that he would have been unwilling to change any views he had formed, were it not that one of his lieutenants, Carlstadt, began to exercise his privilege of judgment by rejecting the Real Presence. Such an act of insubordination aroused the implacable ire of Luther, who denounced his former colleague as a heretic, and pursued him from Wittenberg and Jena, where he had fled for refuge. In the end Carlstadt was obliged to retire to Switzerland, where his doctrine found favour with the Swiss reformers.

From the beginning of his campaign Zwingli realised that the Real Presence was not in harmony with his theory of justification, and hence he was inclined to hold that the Eucharist was a mere sign instituted as a reminder of Christ's death. But in view of the clear testimony of the Holy Scripture he was at a loss how to justify his position. At last by pondering on other passages that he considered similar to the text "This is My body," where the word " is " should be interpreted "signifies," he contended that the true meaning of Christ's words at the Last Supper is, " This signifies My body." Oecolampadius agreed with this interpretation, though for a different reason, comparing the Blessed Eucharist to a ring that a husband going away on a long journey might give to his wife as a pledge and reminder of his affection.*

Luther resented bitterly such a theory as an attack upon his authority, particularly after Zwingli refused to allow himself to be brow-beaten into retracting his doctrine. Instead of submitting to the new religious dictator, Zwingli sought to justify himself by the very principle by which Luther justified his own revolt against the Catholic Church. He contended that Luther's theory of justification involved logically the rejection of the Eucharist as well as of the other Sacraments, that the Scriptural texts could be interpreted as he had interpreted them, and that he was not bound to take any cognisance of the Christian tradition or of the authority of the councils. He complained that Luther treated himself and his followers as heretics with whom it was not right to hold communion, that he proscribed their writings and denounced them to the magistrates, and that he did precisely towards them what he blamed the Pope for doing to himself. Luther found it difficult to meet this line of argument. Much against his will he was obliged to support his opinions by appealing to the tradition of the Church and the writings of the Fathers,

* Schwane, *op. cit.*, p. 349.

which latter he had denounced as "fetid pools whence Christians have been drinking unwholesome draughts instead of slaking their thirst from the pure fountain of Holy Scripture."* "This article (The Eucharist)," he wrote, "is neither unscriptural nor a dogma of human invention. It is based upon the clear and irrefragable words of Holy Writ. It has been uniformly held and believed throughout the whole Christian world from the foundation of the Church to the present time. That such has been the fact is attested by the writings of the Holy Fathers, both Greek and Latin, by daily usage and by the uninterrupted practice of the Church. . . . To doubt it, therefore, is to disbelieve the Christian Church and to brand her as heretical, and with her the prophets, apostles, and Christ Himself, who, in establishing the Church said: 'Behold I am with you all days even to the consummation of the world.'" †

The opposition of Luther did not put an end to the controversy. The Zwinglian theories spread rapidly in Switzerland, whence they were carried into Germany, much to the annoyance of Luther and of the Protestant princes for whom religious unity was necessary at almost any cost. Luther would listen to no schemes of compromise. He denounced the Zwinglians in the most violent terms, as servants of the devil, liars, and heretics for whose salvation no man should pray. Having rejected Transubstantiation in order to rid himself of the sacrificial idea and of the doctrine of a Christian priesthood, he fought strongly for the Real Presence on the ground that Christ's body, being united to the divinity, enjoyed the divine attribute of ubiquity. To this Zwingli made the very effective rejoinder that if the words of Scripture "This is My body and this is My blood" are to be interpreted literally they could bear only the sense put upon them by the Catholics, because Christ did not say "My body is in or under this bread," but rather "This

---

* Döllinger, *Die Reformation*, i., pp. 430-51.
† Alzog, iii., 256-7.

(the bread) is My body." Furthermore, he pointed out that Luther's explanation concerning the ubiquity of Christ's body led clearly to a confusion of the divine and human nature in Christ, and was in consequence only a renewal of the Monophysite heresy, condemned by the whole Christian Church.

This unseemly dispute between the two leaders of the new movement did not please the Protestant princes of Germany, for whom division of their forces might mean political extinction. The Elector of Saxony supported Luther warmly, while Philip of Hesse was more or less inclined to side with Zwingli. A conference was arranged between the two parties at Marburg (1529), at which Luther and Oecolampadius were present to defend their views. On a few secondary matters an agreement was arrived at, but on the main question, the Real Presence, Luther would yield nothing, and so the reformers were divided into two parties, German Lutherans and Swiss Reformed.

(c) NORTHERN EUROPE.

See bibliography, chap. ii. (a). Karup, *Geschichte der Katholischen Kirche in Dänemark*, 1863. Münter, *Kirchengeschichte von Dänemark und Norwegen*, 1823. Theiner-Cohen, *La Suède et la Saint-Siège sous les rois Jean III., Sigismond III., et Charles IX.*, 1842. Butler, *The Reformation in Sweden*, 1884. De Flaux, *La Suède au XVIme siècle*, 1861. Englestoft, *Reformantes et Catholici tempore, quo sacra emendata sunt, in Dania concertantes*, 1836. Schmitt, *Die Verteidigung der Kathol. Kirche in Dänemark gegen die Religionsneuerung im 16en Jahr.* 1899. *Confutatio Lutheranismi Danici*, etc. (written 1530, ed. 1902).

At the beginning of the sixteenth century political power in Denmark was vested to a great extent in the hands of the bishops and nobles. It was by these two parties that the king was elected, and so great was their influence that, as a rule, the candidate chosen by their votes was obliged to accept any conditions they cared to impose. The bishops, as in most countries at the time, held enormous estates, granted to their predecessors by the crown or bequeathed by generous benefactors for the maintenance of religion. Unfortunately, with some exceptions, they were not men zealous for religious interests, or capable of understanding that a serious crisis was at hand. In every direction the need of reform was only too apparent, and, as such a work had not been undertaken by those who should have undertaken it, a splendid opportunity was afforded to the men who desired not the welfare of religion but rather the overthrow of the Church.

Christian II. (1513-23) wished to put an end to the supremacy of the bishops and nobles and to assert for himself and his successors absolute control. He was a man of great ability and determination, well acquainted with the tendencies of the age, and not particularly scrupulous about the means by which the success of his policy might be assured. To such a man Luther's attack on the bishops of Germany seemed to be almost providential. He realised that by embracing the new religious system, which enabled him to seize the wealth of the Church and to concentrate in his own hands full ecclesiastical power, he could rid himself of one of the greatest obstacles to absolutism, and secure for himself and his successors undisputed sway in Denmark. Though his own life was scandalously immoral he determined to become the champion of a religious reformation, and against the wishes of the nobles, clergy, and people he invited a disciple of Luther's to Copenhagen, and placed at his disposal one of the city churches. This step aroused the strongest opposition, but Christian, confident that boldness meant success, adopted stern measures to overcome his opponents. He proclaimed himself the patron of those priests who were willing to disregard their vows of celibacy, issued regulations against the unmarried clergy, and appealed to the people against the bishops and the nobles. As the Archbishop-elect of Lund was unwilling to allow himself to be coerced into betraying the interests confided to his charge, the king commanded that he should be put to death.

By these violent methods he had hoped to frighten his subjects into compliance with his wishes, but he was doomed to speedy and complete disappointment. The bishops and barons, though divided on many questions, were at one in their resistance to such despotism, and they had behind them the great body of the people, who had little if any desire for a religious revolution. Christian II. was deposed, and in his place his uncle, Frederick I. (1523-33), became king of Denmark. At his coronation the new monarch pledged himself to defend the Catholic religion and to suppress heresy. Soon, however, motives similar to those that had influenced his predecessor induced him also to lean towards Lutheranism. At first his efforts for the spread of the new teaching were carried out secretly, but once he felt himself secure on the throne, he proclaimed himself publicly a Lutheran (1526) and invited Lutheran preachers to the capital. A Diet was called in 1527 at Odensee to consider the religious controversy that had arisen. In this assembly the king, basing his defence on the ground that though he had pledged himself to uphold the Catholic Church he was under no obligation to tolerate abuses, contended that the suppression of abuses and the purifying of religion were the only objects he had at heart in the measures that he had taken. Owing mainly to his own stubbornness and the cowardly and wavering attitude of the bishops, it was agreed by the Diet that till a General Council could be convoked full toleration should be given to the Lutheran preachers, that in the meantime no civil disabilities should be inflicted on supporters of the new religion, that those of the clergy who wished to marry should be allowed to do so, that the archbishop should apply no longer to Rome for his pallium, and finally that the confirmation of the appointment of bishops should be transferred from the Pope to the king.

By these measures, to which the bishops offered only a faint opposition, Denmark was separated practically from the Holy See, and the first step was taken on the road that was to lead to national apostasy. The next important measure was the disputation arranged by the king to take place at Copenhagen in 1529. The very fact that at this meeting no Danish ecclesiastic capable of defending the Catholic faith was to be found, and that it was necessary to have recourse to Germany for champions of orthodoxy, is in itself a sufficient indication of the character of the bishops who then ruled in Denmark, and of the state of learning amongst the Danish clergy of the period. Eck and Cochlaeus were invited to come to Copenhagen, but as they had sufficient work to engage their attention at home, the duty of upholding Catholic doctrine devolved upon Stagefyr, a theologian of Cologne.* He could not speak Danish, nor would the Lutheran party consent to carry on the conference in Latin. Furthermore, he claimed that the authority of the Fathers and the decrees of previous General Councils should be recognised, but the Lutherans insisted that the Bible was the only source from which Christians should receive their doctrines. In these circumstances, since a disputation was impossible, both parties agreed to submit a full statement of their views in writing to the king and council, who, as might have been anticipated, decided in favour of Lutheranism.

During the remainder of his reign, Frederick I. spared no pains to secure the victory for the new teaching in his dominions. The nobles were won over to the king's views by promises of a share in the partition of ecclesiastical property, and those who wished to stand well with the sovereign were not slow in having recourse to violence as affording proof that their zeal for Lutheranism was sincere. Consequently the Lutheran party found themselves in a majority in the Diet of 1530, and

* A Franciscan. He was the author of the *Confutatio Lutheranismi Danici*, edited and published 1902.

were powerful enough to do as they pleased. In accordance with the example set in Germany and Switzerland attacks were begun on churches, pictures, and statues, but in many places the people were not prepared for such changes, and bitter conflicts took place between the rival parties. In the confusion that resulted the supporters of the deposed king rose in arms against his successful rival, and the country was subjected to the horrors of civil war. Frederick I. found it necessary to abandon the violent propagation of Lutheranism and to offer toleration to the Catholics.

On his death in 1533 the bishops of Denmark protested against the succession of his son Christian III. (1533-51) who was a personal friend of Luther, and who had already introduced Protestantism into his own state of Holstein; but as the nobles, won over by promises of a share in the spoliation of the Church, refused to make common cause with the bishops, their protest was unheeded. Confident that he could rely on the support of the nobles, the king gave secret instructions to his officials that on a certain day named by him all the bishops of Denmark should be arrested and lodged in prison. His orders were carried out to the letter (1536), and so rejoiced was Luther by this momentous step that he hastened to send the king his warmest congratulations. The bishops were offered release on condition that they should resign their Sees and pledge themselves to offer no further opposition to the religious change. To their shame be it said only one of their number, Rönnow, Bishop of Roskilde, refused to accept liberty on such disgraceful terms, preferring to remain a prisoner until he was released by death (1544). The priests who refused to accept the new religion were driven from their parishes, and several monasteries and convents were suppressed.

To complete the work of reform and to give the Church in Denmark a new constitution Bugenhagen, a disciple of Luther, was invited to the capital (1539). He began

THE RELIGIOUS REVOLUTION 129

by crowning the king according to Lutheran ritual, and by drawing up a form of ecclesiastical government that placed full spiritual power in the hands of the civil ruler. As in Germany, superintendents were appointed in room of the bishops who had resigned. When the work of drawing up the new ecclesiastical organisation had been finished it was submitted to and approved of by the Diet held at Odensee in 1539. In another Diet held in 1546 the Catholic Church in Denmark was completely overthrown, her possessions were confiscated, her clergy were forbidden to remain in the country under penalty of death, and all lay Catholics were declared incapable of holding any office in the state or of transmitting their property to their Catholic heirs. By those measures Catholicism was suppressed, and victory was secured for the Lutheran party.

Norway, which was united with Denmark at this period, was forced into submission to the new creed by the violence of the Danish kings, aided as they were by the greedy nobles anxious to share in the plunder of the Church. Similarly Iceland, which was subject to Denmark, was separated from Rome, though at first the people offered the strongest resistance to the reformers. The execution, however, of their bishop, John Aresen, the example of Denmark and Norway, and the want of capable religious leaders produced their effects, and in the end Iceland was induced to accept the new religion (1551). For a considerable time Catholicism retained its hold on a large percentage of the people both in Norway and Iceland, but the severe measures taken by the government to ensure the complete extirpation of the Catholic hierarchy and priesthood led almost of necessity to the triumph of Lutheranism.

By the Union of Kalmar (1397) Sweden, Norway, and Denmark were united under the rule of the King of Denmark. The Union did not, however, bring about peace. The people of Sweden disliked the rule of a foreigner, and more than once they rose in rebellion

VOL. I.   I against Denmark. In the absence of a strong central authority the clergy and nobles became the dominant factors in the state, especially as they took the lead in the national agitations against King Erik and his successors. As in most other countries at the time, the Church was exceedingly wealthy, the bishoprics and abbacies being endowed very generously, but unfortunately, as elsewhere, the progress of religion was not in proportion to the worldly possessions of its ministers. Endowment had destroyed the liberty of election so essential for good administration, with the result that the bishops and other ecclesiastical dignitaries were selected without much regard for their qualifications as spiritual guides. Yet it must be said that in general the administrators of the ecclesiastical property were not hard task-masters when compared with their lay contemporaries, nor was there anything like a strong popular feeling against the Church. Still the immense wealth of the religious institutions, the prevalence of abuses, and the failure of the clergy to instruct the people in the real doctrines of their faith were a constant source of menace to the Church in Sweden, and left it open to a crushing attack by a leader who knew how to win the masses to his side by proclaiming himself the champion of national independence and of religious reform.

In 1515 Sten Sture, the administrator of Sweden, supported by the Bishop of Linköping as leader of the popular party, made a gallant attempt to rally his countrymen to shake off the Danish yoke. Unfortunately for the success of his undertaking he soon found a dangerous opponent in the person of Gustaf Trolle, Archbishop of Upsala, the nominee and supporter of the King of Denmark. The archbishop threw the whole weight of his influence into the scales for Denmark, and partly owing to his opposition, partly owing to the want of sufficient preparation the national uprising was crushed early in 1520. Christian II. was crowned King of Sweden by the Archbishop of Upsala. He signified his elevation to the throne by a general massacre of his opponents which lasted for two days, and during which many of the best blood of Sweden were put to death (Nov. 1520). The archbishop was rewarded for his services to Denmark by receiving an appointment as regent or administrator of Sweden. He and his party made loud boast of their political victory, but had they been gifted with a little prudence and zeal they would have found good reason to regret a triumph that had been secured by committing the Church to the support of a Danish tyrant against the wishes of the majority who favoured national independence. Religion and patriotism were brought into serious conflict, and, given only a capable leader who would know how to conduct his campaign with skill, it was not difficult to foresee the results of such a conflict.

As it happened, such a leader was at hand in the person of Gustaf Eriksson, better known as Gustavus Vasa. His father had been put to death in the massacre of Stockholm, and he himself when a youth had been given as a hostage to the King of Denmark. He made his escape and fled to Lübeck, where he was kindly received, and remained until an opportunity arose for his return to Sweden. He placed himself immediately at the head of the party willing to fight against Denmark, called upon his countrymen to rally to his standard, and in a short time succeeded in driving the Danish forces from Sweden. He was proclaimed administrator of his country in 1521, and two years later a national Diet assembled at Strengnäs offered him the crown.

Such an offer was in exact accordance with his own wishes. But he had no intention of becoming king of Sweden merely to remain a tool in the hands of the spiritual and lay lords as the kings of Denmark had remained. Determined in his own mind to make himself absolute ruler of Sweden by crushing the bishops and barons, he recognised that Luther's teaching, with which he was familiar owing to his stay at Lübeck, held out good hopes for the success of such a project. The warm attachment of the Archbishop of Upsala for the Danish faction had weakened the devotion of the people to the Church, and had prepared the way for the change which Gustavus contemplated. Some of the Swedish ecclesiastics, notably the brothers Olaf and Laurence Peterson, both students of Wittenberg, the former a well-known preacher at Stockholm, the latter a professor at Upsala, were strongly Lutheran in their tendencies and were ready to assist the king. Though in his letters to Rome and in his public pronouncements Gustavus professed himself to be a sincere son of the Church, anxious only to prevent at all costs the spread of Lutheranism in his dominions, he was taking steps secretly to encourage his Lutheran supporters and to rid himself of the bishops and members of the religious orders from whom he feared serious opposition. As was done elsewhere, he arranged for a public disputation at which Olaf Peterson undertook to defend the main principles advocated by Luther, but the results of the controversy were not so satisfactory for his party as he had anticipated.

Gustavus now threw off the mask of hypocrisy, and came forward boldly as the champion of the new religion. He removed those bishops who were most outspoken in their opposition, banished the Dominicans who stood loyal to Rome, and tried to force the clergy to accept the change. Anxious to enrich his treasury by confiscating the wealth of the Church he scattered broadcast Luther's pamphlet on the confiscation of ecclesiastical property, and engaged the professors of the University of Upsala to use their efforts to defend and popularise the views it contained. A commission was appointed to make an inventory of the goods of the bishops and religious institutions and to induce the monasteries to make a voluntary surrender of their property. By means of threats and promises the commissioners secured compliance with the wishes of the king in some districts, though in others, as for example in Upsala, the arrival of the commission led to scenes of the greatest violence and commotion. More severe measures were necessary to overawe the people, and Gustavus was not a man to hesitate at anything likely to promote the success of his plans. Bishop Jakobson and some of the clergy were arrested, and after having been treated with every species of indignity were put to death (1527).

In this year, 1527, a national Diet was held at Vesteräs principally for the discussion of the religious difficulties that had arisen. Both parties, the supporters of the old and of the new, mustered their forces for a final conflict. Gustavus took the side of the so-called reformers, and proposed the measures which he maintained were required both in the interests of religion and of the public weal. The Catholic party were slightly in the majority and refused to assent to these proposals. Gustavus, though disappointed at the result, did not despair. He announced to the Diet that in view of its refusal to agree to his terms he could undertake no longer the government and defence of the country. A measure such as this, calculated to lead to anarchy and possibly to a new subjugation of the country by Denmark, was regarded by both sides as a national disaster, and secured for the king the support of the waverers. The masses of the people were alarmed lest their opposition might lead to the restoration of Danish tyranny, while the support of the nobles was secured by the publication of a decree authorising them to resume possession of all property handed over by their ancestors to religious institutions for the last eighty years. The remainder of the possessions of the Church were appropriated for the royal treasury. The king now issued a proclamation in favour of the new religion, insisted on the adoption of a liturgy in the vulgar tongue, and abolished clerical celibacy. At the National Assembly of Örebro (1529) the Catholic religion was abolished in favour of Lutheranism, and two years later Laurence Peterson was appointed first Lutheran Archbishop of Upsala.

Though the Lutheran teaching had been accepted, great care was taken not to shock the people by any violent change. Episcopal government of the Church was retained; most of the Catholic ritual in regard to the sacraments and the Mass was adopted in the new liturgy, and even in some cases the pictures and statues were not removed from the churches. But the revolution that Gustavus had most at heart was fully accomplished. The authority of the Pope had been overthrown, and in his place the king had been accepted as the head of the Swedish Church. Nor did the Lutheran bishops find themselves in the enjoyment of greater liberty and respect as a result of their treason to the Church. Gustavus warned them that they must not carry themselves like lords, and that if they should attempt to wield the sword he would know how to deal with them in a summary manner. Resenting such dictation and tyranny they began to attack Gustavus in their sermons and to organise plots for the overthrow of his government. The conspiracy was discovered (1540). Olaf and Laurence Peterson, the two prominent leaders of the reforming party, were condemned to death, but were reprieved on the payment of a large fine. Laurence was, however, removed from his position as Archbishop of Upsala. In the Diet of Vesterås in 1544 the crown of Sweden was declared to be hereditary, and was vested in the family and heirs of Gustavus. Thus the well-considered policy of Gustavus was crowned with success. By means of the Lutheran revolt he had changed the whole constitution of the country, had made himself absolute master of Sweden, and had secured the succession to the throne for his own family.

But he had not broken the power of his opponents so completely as to bring peace to his country, nor, if credence be given to the proclamations in which he bewailed the increase of evil under the plea of evangelical freedom, did the reformed religion tend to the elevation of public morals. On his death in 1560 he was succeeded by his son Erik XIV. (1560-69). Hardly had the new king been proclaimed than the principle of private judgment introduced by the reformers began to produce its natural results. Calvinism, which was so opposed to Lutheranism both in doctrine and in church government, found its way into Sweden, and attracted the favourable notice of the king. Regardless for the time being of the Catholic Church, which to all appearances was dead in Sweden, the two parties, Lutherans and Calvinists, struggled for supremacy. Erik was won over to the side of the Calvinists, and measures were taken to overcome the Lutherans by force, but the king had neither the capacity nor the energy of his father. The plan miscarried; the Calvinists were defeated (1568), and Erik was deposed and imprisoned.

His younger brother John succeeded to the throne under the title John III. He was a man of considerable ability, and was by no means satisfied with the new religion. His marriage with Catharine, sister of Sigismund, King of Poland, herself a devoted Catholic, who stipulated for liberty to practise her religion, helped to make him more favourable to a Catholic revival. He set himself to study the Scriptures and writings of the Fathers under the guidance of Catharine's chaplains, and convinced himself that he should return to the Catholic Church and endeavour to rescue his country from the condition of heresy into which it had fallen. He allowed the monks and nuns who were still in Sweden to form communities again, and endeavoured to win over the clergy by a series of ordinances couched in a Catholic tone which he issued for their guidance. In 1571 he induced the Archbishop of Upsala to publish a number of regulations known as the *Agenda,* which both in ritual and doctrine indicated a return to Rome, and he employed some Jesuit missionaries to explain the misrepresentations of Catholic doctrine indulged in by the Lutheran and Calvinist leaders. His greatest difficulty in bringing about a reunion was the presence of

Lutheran bishops, but fortunately for him many of them were old men whose places were soon vacant by death, to whose Sees he appointed those upon whom he could rely for support. When he thought the time was ripe he summoned a National Synod in 1574, where he delivered an address deploring the sad condition to which religious dissensions had reduced the country. He pointed out that such a state of affairs had been brought about by the Reformation and could be remedied only by a return to the Church. The address received from the clergy a much more favourable reception than he had anticipated. As the Archbishopric of Upsala was vacant, he secured the election of an archbishop, who gave his adhesion to seventeen articles of faith wholly satisfactory to Catholics, and who allowed himself to be consecrated according to the Catholic ritual. He promised also to use his influence to secure the adhesion of the other bishops. In 1576 the king issued a new liturgy, *The Red Book of Sweden,* which was adopted by the Diet in 1577, and accepted by a large body of the clergy. Its principal opponent was the king's brother, Karl, Duke of Suthermanland, who for political reasons had constituted himself head of the Lutheran party, and who refused to agree with the Roman tendencies of the king on the ground that they were opposed to the last wishes of Gustavus and to the laws of Sweden. A disputation was arranged to take place at Upsala, where the Belgian Jesuit, Laurence Nicolai, vindicated triumphantly against his Lutheran opponents the Catholic teaching on the Church and the Mass. Copies of the celebrated catechism of the Blessed Peter Canisius were circulated throughout Sweden, and made an excellent impression on the people.

Encouraged by these hopeful signs, the king despatched an embassy to Rome to arrange for the reconciliation of Sweden to the Church. The royal commissioners were instructed to request, that owing to the peculiar circumstances of the country, permission

THE RELIGIOUS REVOLUTION   137

should be given for Communion under both kinds, for the celebration of the Mass in the Swedish language, and for the abrogation of the law of celibacy at least in regard to the clergy who were already married. Gregory XIII., deeply moved by the king's offer of a reunion, sent the Jesuit, Anthony Possevin, as his legate to discuss the terms. John set an example himself by abjuring publicly his errors and by announcing his submission to the Church (1578).

A commission was appointed at Rome to discuss the concessions which the king demanded, and unfortunately the decision was regarded in Sweden as unfavourable. A warm controversy, fomented and encouraged by the enemies of reunion, broke out between the opponents and supporters of the new liturgy. Duke Karl, who had now become the hope of the Lutheran party, did everything he could to stir up strife, while at the same time Rome refused to accept the terms proposed by the king. Indignant at what he considered the unreasonable attitude of the Roman authorities, John began to lose his enthusiasm for his religious policy, and after the death of his wife who was unwavering in her devotion to her religion, there was no longer much hope that Sweden was to be won from heresy (1584). The king married another who was strongly Lutheran in her sympathies, and who used her influence over him to secure the expulsion of the Jesuits. Though John III. took no further steps to bring about reunion he could not be induced to withdraw the liturgy, the use of which he insisted upon till his death in 1592.

His son Sigismund III. should have succeeded. He was an ardent Catholic as his mother had been, but as he had been elected King of Poland (1586) he was absent from Sweden when the throne became vacant by the death of his father. Duke Karl and his friends did not fail to take advantage of his absence. When the Synod met the senators demanded that Sigismund should accept the Augsburg Confession as a condition for his election

to the throne. To this Sigismund sent the only reply
that a good Catholic and an honest man could send,
namely, a blunt refusal. His uncle, Duke Karl, the
acting regent of Sweden, took steps to seduce the
Swedish people from their allegiance to their lawful
king, and to prepare the way for his own accession. He
proclaimed himself the protector of Lutheranism and
endeavoured to win over the bishops to his side. In a
national Assembly held at Upsala (The " Upsala-möte "
1593) after a very violent address from the regent against
the Catholic Church, the bishops confessed that they had
blundered in accepting the liturgy of John III., and the
Assembly declared itself strongly in favour of the Augsburg Confession.

When, therefore, Sigismund returned to claim the
throne he found that Lutheranism was entrenched
safely once more, and that even the most moderate of the
bishops appointed by his father must be reckoned with
as opponents. The clergy united with Duke Karl in
stirring up the people against him. In these conditions
he was forced to abandon his projects of reform, and to
entrust his uncle with the administration of Sweden when
he himself was obliged to return to Poland. While
Sigismund was engaged in Poland, the regent conducted
a most skilful campaign, nominally on behalf of Protestantism, but in reality to secure the deposition of
Sigismund and his own election to the throne. In the
Diet of Süderköping (1595) Sigismund was condemned
for having bestowed appointments on Catholics and for
having tolerated the Catholic religion in his kingdom of
Sweden, and it was ordered that all who professed the
doctrines of Rome should abandon their errors within
six months under pain of expulsion from the country.
The Archbishop of Upsala made a visitation of the
churches, during which he ordered that all those who
absented themselves from the Lutheran service should be
flogged in his presence, that the pictures, statues, and
reliquaries should be destroyed, and that the liturgy

THE RELIGIOUS REVOLUTION 139

introduced by John III. should be abolished. The greatest violence was used towards the supporters of King Sigismund, most of whom were either Catholic or at least favourably inclined towards Catholicism.

Enraged by a decree that no edict of the king should have any binding force unless confirmed by the Swedish Diet, and driven to desperation by the tyranny and oppression of the regent, some of Sigismund's followers raised the standard on behalf of their king, and Sigismund returned to Sweden with an army of five thousand men. He found himself opposed by the forces of the regent against whom he was at first successful, but in his treatment of his uncle and his rebel followers he showed himself far too forgiving. In return for his kindness, having strengthened themselves by a large army they forced him to submit to the decision of a national Assembly to be held at Jonköping (1599). At this meeting Duke Karl accused the king of endeavouring to plunge Sweden once more into the errors from which it had been rescued by the reformers. In May of the same year a resolution was passed declaring that the king had forfeited the allegiance of his subjects unless he yielded to their demands, and more especially unless he handed over his son and heir to be reared by the regent as a Protestant. Many of his supporters, including nine members of the Council of State, were put to death. Finally in 1604 Sigismund was formally deposed, and the crown was bestowed on his uncle, Duke Karl, who became king under the title of Charles IX. Protestantism had triumphed at last in Sweden, but even its strongest supporters would hardly like to maintain that the issue was decided on religious grounds, or that the means adopted by Charles IX. to secure the victory were worthy of the apostle of a new religion.

CHAPTER III.

PROGRESS OF CALVINISM

(a) IN SWITZERLAND

Calvini Joannis, Opera quae supersunt in the *Corp. Reformatorum*, vols. xxix.-lxxxvii. Doumergue, *Jean Calvin, les hommes et les choses de son temps*, 1900-5. Kampschulte, *Johann Calvin, seine Kirche und sein staat in Genf,* 1899. Fleury, *Histoire de l'Église de Genève*, 3 vols., 1880. Mignet, *Établissement de la réforme religieuse et constitution du calvinisme à Genève*, 1877. Choisy, *La théocratie à Genève au temps de Calvin*, 1897. *Cambridge Mod. History*, ii., chap. xi. (Bibliography, 769-83). For complete bibliography, see *Diction. Théologique* (art. Calvin).

JOHN CALVIN, from whom the heresy takes its name, was born at Noyon in Picardy in 1509. In accordance with the wishes of his father he studied philosophy and theology at the University of Paris, where he was supported mainly from the fruits of the ecclesiastical benefices to which he had been appointed to enable him to pursue his studies. Later on he began to waver about his career in life, and without abandoning entirely his hopes of becoming an ecclesiastic he turned his attention to law in the Universities of Orleans and Bourges. In French intellectual centres at this period a certain spirit of unrest and a contempt for old views and old methods might be detected. The Renaissance ideas, so widespread on the other side of the Alps, had made their way into France, where they found favour with some of the university professors, and created a feeling of distrust and suspicion in the minds of those to whom Scholasticism was the highest ideal. Margaret of Navarre, sister of the king, showed herself the generous patron and defender of the new movement, and secured for it the sympathy and to some extent the support of Francis I. A few of the friends of the Renaissance in France were not slow to adopt the religious ideas of Luther, though not all who were suspected of heresy by the extreme champions of Scholasticism had any intention of joining in a movement directed against the defined doctrines or constitution of the Catholic Church.

As a student at Bourges, Calvin was brought into close relations with Melchior Wolmar, a German Humanist, who was strongly Lutheran in his tendencies, and through whom he became enamoured of Luther's teaching on Justification. On his return to Paris he was soon remarkable as a strong partisan of the advanced section of the university, and by his ability and determination he did much to win over the Renaissance party to the religious teaching that had become so widespread in Germany. As a result of an address delivered by Nicholas Cop, rector of the university, and of several acts of violence perpetrated in the capital by the friends of heresy Francis I. was roused to take action. Calvin, fearing death or imprisonment, made his escape from Paris to Basle (1534). Here he published his first and greatest theological treatise, *Christianœ Religionis Institutio,* which he dedicated to the King of France (1536). The work was divided into four sections, namely, God the Creator, God the Redeemer, Grace, and the External Means for Salvation. Both in its style and in its arguments drawn from the Scriptures, the Fathers, and the theologians of the Middle Ages, it was far superior, at least for educated readers, to the best that had been produced by Luther and even to the *Loci Communes* of Melanchthon.

He arrived at Basle at a time when a crisis had arisen in the political and religious development of Geneva. For a long period the House of Savoy was seeking for an opportunity to annex the territory of Vaud extending along the Lake of Geneva, and the episcopal cities of

Geneva and Lausanne. Berne, too, had aspirations of a similar kind. The authorities of Berne, having adopted the Zwinglian doctrine, thought that in it they had a means at their hand to detach Geneva and Lausanne from any sympathy with Savoy and to secure these territories for themselves. They despatched preachers to Geneva, where there were already two political factions, one advocating a closer alliance with Savoy, another clamouring for a union with Berne. The supporters of Berne rallied round William Farel and the Zwinglian ministers, while the friends of Savoy undertook to champion the old religion. The whole struggle was at bottom political rather than religious, but the triumph of the republican adherents of Berne meant victory for the reforming party in Geneva. The Duke of Savoy issued a declaration of war against the rebels to whom the Canton of Berne had pledged support (1534). As a result the forces of Savoy were driven out of Geneva and the Vaud, a close union was formed between Geneva and Berne, and every effort was made to spread the new religion in the city and among the Vaudois. A Zwinglian university was established at Lausanne, which exercised a great influence in propagating the new doctrine, and which had the honour of counting among its students Theodore Beza * the most gifted and learned assistant of Calvin.

But though the Vaudois had been won over, Geneva was by no means secured for the reformers. Farel and his followers, finding themselves involved in serious difficulties, appealed to Calvin to help them in completing the work they had begun. In 1536 Calvin accepted this invitation, and took up his residence at Geneva. Gifted with great powers as an organiser and administrator he soon restored order in the city, and won over the people to his doctrines. Himself a man of very strict notions, in whose eyes all even the most harmless amusements appeared sinful or dangerous, he was determined that

* Baird, *Theodore Beza, Counsellor of the French Reform*, 1900.

his followers must accept his views. Under his rule Geneva, formerly so gay, became like a city of death, where all citizens went about as if in mourning. Such an unnatural condition of affairs could not be permanent. The people soon grew tired of their dictator and of his methods; the authorities of Berne were roused to hostility by his refusal to accept their doctrinal programme or their model religious organisation; the Synod of Lausanne declared against him for a similar reason, and in 1538 he and his principal supporters were driven from the city. Cardinal Sadoleto took occasion to address a stirring appeal to Geneva to return to the old faith, but his appeal fell upon deaf ears.

Calvin retired at first to Strassburg, and later he took charge of a parish in France. During the interval he devoted himself to a closer study of the disputed religious questions, and wrote much in favour of the Reformation. It was at this time (1540) that he married the widow of one of the Anabaptist leaders. Meanwhile Geneva was torn by disputes between two factions, the Libertines as they were called, who were opposed to Calvin, and the Guillermins, who clamoured for his return. The latter body gained ground rapidly, and a decree was issued recalling Calvin to Geneva (October 1540). Knowing well that his presence was necessary to restore peace to the city he refused to return unless the conditions imposed by him should be accepted. In the end he went back to Geneva practically as its religious and political dictator (1541).

The form of government introduced was theocratic. Calvin was recognised as the spiritual and temporal ruler of the city. He was assisted in the work of government by the Consistory, which was composed of six clerics and twelve laymen. The latter was the worst form of inquisition court, taking cognisance of the smallest infractions of the rules laid down for the conduct of the citizens, and punishing them by the severest form of punishment. Any want of respect for the Consistory or opposition to its authority was treated as a rebellion against God. Calvin formulated a very severe code of rules for the guidance of the people not merely in their duties as citizens and as members of his religious organisation, but also in their social intercourse with one another. Even the privacy of family life was not sacred in his eyes. All kinds of amusements, theatres, dances, cards, &c., were banned as ungodly, as were also extravagance in dress and anything savouring of frivolity. Nobody was allowed to sell wine or beer except a limited number of merchants licensed to do so by the Consistory.

Nor were these mere empty regulations designed only to keep religion before the eyes of the people without any intention of enforcing them. The preachers were invested with extraordinary powers, and were commissioned to make house to house visitations, to inquire about violations of the rules. In their reports to the Congregation and to the Consistory they noted even the most minute transgressions. Not content with this Calvin had his spies in all parts of the city, who reported to him what people were saying about his methods and his government. The punishment meted out by the courts were of a very severe and brutal kind. No torture that could be inflicted was deemed too much for any one bold enough to criticise the Consistory or the dictator.

It was natural that such methods should be highly distasteful to those of the citizens of Geneva who were not religious fanatics. A strong party tried to resist him. They accused him of being much more tyrannical than the Pope, but Calvin denounced such opponents as libertines, heretics, and atheists. He handed them over to the devil at least in so far as his ecclesiastical censures were effective,* threatened the severest spiritual punishment against their aiders and abettors, and when all such means of reproof failed he had recourse to the secular arm.

* Galli, *Die Lutheran. und Calvinist. Kirchenstrafen im Reformationszeitalter*, 1878.

Sebastian Castellio, a well-known preacher and Scriptural scholar, was punished because he could not agree with Calvin's teaching on predestination, as was also the physician Bolsec; Ameaux one of the members of the Council was put to death because he denounced the tyranny of Calvin and of the Consistory; Gentilis was condemned to execution for differing with Calvin's teaching on the Trinity, and was compelled to make a most abject public retraction before he could obtain a reprieve. Several of the citizens were punished with long imprisonment for dancing even on the occasion of a wedding, as happened in the case of Le Fèvre, whose son-in-law was obliged to flee to France because he resented warmly such methods of promoting religion. In Geneva and in the adjoining territory all Catholic practices were put down by violence, and the peasants were allowed no choice in their religious views. Possibly, however, the most glaring example of Calvin's tyranny and highhanded methods was his treatment of Michael Servetus, a Spaniard who had written against the Trinity. He was on a journey through the territory of Geneva and was doing nothing to spread his doctrines nor acting in any way likely to bring him under the ire of Calvin. The latter having heard of his presence there had him arrested, tried, and condemned to death. To justify such harshness he published a pamphlet in which he advocated death as the only proper remedy for heresy. Theodore Beza wrote strongly in support of this opinion of his master's, as did also Melanchthon who, though differing from Calvin on so many points, hastened to forward his warmest congratulations on the execution of Servetus.*

Calvin's acts of cruelty were not the result of violent outbursts of temper. By nature cold and immovable, he

* Rouquette, *L'Inquisition protestante. Les victimes de Calvin*, 1906. Galiffe, *Quelques pages d'histoire exacte sur les procès intentés à Genève*, 1862. Paulus, *Luther und Gewissensfreiheit*, 1905. Id., *Melanchthon und Gewissensfreiheit* (*Katholik*, i., 546 *sqq.*).

did not allow himself to be hurried to extremes either by anger or by passion. How he succeeded in maintaining his position for so many years in Geneva is intelligible only to those who understand the strength of the religious fanaticism that he was able to arouse amongst his followers, the terror which his spiritual and temporal punishments inspired among his opponents, his own wonderful capacity for organisation and administration, the activity of his ministers and spies, and the almost perfect system of repression that he adopted in his twofold character of religious and political dictator.

To strengthen his position and to provide for the continuance of his system he established an academy at Geneva (1558) principally for the study of theology and philosophy. It was attended by crowds of scholars from Switzerland, France, Germany, the Netherlands, England, and Scotland. By means of the academy, Calvinism was spread throughout Switzerland notwithstanding the opposition of the Zwinglian preachers, and Calvin's system of ecclesiastical organisation became the model aimed at by his disciples in most countries of Europe, notably France, the Netherlands, and Scotland. The Zurich school, at the head of which stood Bullinger, did not yield ground to the new teaching without a severe struggle, and Calvin found himself obliged to come to terms with them in the *Consensus Tigurninus* (1549). In his desire to secure the religious unity of Switzerland he had no difficulty in abandoning or minimising his own doctrine in the hope of overcoming or winning over his opponents. After a life of tireless energy his health began to fail in 1561, and three years later he passed away (1564).

Calvin was a man of morose and gloomy temperament, severe even to harshness with his followers, and utterly devoid of human sympathy. Not so however his disciple and assistant Theodore Beza. The latter was born in Burgundy in 1519, and after completing his classical studies at Orleans he drifted to Paris, where he plunged into all the pleasures and dissipations of the capital, and where at first he was remarkable more for his love songs than for his theology. He devoted himself to the study of law, and in 1539 he took his licentiate at Paris. Having become attached to the opinions of the Swiss Reformers he left Paris and settled at Geneva, where he fell completely under the influence of Calvin, but not even Calvin's temperament and system could change his naturally gay and sympathetic disposition. For this reason he became a general favourite, and did much to win the good-will of those who felt themselves repelled by the harshness of the dictator. Beza was, besides, a man of very superior ability, and had been especially well equipped in Hebrew and in the classics. He was master of a striking style whether he wrote in French or in Latin, eloquent beyond most of his contemporaries, and in every way capable of making a good impression not merely on the ordinary citizen but on the more educated classes. His writings in defence of Calvin's system and his translations of the Scriptures gave him a great reputation throughout Europe, and gained for him a commanding position in Geneva, where he died in 1605.

Calvin's system was modelled to a great extent on the doctrines of Luther and Zwingli, but it was coloured largely by his own harsh and morose disposition. For the distinguishing feature of his system, namely, absolute predestination, he was dependent largely upon the works of Wycliffe. Like Luther, he began with the assumption that the condition of man before the Fall was entirely natural, and that consequently by the Fall he was deprived of something that was essential to his nature and without which human nature was completely corrupted. Man was no longer free, and every act of his was sinful. His want of freedom was the result of the play of external forces directed and arranged by God, rather than of any internal necessity by which he was forced to sin. God is, according to Calvin, the author of sin, in the sense that he created a certain number of men to work evil through them in order that He might have an opportunity of displaying the divine attribute of mercy. Hence the motive of God in bringing about evil is different from the motive of the sinner, and therefore though the sinner is blameworthy God is nowise responsible for his crime.

Adam sinned because it was decreed by God that he should fall in order that the divine mercy should be manifested to the world. For the same reason God did not intend that all should be equally good or that all should be saved. He created some men that they might sin and that their punishment might afford an example of God's justice, while He made others that they might be saved to show His overwhelming mercy. The former are condemned to hell by an irreversible decree, the others, the elect, are predestined absolutely to glory. The elect are assured of justification through the merits of Christ, and once justified they are always justified, for justification cannot be lost. Faith such as that advocated by Luther was the means of acquiring justification, but, mindful of his other doctrine that even the best of men's works are sinful, Calvin took care to explain that justifying faith was only the instrument by which a man laid hold of the merits of Christ. It was like a vessel which, though containing some priceless treasure, was in itself worthless.

As might be expected, Calvin refused to admit that the sacraments were endowed with any objective power of conferring Grace. In the case of their reception by the elect, however, he held that they were the means of strengthening the faith by which justification is acquired, but for those predestined to damnation they were mere signs without any spiritual effect. In regard to the Eucharist, while he rejected the Catholic view of Transubstantiation, he maintained against the Lutherans that Impanation or Companation was equally absurd. Nor did he agree with Zwingli that the Eucharist is a mere sign of Christ's love for men. According to him Christ is really present, in the sense that though the bread and wine remain unchanged, the predestined receive with the Eucharistic elements a heavenly food that proceeds from the body of Christ in Heaven.

Like Luther he contended that the true Church of Christ is invisible, consisting in his view only of the predestined, but, realising the necessity for authority and organisation, he was driven to hold that the invisible Church manifested itself through a visible religious society. Unlike Luther, however, he was unwilling to subordinate the Church to the civil power, believing as he did that it was a society complete in itself and entirely independent of temporal sovereigns. Each Calvinistic community should be to a great extent a self-governing republic, all of them bound together into one body by the religious synods, to which the individual communities should elect representatives. The churches were to be ruled by pastors, elders, and deacons. Candidates for the sacred ministry were to receive the confirmation of their vocation by a call from some Calvinistic church body, and were to be ordained by the imposition of the hands of the presbyters or elders. For Calvin as for Luther the Holy Scriptures were the sole rule of faith to be adopted by both the preachers and the synods. The special illumination of the Holy Ghost was sufficient to guard individuals from being deceived either in determining what books are inspired, or what is the precise meaning which God wished to convey in any particular book or passage.*

* Schwane, *Dogmengeschichte der neuerenzeit.* Cunningham, *The Reformers and the Theology of the Reformation,* 1862.

(b) CALVINISM IN FRANCE.

Lavisse, *Histoire de France* (vols. v.-vi.), 1904-5. De Meaux, *Les luttes religieuses en France au XVIe siècle*, 1879. Imbart de la Tour, *Les origines de la Réforme*, vols. i.-ii., 1904-9. Hauser, *Études sur la Réforme française*, 1909. Capefigue, *Histoire de la réforme, de la ligue et du règne de Henri IV.*, 4 vols., 1834. Maimbourg, *Histoire du Calvinisme*, 1682. Soldan, *Geschichte des Protestantismus in Frankreich bis zum Tode Karls ix.*, 2 Bde, 1855. Baird, *History of the Rise of the Huguenots in France*, 2 vols., 1879. See also bibliography, chap. iii. (a).

Many causes combined to favour the introduction of the reformed doctrines into France. Owing to the anti-papal attitude adopted by the French theologians during the Great Western Schism, there was still lurking in many circles a strong feeling against the Holy See and in favour of a national Church, over which the Pope should retain merely a supremacy of honour. Besides, the influence of the old sects, the Albigenses and the Waldenses, had not disappeared entirely, and the principles of the French mystics favoured the theory of religious individualism, that lay behind the whole teaching of the reformers. The Renaissance, too, was a power in France, more especially in Paris, where it could boast of powerful patrons such as Margaret of Navarre, sister of Francis I. and wife of the King of Navarre, the king's mistress, his favourite minister Du Bellay, and the latter's brother, the Bishop of Paris. Not all the French Humanists, however, were equally dangerous. A few of them were undoubtedly favourable to Luther's views, while many others, infuriated by the charges of unorthodoxy levelled against them, were inclined to look with complacency on whatever was condemned by their Scholastic opponents. The proximity of Strassburg, where Lutheran and Zwinglian doctrines found support, and the close relations existing between the Paris University and German scholars helped to disseminate among

Frenchmen the writings of Erasmus, Luther, and Melanchthon and with them the new religious views.

Against the success of the Reformation in France was the fact that the people, Latin rather than Teuton in their sympathies, were thoroughly devoted to their religion and to the Holy See, that the bishops though nominated by the king according to the Concordat of 1516, were more zealous than their German brethren, that in the main Paris University, then the great centre of intellectual life in France, was thoroughly Catholic, and that the queen-mother, the chancellor of state, the leading ministers both lay and ecclesiastic, and the parliamentary authorities could be relied upon to offer Lutheranism their strongest opposition. Nor, however much Francis I. might be inclined to vacillate in the hope of securing the help of the German Protestant princes in his struggle with the empire, had he any desire to see his kingdom convulsed by the religious strife raging on the other side of the Rhine.

In 1521 the Parliament of Paris with the approval of the king forbade the publication of writings dealing with the new religious views. Luther's books were condemned, and the Paris University drew up a list of erroneous propositions extracted from the works of the German theologians (1523). At the request of the queen-mother the theological faculty of Paris formulated a plan for preventing the spread of the German errors in France, the main points of which were that heretical books should be forbidden, that the bishops should be exhorted to seek out such works in their dioceses and have them destroyed, and that the Sorbonne should have a free hand in maintaining religious unity. Yet in spite of these precautions a Lutheran community was formed at Meaux in the vicinity of Paris, and in the South of France, where the Waldensian party was still strong, Lutheran teaching found many supporters. In some places various attempts were made to imitate the tactics adopted so successfully at Wittenberg and Berne to bring about by force the discontinuance of Catholic worship. But these attempts failed, owing mainly to the independent attitude of the local parliaments and to the energy of the bishops, who removed one of the most dangerous weapons wielded by the heretics by insisting on a thorough reform of the clergy.

But though Francis I. had been moved to take action against the sectaries, and though Calvin and other leaders were obliged to leave France, the reforming party, relying on the influence of patrons like Margaret of Navarre * and on the Humanist section at the university and at the newly established Collège de France, felt confident of ultimate success. They realised that the king was most anxious to arrive at an understanding with the Protestant princes of Germany against Charles V., and that therefore it was unlikely that he would indulge in a violent persecution of their co-religionists at home. They knew, too, that Francis I. had set his heart on securing complete control of the Church in his own dominions, as was evident by the hard bargain which he drove with Leo X. in the Concordat of 1516,† and they were not without hope that Luther's teaching on the spiritual supremacy of the civil rulers might prove an irresistible bait to a man of such a temperament. Negotiations were opened with Francis I. by some of the German reformers, who offered to accept most of the Catholic doctrines together with episcopal government if only the king would support their cause (1534). As it was impossible to arrange for a conference, the Lutheran party submitted a summary of their views embodied in twelve articles to the judgment of the Sorbonne. In reply to this communication the doctors of the Sorbonne, instead of wasting their energies in the discussion of particular tenets, invited the Germans to state explicitly whether or not they accepted the authority of the Church and the writings of the Fathers. Such an attitude put

* Lefranc, *Les idées religieuses de Marguerite de Navarre*, 1898.
† Thomas, *Le Concordat de 1516*, 3 vols., 1910.

PROGRESS OF CALVINISM 153

an end to all hopes of common action between the French and German theologians, but at the same time Francis I. was not willing, for political reasons, to break with Protestantism. The publication, however, of a particularly offensive pamphlet against Catholicism, printed in Switzerland and scattered broadcast throughout France, served as a warning to the king that his own country was on the brink of being plunged into the civil strife which Protestantism had fomented in Germany, and that if he wanted to preserve national unity and peace the time for decisive action had arrived. Many of the leading reformers were arrested and some of them were put to death, while others were banished from France (1535).

From this time the Lutherans began to lose hope of securing the active co-operation of Francis I., but the friendly political relations between the king and the German Protestant princes, together with the close proximity of Strassburg, Geneva, and Berne, from which preachers and pamphlets made their way into France, helped to strengthen the heretical party in the country despite the efforts of the ecclesiastical and lay authorities. In the South many of the Waldenses in Dauphiny and Provençe went over formally to the side of the Calvinists. In places where they possessed considerable strength they indulged in violent attacks on the clergy, for which reason severe measures of repression were adopted by the local administrators and by the king. As in Switzerland, so too in France Calvinism proved to be the most attractive of the new religious systems. Calvinistic communities were formed at Paris, Rouen, Lyons and Orleans, all of which looked to Geneva for direction. The name given to the French followers of Calvin was Huguenots.

Henry II. (1547-59), who succeeded on the death of Francis I. had no difficulty in allying himself with the German Protestants, and in despatching an army to assist Maurice of Saxony in his rebellion against the

Emperor, while at the same time taking every precaution against the spread of heresy at home. He established a new inquisition department presided over by a Dominican for the detection and punishment of the Huguenots, and pledged the civil power to carry out its decisions. In this attitude he was supported strongly by the University of Paris, which merited the heartiest congratulations of Julius III. by its striking defence of Catholic doctrines, especially the necessity of obedience to the Holy See. Yet notwithstanding all measures taken against them the Huguenots continued to increase in numbers. The Bishop of Navarre went over to their side, as did a certain number of the clergy, and the attitude of some of the others was uncertain. So strong did the Huguenot party find itself in France that a Synod representing the different reformed communities was held in Paris in 1559, at which the doctrine and ecclesiastical organisation introduced by Calvin into Switzerland were formally adopted. The accession of Elizabeth to the throne in England, and the hopes entertained in France of detaching that country from Spain made the French government less anxious to adopt severe measures against the Protestants. After the Peace of Cateau Cambrésis (1559), when Henry determined to make a great effort to extirpate Calvinism, he was prevented by death.

Francis II. who lived only one year (1559-60) succeeded, and he was followed by Charles IX. (1560-74). The latter of these was a mere child, and during the minority the government of the country was in the hands of Catharine de'Medici, his mother, who became regent of France. At the court two parties struggled for supremacy, the family of Guise which stood for Catholicism, and the Bourbons who favoured Calvinism. The regent, not being a woman of very decided religious convictions or tendencies, set herself to play off one party against the other so as to increase her own power, and in this way a splendid opportunity was given to the

Calvinists to pursue their religious campaign. Several of the more powerful people in the kingdom favoured their schemes solely out of hatred to the Duke of Guise * and with the hope of lessening his power. Amongst the prominent Calvinist leaders at this period were Antoine de Bourbon,† King of Navarre, and his brother Louis Prince de Condé, the Constable de Montmorency and Admiral Coligny,‡ the recognised head and ablest leader of the Huguenot party.

Taking advantage of the bitter feeling aroused amongst their followers by the execution of some of their number, the Huguenots formed a conspiracy (Tumult of Amboise 1560) to seize the young king, to overthrow the Duke of Guise, and to set up in his place the Prince de Condé. The Calvinist theologians, having been consulted about the lawfulness of such an enterprise, declared that the conspirators might proceed without fear of sinning so long as a prince of the royal family was amongst their leaders. The plot was discovered, however, before their plans were matured, and several of those who took part in it were put to death. Instead of weakening, it served only to strengthen the family of Guise. Francis, Duke of Guise, was appointed a lieutenant-general of France with the title of saviour of his country, while his brother, the Cardinal of Lorraine, became chief inquisitor and one of the papal legates appointed for the reform of abuses in France. The King of Navarre, to whom Pius IV. addressed a personal appeal, professed his unfaltering loyalty to the Catholic religion, although at the same time he was doing much to spread Calvinism in his own dominions and throughout the South of France.

Though the royal edict against the Calvinists, published in 1560, was severe, yet little was done to enforce its terms except against those who had recourse to arms.

* Forneron, *Les Ducs de Guise*, 1877.
† De Ruble, *Antoine de Bourbon*, 2 vols., 1881-2.
‡ Marcks, *Gaspard von Coligny*, 1892. Delaborde *Gaspard de Coligny*, 3 vols., 1879-83.

The Prince de Condé organised a new conspiracy and attempted to capture Lyons. He was arrested, tried, and condemned to death, but before the sentence could be carried out Francis II. passed away.

A new grouping of parties now took place. The regent, Catharine de'Medici, alarmed at the growing influence of the Guise faction, threw the whole weight of her influence into the scales in favour of the Prince de Condé and of the Huguenots. A royal edict was issued suspending all prosecutions against heretics and ordering the release of all prisoners detained on account of their religion (1561). The regent wrote to the Pope praising the religious fervour of the Calvinists, and calling upon him to suppress several Catholic practices to which the heretics had taken exception. She professed herself anxious for a national council to settle the religious differences, and failing this she insisted upon a religious disputation at Poissy. The disputation ("Colloquy" of Poissy) took place (1561) in presence of the young king, his mother, and a large number of cardinals, bishops, and ministers of state. The Catholics were represented by the Cardinal of Lorraine, the Jesuit General Lainez, and other distinguished clergy, while the Calvinists sent a large number of their ablest leaders, conspicuous amongst whom were Theodore Beza and François de Morel. The principal doctrines in dispute, notably the authority of the Church and the Eucharist, were discussed at length without result. Then a small committee, composed of five theologians representing each side, was appointed, but without any better success. In the end, as no agreement could be secured, the conference was dismissed.

Owing to the close alliance between the regent and the Prince de Condé the former issued a new edict, in which she allowed the Calvinists free exercise of their religion outside the cities provided that they assembled unarmed, commanded them to restore the goods and churches they had seized, and forbade them to have

PROGRESS OF CALVINISM

recourse to violence or to conspiracies to promote their views (1562). Encouraged by these concessions, the Calvinists especially in the South of France attempted to force their religion on the people. They attacked churches, profaned the Blessed Sacrament, murdered several priests and laymen, and obliged the peasants to listen to their preachers. Feeling between the two parties was extremely bitter, and the Catholics were specially incensed that a small minority should be allowed to have their own way regardless of the opinions of the vast body of the French people.

In these circumstances it required very little to lead to serious conflict. At Vassy some soldiers accompanying the Duke of Guise quarrelled with a party of Calvinists, whose psalm-singing was disturbing the Mass at which the Duke was assisting. The latter, hearing the noise, hastened out to restore peace, and was struck with a stone. His followers, incensed at this outrage, drew their swords and killed a large number of the Calvinists. This incident, referred to generally as the massacre of Vassy, led to a new civil war (1562). The Calvinists hastened to take up arms, and the Prince de Condé was assured of English assistance. A large army attacked Toulouse, but after a struggle lasting four days the Calvinists were defeated and driven off with severe loss. In Normandy and other centres where they were strong they carried on the war with unheard of cruelty; but as they were in a hopeless minority and as the English failed to give them the necessary assistance they lost many of their strongholds, and finally suffered a terrible defeat at Dreux where the Prince de Condé was taken prisoner (Dec. 1562). Coligny escaped to Orleans, which city was besieged by the Duke of Guise, who was murdered during the siege by one of the followers of Coligny.* Before his execution the prisoner accused Coligny and Beza as being accessories to his crime, but it is only fair to say that Coligny denied under oath the truth of this statement.

* De Ruble, *L'assassinat de François de Lorraine*, 1898.

Though the Catholics were victorious the awful struggle had cost them dearly. Their ablest leader the Duke of Guise had fallen, as had also Antoine de Bourbon, King of Navarre, who had been converted from Calvinism; many of their churches and most valuable shrines were destroyed; and to make matters worse they recognised that the struggle had been fought in vain, as the regent proclaimed a general amnesty and concluded a peace with the Huguenots (Peace of Amboise, 1563), whereby Calvinist nobles and their followers were allowed free exercise of their religion with certain restrictions.

Neither side was satisfied with these terms. Coligny and the Prince de Condé were annoyed furthermore by the fact that the regent broke off her close relations with them, and began to lean towards the Catholic side and towards an alliance with Spain. After raising large sums of money and arming their forces for a new effort they determined to seize the king and his court at Monceau, but the Constable de Montmorency with six thousand trusty Swiss soldiers hastened to the king's defence, and brought him safely from the midst of his enemies (1567). This attempt together with the terrible slaughter of Catholics at Nîmes (29 Sept.)* led to the outbreak of the second civil war. The Catholic forces were successful at St. Denis though they lost one of their ablest generals, the Constable de Montmorency, and were deprived of the fruits of their victory by the intervention of the Elector of the Palatinate. Owing to the mediation of the latter a new treaty was made in 1568, but as the Huguenots continued to seek alliances with England, Germany, and the Netherlands, Charles IX. recalled the concessions he had made, and forbade the exercise of Calvinist worship under penalty of death.

Thereupon the third civil war broke out (1569). The Huguenots received assistance from England, the

---

* Rouquette, *L'inquisition protestante, Les Saint-Barthélemy calvinistes*, 1906.

Netherlands, and Germany, while the Catholics were supported by Spain and the Pope. The war was carried on with relentless cruelty on both sides. In the battle of Jarnac the Huguenot forces were defeated, and the Prince de Condé was slain (1569). The struggle was however continued by Coligny supported by Henry King of Navarre and the young de Condé. By wonderful exertions Coligny put a new army into the field only however to suffer another terrible defeat at Moncontour, where the Huguenots were almost annihilated. It seemed that the long struggle was to end at last and that peace was to be restored to France. But unfortunately at this juncture some of his courtiers succeeded in convincing Charles IX. that his brother, the Duke of Anjou, who with the young Duke of Guise was mainly responsible for the Catholic victories, might use his recognised military ability and his influence with the people to make himself king of France. Alarmed by the prospect of such a contingency Charles IX., already jealous of his brother's triumphs, turned against the Catholic party and concluded the Peace of St. Germain-en-Laye with the Huguenots (1570).

According to the terms of this Peace the Huguenots were allowed free exercise of their religion in France with the sole exception of the capital. They were not to be excluded from any office of the state, and four of the strongest fortresses of the country, La Rochelle, Montauban, Cognac, and La Charité were to be delivered to them for their protection and as a guarantee of good faith. The whole policy of Charles IX. underwent a complete change. Obsessed with the idea that the Catholic party, led by the Duke of Anjou was becoming too powerful to be trusted, he turned to Coligny and the Calvinists, broke off the alliance concluded with Spain the previous year, and sought to bring over France to the side of England and of the rebel subjects of Spain in the Netherlands. Coligny was invited to court, where he soon became the most trusted and influential councillor of the king. He endeavoured to embitter the mind of Charles IX. against his mother, against the Duke of Anjou and the family of Guise. No effort was spared by him to bring France into the closest relations with England and the Netherlands against Spain, and as a sign of the reconciliation that had been effected between the court and the Huguenots a marriage was arranged between Henry, the Calvinist King of Navarre and Margaret of Valois, the sister of Charles IX.

The Catholics were highly indignant at this sudden change of policy. Mindful of the misfortunes brought upon their country by the Huguenots and of the losses and cruelties they had suffered at the hands of this implacable minority, they resented the domination of Coligny, whom they regarded as their most dangerous enemy, and they were embittered by the thought that the victories they had won at so much cost had resulted only in their own downfall and in the triumph of their worst enemies. Catharine de'Medici, the queen-mother, felt more acutely than the rest the influence of Coligny. She believed that he was using his power to alienate the affections of the young king from herself, and to win him from the policy she had advocated. She was only waiting an opportunity to wreak her vengeance on Coligny and on the whole Huguenot party, knowing well as she did that she could count upon the popular feeling of the nation to support her.

The opportunity came on the occasion of the marriage between the King of Navarre and Margaret of Valois. The leading Calvinists anxious to take part in the ceremony flocked to Paris, where they and their followers paraded the streets armed to the teeth and with the air of conquerors. Catharine de'Medici took steps to secure the murder of Coligny on the 22nd August, 1572, but the attempt failed. Such a step served, however, to embitter feeling on both sides, and to arouse the queen-mother to make one final effort for the destruction of her Huguenot opponents. In an audience with the king she represented to him that the Calvinists were plotting to take his life, and that the only way to secure himself against them was to anticipate them. In view of the previous history of the party and the suspicious temperament of the king it required little to convince him of the truth of this allegation, and at last he signed an order that on a certain pre-arranged signal having been given the soldiers should be let loose on the Huguenots. On the night preceding the feast of St. Bartholomew (23-24 Aug.) the bells of the church of St. Germain-en-Laye were rung, and the troops sallied forth to carry out their instructions. Rumours of a Huguenot plot had been spread through the city. The people were alarmed, and the general body of the citizens took up arms to support the soldiers. In the melée that followed over a thousand Calvinists including Coligny were put to death. The movement spread through the provinces where about the same number suffered as in the capital, though many of the Catholic clergy, as for example, the Bishop of Lisieux, exerted themselves to put an end to the butchery.

This event is known in history as the massacre of St. Bartholomew. The massacre was in no sense a premeditated affair. It was a sudden outburst of popular indignation brought about by the machinations of the queen-mother, and was neither encouraged nor approved by the bishops of the Catholic Church. The king presented himself before the Parliament of Paris on the day following the massacre, and declared that he alone was responsible for what had happened. He explained that a plot had been formed against his life and that he had taken the only measures that it was possible for him to take. This was the account of the affair that was forwarded to the French diplomatic representatives abroad, and which they gave at the courts to which they were accredited. Gregory XIII., acting on the report of the French ambassador, ordered that a *Te Deum* should be sung in thanksgiving for the safety of the king and royal family, and not, as has been so often alleged, as a sign of rejoicing for the murder of the Calvinists. On the contrary he was deeply pained when he learned the true state of affairs. The massacre of St. Bartholomew was indeed unjustifiable, but it was done neither to promote religion nor at the instigation of the Church. It was merely political in its object as far as the king and the queen-mother were concerned, and was a sudden popular outburst in so far as the citizens of Paris or the people of the country took part in it. In judging the responsibility and blame for what took place nobody can put out of mind the terrible excesses, of which the Huguenots had been guilty during their long struggle against their own countrymen. The German Lutherans, who looked upon the slaughter as a judgment from Heaven on the Calvinist heretics, were rejoiced at their extinction.*

The Huguenots flew to arms to avenge their brethren who had fallen, and the fourth civil war began. The Duke of Anjou laid siege to their strongest fortress, La Rochelle, but failed to take it, and on his election as King of Poland (1573) a treaty was concluded according to which the Huguenots were allowed free exercise of their religion. A large number of French politicians were at last growing tired of a struggle which was costing their country so dearly, and were anxious to conclude peace even though it were necessary to yield to the demands of the Huguenots. At the head of this party stood some of the most powerful nobles of France including the Duc d'Alençon, and when on the death of Charles IX. the Duke of Anjou succeeded as Henry III. (1575-89) his sympathies were entirely with the party of

* On the massacre of St. Bartholomew, *cf.* De la Ferrière, *La St. Barthélemy*, 1892. Fauriel, *Essai sur les évènements qui ont précédé et amené la St. Barthélemy*, 1838. Bordier, *La St. Barthélemy et la critique moderne*, 1879. Hanoteaux, *Études historiques sur le XVIe et le XVIIe siècle en France*, 1886. Vacandard, *Études de critique et d'histoire religieuse*, 1905. *Id., Les papes et la St. Barthélemy* (*Rev. du Cler. Français*, 1904).

PROGRESS OF CALVINISM 163

the moderates as against the extremists of both sides. By the terms of the Peace of Beaulieu (1576) the Huguenots were assured of complete freedom except in Paris and at the French Court, and of full civil rights, and as a guarantee of good faith they were continued in possession of their fortresses.

Indignant at such concessions the Catholic party formed the League * with the young Duke of Guise at its head. Henry III., finding that it was impossible to oppose this combination with any hope of success, determined to control it by becoming himself its leader. The concessions made to the Huguenots were recalled (1577), and the fifth civil war broke out. This was brought to an end by the Peace of Poitiers (1577). The Huguenot party, under the King of Navarre and the young Prince de Condé, continued to make headway against the League, and sought to strengthen themselves by an alliance with England and the Netherlands.

The question of the succession to the French throne became serious for both parties. Henry III. was childless, and on the death of the heir-apparent, his brother the Duke of Anjou (Alençon, 1584), the succession devolved apparently on Henry King of Navarre, but as he was a Calvinist the Catholics were unwilling to recognise him. The League declared Cardinal de Bourbon son of the Duke of Vendôme as the lawful heir to the French throne, though many of its out and out supporters were strongly in favour of the Duke of Guise. An attempt was made to get the approval of the Pope for the League and its policy, but both Gregory XIII. and Sixtus V. were not inclined to support its pretensions. At the earnest request of Spain the latter, however, issued a constitution in 1585, by which he declared that Henry of Navarre and the Prince de Condé, as notorious heretics excommunicated by the Church, had forfeited all claim to the throne

* Richard, *La papauté et la ligue française*, 1901. De Chalambert, *Histoire de la Ligue sous Henri III. et Henri IV.*, 1898. De l'Epinois, *La Ligue et les papes*, 1886.

of France. Henry of Navarre lodged a solemn protest in Rome, and he appealed to the Parliament of Paris, which refused to approve of the publication of the papal document. Both sides had recourse once more to arms, and the Huguenots under the leadership of Henry of Navarre were victorious in the battle of Coutras (1587). The League however continued the struggle, captured some of the principal cities such as Lyons, Orleans, and Bourges, while Henry III. favoured both parties in turn. Overawed by the successful exploits of the Duke of Guise he pledged himself to put down the Huguenots, and the French people were called upon by royal proclamation to swear that they would never accept a heretic as their king (1588).

But in his heart Henry III. favoured the cause of the King of Navarre, if for no other reason because he wished to escape from the dictatorship of the Duke of Guise. In 1588 he procured the murder of the two greatest leaders of the League, Henry Duke of Guise and his brother Louis the Cardinal-archbishop of Lyons. This outrage drew upon him the wrath of the League and of the great body of French Catholics. Charles de Lorraine, brother of the murdered Duke of Guise, put himself at the head of the king's enemies. Sixtus V. issued a strong condemnation of the murder of the cardinal-archbishop, and the Sorbonne declared that the nation no longer owed any allegiance to the king. The war was renewed vigorously on both sides, the League being supported by Philip II. of Spain and its opponents by Protestant troops from Germany and Switzerland. While the combined forces of Henry III. and of the King of Navarre were besieging Paris, Henry III. was assassinated (1589).

Thereupon Henry of Navarre had himself proclaimed King of France under the title of Henry IV., but the League refused to recognise his claims and put forward instead the aged Cardinal de Bourbon, then a prisoner in the hands of the King of Navarre. The Cardinal also

PROGRESS OF CALVINISM

was proclaimed king (Charles X.). Spain, too, refused to acknowledge Henry IV., and assisted the League with both money and soldiers. The Popes, Sixtus V. Gregory XIV. and Clement VIII. adopted an attitude of great reserve. While they were not inclined to support the demands of the League in their entirety they were unshaken in their resolve to acknowledge no heretic as king of France. Henry IV., though supported by many of the moderate Catholics (*Les Politiques*), began to recognise that as a Calvinist he could never hope for peaceful possession of the French throne. He determined, therefore, to yield to the entreaties of his most powerful supporters and to make his submission to the Catholic Church. In July 1593 he read a public recantation in the Church of St. Denis, and was absolved conditionally from the censures he had incurred. The following year he made his formal entrance into Paris, where he was welcomed by the people, and acknowledged as lawful king of France by the Sorbonne. Having pledged himself to accept the decrees of the Council of Trent, to abide by the terms of the Concordat of 1516, and to rear his heir and successor as a Catholic he was reconciled to the Holy See. The League dissolved itself in a short time, and so far as Catholics were concerned peace was restored to France.

The Huguenots, Henry IV.'s former co-religionists, were deeply pained at the step taken by their leader, and they insisted that their demands must be satisfied. Henry IV., more anxious for the unity and welfare of France than for the triumph of either religious party, determined to put an end to the civil strife by the publication of the Edict of Nantes (1598). The principal articles of the Edict of Nantes were that the Calvinists should enjoy freedom of worship throughout the greater part of the kingdom, that they should be eligible for all positions of honour and trust in the state, that they should have for their own use the Universities of Montauban, Montpelier, Sedan, and Samur, that the funds for the upkeep of these universities and for the maintenance of their religion should be supplied by the state, and that for a period of eight years they should have possession of some of the principal fortresses. On their side they engaged to break off all alliances with foreigners, to allow Catholic worship to be restored in the places where it had been suppressed, to observe the marriage laws of the Catholic Church, and to abstain from anything that might be regarded as a violation of Catholic holidays. Such concessions were regarded with great disfavour by the Pope, the clergy, and the vast majority of the French people as being opposed to the entire national tradition of France, and it required all the efforts of the king to secure for them the approval of the Paris Parliament (1599). Similarly the Calvinists were not content with what had been conceded to them, nor were they willing to abide by the terms of the Edict of Nantes in so far as to allow the establishment of Catholic worship in the places which were under their control. Their public attacks on the Blessed Eucharist and on the Pope were very irritating to their countrymen, but Henry IV., who was a good king deeply interested especially in the welfare of the lower classes, continued to keep the peace between both parties. His sympathies were, however, with the Protestants of Germany, and he was actually on his way to take part in a war against the Emperor when he was assassinated (1610).

He was succeeded by his son Louis XIII. (1610-43) who was then a boy of nine years. His mother Mary de' Medici, who acted as regent approved of the terms of the Edict of Nantes, but the Huguenots relying on the weakness of the government refused to carry out those portions of the Edict favourable to Catholics, and made demands for greater privileges. They rose in rebellion several times especially in the South, entered into alliance with every rebel noble who took up arms against the king, and acted generally as if they formed a state within a state. Cardinal Richelieu who was for years the actual ruler of France (1624-42),* inspired solely by political motives, determined to put an end to a condition of affairs that was highly dangerous to the strength and national unity of the kingdom. He saw that it was impossible for France to extend her power so long as there existed at home a well-organised body of citizens prepared to enter into treasonable relations with foreign enemies, and to turn to their own advantage their country's difficulties. His opportunity came when the Huguenots having concluded an alliance with England rose in rebellion (1627). He laid siege to their strongest fortress, La Rochelle, drove back the fleet which England sent to their assistance, and compelled the city to surrender (1628). By this strong measure he put an end to the power of the Huguenots in France and secured peace and unity for the country, while at the same time he treated the conquered with comparative mildness, confirming the Edict of Nantes (Edict of Nîmes, 1629), proclaiming a general amnesty, and restoring the leaders of the rebellion to the property and positions they had forfeited.

During the reign of Louis XIV. (1643-1715) the whole tendency of the government was dangerous to the Huguenots. Louis XIV. was determined to make himself absolute ruler of France, and, therefore, he could regard only with the highest disfavour the presence in his territories of a well-organised privileged party like the Huguenots. An opportunity of carrying out his designs came in 1659, when with the approval of the Synod of Montpazier they attempted to negotiate an alliance with England. They were punished with great severity, forbidden to preach in any place without express permission, to attack Catholic doctrines publicly, or to intermarry with Catholics. Converts from Calvinism were encouraged by promises of special concessions. Owing to the disfavour of the king and the energetic

* Caillet, *L'Administration en France sous le ministère du cardinal de Richelieu*, 2 vols., 1863.

action of the clergy and bishops, whose education and culture at that time stood exceedingly high, large numbers of the Huguenots returned to the Church so that in some places, as for example in Normandy, where once they could boast of considerable influence, the sect became almost extinct.

The severity of the measures taken by Louis XIV. led to new rebellions, which were suppressed with great severity. Finally in 1685 a royal proclamation appeared announcing the revocation of all the privileges granted to the Huguenots and more particularly all those contained in the Edict of Nantes (1685). The churches which they had built recently were to be destroyed, their religious assemblies were forbidden, and their clergy were offered their choice between submission to the Church or exile. The prime minister Louvois sent soldiers to enforce this proclamation, and the unfortunate Huguenots were treated with great harshness and cruelty. Many of them, unwilling to change their religion and unable to endure their hard lot at home, left the country and sought refuge in England, Germany, Denmark, and Holland. The revocation of the Edict of Nantes was not due to the religious zeal of Louis XIV. or of his ministers. Indeed at the very time that Louis XIV. was engaged in dragooning the Huguenots into the Catholic Church he was in bitter conflict with the Pope, and was committed to a policy that seemed destined to end in national schism. Some of the French bishops, notably Fénelon, disapproved of this attempt at conversion by violence, and Pope Innocent XI., having no representative in Paris at the time, instructed his nuncio at London to induce James II. of England to bring pressure to bear on Louis XIV. to favour the Huguenots.* Several times during the reign of Louis the Calvinists rose in arms to defend their religion but without effect. After his death the decrees against them were not enforced with much

* Gérin, *Le Pape, Innocent XI. et la Révocation de l'Édit de Nantes* (*Rev. des Quest. Historiques*, xxiv.).

severity, but it was only in 1787 that a measure of almost complete political equality was granted to them by Louis XVI.

(c) CALVINISM IN THE NETHERLANDS.

Cramer-Piper, *Bibliotheca Reformatoria Neerlandica*, 1903-11. Juste, *Histoire de la révolution des Pays Bas sous Philippe II.*, 2 vols., 1863-7. De Lettenhove, *Les Huguenots et les Gueux*, 6 vols., 1882-85. Gossart, *La domination espagnole dans les Pays Bas à la fin du règne de Philippe II.*, 1906. Holzwarth, *Der Abfall der Niederlanden*, 2 Bde, 1865-72.

The Netherlands formed part of the vast territories ruled over by Charles V. For many reasons it was not to be wondered at that the people should sympathise with the great religious revolt in Germany. They were allied closely with the Germans by blood and language. Like them, too, they looked upon Spain and upon the Spaniards with feelings of distrust. Again, as in other parts of the world, so too in the Netherlands the wealth of the Church had led to grave abuses as well as to a loss of respect for ecclesiastical authority, the latter of which was fostered in the minds of some by the spirit of mysticism that flourished in the land of St. Thomas à Kempis.

Yet, notwithstanding these favourable circumstances, the Reformation made little progress in the Netherlands during the reign of Charles V. He was a man who understood the people and who respected their rights and privileges. He visited the country frequently, was always ready to listen to their demands, and he took care not to offend their national instincts by a display of Spanish troops or Spanish officials. Besides, having a freer hand to deal with the new religious movement in the Netherlands than he had in Germany, he was determined to preserve his hereditary dominions from the dissensions and civil strife that had done so much to weaken the empire. He insisted on the proclamation and execution of the decree of the Diet of Worms against

Luther, forbade the spread of heretical writings, introduced the Inquisition, and punished with great severity those who were found guilty of attempting to tamper with the faith of the people. But despite his efforts the trouble that had broken out in the neighbouring countries, France and Germany, could not fail to find an echo in the Netherlands, and the views of Calvin and Luther found some support.

In 1555 Charles retired and was succeeded by his son Philip II. (1555-98). The new ruler unlike his father made no effort to win the affections of his subjects in the Netherlands, or to attach them to himself by bonds of loyalty. On the contrary he came amongst them only too seldom, and after 1559 he never set foot in the country. He showed himself careless about their commercial interests, regardless of their constitutional rights and privileges, and indifferent to their national prepossessions. Instead of relying on the native officials and nobles to carry on the administration of the kingdom, he sought to strengthen his own power by appointing Spaniards to offices of trust and by sending Spanish troops to suppress all symptoms of discontent. He set aside the Grand Council which by custom had the rights of a parliament, and without consultation with the authorities in the Netherlands he decided upon a new ecclesiastical division of the country. Hitherto there were only four bishops, whose Sees were subject to foreign metropolitans. Philip decided that the time had come when the number of bishoprics should be increased, and the jurisdiction of foreign metropolitans should be abolished. The main reason that influenced him to adopt this decision was the fact that, as things stood, a complete and far-reaching scheme of reform could not be put into operation. In conjunction with Pope Paul IV. he arranged (1559) that the Spanish Netherlands should be divided into seventeen dioceses, that these should be placed under the three newly-erected archiepiscopal Sees of Utrecht, Cambrai, and Mechlin, and that suitable pro-

PROGRESS OF CALVINISM

vision should be made for the maintenance of the new bishops out of the possessions of the monasteries and of the ecclesiastical institutions as well as from the contributions of the laity.

Many of the nobles were already tired of the Spanish rule, and were not unwilling to look favourably on the religious struggle as a means of securing independence. They objected to several unconstitutional acts of which the government of Philip II. had been guilty. They disliked Cardinal de Granvelle, the prime minister in the Netherlands and insisted on his recall. They objected to the introduction of the Inquisition, and they protested against the new diocesan division as unnecessary, burdensome to the country, and an infringement of the rights and privileges of certain individuals. The clergy and people, whose positions were affected by the new arrangement, supported them strongly in their opposition to this measure. The leaders of this movement were the Count of Egmont and William of Orange,* the latter of whom was a clever politician of boundless ambitions, who was not without hope that a rebellion against Spain might be the means of securing supreme power in the Netherlands. His brother, the Prince of Nassau, had adopted Calvinism, and William himself was not troubled with any particularly strong religious convictions. By his marriage with the daughter of Maurice of Saxony he sought to assure himself of the support of the German Protestant princes, while at the same time he was intimately connected with the Huguenots of France, and was on terms of the closest friendship with Counts Egmont and Horn, both of them, though for different reasons, hostile to Philip II. For William and for many of his abettors religion was but a secondary issue, provided only that by means of a religious revolution the power of Spain could be overthrown. Cardinal Granvelle, the minister of the Duchess of Parma,† who

---

* Lacheret, *L'évolution religieuse de Guillaume le Taciturne*, 1904.
† Rachfal, *Margareta von Parma*, 1898.

was then regent of the country, was a strong man and a dangerous opponent, for whose removal the party of William of Orange strove with all their might. They succeeded at last in 1564, but despite all their efforts they could not prevent the publication of the decrees of the Council of Trent. They met together in the following year (1565) and formed the union known as the Compromise of Breda, nominally for the preservation of their constitutional rights but in reality to promote a political and religious rebellion. Many earnest Catholics unaware of the motives that inspired the leaders of this movement lent them their support. Having strengthened themselves by negotiations with some of the Protestant princes of Germany, the revolutionary party presented themselves before Margaret of Parma at Brussels to demand redress (1566). During the course of the interview Count de Berlaymont referred to them as a crowd of " gueux " or beggars, and this was the name they adopted to designate their party (*Les Gueux*).

Though they professed themselves willing to maintain the Catholic religion the friends of William of Orange had strong leanings towards Protestantism. Calvinist preachers flocked in from France; Calvinist communities began to be formed; and in districts where the party found itself powerful enough to do so, attacks were made on Catholic churches and Catholic worship. These outrages served to indicate the real tendency of the movement, and to drive into the opposite camp many Catholics who had joined the party merely to secure redress of political grievances. The Duchess of Parma, having failed to put an end to the disturbances by friendly negotiations, determined to employ force against the rebels. She was completely successful. William of Orange fled to Germany, and Counts Egmont and Horn surrendered themselves to the mercy of the king (1567). Had Philip II. known how to take advantage of this victory he might have put an end to Calvinism in the Netherlands, for as yet the vast majority of the inhabitants were at heart loyal to the Church.

PROGRESS OF CALVINISM 173

But instead of coming to make a personal appeal for the allegiance of his subjects and of trying to win over the malcontents by a policy of moderation Philip II., more concerned for the suppression of heresy than for the maintenance of Spanish rule, sent the Duke of Alva * (1567-72) with an army of ten thousand men to punish the offenders and to wipe out all traces of Calvinism. Alva was a soldier who had distinguished himself on many a field in the wars against the Turks and against France. His character is sufficiently indicated by the title "the iron duke" given him by those who knew him best. He had no faith in diplomacy or concession. For him martial law was the only means of reducing rebels to subjection. The Duchess of Parma, unwilling to share the responsibility of government with such an associate, petitioned for her recall, and the Duke of Alva was appointed regent of the Netherlands. Two leaders of the rebellion, Counts Egmont and Horn, were tried and put to death (1568), as were also many of their followers. The goods of the rebels were confiscated, soldiers were quartered on the districts which were supposed to be sympathetic with the movement, and martial law became the order of the day. But the cruel measures adopted by the Duke of Alva did not put an end to the rebellion in the Netherlands. On the contrary, the contempt shown by him for the constitution of the country and the rights of individual citizens, the excessive taxation, and the license given to the soldiers in their treatment of civilians served only to embitter the issue and to drive even moderate men into the path of rebellion. William of Orange, backed by his brother, Louis of Nassau, made descents upon the country, while vessels manned by their supporters set themselves to do as much harm as possible to Spanish trade. With the aid of England they managed to capture the city and port of Briel (1572). Several of the northern states threw off the yoke of Spain and acknowledged William of Orange as their ruler, so

* *Vita Ferdinandi Toletani, ducis Albani,* 1669.

that in a short time the Provinces of Holland and Zeeland were practically lost to Philip II. William of Orange tried to obscure the religious nature of the campaign by proclaiming religious freedom, but his followers could not be restrained. The Catholic churches were attacked, the clergy were expelled, and in 1572 nineteen priests were martyred for the faith at Gorcum. Holland and Zeeland went over completely to Calvinism, nor were the southern provinces, which were still Catholic, contented with the rule of Alva. Driven to desperation by his taxation and unconstitutional policy they formed a league with the followers of William of Orange to put an end to Spanish rule in the Netherlands. Philip II. began to realise that he had been unfortunate in the selection of a governor. A deputation that was sent from the insurgents was received kindly, and Alva's resignation of his office was accepted.

In his place Don Luis Requesens was sent as governor of the Netherlands (1573-75). Though inferior to Alva in military skill he was much superior to him in the arts of diplomacy and conciliation. He withdrew promptly the financial decrees that had caused such general discontent, yielded to most of the demands made by the people, and offered a general amnesty to those who would return to their allegiance. It required all the skill of William of Orange to prevent the submission of his adherents. Disappointed by the removal of the grievances that had provoked a national uprising, he was forced to have recourse more and more to the religious issues in order to maintain his power. He proclaimed himself the protector and champion of Calvinism, and as such he could still count on the aid of the northern provinces. Unfortunately, too, at the very time when the success of his policy of mildness seemed assured, Requesens died leaving it to his successor to complete his work.

Don Juan of Austria, the natural son of Charles V.,

who had won renown throughout the world by his annihilation of the Turkish fleet at Lepanto, was appointed in his place. Before his arrival the southern and northern provinces had bound themselves together in the Pacification of Ghent (1576). Don Juan was obliged to accept the terms of the Pacification and to dismiss the Spanish troops before his authority would be recognised. William of Orange, secure in the north, determined to occupy the southern provinces, but his public profession of Calvinism and the religious intolerance of his followers prevented a combined national effort. The Catholic nobles of the Walloon provinces objected to the Protestant campaign that was being carried on in the name of liberty, and showed themselves not unwilling to come to terms with Don Juan. The latter, only too glad to meet them half-way, issued a very conciliatory decree (1577), which secured him the support of many of the Catholic party, and partly by force partly by negotiation he succeeded in winning back much of what had been lost.

On the death of Don Juan (1578) Alexander Farnese, son of the former regent Margaret of Parma, was appointed his successor. Being something of a statesman as well as a soldier he lost no opportunity of endeavouring to break the power of the Prince of Orange. He devoted a great deal of his energies to the work of detaching the southern provinces, which still remained Catholic, from the northern, which had gone over to Calvinism. The intolerance of the Calvinists and their open violation of the religious freedom guaranteed to all parties tended to the success of his plans. During his term of office Belgium returned to its allegiance to Spain, and this step put an end to the hopes entertained by the Calvinists of winning that country to their side. Meanwhile the northern provinces were entirely in the hands of William of Orange. In 1579 the five provinces Holland, Zeeland, Friesland, Geldern, and Zutphen bound themselves together by a solemn compact in the Union of Utrecht under the name of the United Provinces, and practically speaking established a Dutch republic. They agreed to make common cause in war and in peace, and appointed William of Orange as Stadtholder for life. A short time later (1581) William of Orange, notwithstanding all his proclamations regarding religious liberty, forbade the public exercise of the Catholic religion, and refused to allow the new Archbishop of Utrecht to take possession of his See. In these circumstances nothing remained for the Pope except to appoint a vicar-apostolic to take charge of the religious interests of the Catholics, who formed two-fifths of the population of Holland, but even the vicar-apostolic was soon banished from the country.

In 1584 William of Orange was assassinated, and his son Maurice was appointed to succeed him. The English Government anxious to strike a blow at Spain encouraged the Dutch to continue the war, and despatched troops to their assistance. After the defeat of the Spanish Armada the situation was much more favourable to the rebels, and at last in 1609 a twelve years' truce was concluded. On the expiration of the truce the war was renewed without any very striking success on either side. Finally in the Peace of Westphalia (1648) the independence of the Dutch republic was acknowledged by Spain. From the very beginning of the religious revolt in the Netherlands Calvinism was the sect most favoured by the people, as is evidenced by the *Confessio Belgica* in 1562. The University of Leyden decided in its favour, as did also the Synods of Dordrecht in 1574 and 1618. The Catholic minority in Holland were treated with the greatest severity, but in spite of all the efforts to induce them to change their faith many of the districts remained completely Catholic.

The Catholic provinces, which remained true to Spain and to the Catholic Church, suffered very severely from the long-drawn-out struggle, but despite the ravages of war they were soon the centre of a great religious, literary and artistic revival. The University of Louvain, founded in 1425, developed rapidly under the generous patronage of the civil rulers. During the sixteenth century it was recognised as an important centre of learning whither scholars flocked not merely from the Low Countries but from all parts of Europe. Throughout the Reformation struggle Louvain and Douay, the latter of which was founded in 1562 by Philip II. to assist in stemming the rising tide of Calvinism, remained staunch defenders of Catholic orthodoxy, though the unfortunate controversies waged round the doctrines of Baius and Jansenius did something to dim the glory of the university to which both belonged. The Jesuits, too, rendered invaluable service to religion and learning, particularly the men who hastened to offer their services to Father van Bolland in his famous *Acta Sanctorum.* Nor can it be forgotten that it was in these days Catholic Belgium gave to the world the great Flemish school of artists, amongst whom must be reckoned such men as Rubens, Van Dyck, and Jordaens.

CHAPTER IV

THE COUNTER-REFORMATION

FOR more than thirty years the new religious movement continued to spread with alarming rapidity. Nation after nation either fell away from the centre of unity or wavered as to the attitude that should be adopted towards the conflicting claims of Rome, Wittenberg, and Geneva, till at last it seemed not unlikely that Catholicism was to be confined within the territorial boundaries of Italy, Spain, and Portugal. That the world was well prepared for such an outburst has been shown already,* but it is necessary to emphasise the fact that the real interests of religion played but a secondary part in the success of the Protestant revolt. Luther, Calvin, Zwingli, and Knox may be taken as typical of the new apostles, and however gifted or energetic these men may have been, yet few would care to contend that either in their own lives or in the means to which they had recourse for propagating their views they can be regarded as ideal religious reformers.

Protestantism owed its success largely to political causes, and particularly in the case of Lutheranism to its acknowledgment of the principle of royal supremacy. At its inception it was favoured by the almost universal jealousy of the House of Habsburg and by the danger of a Turkish invasion. If attention be directed to the countries where it attained its largest measure of success, it will be found that in Germany this success was due mainly to the distrust of the Emperor entertained by the princes and their desire to

* Chap. I.

THE COUNTER-REFORMATION 179

strengthen their own authority against both the Emperor and the people; in Switzerland to the political aspirations of the populous and manufacturing cantons and their eagerness to resist the encroachments of the House of Savoy; in the Scandinavian North to the efforts of ambitious rulers anxious to free themselves from the restrictions imposed upon their authority by the nobles and bishops; in the Netherlands to the determination of the people to maintain their old laws and constitution in face of the domineering policy of Philip II.; in France to the attitude of the rulers who disliked the Catholic Church as being the enemy of absolutism, and who were willing to maintain friendly relations with the German Protestants in the hope of weakening the Empire by civil war; in England, at first to the autocratic position of the sovereign, and later to a feeling of national patriotism that inspired Englishmen to resent the interference of foreigners in what they regarded as their domestic affairs; and in Scotland to the bitter rivalry of two great factions one of which favoured an alliance with France, the other, a union with England. In all these countries the hope of sharing in the plunder of the Church had a much greater influence in determining the attitude of both rulers and nobles than their zeal for reform, as the leaders of the so-called Reformation had soon good reason to recognise and to deplore.

Protestantism had reached the zenith of its power on the Continent in 1555. At that time everything seemed to indicate its permanent success, but soon under the Providence of God the tide began to turn, and instead of being able to make further conquests it found it impossible to retain those that had been made. The few traces of heresy that might have been detected in Italy, Spain, and Portugal disappeared. France, thanks largely to the energy of the League and the political schemes of Cardinal Richelieu, put an end to the Calvinist domination. Hungary and Poland were wrested to a great extent from the influence of the Protestant preachers by the labours of the Jesuits. Belgium was retained for Spain and for Catholicity more by the prudence and diplomacy of Farnese than by the violence of Alva; and in the German Empire the courageous stand made by some of the princes, notably Maximilian of Bavaria, delivered Austria, Bohemia, Bavaria and the greater part of Southern Germany from Protestantism.

Many causes helped to bring about this striking reaction towards Catholicism. Amongst the principal of these were the reforms initiated by the Council of Trent, the rise of zealous ecclesiastics and above all of zealous popes, the establishment of new religious orders, especially the establishment of the Society of Jesus, and finally the determination of some of the Catholic princes to meet force by force. Mention should be made too of the wonderful outburst of missionary zeal that helped to win over new races and new peoples in the East and the West at a time when so many of the favoured nations of Europe had renounced or were threatening to renounce their allegiance to the Church of Rome.

(a) THE COUNCIL OF TRENT

Le Plat, *Monumentorum ad historiam concilii Tridentini spectantium amplissima collectio*, 7 vols., 1781-5. Theiner, *Acta genuina S. oecumenici Concilii Tridentini*, etc., 1874. *Concilium Tridentinum Diariorum, Actorum, Epistularum, Tractatuum Nova Collectio Edidit Societas Goerresiana*, vols. i., ii., iii. (*Diariorum*), iv., v. (*Actorum*), 1901-14. Pallavicino, *Istoria del Concilio di Trento*, 3 vols., 1664. Maynier, *Étude historique sur le concile de Trent*, 1874. Mendham, *Memoirs of the Council of Trent*, 1834. Marchese, *La riforma del clero secondo il concilio de Trento*, 1883. Deslandres, *Le concile de Trente, et la réforme du clergé*, 1906. *Canones et decreta sacrosancti oecumenici concilii Tridentini*.

For more than a century and a half reform of the Church "in its head and members" was the watchword both of the friends and the enemies of religion. Earnest men looked forward to this as the sole means of stem-

THE COUNTER-REFORMATION 181

ming the tide of neo-paganism that threatened to engulf the Christian world, while wicked men hoped to find in the movement for reform an opportunity of wrecking the divine constitution that Christ had given to His Church. Popes and councils had failed hitherto to accomplish this work. The bishops had met at Constance and Basle, at Florence and at Rome (5th Lateran Council), and had parted leaving the root of the evil untouched. Notwithstanding all these failures the feeling was practically universal that in a General Council lay the only hope of reform, and that for one reason or another the Roman Curia looked with an unfavourable eye on the convocation of such an assembly. Whether the charge was true or false it was highly prejudicial to the authority of the Holy See, and as a consequence of it, when Luther and his followers appealed from the verdict of Leo X. to the verdict of a General Council, they evoked the open or secret sympathy of many, who had nothing but contempt for their religious innovations. Charles V., believing in the sincerity of their offer to submit themselves to the judgment of such a body, supported strongly the idea of a council, as did also the Diets held at Nürnberg in 1523 and 1524.

The hesitation of Adrian VI. (1522-23) and of Clement VII. (1523-34) to yield to these demands was due neither to their inability to appreciate the magnitude of the abuses nor to their desire to oppose any and every proposal of reform. The disturbed condition of the times, when so many individuals had fallen away from the faith and when whole nations formerly noted for their loyalty to the Pope threatened to follow in their footsteps, made it difficult to decide whether the suggested remedy might not prove worse than the disease. The memory, too, of the scenes that took place at Constance and Basle and of the revolutionary proposals put forward in these assemblies, made the Popes less anxious to try a similar experiment with the possibility of even worse results, particularly at a time when the unfriendly relations existing between the Empire, France, and England held out but little hope for the success of a General Council. As events showed the delay was providential. It afforded an opportunity for excitement and passion to die away; it helped to secure moderation in the views both of the radical and conservative elements in the Church; and it allowed the issues in dispute to shape themselves more clearly and to be narrowed down to their true proportions, thereby enabling the Catholic theologians to formulate precisely the doctrines of the Church in opposition to the opinions of the Lutherans.

Clement VII. (1523-34), one of the de'Medici family, succeeded to the Papacy at a most critical period in the civil and religious history of Europe. The time that he spent at the court of his cousin, Leo X., and the traditions of his family and of his native city of Florence made it almost impossible for him to throw himself into the work of reform or to adopt the stern measures that the situation demanded. Instead of allying himself closely with Charles V. or Francis I. of France, or better still of preserving an attitude of strict neutrality towards both, he adopted a policy of vacillation joining now one side now the other, until the terrible sack of Rome by the infuriated and half-savage soldiery of Germany forced him to conclude an agreement with the Emperor. During the earlier years of Clement VII.'s reign the German people, Catholic as well as Lutheran, demanded the convocation of a general or at least a national council, and their demands met with the approval of Charles V. The naturally indolent temperament of the Pope, the fear that the eagerness for reform might develop into a violent revolution, and the danger that a council dominated by the Emperor might be as distasteful to France and England as dangerous to the rights and prerogatives of the Holy See, made him more willing to accept the counsels of those who suggested delay. When peace was at last concluded between the Pope and the Emperor (1529) Charles V. had changed his mind about the

THE COUNTER-REFORMATION 183

advisability of a General Council, having convinced himself in the meantime that more could be done for the cause of peace in his territories by private negotiations between the different parties.

It was only on the accession of Paul III. (1534-49) that a really vigorous effort was made to undertake the work of reform. The new Pope, a member of the Farnese family, was himself a brilliant Humanist, a patron of literature and art, well known for his strict and exemplary life as a priest, and deservedly popular both with the clergy and people of Rome. His one outstanding weakness was his partiality towards his own relatives, on many of whom he conferred high positions both in church and state. In justice to him it should be said, however, that the position of affairs in Rome and in Italy made such action less reprehensible than it might seem at first sight, and that he dealt severely with some of them, as for example, the Duke of Parma and Piacenza, once he discovered that they were unworthy of the confidence that had been reposed in them. He signalised his pontificate by the stern measures he took for the reform of the Roman Curia, by the appointment of learned and progressive ecclesiastics like Reginald Pole, Sadoleto, Caraffa, and Contarini to the college of cardinals, and by the establishment of special tribunals to combat heresy.

After a preliminary agreement with the Emperor, Paul III. convoked the General Council to meet at Mantua in 1537; but the refusal of the Lutheran princes to send representatives, the prohibition issued by Francis I. against the attendance of the French bishops, and the unwillingness of the Duke of Mantua to make the necessary arrangements for such an assembly in his territory unless under impossible conditions, made it necessary to prorogue the council to Vicenza in 1538. As hardly any bishops had arrived at the time appointed it was adjourned at first, and later on prorogued indefinitely. Negotiations were, however, continued regarding the place of assembly. The Pope was anxious that the council should be held in an Italian city, while Charles V., believing that the Lutherans would never consent to go to Italy or to accept the decrees of an Italian assembly, insisted that a German city should be selected. In the end as a compromise Trent was agreed upon by both parties, and the council was convoked once more to meet there in 1542. The refusal of the Lutherans to take part in the proposed council, the unwillingness of Francis I. to permit any of his subjects to be present, and the threatened war between France and the Empire, made it impossible for the council to meet. Finally, on the conclusion of the Peace of Crépy (1544), which put an end to the war with France, the council was convoked to meet at Trent in March 1545, and Cardinals del Monte, Reginald Pole, and Marcello Cervini were appointed to represent the Pope. When the day fixed for the opening ceremony arrived, a further adjournment was rendered imperative owing to the very sparse attendance of bishops. The First Session was held on the 13th December 1545, and the second in January 1546. There were then present in addition to the legates and theologians only four archbishops, twenty-one bishops, and five generals of religious orders.

These two preliminary sessions were given over almost entirely to a discussion of the procedure that should be followed. In the end it was agreed that the legates should propose to the council the questions on which a decision should be given, that these questions should be examined by committees of bishops aided by theologians and jurists, that the results of these discussions should be brought before a full congregation of the bishops, and that when a decision had been agreed to the formal decrees should be promulgated in a public session. The novel method of voting by nations, introduced for the first time at Constance and Basle, was rejected in favour of individual voting, a definitive vote being allowed only to bishops, generals of religious orders and abbots (one vote to every three abbots). Procurators of absent bishops were not allowed to vote, though later on a special concession was made in favour of some German bishops detained at home by the serious religious condition of their dioceses. The legates were anxious that the dogmatic issues raised by the Lutherans should be dealt with at once, while the Emperor was strongly in favour of beginning with a comprehensive scheme of reform. By this time he had made up his mind to put down his opponents in Germany by force of arms, and he believed that if nothing were done in the meantime to widen the breach the defeat of the Lutheran princes might make them more willing to take part in the council. As a compromise it was agreed that doctrine and discipline should be discussed simultaneously, and, hence, at most of the public sessions two decrees were published, one on matters of faith, the other on reform (*De Reformatione*).

It was only at the 4th public session (8th April 1546) that the first doctrinal decree could be issued. Since the Lutherans had called in question the value of Tradition as a source of divine revelation, and had denied the canonicity of several books accepted hitherto as inspired, it was fitting that the council should begin its work by defining that revelation has been handed down by Tradition as well as by the Scriptures, of which latter God is the author both as regards the Old Testament and the New. In accordance with the decrees of previous councils a list of the canonical books of the Scriptures was drawn up. Furthermore, it was defined that the sacred writings should not be interpreted against the meaning attached to them by the Church, nor against the unanimous consent of the Fathers, that the Vulgate Version, a revised edition of which should be published immediately, is authentic, that is to say, accurate as regards faith and morals, and that for the future no one was to print, publish, or retain an edition of the Scriptures unless it had been approved by the local bishop.

The next subject proposed for examination was Original Sin. The Emperor showed the greatest anxiety to secure a delay, and at a hint from him several of the Spanish bishops tried to postpone a decision by prolonging the discussions and by raising the question of the Immaculate Conception of the Blessed Virgin. That the Fathers of Trent were not opposed to this doctrine is clear enough from the decrees they formulated, but the majority of them were of opinion that purely domestic controversies among Catholic theologians should be left untouched. In the fifth general session (17th June 1546) it was defined that by his transgression of the commandment of God the head of the human race had forfeited the sanctity and justice in which he had been created, and had suffered thereby in both soul and body, that in doing so he had injured not merely himself but all his descendants, to whom Original Sin is transmitted not by imitation merely but by propagation, that the effects of this sin are removed by the sacrament of Baptism, necessary alike for adults and infants, and that the concupiscence, which still remains in man even after baptism has produced its effects, is not in itself sinful. It was declared, furthermore, that in the decrees regarding the universality of Original Sin it was not intended to include the Blessed Virgin or to weaken the binding force of the decrees issued by Sixtus IV. regarding her Immaculate Conception.

The way was now cleared for the question of Justification.* This was the doctrine on which Luther first found himself in disagreement with the Church, and which he put forward in his sermons as the foundation of his new gospel. The importance of the subject both in itself and in the circumstances of the time cannot be exaggerated, nor can it be contended that the Fathers at Trent failed to realise their responsibilities or to give it the attention it deserved. Had they done nothing else

* Hefner, *Die Enstehungsgeschichte des trienter Rechtfertigungsdekrets*, 1909.

THE COUNTER-REFORMATION 187

except to give to the world such a complete and luminous exposition of the Catholic teaching on Justification their meeting would not have been held in vain. In the 6th public session (13th January 1547), at which there were present besides the legates, ten archbishops, forty-two bishops, two procurators, five generals of religious orders, two abbots and forty-three theologians, it was defined that, though by the sin of Adam man had lost original justice and had suffered much, he still retained free-will, that God had been pleased to promise redemption through the merits of Jesus Christ, and that baptism or the desire for baptism is necessary for salvation. The decrees dealt also with the method of preparing for Justification, with its nature, causes; and conditions, with the kind of faith required in opposition to the confidence spoken of by the Reformers, with the necessity and possibility of observing the commandments, with the certainty of Justification, perseverance, loss of Grace by mortal sin, and with merit. The 7th public session (3rd March) was given to decrees regarding the Sacraments in general and Baptism and Confirmation in particular.

Meanwhile the long-expected civil war had begun in Germany, and Europe awaited with anxiety the result of a struggle upon which such momentous interests might depend. Charles, supported by most of the Catholic and not a few of the Protestant princes, overthrew the forces of the Elector of Saxony and of Philip of Hesse (1547) and by his victory found himself for the first time master in his own territories. Coupled with rejoicing at the success of the imperial arms there was also the fear in many minds that the Emperor might use his power to overawe the Council, and force it to agree to compromises, which, however useful for the promotion of unity in Germany, might be subversive of the doctrine and discipline of the Church and dangerous to the prerogatives of the Holy See. The selection of Trent as the place of assembly for the council was never very satisfactory to the Pope, but now in the changed circumstances of the Empire it was looked upon as positively dangerous. An epidemic that made its appearance in the city afforded an excellent pretext for securing a change of venue, and at the 8th public session (11th March 1547) a majority of the members present voted in favour of retiring to Bologna. The legates accompanied by most of the bishops departed immediately, while the bishops who supported the Emperor remained at Trent. For a time the situation was critical in the extreme, but under the influence of the Holy Ghost moderate counsels prevailed with both parties, and after a couple of practically abortive sessions at Bologna the council was prorogued in September 1549. A few months later, November 1549, Paul III. passed to his reward.

In the conclave that followed the cardinals were divided into three parties, namely, the Imperial, the French, and the followers of the Farnese family. By an agreement between the two latter Cardinal del Monte was elected against the express prohibition of Charles V., and took as his title Julius III.* (1550-55). He was a man of good education, of sufficiently liberal views, and with a rather large experience acquired as a prominent official in Rome and as one of the legates at the Council of Trent. While acting in the latter capacity he had come into sharp conflict with the Emperor, but as Pope he found himself forced by the conduct of the Farnese family to cultivate friendly relations with his former opponent. The alliance concluded with the Emperor turned out disastrously enough owing to the French victories in Italy during the campaign of 1552, and in consequence of this Julius III. ceased to take an active part in the struggle between these two countries. During the earlier years of his reign the Pope took earnest measures to push forward the work of reform, patronised the Jesuits, established the *Collegium Germanicum* at Rome for the use of ecclesiastical students from Germany,

* Pastor, *op. cit.*, v. Ciacconius, *Vitae et res gestae Pontificum Roman.* 1677. (741-98).

and succeeded in restoring England to communion with the Holy See, but as time passed, discouraged by the failure of his cherished projects, he adopted a policy of *laissez-faire,* and like many of his predecessors laid himself open to damaging though to a great extent unfounded charges of nepotism.

Julius III. was anxious to continue the work of reform that had been begun in Trent. In 1550 he issued a Bull convoking the council to meet once more in Trent on the 1st May 1551. When the papal legates attended at the time fixed for the opening of the council they found it necessary owing to the small numbers present to adjourn it at first till the 1st September, and later till the 11th October. On account of the unfriendly relations existing between France and the Empire regarding the Duchy of Parma, and to the alliance of the Pope and the Emperor, the King of France would not permit the French bishops to attend. The majority of the bishops present were from Italy, Germany, and Spain. In the 13th public session (11th Oct. 1551), at which there were present in addition to the legates, ten archbishops and fifty-four bishops, decrees were passed regarding the Real Presence of Christ in the Eucharist, Transubstantiation, the institution, excellence and worship of the Eucharist, its reservation and the conditions necessary for its worthy reception. In the 14th public session (25th Nov. 1551) the council dealt with the sacraments of Penance and Extreme Unction. In the meantime the Emperor was negotiating with the Lutherans with the object of inducing them to send representatives to Trent. Some of their procurators had arrived already, amongst them being the well-known theologian and historian John Sleidanus of Strassburg, but their demands, including the withdrawal of the decrees contravening the articles of the Augsburg Confession and the submission of the Pope to the authority of a General Council, were of such an extravagant character that they could not be entertained. While the subject was under consideration news arrived that Maurice of Saxony had gone over to the side of the Lutherans, that there was no army in the field to hold him in check, that the passes of the Tyrol were occupied by his troops, and that an advance upon Trent was not impossible. Many of the bishops took their departure immediately, and in April 1552 against the wishes of a few Spanish bishops the council was suspended for two years. As a matter of fact close on ten years were to elapse before the work that had been interrupted could be resumed.

On the death of Julius III. (1555) Marcellus II. succeeded, but his reign was cut short by death (22 days). In the conclave that followed Cardinal Pietro Caraffa, the first general and in a certain sense the founder of the Theatines, received the required majority of votes notwithstanding the express veto of the Emperor. He was proclaimed Pope under the title of Paul IV.* (1555-59). During his life as an ecclesiastic the new Pope had been remarkable for his rigid views, his ascetic life, and his adherence to Scholastic as opposed to Humanist views. As nuncio in Spain he had acquired a complete distrust of the Spanish rulers, nor was this bad impression likely to be removed by the treatment he received from the Austro-Spanish party when appointed Archbishop of Naples. The conclusion of the religious peace of Augsburg (1555) and the proclamation of Ferdinand I. were not calculated to win the sympathy of Paul IV. for the House of Habsburg. Hence, he put himself into communication with the Italian opponents of Philip II. of Spain, and concluded an alliance with France. The French army despatched to Naples under the leadership of the Duke of Guise was out-manœuvred completely by the Spanish viceroy, the Duke of Alva, who followed up his success by invading the Papal States and compelling the Pope to sue for peace (1556). The unfriendly relations existing between Paul IV. and Philip II. of Spain, the husband of Queen Mary I., ren-

* Bromato, *Storia di Paolo IV.*, 1748.

dered difficult the work of effecting a complete reconciliation between England and the Holy See. Owing to the disturbed condition of Europe and the attitude of the Emperor and the King of Spain, it would have been impossible for the Pope even had he been anxious to do so to re-convoke the council. He would not so much as consider the idea of selecting Trent or any German city as a fit place for such an assembly, while the Austro-Spanish rulers were equally strong against Rome or any other place in Italy. But of his own initiative Paul IV. took strong measures to reform the Roman Curia, established a special commission in Rome to assist him in this work, stamped out by vigorous action heretical opinions that began to manifest themselves in Italy, and presided frequently himself at meetings of the Inquisition. He even went so far as to arrest Cardinal Morone on a suspicion of heresy, and to summon Cardinal Pole to appear before the tribunal of the Inquisition. By the Romans he had been beloved at first on account of his economic administration whereby the taxes were reduced considerably, but the disastrous results of the war against Philip II. in Naples effaced the memory of the benefits he had conferred, and he died detested by the people. After his death the city was at the mercy of the mob, who plundered and robbed wholesale for close on a fortnight before order could be restored.

In the conclave that followed the two great parties among the cardinals were the French and the Austro-Spanish, neither of which, however, was strong enough to procure the election of its nominee. After a struggle lasting three months Cardinal Giovanni Angelo de' Medici, who was more or less neutral, was elected by acclamation. He was proclaimed under the title of Pius IV. (1559-65). The new Pope had nothing of the stern morose temperament of his predecessor. He was of a mild disposition, something of a scholar himself, inclined to act as a patron towards literature and art, and anxious to forward the interests of religion by kindness rather than by severity. He was determined to proceed with the work of the council at all cost, and as a first step in that direction he devoted all his energies to the establishment of friendly relations with the Emperor Ferdinand I. and with Spain. In all his schemes for reform he was supported loyally by his nephew, Charles Borromeo, whom he created cardinal, and to whom he entrusted the work of preparing the measures that should be submitted to the future council.

When all arrangements had been made the Bull of re-convocation, summoning the bishops to meet at Trent at Easter 1561, was published in November 1560. Though not expressly stated in the document, yet it was implied clearly enough that the assembly was not to be a new council but only the continuation of the Council of Trent. This was not satisfactory to France, which demanded a revision of some of the decrees passed previously at Trent, and which objected strongly to the selection of Trent as the meeting-place. The Emperor Ferdinand I. and Philip II. expressed their anxiety to further the project of the Pope. Delegates were sent from Rome to interview the Lutheran princes and theologians, but only to meet everywhere with sharp rebuffs. In an assembly held at Naumburg in 1561 the Lutherans refused to attend the council, unless they were admitted on their own terms, while many of the Catholic princes and bishops showed no enthusiasm to respond to the papal convocation. When the legates arrived to open the council they found so few bishops in attendance that nothing could be done except to prepare the subjects that should be submitted for discussion.

It was only on the 15th January 1562 the first (17th) public session could be held. There were present in addition to the legates, three patriarchs, eleven archbishops, forty bishops, four generals of religious orders, and four abbots. From the very beginning the legates found themselves in a very difficult position owing to the spirit of hostility against the Holy See manifested by

THE COUNTER-REFORMATION

some of the bishops and representatives of the civil powers. At this session very little was accomplished except to announce the formal opening of the council, to fix the date for the next public session, and to prepare safe conducts for the delegates of the Protestant princes. Similarly in the 18th public session (25th February) no decrees of any importance could be passed. Despite the earnest efforts of the presidents it was found impossible to make any progress. Grave differences of opinion manifested themselves both within and without the council. The question whether bishops are bound to reside in their dioceses by divine or ecclesiastical law gave rise to prolonged and angry debates. Spain demanded that it should be stated definitely that the council was only a prolongation of the council held previously at Trent, while France insisted that it should be regarded as a distinct and independent assembly. The Emperor put forward a far-reaching scheme of reform parts of which it was entirely impossible for the legates to accept.* At length after many adjournments the 21st public session was held (16th July 1562), in which decrees regarding the Blessed Eucharist were passed. It was defined that there was no divine law obliging the laity to receive Holy Communion under both kinds, that the Church has power to make arrangements about Communion so long as it does not change the substance of the sacrament, that Christ is really present whole and entire both under the appearance of bread and under the appearance of wine, that infants, who have not come to the use of reason, are not bound to receive Holy Communion because they have been regenerated already by baptism. At this session there were present six cardinals, three patriarchs, nineteen archbishops, and one hundred and forty-eight bishops.

In the 22nd public session (17th Sept. 1562) decrees were published concerning the Holy Sacrifice of the

* Kassourtz, *Die Reformvorschläge Kaiser Ferdinands I. auf dem Konzil von Trient*, 1906.

Mass. It was laid down that in place of the sacrifices and the priesthood of the Old Law Christ set up a new sacrifice, namely the Mass, the clean oblation foretold by the prophet Malachy (Mal. I., 11) and a new priesthood, to whom the celebration of the Mass was committed, that the sacrifice of the Mass is the same sacrifice as that of the Cross having the same high priest and the same victim, that the Mass may be offered up for the dead as well as for the living, that it may be offered up in honour of the Saints, that though the faithful should be advised to receive Holy Communion whenever they assist at Mass, yet private Masses at which nobody is present for Communion are not unlawful, and that, though it was not deemed prudent to allow the sacrifice to be offered up in the vulgar tongue, it was the earnest wish of the council that priests should explain the ceremonies of the Mass to the people especially on Sundays and holidays. The question of allowing the laity to receive the chalice was discussed at length, and it was decided finally to submit it to the decision of the Pope. Pius IV. did, indeed, make a concession on this point in favour of several districts in Austria; but as the Catholics did not desire such a concession and the Lutherans refused to accept it as insufficient the indult remained practically a dead-letter, and later on was withdrawn.

The next session was fixed for November 1562 but on account of very grave difficulties that arose a much more prolonged adjournment was rendered necessary. During this interval the old controversies broke out with greater violence and bitterness, and more than once it appeared as if the council would break up in disorder; but the perseverance, tact, and energy of the new legates, Cardinals Morone and Navagero, strengthened by the prudent concessions made by the Pope, averted the threatened rupture, and made it possible for the Fathers to accomplish the work for which they had been convoked. Cardinal Guise* (de Lorraine) accompanied by

* Guillemin, *Le Cardinal de Lorraine, son influence politique et religieuse*, 1881.

THE COUNTER-REFORMATION 195

a number of French bishops and theologians arrived at Trent in November 1562. His arrival strengthened the hands of those Spanish bishops who were insisting on having it defined that the obligation of episcopal residence was *de jure divino*. The question had been adjourned previously at the request of the legates, but with the advent of the discussion on the sacrament of Orders further adjournment was impossible. Several of the bishops maintained that the obligation must be *jure divino*, because the episcopate itself was *de jure divino*. From this they concluded that the bishops had their jurisdiction immediately from Christ, not mediately through the Pope as some of the papal theologians maintained. Consequently they asserted that the subordination of the bishops to the Pope was not, therefore of divine origin, thereby raising at once the whole question of the relations of a general council to a Pope and the binding force of the decrees regarding the superiority of a council passed at Constance and Basle.

At the same time danger threatened the council from another quarter. The Emperor, Ferdinand I. had put forward a very comprehensive scheme of reform. Some portions of this were considered by the legates to be prejudicial to the rights of the Holy See, and were therefore rejected by them after consultation with the Pope. Ferdinand annoyed by their action asserted that there was no liberty at the council, that it was being controlled entirely from Rome, and that the assembly at Trent had become merely a machine for confirming what had been decreed already on the other side of the Alps. At his request several of his supporters left Trent and joined him at Innsbruck, where a kind of opposition assembly was begun. Cardinal Morone, realising fully the seriousness of the situation, betook himself to Innsbruck (April 1563) for a personal interview with the Emperor. The meeting had the result of clearing away many of the misunderstandings that had arisen, and of bringing about a compromise. At the same time the

Pope wrote a letter pointing out that it was only reasonable that the Head of the Church, not being present at the council, should be consulted by his legates in all important matters that might arise.

Meanwhile the council was still engaged in discussing the authority of the bishops. On the ground that the Fathers should define at one and the same time both the rights of the bishops and the rights of the Holy See Cardinal Guise, who represented the Gallican school of thought, brought forward certain proposals highly derogatory to the prerogatives of the Pope. In face of this counter-move the legates were firm but conciliatory. They pointed out that the whole question of the jurisdiction of the Holy See had been decided already by the Council of Florence and that the decrees of Florence could not be watered down at Trent. On this question the Italian bishops found themselves supported by the vast majority of the Spanish, Austro-German and Portuguese representatives; but in deference to the request of the Pope, who wished that nothing should be defined unless with the unanimous consent of the Fathers, and to the feelings of the French, whose secession from the council was anticipated, it was agreed to issue no decree on the subject. As the supreme authority of the Pope had been recognised implicitly by the council* no definition was required.

As a result of the negotiations inside and outside the council it was possible to hold the 23rd public session on the 15th July 1563. In this it was defined that the priesthood of the New Law was instituted by Christ, that there are seven orders in the Church about two of which, the priesthood (*de sacerdotibus*) and the diaconate (*de diaconis*) express mention is made in the Scriptures, that the bishops who have succeeded to the place of the Apostles pertain especially to the hierarchy and are superior to priests, that neither the consent of the people nor of the civil power is necessary for the valid reception

* Denzinger, *Enchiridion*, 11th edition, 1908 (nos. 859, 903, 968, etc.)

THE COUNTER-REFORMATION 197

of orders, and that bishops who are appointed by the authority of the Roman Pontiff are true bishops.* The question whether the duty of episcopal residence is *de jure divino*, about which such a protracted and heated controversy had been waged, was settled amicably by deciding that the bishops as pastors are bound by divine command to know their flocks, and that they cannot do this unless they reside in their dioceses. At this session there were present four cardinals, three patriarchs, twenty-five archbishops and one hundred and ninety-three bishops.

Many of the bishops were anxious to return to their dioceses, and nearly all of them hoped for a speedy conclusion of the council. The Pope, the Emperor, and the King of France were in agreement, though for different reasons, in endeavouring to dissolve the assembly as soon as possible. The sacrament of Matrimony was next proposed for discussion. The French party wished that marriages contracted without the consent of the parents as well as clandestine marriages should be declared invalid, but the council refused to make the validity of marriage dependent upon parental consent. In deference to the wishes of Venice, which stood in close relation to the Greeks, it was agreed to define merely that the Church does not err when she states in accordance with the apostolic and evangelic teaching that the bond of marriage is not broken by adultery. In the 24th public session (11th Nov. 1563) the decrees on Matrimony were proclaimed.

The greatest anxiety was displayed on all sides to bring the work to a conclusion. The action of the papal legates in proposing that the interference of Catholic rulers in ecclesiastical affairs should be considered and if necessary reformed did not tend to delay the dissolution. The princes were most anxious to reform the Pope and clergy, but they were determined not to allow any weakening of their own so-called prerogatives. In

* *Op. cit.*, nos. 958-69.

accordance with the general desire the addresses were cut short, and so rapid was the progress made that the last public session was held on the 3rd and 4th December 1563. The decrees on Purgatory, on the honour to be paid to relics and images of Saints and on Indulgences were passed. It was agreed, furthermore, that in regard to fast days and holidays the usage of the Roman Church should be followed, and that the Holy See should undertake the preparation of a new edition of the missal and breviary. The decrees that had been passed under Paul III. and Julius III. were read and approved. The legates were requested to obtain the approval of the Holy Father for the decisions of the council, and Cardinal Guise in the name of the bishops returned thanks to the Pope, the Emperor, the ambassadors of the Catholic nations, and to the legates. Finally the Fathers subscribed their names to the acts of the council. There were then present six cardinals, three patriarchs, twenty-five archbishops, one hundred and sixty-seven bishops, and nineteen procurators.

The Council of Trent met in peculiarly difficult circumstances, and it carried on its work in face of great opposition and disappointments. More than once it was interrupted for a long period, and more than once, too, it was feared by many that it would result in promoting schism rather than unity. But under the Providence of God the dangers were averted, the counsels of despair were rejected, the arms of its enemies were weakened, and the hearts of the faithful children of the Church throughout the world filled with joy and gratitude. It found itself face to face with a strong and daily increasing party, who rejected the authority that had been accepted hitherto without difficulty, and who called in question many of the most cherished doctrines and practices of the Catholic world. Without allowing themselves to be involved in purely domestic disputes among Catholic theologians or to be guided by the advice of those who sought to secure peace by means of dishonourable compromises, the Fathers of Trent set themselves calmly but resolutely to sift the chaff from the wheat, to examine the theories of Luther in the light of the teaching of the Scriptures and the tradition of the Church as contained in the writings of the Fathers, and to give to the world a clear-cut exposition of the dogmas that had been attacked by the heretics. Never had a council in the Church met under more alarming conditions; never had a council been confronted with more serious obstacles, and never did a council confer a greater service on the Christian world than did the 19th ecumenical council held at Trent (1545-63).

It was of essential importance that the council should determine the matters of faith that had been raised, but it was almost equally important that it should formulate a satisfactory scheme of reform. Reform of the Church in its Head and members was on the lips of many whose orthodoxy could not be suspected long before Luther had made this cry peculiarly his own, the better thereby to weaken the loyalty of the faithful to the Holy See. As in matters of doctrine so also in matters of discipline the Council of Trent showed a thorough appreciation of the needs of the Church, and if in some things it failed to go as far as one might be inclined to desire the fault is not to be attributed to the Popes or the bishops, but rather to the secular rulers, whose jealousies and recriminations were one of the greatest impediments to the progress of the council, and who, while calling out loudly for the reform of others, offered a stubborn resistance to any change that might lessen their power over the Church, or prevent the realisation of that absolute royalty, towards which both the Catholic and Protestant rulers of the sixteenth century were already turning as the ultimate goal of their ambitions.

The council struck at the root of many of the abuses that afflicted the Christian world by suppressing plurality of benefices, provisions, and expectancies, as well as by insisting that, except in case of presentation by a university, nobody could be appointed to a benefice unless he had shown that he possessed the knowledge necessary for the proper discharge of his duty. It determined the method of electing bishops, commanded them to reside in their dioceses unless exempted for a time on account of very special reasons, to preach to their people, to hold regular visitations of their parishes, to celebrate diocesan synods yearly, to attend provincial synods at least once in three years, and to safeguard conscientiously the ecclesiastical property committed to their charge.

It put an end to abuses in connexion with the use of ecclesiastical censures, indulgences, and dispensations, and ordained that all causes of complaint should be brought before the episcopal court before being carried to a higher tribunal. It made useful regulations concerning those who should be admitted into diocesan chapters, defined the relations between the bishop and his canons, and arranged for the administration of the dioceses by the appointment of vicars-capitular to act during the interregnum. It ordered the secular clergy to be mindful always of the spiritual dignity to which they had been called, not to indulge in any business unworthy of their sacred office, condemned concubinage in the strongest terms, and commanded priests to look after the religious education of the young, to preach to their flocks on Sundays and holidays, and to attend zealously to the spiritual wants of the souls committed to their charge.

The council recognised, futhermore, that the best method of securing a high standard of priestly life was the careful training of ecclesiastical students. Hence it ordained that in the individual dioceses seminaries should be established, where those who were desirous of entering the clerical state should live apart from the world, and where they should receive the education and discipline necessary for the successful discharge of their future obligations. It put an end to many abuses of

THE COUNTER-REFORMATION

monastic life, suppressed questing for alms, drew up rules for the reception of novices, gave the bishop power to deal with irregularities committed outside the monasteries, and subjected all priests both regular and secular to episcopal authority by insisting on the necessity of Approbation for all who wished to act as confessors. Finally, in order to apply a remedy against the many scandals and crimes that resulted from secret marriages, the Council of Trent laid it down that those marriages only should be regarded as valid which should be contracted in the presence of the parish priest of one of the contracting parties and two witnesses.

On the conclusion of the Council of Trent Cardinal Morone hastened to Rome with the decrees to seek the approval of the Pope. Some of the Roman officials, who felt themselves aggrieved by the reforms, advised the Pope to withhold his approval of certain decrees, but Pius IV. rejected this advice. On the 26th January 1564 he issued the Bull of confirmation, and set himself to work immediately to put the reforms into execution. To assist him in this design he appointed a commission, one of the ablest members of which was his own nephew, Charles Borromeo, and he despatched representatives to the princes and bishops to ensure their acceptance of the decrees. As an example to others he established the Roman Seminary for the education of priests for the city. All the princes of Italy received the decrees in a friendly spirit and allowed their publication in their territories, as did also the King of Portugal. Philip II. acted similarly except that he insisted upon the addition of a saving clause "without prejudice to royal authority." The Emperor Ferdinand I. hesitated for some time, but at last he accepted them in 1566. In France very little opposition was raised to the dogmatic decrees, but as several of the practical reforms, notably those relating to marriage, benefices, ecclesiastical punishments, etc., were opposed to the civil law, permission to publish them was refused.

A profession of faith based on the decrees of the Council of Trent and of previous councils was drawn up by Pius IV. (13th Nov. 1564), and its recitation made obligatory on those who were appointed to ecclesiastical benefices or who received an academic degree as well as on converts from Protestantism. The Cathechism of the Council of Trent (*Catechismus Romanus*)* was prepared at the command of Pius V. and published in 1566. It is a valuable work of instruction, approved by the highest authority in the Church, and should be in the hands of all those who have care of souls.

(b) THE REFORMING ACTIVITY OF THE POPES

Pastor, *Geschichte der Päpste im Zeitalter der Renaissance und der Glaubenspaltung* (Eng. Trans. *History of the Popes*). Ciacconius, *Vitae et res gestae Roman. Pontificum*, 1688. Ranke, *Die Römischen Päpste* (vols. 37-39), 1894 (Eng. Trans., 1847). Von Reumont, *Geschichte der Stadt Rom.*, 3 Bde, 1867-70. Artaud de Montor, *History of the Popes*, 1867. Theiner, *Annales ecclesiastici*, etc., Rome, 1856.

The Council of Trent had accomplished the work for which it was called. Though it failed to extinguish the rising flames of heresy or to restore peace to the Christian world, it had swept away most of the glaring abuses that had proved the main source of Luther's success, and rendered impossible for the future any misunderstanding about the doctrines that had been called in question. The Catholic Church, purified by the severe trials through which she had passed, stood forth once again active and united under the leadership of the Successor of St. Peter, still face to face it is true with a powerful opposition, but an opposition on which the disintegrating influence of private judgment was already making itself felt. Thus the foundations of the great Catholic Counter-Reformation were laid securely, and a

---

* English translations by Donovan (1829), Buckley (1852), and Dr. Hagan (1912).

THE COUNTER-REFORMATION 203

movement was begun which stayed the further advance of Protestantism, secured the allegiance of individuals and nations that were wavering, and won back many who had been seduced from the faith during the early days of the religious upheaval.

But if the labours of the Fathers of Trent were to be productive of the good results that might be anticipated, earnest, religious, energetic Popes were required to give a lead to their spiritual children, whose courage had been damped by over thirty years of almost uninterrupted defeats, to put into force the valuable reforms that had been planned with such minute care, and above all to make the court and city of Rome an example for the princes and people of the world. Here, again, the providence of God watching over His Church was manifested in a striking manner. Pius IV. deserves to be remembered with gratitude by all future generations for the part that he took in bringing to a successful conclusion the Council of Trent in face of almost insuperable difficulties, for having taken such energetic and withal such prudent action to secure the acceptance of its decrees and their reduction into practice, and for having given to Rome and to the Catholic Church so gifted, so saintly, and so disinterested an ecclesiastic as his nephew, the Cardinal-Archbishop of Milan, St. Charles Borromeo.

On the death of Pius IV. the conclave, mainly through the exertions of Cardinal Borromeo, elected Cardinal Ghisleri, who took the title of Pius V.* (1566-72) in memory of his predecessor. In his youth the future Pope joined the Order of St. Dominic, and for years had acted as professor of theology, master of novices, and prior. He was noted specially for his simplicity and holiness of life, a holiness which it may be remarked had nothing in common with the morose rigour of Paul

---

* *Catena, Vita del gloriossisimo Papa Pio V.*, 1587. Gabutius, *De Vita et rebus gestis Pii V.*, 1605. Antony, *Saint Pius V.*, 1911. Grente, *Saint Pie V.*, ("*Les Saints*"), 1914.

IV., for his humility, his love of silence and meditation, and for his kindness towards the poor and the suffering. As a man of good education and of conservative tendencies he was summoned to assist Cardinal Caraffa, then president of the Holy Office, and when the latter became Pope he was created cardinal and appointed Grand Inquisitor. After his election Pius V. followed still the strict life of fasting and prayer to which he had been accustomed as a Dominican friar. He did not seek to create positions, or to carve out estates from the papal territories for his relatives. Anxious to promote the temporal as well as the spiritual welfare of the people in his temporal dominions he took steps to see that justice was meted out to poor and rich, banished women of loose character from the streets, put an end to degrading amusements, enforced the observance of the Sunday, and, backed by St. Charles Borromeo and the princes of Italy, he changed the whole face of the capital and the country. Rome was no longer the half-pagan city of the days of Leo X., nor yet did it partake of the savage rigour of Geneva.

Pius V. was most anxious to enforce the decrees of Trent, and it was for the accomplishment of this object that he had prepared for the instruction of pastors the Catechism of the Council of Trent. In compliance with the wishes of the bishops he published also a revised edition of the Roman Breviary and of the Missal. With the Catholic princes of Europe he maintained very friendly relations. He furnished supplies to Charles IX. of France in his struggle with the Huguenots, and to Philip II. of Spain in his wars against the Calvinists of the Netherlands. He encouraged the Emperor, Ferdinand I., and Maximilian of Bavaria to stand firm against the further encroachments of the Lutherans, and sympathised actively with the unfortunate Queen of Scotland. Having realised that Queen Elizabeth was lost hopelessly to the Church and that she was making every effort to involve the whole English nation in

THE COUNTER-REFORMATION 205

heresy, he directed against her a Bull of excommunication and deposition. But though he endeavoured to cultivate friendly relations with the Catholic rulers he had no intention of abandoning the rights of the Church or of yielding in the slightest to the increasing demands of the civil power. Against the wishes of some of his advisers and to the no small annoyance of the Catholic princes he republished the Bull, known as the *In Coena Domini*, because he commanded that it should be read in all churches on Holy Thursday.

Like his great namesake Pius II. he had especially at heart the defence of Europe against invasion by the Turk. Owing to the religious controversies and the eagerness of some of the princes to ally themselves with the Sultan the followers of Islam had grown bolder, and had shown that they dreamed still of overcoming Western Europe and of planting the crescent even in the very city of the Popes. Pius V. appealed to the rulers of Europe to close up their ranks against their common enemy. He granted generous subsidies to the Knights of Malta and the rulers of Venice and Hungary upon whom the brunt of the struggle must inevitably fall. When on the accession of Selim II. in 1570 the danger was pressing, the Pope succeeded in bringing about a Christian confederacy composed of Spain, Venice, and the Papal States with Don Juan of Austria in command of the Christian forces. For the success of the enterprise the Pope ordered that public prayers and particularly the Rosary should be recited in the churches throughout the world. The decisive struggle between the two forces, as a result of which the Turkish fleet was almost completely annihilated, was fought in the Bay of Lepanto on Sunday, 7th October 1571.* In memory of this great victory the Pope instituted the Feast of the Holy Rosary to be celebrated for ever on the first Sunday of October. While he was engaged in making arrange-

* Julien, *Papes et Sultans*, 1880. De la Gravière, *La Guerre de Chypre et la bataille de Lépante*, 1888.

ments to follow up his success by driving the Turks beyond the Bosphorus he was called to his reward. Even by his contemporaries Pius V. was regarded as a saint. It is not to be wondered at, therefore, that one hundred years after his death he was beatified, and forty years later, in 1712, he was canonised formally by Clement XI.

When the cardinals met in conclave, mainly by the intervention of Cardinal Granvelle, viceroy of Philip II. in Naples, Cardinal Buoncompagni was elected almost immediately, and proclaimed under the title of Gregory XIII. (1572-85). He had been a distinguished student and professor of law at the University of Bologna, where he had the honour of having as his pupils many of the ablest ecclesiastics of the age. Later on he was sent as confidential secretary to the Council of Trent. On his return from this assembly he was created cardinal, and appointed papal legate in Spain. At the time of his election to the Papacy he had reached his seventieth year. As a young man his life was not blameless from the point of view of morality, but after he became a priest nothing could be urged against his conduct even by his worst enemies. Though it must be admitted that he was not of such an ascetic and spiritual temperament as his predecessor, he was a man of irreproachable character, not over anxious to promote his own relatives, and determined to strengthen the Catholic Church by raising the standard of education and by appointing to the episcopate none but the most worthy ecclesiastics. Hence he drew lavishly upon the funds of the Holy See to erect Catholic Colleges in Rome and in several countries of Europe. He founded the magnificent *Collegium Romanum* for the education of students from all parts of the world, and placed it under the administration of the Jesuits, in whom he reposed the most signal confidence. As the circumstances that led to the establishment of the *Collegium Germanicum* had not improved, he conferred on it more generous endowments, and united with it later on the college which he had founded for the Hungarians. Owing to the persecutions in England and Ireland and the suppression of institutions for the education of the clergy, Gregory XIII. founded an English College (1579) and provided funds for the erection of an Irish College. The money intended for this latter institution was spent in assisting the Irish in their wars against Elizabeth. In addition to this, more than twenty colleges situated in various parts of Europe, amongst them being the Scotch College at Pont-à-Mousson, owe their origin in whole or in part to his munificence. He was, also, very determined that none but the most worthy men should be appointed to episcopal sees, and with this object in view he took pains to inquire personally about the merits of distinguished ecclesiastics in each country, and to prepare lists of them for use as vacancies might arise. He was equally careful in the appointments which he made to the college of cardinals. In order to keep in touch with the progress of affairs in Germany he established a nunciature at Vienna in 1581, and another at Cologne in the following year. The results of this experiment were so successful that in a short time nunciatures were established in nearly all the Catholic countries.*

Like his predecessor he was resolved to continue the war against the Turks, but the circumstances were unfavourable in France and in the Empire, while Venice and Spain, the former allies of the Holy See, concluded peace with the Sultan. In England and Ireland neither by peaceful measures nor by the expeditions fitted out by him in connexion with the Desmond Rebellion was he able to achieve any lasting results. His legates succeeded in inducing John III. of Sweden to abjure heresy and to return to the bosom of the Catholic Church, but, unfortunately, the conversion lasted only until political circumstances demanded another change. In Russia

* Pieper, *Zur Enstehungsgeschichte der ständigen Nuntiaturen*, 1894.

his representatives arranged a peace with Poland, and put an end for the time to any active persecution of Catholicism within the Russian dominions.* In all parts of Europe, where Catholic rulers found themselves in difficulties, subsidies were sent by Gregory XIII. to their assistance. Charles IX. in France, Philip II. of Spain, Austria, the Knights of Malta, and the Catholics of England and Ireland shared largely in his munificence.

He issued a new edition of the Roman Martyrology in 1584, and directed that it should be used to the exclusion of all others. His predecessor had appointed a committee of jurists to prepare a revised edition of the Decrees of Gratian. He had been a member of that commission, and as Pope he brought the work to a successful conclusion. But the achievement for which he will be best remembered is undoubtedly the Gregorian Calendar. The errors of the calendar had been noticed by many, but how to correct them and prevent them for the future was the problem that was still unsolved. Gregory XIII. appointed a body of experts to examine the subject, the most prominent of whom were the Jesuit Father Clavius and Cardinal Sirleto. The committee had the advantage of having before them the papers of the Italian scientist, Lilius, and the suggestions of the Catholic universities. In 1582 the Gregorian Calendar was published, and was accepted generally in all the Catholic countries of Europe. But for a long time the Protestant countries, believing that nothing good could come from Rome, remained attached to the old style. It was only in 1700 that the Gregorian Calendar was accepted in Germany and Holland, and at a still later period (1752) England consented to the change. The following year Sweden followed suit, and by 1775 the use of the new calendar had become general outside Russia and the

* Pierling, *Grégoire XIII. et Ivan le Terrible* (*Revue des Quest. Histor.*, 1886).

THE COUNTER-REFORMATION

other countries involved in the Eastern schism, in which the old style is followed till the present day.

The immense sums expended by Gregory XIII. in endowing colleges and subsidising Catholic sovereigns proved too great a strain on the resources of the papal treasury. To raise funds the Pope was obliged to increase the taxes, to impose tariffs on imports and exports, to curtail the privileges of certain sections of his subjects, and to recall many of the fiefs granted to feudal proprietors. These measures led to grave discontent among all classes. Secret societies were formed, in which the dispossessed nobles encouraged their poorer followers to acts of violence. Robber bands led by some of the younger barons made their appearance in all parts of the Papal States, so that even in the very streets of Rome the lives of the papal officials were not secure. Gregory XIII. was too old to cope with such a serious situation. Before order could be restored he passed away leaving to his successor a very difficult task.

After a conclave lasting only four days Cardinal Felice Peretti, better known as the Cardinal di Montalto, secured the required majority of votes, and ascended the papal throne under the name of Sixtus V.* (1585-90). He belonged to a very poor family in Italy, had joined the Franciscans as a boy, and had risen from office to office till at last in 1570 he was created cardinal. At the time of his election he was practically unknown, partly because he was not a scion of one of the leading families of Italy, partly, also, because during the reign of Gregory XIII. with whom he was in disagreement he lived a retired life, devoting himself almost completely to the preparation of an edition of the works of St. Ambrose. Throughout the Catholic world the news of his elevation was received with joy. He was a man of strict life and tireless activity, more inclined to act than to speak, unwilling to burthen his spiritual or temporal subjects with new laws, but fully determined

* Hübner, *Sixte-Quint*, 3 vols., 1870.

to enforce those already made, and almost unchangeable in his views once his decision had been given.

The restoration of order in the Papal States and the suppression of the robbers who terrorised peaceful citizens were the first work to which he directed his attention. Nor was it long till the severe and almost extreme measures he adopted, and in which he was supported by the Italian princes, produced their effect. The bankrupt condition of the papal treasury necessitated a close revision of the papal finances, and so well did Sixtus V. succeed in this respect that he was able to bequeath to his successor immense reserves. Though very careful about expenditure for his own uses or on the papal court he spent money freely on the erection and decoration of churches, and on the improvement of the city of Rome. He extended the Vatican Library, in connexion with which he established a new printing-press, provided a good water supply (*Acqua Felice*), built the Lateran Palace, completed the Quirinal, restored the columns of Trajan and Antoninus, erected the obelisks of the Vatican, St. Mary Major, the Lateran and Santa Maria del Popolo, and built several new streets to beautify the city and to prevent congestion.

His administrative ability manifested itself in the establishment of various congregations, to each of which was committed some particular department of work in the administration of the Church and of the Papal States. Hitherto most of this work had been done by the *auditores* or the *penitentiarii* according as it belonged to the external or internal forum, or else in consistories of the cardinals. The idea of Sixtus V. was not entirely a novel one. The Congregation of the Index (1571) and the Holy Office (1588) had been established already, as also a commission to watch over the execution of the decrees of the Council of Trent (1564). By the Bull, *Immensa Aeterni Dei** (11th Feb. 1588) Sixtus V. established fifteen different congregations, the most important

* *Bullar. Rom.*, iv., 4, 392.

THE COUNTER-REFORMATION

of which were the Congregation of the Index, of the Inquisition, of the Signatura, of the Council of Trent, of Rites and Ceremonies, and of Bishops and Regulars. By means of these various bodies the work was done better and more expeditiously without impairing in the slightest the authority of the Pope. In 1586 he issued the Bull, *Postquam verus* by which he fixed the number of cardinals at seventy, namely, six cardinal-bishops, fifty cardinal-priests and fourteen cardinal-deacons. He had prepared and published a new edition of the Septuagint (1588) as a preparation for the revised edition of the Vulgate, which was brought out later, and was of so faulty a character that it was necessary to withdraw it from circulation.

Sixtus V. had great hopes of inducing the princes of Europe to form an alliance against the Turks, and, indeed, it was with a view to some such struggle that he laid aside such immense reserves, but his hopes were doomed to disappointment. In England no progress could be made, more especially as the defeat of the Spanish Armada served only to strengthen the throne of Elizabeth. The condition of affairs in France was calculated to cause the Pope great anxiety. The murder of the Catholic leaders and the alliance of Henry III. with the Calvinist King of Navarre compelled the Pope to espouse warmly the cause of Spain and the League. But towards the end of his reign Sixtus V. began to realise that Spain's intervention in favour of the League was not nearly so disinterested as it might seem, and that the aim of Spanish statesmen was the union of the two countries in one great empire, an event which, were it to come to pass, might be as dangerous for the Holy See as for the succession of Henry of Navarre. He was, therefore, more inclined to compromise than to fight.

After the death of Urban VII., Gregory XIV., and Innocent X., who followed one another in rapid succession, a large number of the cardinals, determined to put an end to the dominating influence of Spain, put forward as the candidate of their choice Cardinal Aldobrandini, whose election had been vetoed twice before by the Spanish representatives. Notwithstanding the opposition of Spain they succeeded in their effort, and Cardinal Aldobrandini was proclaimed under the title Clement VIII.* (1592-1605). The character of the new Pope both as a man and an ecclesiastic was beyond the shadow of reproach. He was the special disciple and friend of St. Philip Neri who acted as his confessor for thirty years. As Pope his choice of a confessor fell upon the learned and saintly Baronius whom he insisted upon creating cardinal. His activity and zeal were manifested soon in the visitation which he undertook of the churches and institutions of Rome, and during the course of which he suppressed many abuses.

The situation in France was sufficiently delicate. Henry IV. was beginning to recognise that notwithstanding his victories he could never reign as a Calvinist over a united France. Clement VIII. was very decidedly in favour of a solution that would put an end to the war and would prevent France from degenerating into a Spanish province. Hence as soon as the conversion of Henry IV. was proved to be genuine the Pope acknowledged his title as king of France, and exhorted French Catholics to receive him as their ruler. Such a course of action was of necessity displeasing to Spain, but a few years later the Pope had the happiness of putting an end to the struggle between these two countries. During his term of office Clement VIII. founded at Rome a national college for providing priests for the mission in Scotland, issued a revised edition of the Vulgate (1598), of the Breviary, the Missal, the Caerimonial and the Pontifical, and instituted the *Congregatio de Auxiliis* to investigate the matters in dispute between the Thomists and the Molinists. He presided personally at many of its sessions though he never issued a definite sentence. It was also during his reign that the infamous

* Wadding, *Vita Clementis VIII.*, Rome, 1723.

THE COUNTER-REFORMATION

ex-monk Giordano Bruno was condemned by the Inquisition, handed over to the secular power, and burned at the stake (17th Feb. 1600). In his youth Giordano joined the Dominicans, from which order he fled because definite charges of heresy, the truth of which he could not deny, were brought against him. Later on he was excommunicated by the Calvinists of Geneva and the Lutherans of Germany, and refused permission to lecture by the professors of Oxford when he visited that seat of learning. Many of his writings are strongly anti-Christian, and some of them thoroughly indecent. He was condemned to die solely on account of his denial of the Divinity of Christ and other heretical views and not, as is said by some, because he defended the Copernican system.*

Leo XI. succeeded, but survived his election less than a month. The choice of the conclave then fell upon Cardinal Borghese who took as his title Paul V.† (1605-21). He had been a distinguished law student of Bologna and Padua, a papal legate in Spain, and under Clement VIII. cardinal-vicar of Rome. He was a man of great energy and zealous for the promotion of religion. During his reign he canonised St. Charles Borromeo and issued a decree of beatification in favour of Ignatius of Loyola, Francis Xavier, and Philip Neri, provided generous subsidies for the advancement of the missions, endeavoured to bring about a re-union with some of the separated religious bodies in the East, and spent money freely on the decoration of the Roman churches, notably St. Peter's, which he had the honour of completing. Like his predecessors he was desirous of continuing the war against the Turks, but the state of affairs in western Europe rendered such a scheme impossible of realisation. With France and Spain he preserved friendly relations, tried to put an end to the rivalries that weakened the House of Habsburg and the Catholic

* McIntyre, *Giordano Bruno*, 1903.
† Bzovius, *Vita Pauli V.*, 1625.

cause in the Empire, and despatched supplies of both men and money to the assistance of Ferdinand II. in his struggle with the Protestants. He wrote to James I. of England (1606) congratulating him on his accession and his escape from death and asking for toleration of the Catholic religion, in return for which he promised to induce the Catholics to submit in all things not opposed to the law of God. The reply of the king to this overture was the well-known Oath of Allegiance, that led to such ugly controversies among the Catholic body.

As an earnest student of canon law Paul V. was too inclined to maintain all the rights and privileges of the Church as they were expounded in the decretals of the Middle Ages. This attitude of mind brought him into a prolonged and inglorious conflict with the republic of Venice. This latter state, regardless of the *privilegium fori* imprisoned two clerics without reference to the ecclesiastical authorities, and about the same time gave great offence by passing laws rendering it difficult for the Church to acquire ownership of landed property, to build new churches or monasteries, or to found new religious orders or societies. Paul V. lodged a solemn protest against these innovations. When his demands were not complied with he issued a sentence of excommunication against the Doge, Senate, and Government, and later on he placed Venice under interdict (1606). The quarrel was so bitter that at one time it was feared that it might end in separating the republic from the centre of unity. Cardinals Baronius and Bellarmine entered the lists in defence of the Pope, while the notorious ex-Servite, Paul Sarpi* (1552-1623), undertook to reply to them on behalf of Venice. The government forbade the promulgation of the interdict, and threatened the most severe punishment against all clergy who should observe it. With the exception of the Jesuits, Capuchins, and Theatines who were expelled, the clergy both

* Campbell, *Vita di Fra Paolo Sarpi*, 1875. *Irish Ecc. Record* xv., 524-40.

THE COUNTER-REFORMATION 215

secular and regular took no notice of the interdict. It was feared that in the end the issues could be decided only by war in which Spain was prepared to support the Pope, but through the friendly intervention of Henry IV. of France peace was concluded without any very decisive victory on either side (1607). The clergy who were expelled for obeying the interdict were allowed to return except the Jesuits. These latter were permitted to settle in Venice again only in 1657.

On the death of Paul V. Cardinal Ludovisi ascended the papal throne under the title of Gregory XV. (1621-23). The new Pope had been educated by the Jesuits, and had risen rapidly in the service of the Church. At the time of his election he was old and infirm, but by the appointment of his nephew Ludovico to the college of cardinals he secured for himself an able and loyal assistant. To put an end to several abuses that had taken place in connexion with papal elections he published the Bull, *Decet Romanum Pontificem* (1622), in which were laid down minute regulations about conclaves, the most important of which were that the cardinals should vote secretly, that they should vote only for one candidate, and that no elector should vote for himself.* In providing funds for the assistance of the Catholic missions Gregory XV. was very generous as was also his cardinal-nephew. The success of the missionaries had been so great, and the conditions of the various countries in which they laboured so different, that proper supervision of the new provinces of the Church was by no means easy. Gregory XIII. and Clement VIII. had appointed commissions to look after the spiritual wants of particular districts, but it was reserved for Gregory XV. to establish a permanent congregation, *De Propaganda Fide* (Bull, *Inscrutabili*, 1622) to superintend the entire field of Catholic missions. He had the honour, too, of canonising St. Ignatius of Loyola, St. Francis Xavier, and St. Philip Neri, and of approving the foundation of several new religious orders.

* *Bullar. Romanum* (xii., 662 *sqq.*).

During the Thirty Years' War he afforded every possible assistance to Ferdinand II., and helped to secure the Palatinate for Maximilian of Bavaria on the expulsion of Frederick. In return for this favour Maximilian presented the Pope with a goodly portion of the library of Heidelberg. By the judicious interposition of Gregory XV. war was averted between Spain and Austria on the one side and France, Venice, and Savoy on the other regarding the possession of the Valtelline, while in England, though the Spanish Match which he favoured was broken off, he succeeded in securing some respite for the persecuted Catholics.

In the conclave that followed upon the death of Gregory XV. Cardinal Barberini received the support of the electors and was proclaimed Pope as Urban VIII. (1623-44). The new Pope was a man of exemplary life whose greatest fault was his excessive partiality towards his relatives, though it must be said that some of the relatives on whom he bestowed favours were by no means unworthy of them. As a native of Florence he seems to have caught up something of the spirit of classical learning for which that city had been so renowned, as was shown unfortunately too clearly in the Breviary that he published in 1632. He issued the Bull, *In Coena Domini* in its final form, founded a national college in Rome for students from Ireland, and issued a series of strict and minute regulations on canonisation and beatification, many of which remain in force till the present time. The interests of the foreign missions were specially dear to the heart of Urban VIII. To provide a supply of priests for them he established the celebrated *Collegium Urbanum* (1627), and established there a printing-press for the use of the missionaries. He reduced the number of holidays of obligation, opened China and Japan, till then reserved for the Jesuits, to all missionaries, and forbade slavery of whatsoever kind in Paraguay, Brazil and the West Indies.

For many reasons the political policy of Urban VIII.

THE COUNTER-REFORMATION 217

has been criticised very severely. Too much money was wasted by him in fortifying the Papal States and on the disastrous war with the Duke of Parma (1641-44). He has been blamed also for his failure to support Ferdinand II. more energetically during the Thirty Years' War, but in reality this hostile verdict is based largely on a distorted view of the war itself and of the policy of the Pope. It is not true that the Pope sympathised with Gustavus Adolphus or that he grieved over his death. Neither is it true that he procured the dismissal of Wallenstein from the imperial service. It is a fact undoubtedly that he did not take energetic measures to prevent the French from assisting the Protestant princes and the Swedes against the Emperor, but it remains to be proved that any remonstrances from the Pope, however strong, would have proved effectual in the circumstances. In the later stages at any rate the war could not be regarded at first sight as a religious one, but at the same time it is to be regretted that Urban VIII. did not recognise that the triumph of the enemies of the Emperor meant a triumph for Lutheranism. In the war between Spain and Portugal consequent upon the proclamation of the Duke of Braganza he endeavoured to preserve an attitude of neutrality by refusing to appoint to episcopal sees in Portugal the candidates presented by the new king. The policy of Urban VIII. in regard to England and Ireland will be dealt with under these countries.

When the conclave met to elect a successor to Urban VIII. it was soon discovered that some of the cardinals wished to elect a Pope friendly to Spain, while others favoured a pro-French Pope. At length, as neither party was sufficiently strong to ensure the required majority for its nominee, a more or less neutral candidate was found in the person of Cardinal Pamfili who took the title of Innocent X. (1644-55).* He was a man of

* Chinazzi, *Sede vacante per la morte del papa Urbano VIII. e conclave di Innocenzo X.*, 1904.

advanced years, who had served in many offices with success, and who possessed many of the qualifications required in a good ruler of the Church. Unfortunately, however, his flagrant nepotism did him much harm and gave occasion to ugly rumours utterly devoid of truth. Finding the papal treasury empty after his election and believing that the relatives of the late Pope were responsible for this, he took steps to secure a return from them; but they fled to France, where they placed themselves under the protection of Cardinal Mazarin, who succeeded in bringing about a reconciliation. Innocent X. restored order in the Papal States, punished the Duke of Parma for his crimes, especially for his supposed connexion with the murder of the Bishop of Castro, and maintained friendly relations with Venice, which he assisted against the Turks. He was deeply pained by the terms of the Peace of Westphalia (1648) against which his representatives had protested in vain, and which he condemned in the Bull, *Zelus Domus Dei* published in November 1648.

(c) The Religious Orders and the Counter-Reformation

NEW RELIGIOUS ORDERS

Hélyot, *Histoire des ordres monastiques religieux*, etc., 8 vols., 1714-19 Heimbucher, *Die Orden und Kongregationen der Katholischen Kirche*, 1907-8. Mabillon, *Annales Ordinis Sancti Benedicti*, 1703-39. Albers, *Zur Reformgeschichte des Benediktiner-ordens im 16 Jahrhundert* (*Stud. u-Mitteil*, 1900, 1901). Daurignac, *Histoire de la comp. de Jésus*, 1862. Crétineau-Joly, *Histoire religieuse, politique et littéraire de la comp. de Jésus*, 1859. Huber, *Der Jesuitenorden*, Duhr, *Jesuitenfabeln*, 1904. Abelly, *Vie du Vén. serviteur de Dieu, Vincent de Paul*, 1891. Bougaud-Brady, *History of St. Vincent de Paul*, etc., 1908. Boyle, *St. Vincent de Paul, and the Vincentians in Ireland, Scotland, and England*, 1909.

The religious orders, like most other institutions of the age preceding the Reformation, stood badly in need of re-organisation and reform. Various causes had combined to bring about a relaxation of the discipline prescribed by their holy founders, and to introduce a spirit of worldliness, that boded ill both for the individual members as well as for the success of the work for which these orders had been established. The interference of outside authorities lay or ecclesiastical in the appointment of superiors, the union of several houses under one superior, the accumulation of wealth, the habitual neglect of the superiors to make their visitations, and a general carelessness in the selection and training of the candidates to be admitted into the various institutions, were productive of disastrous results. It is difficult, however, to arrive at a correct estimate as to the extent of the evil, because the condition of affairs varied very much in the different religious orders and in the different provinces and houses of the same order. At all times a large proportion of the religious of both sexes recognised and deplored the spirit of laxity that had crept in, and laboured strenuously for a return to the old ideals long before the Lutheran campaign had made it necessary to choose between reform and suppression.

The Benedictines, who had done excellent work for the promotion of the spiritual and temporal welfare of the people amongst whom they laboured, suffered more than any other body from the interference of lay patrons in the appointment of abbots, as well as from the want of any central authority capable of controlling individual houses and of insisting upon the observance of the rules and constitution. Various efforts were made, however, to introduce reforms during the sixteenth century. In France the most important of these reforms was that begun in the abbey of St. Vannes by the abbot, Didier de la Cour. Recognising the sad condition of affairs he laboured incessantly to bring about a return to the strict rule of St. Benedict. His efforts were approved by Clement VIII. in 1604. Many houses in France having accepted the reform, it was resolved to unite them into one congregation under the patronage of St. Maur, the disciple of St. Benedict.* The new congregation of St. Maur was sanctioned by Louis XIII. and by Pope Gregory XV. (1621). The Maurists devoted themselves to the study of the sacred sciences, more especially to history, liturgy and patrology, and set an example of thorough scholarship which won for them the praise of both friends and foes. The names of D'Achéry, Mabillon, Ruinart, Martène, Thierry, Lami and Bouquet are not likely to be forgotten so long as such works as the *Amplissima Collectio Veterum Scriptorum, Thesaurus Anecdotorum, Gallia Christiana, Histoire Littéraire de la France, De Re Diplomatica, L'Art de vérifier les dates,* the *Recueil des historiens des Gaules,* etc., survive to testify to the labours and research of the Congregation of St. Maur.†

The reform movement among the Dominicans had made itself manifest from the days of Raymond of Capua (1390), who ordered that in every province there should be at least one house where the rule of St. Dominic might be observed in its original strictness. The success of the reform varied in the different countries and even in the different houses of the same province, but in the sixteenth century the general tendency was undoubtedly upwards. The religious rebellion inflicted serious losses on the order and led to the almost complete extinction of provinces that once were flourishing; but the Spanish and Portuguese discoveries in America and the spread of the missionary movement opened up for the order new fields, where its members were destined to do lasting service to religion and to win back in the New World more than they had lost in the Old. Discipline among the Cistercians, too, had become relaxed, but a general improvement set in which led to the formation of new congregations, the principal of which were the Congregation of the Feuillants approved by Sixtus V.

* *Histoire du Vén Didier de la Cour, réformateur des Bénédictins,* 1772
† De Lama, *Bibliothèque des écrivains de la congrégation de St. Maur,* 1882.

THE COUNTER-REFORMATION

(1587), and of the Trappists, which take their name from the monastery of La Trappe and owe their origin to the zealous efforts of the Abbot de Rancé (1626-1700).

The Franciscans were divided already into the Observants and the Conventuals, but even among the Observants the deteriorating influence of the age had made itself felt. Matteo di Bassi set himself in the convent of Monte Falco to procure a complete return to the original rule of St. Francis, and proceeded to Rome to secure the approbation of Clement VII. In 1528 by the Bull, *Religionis Zelus* the Pope permitted himself and his followers to separate from the Observants, to wear the hood (*cappuccio*, hence the name Capuchins*) which Matteo claimed to have been the dress of St. Francis, to wear the beard, to found separate houses in Italy, and to preach to the people. Soon the Capuchins spread through Italy, and so popular did they become that Gregory XIII. withdrew the regulations by which they were forbidden to found separate houses outside of Italy. The new order suffered many trials more especially after the apostasy of its vicar-general Ochino in 1544, but with the blessing of God these difficulties were overcome. The Capuchins rendered invaluable service to religion by their simple straightforward style of preaching so opposed as it was to the literary vapourings that passed for sermons at the time, by their familiar intercourse with the poor whom they assisted in both spiritual and temporal misfortunes, by their unswerving loyalty to the Pope and by the work they accomplished on the foreign missions, more especially in those lands which had once been the glory of the Church but where religion had been extinguished almost completely by the domination of the Saracen.

The revival was not confined, however, merely to a reform of the older religious orders. The world had changed considerably since the constitutions of these bodies had been formulated by their holy founders. New con-

* Da Forli, *Annali Cappuccini*, 1882.

ditions and new dangers necessitated the employment of new weapons and new methods for the defence of religion. Fortunately a band of zealous men were raised up by God to grapple with the problems of the age, and to lay the foundation of religious societies, many of which were destined to confer benefits on religion hardly less permanent and less valuable than had been conferred in other times by such distinguished servants of God as St. Benedict, St. Dominic, and St. Francis of Assisi.

The Theatines, so called from Chieti (Theate) the diocese of Peter Caraffa, had their origin in a little confraternity founded by Gaetano di Tiene* a Venetian, who gathered around him a few disciples, all of them like himself zealous for the spiritual improvement of both clergy and people (1524). During a visit to Rome Gaetano succeeded in eliciting the sympathy of Peter Caraffa (then bishop of Theate and afterwards cardinal and Pope) and in inducing him to become the first superior of the community. The institution was approved by Clement VII. in 1524. Its founders aimed at introducing a higher standard of spiritual life amongst both clergy and laity by means of preaching and by the establishment of charitable institutions. The order spread rapidly in Italy, where it did much to save the people from the influence of Lutheranism, in Spain where it was assisted by Philip II., in France where Cardinal Mazarin acted as its patron, and in the foreign missions, especially in several parts of Asia, the Theatines won many souls to God.

The Regular Clerics of St. Paul, better known as the Barnabites from their connexion with the church of St. Barnabas at Milan, were founded by St. Anthony Maria Zaccaria† of Cremona, Bartholomew Ferrari and Jacopo Morigia. Shocked by the low state of morals then prevalent in so many Italian cities, these holy men gathered around them a body of zealous young priests,

---

* Dumortier, *Saint Gaëtan di Thiene*, 1882.

† Dubois, *Le bienheureux A. M. Zaccaria fondateur des Barnabites*, 1896.

THE COUNTER-REFORMATION 223

who aimed at inducing the people by means of sermons and instructions to take advantage of the sacrament of Penance. The order was approved by Clement VII. in 1533, and received many important privileges from his successors. Its members worked in complete harmony with the secular clergy and in obedience to the commands of the bishops. They bound themselves not to seek or accept any preferment or dignity unless at the express direction of the Pope. In Milan they were beloved by St. Charles Borromeo who availed himself freely of their services, and they were invited to Annecy by St. Francis de Sales. Several houses of the Barnabites were established in Italy, France, and Austria. In addition to their work of preaching and instructing the people they established many flourishing colleges, and at the request of the Pope undertook charge of some of the foreign missions.

The founder of the Oblates was St. Charles Borromeo* (1538-84) who was created cardinal by his uncle Pius IV., at the age of twenty-three, and who during his comparatively short life did more for the reform of the Church and for the overthrow of Protestantism than any individual of his age. It was due mainly to his exertions that the Council of Trent was re-convoked, and to his prudent advice that it was carried to a successful conclusion. Once the decrees of the Council had received the approval of the Pope St. Charles spared no pains to see that they were put into execution not only in his own diocese of Milan but throughout the entire Church. For a long time personal government of his diocese was impossible as his presence in Rome was insisted upon by the Pope; but as soon as he could secure permission he hastened to Milan, where he repressed abuses with a stern hand, introduced regular diocesan and provincial synods, visited in person the most distant parts of the diocese, won back thousands who had gone over to heresy in the valleys of Switzer-

* Sylvain, *Histoire de St. Charles Borromée*, 3 vols., 1884.

land, and defended vigorously the rights and the liberties of the Church against the Spanish representatives. In all his reforms he was supported loyally by the religious orders, more especially by the Jesuits and the Barnabites, with whom he maintained at all times the most friendly relations. At the same time he felt the need of a community of secular priests, who while remaining under the authority of the bishop would set an example of clerical perfection, and who would be ready at the request of the bishop to volunteer for the work that was deemed most pressing. He was particularly anxious that such a body should undertake the direction of the diocesan seminary, and should endeavour to send forth well educated and holy priests. With these objects in view he established the Oblates in 1578, and the community fully justified his highest expectations.

The Oratorians* were established by St. Philip Neri (1515-95) the reformer and one of the patrons of Rome. He was a native of Florence, who when still a young man turned his back upon a promising career in the world in order to devote himself entirely to the service of God. Before his ordination he laboured for fifteen years visiting the sick in the hospitals, assisting the poorer pilgrims, and instructing the young. He formed a special confraternity, and gathered around him a body of disciples both cleric and lay. After his ordination they were accustomed to hold their conferences in a little room (*Oratorium,* Oratory) over the church of St. Girolmao. Here sermons and instructions were given on all kind of subjects, particularly on the Sacred Scriptures, the writings of the Fathers, and the leading events in the history of the Church. The society was approved by Gregory XIII. (1575) under the title of the Congregation of the Oratory. It was to be composed of secular priests living together under a rule, but bound by no special vows. St. Philip Neri was convinced that the style of preaching in vogue at the time was responsible

* Perraud, *L'Oratoire de France au XVIIe et au XVIIIe siècle.*

in great measure for the decline of religion and morality. Being a man of sound education himself he insisted that his companions should devote themselves to some particular department of ecclesiastical knowledge, and should give the people the fruits of their study. Baronius for example, the author of the celebrated *Annales Ecclesiastici,* is said to have preached for thirty years on the history of the Church. In this way St. Philip provided both for sound scholarship and useful instruction. Many branches of the Oratory were founded in Italy, Spain, Portugal, and in the Spanish and Portuguese colonies in South America.

Recognising the need for an improvement in the education and lives of the French clergy and mindful of the benefits conferred on Rome by the community of St. Philip Neri, the Abbé, afterwards Cardinal, Pierre de Bérulle determined to found an Oratory in Paris.* The Paris Oratorians were a community of secular priests bound by no special vows, but living under a common rule with the object of fulfilling as perfectly as possible the obligations they had undertaken at their ordination. The project received the warm support of Cardinal Richelieu and was approved by Paul V. in 1513. At the time clerical education in Paris and throughout France was in a condition of almost hopeless confusion. The French Oratorians, devoted as they were themselves to study, determined to organise seminaries on the plan laid down by the Council of Trent, and to take charge of the administration of such institutions. In philosophy the Oratory produced scholars such as Malebranche, in theology Thomassin and Morin, in Scripture Houbigant and Richard Simon, and in sacred eloquence such distinguished preachers as Lajeune and Massillon. The Oratorians survived the stormy days of the Jansenist struggle though the peace of the community was disturbed at times by the action of a few of its members, but it went down before the wild onslaught of the

* Perraud, *L'Oratoire de France au XVIIe et au XVIIIe siècle,* 1866.

Revolution. It was revived, however, by Père Gratry in 1852.

The Brothers of Charity were founded by a Portuguese,* who having been converted by a sermon of St. John d'Avila, devoted himself to the relief of human suffering in every form. On account of his great charity and zeal for souls he received the surname, St. John of God. He gathered around him a band of companions who assisted him in caring the sick in the hospital he had founded at Granada. After his death in 1550 the work that he had begun was carried on by his disciples, whose constitutions were approved by Pius V. in 1572. Soon through the generosity of Philip II. and of the Spanish nobles hospitals were established in various cities of Spain, and placed under the control of the Brothers of St. John of God. They were invited by the Pope to open a house in Rome, and they went also to Paris on the invitation of the queen (1601). At the time of the French Revolution they had charge of forty hospitals, from all of which they were expelled. The founder was canonised in 1690, and named as patron of hospitals by Leo XIII. in 1898.

The Piarists or Patres Piarum Scholarum were founded by St. Joseph Calasanza† (1556-1648), who had been vicar-general of the diocese of Urgel in Spain, an office which he resigned in order to betake himself to Rome. Here he began to gather the poorer children for instruction, and as the teachers were unwilling to assist him unless they were given extra remuneration, he opened a free school in Rome in 1597. The school was taught by himself and two or three priests whom he had interested in the work. From these unpretentious beginnings sprang the society of the Fathers of the Pious Schools. The object of the society, which was composed of priests, was the education of the young both in primary and secondary schools. The society was approved by Paul

---

* Girard, *La vie de St. Jean de Dieu*, 1691.
† Hubert, *Der hl. Joseph Calasanza, stifter der frommen Schulen*, 1886.

THE COUNTER-REFORMATION

V., and established finally as a recognised institution by Gregory XV. (1621). It spread rapidly in Italy, Austria, and Poland. Somewhat akin to the Piarists were the Fathers of Christian Doctrine, founded by Caesar de Bus for the purpose of educating the young. The society was composed of priests, and received the approval of Clement VIII. in 1597. Later on it united with the Somaschans, who had been established by St. Jerome Aemilian with a similar purpose, but on account of certain disputes that arose the two bodies were separated in 1647.

The Brothers of the Christian Schools were founded by John Baptist de la Salle* (1651-1719). The founder was a young priest of great ability, who had read a distinguished course in arts and theology before his ordination. Having been called upon to assist in conducting a free school opened at Rheims in 1679 he threw himself into the work with vigour, devoting nearly all his energies to the instruction of the teachers. These he used to gather around him after school hours to encourage them in their work, to suggest to them better methods of imparting knowledge and generally to correct any defects that he might have noticed during the course of his daily visits to the schools. In this way he brought together a body of young men interested in the education of the children of the poor, from which body were developed the Brothers of the Christian Schools. At first he intended that some of the congregation should be priests, but later on he changed his mind, and made it a rule of the institute that none of the Brothers should become priests, nor should any priest be accepted as a novice. For a long time the holy founder was engaged in an uphill struggle during which the very existence of the institute was imperilled. Distrusted by some of the ecclesiastical authorities,

---

* Ravelet-O'Meara, *The Life of the Blessed John Baptist de la Salle*, 1888. Lucard, *Annales de l'Institut des Frères des Écoles Chrétiennes*, 1883.

attacked by enemies on all sides, deserted by a few of his own most trusted disciples, a man of less zeal and determination would have abandoned the project in despair. But de la Salle was not discouraged. He composed a constitution for his followers, and in 1717 he held a general chapter, in which he secured the election of a superior-general. From this time the Institute of Christian Brothers progressed by leaps and bounds. The holy founder of the society was a pioneer in the work of primary education. In teaching, in the grading of the pupils, and in constructing and furnishing the schools new methods were followed; more liberty was given in the selection of programmes to suit the districts in which schools were opened; normal schools were established to train the young teachers for their duties, and care was taken that religious and secular education should go forward hand in hand. The society spread rapidly in France, more especially after it had received the approval of Louis XV., and had been recognised as a religious congregation by Benedict XIII. (1725). During the Revolution the society was suppressed, and the Brothers of the Christian Schools suffered much rather than prove disloyal to the Pope. In 1803 the institute was re-organised, and since that time houses have been opened in nearly every part of the world. John Baptist de la Salle was canonised by Leo XIII. in 1900.

The Congregation of the Priests of the Mission, better known as Lazarists from the priory of St. Lazare which they occupied in Paris, and as Vincentians from the name of their founder, St. Vincent de Paul, was established in 1624. St. Vincent was born at Pouy in Gascony in 1576, received his early education at a Franciscan school, and completed his theological studies at the University of Toulouse, where he was ordained in 1600. Four years later the ship on which he journeyed from Marseilles having been attacked by Barbary pirates, he was taken prisoner and brought to Tunis, where he was sold as a slave. He succeeded in making his

THE COUNTER-REFORMATION

escape from captivity (1607) by converting his master, a Frenchman who had deserted his country and his religion. He went to Rome, from which he was despatched on a mission to the French Court, and was appointed almoner to queen Margaret of Valois. Later on he became tutor to the family of the Count de Gondi, the master of the French galleys. During his stay there St. Vincent found time to preach to the peasants on the estate of his employer, and to visit the prisoners condemned to the galleys. The splendid results of his labours among these classes bore such striking testimony to the success of his missions that St. Vincent was induced to found a congregation of clergymen for this special work. Something of this kind was required urgently in France at this period. The absence of seminaries and the want of any properly organised system of clerical education had produced their natural consequences on the clergy. In the country districts particularly, the priests had neither the knowledge nor the training that would enable them to discharge their sacred functions. From this it followed that the people were not instructed, and the sacraments were neglected.

By opening a house in Paris in 1624 St. Vincent took the first practical step towards the foundation of a religious congregation, that was destined to renew and to strengthen religion in France. Later on the society received the sanction of the Archbishop of Paris,* and of Louis XIII., and finally it was approved by Urban VIII. in the Bull, *Salvatoris Nostri,* dated 12th January 1632. In the same year St. Vincent took possession of the priory of St. Lazare placed at his disposal by the canons regular of St. Victor. The Congregation of the Mission was to be a congregation of secular clergymen, bound by simple religious vows. Its principal work, besides the sanctification of its own members, was to give missions to the poor particularly in country districts, and to promote a high standard of clerical life.

* Paris became an archiepiscopal See in 1622.

The bishops of France were delighted with the programme of the new congregation. Invitations poured in from all sides on the disciples of St. Vincent asking them to undertake missions, and wherever they went their labours were attended with success. As a rule St. Vincent established a confraternity of charity in the parishes that he visited to help the poor and above all to look after the homeless orphans.*

It was not long until he discovered that, however successful his missions might be, they could effect little permanent good unless the priests in charge of the parishes were determined to continue the work that had been begun, and to reap the harvest which the missioners had planted. At that time there were no seminaries in France, so that candidates for the priesthood were ordained on the completion of their university course without any special training for their sacred office. At the request of some of the bishops St. Vincent determined to give retreats to those who were preparing for Holy Orders. At first these retreats lasted only ten days, but they were productive of such splendid results that they were extended to several months. Finally they led to the establishment of clerical seminaries, of which institutions St. Vincent and his associates took charge in several of the dioceses of France. Before his death they had control of eleven French seminaries; and at the time of the Revolution fully one-third of the diocesan seminaries were in the hands of his disciples.† By means of retreats for the clergy, and spiritual conferences organised for their improvement St. Vincent kept in close touch with those whom he had trained, and afforded them an opportunity of renewing their fervour and completing their education.

It was fortunate for France that God had raised up a man so prudent and zealous as St. Vincent to be a guide to both priests and people during the difficult times

* **Lorti**, *Saint Vincent de Paul et sa mission sociale*, 1880.
† **Degert**, *Histoire des séminaires français*, 1912.

THE COUNTER-REFORMATION 231

through which the country was then passing. From without, danger threatened the Church on the side of the Huguenot heretics, and from within, Jansenism and Gallicanism bade fair to captivate the sympathy of both clergy and people. At first St. Vincent was on friendly terms with the Abbot de St. Cyran, the leader of the Jansenists in France, but once he realised the dangerous nature of his opinions and the errors contained in such publications as the *Augustinus* of Jansen and the *Frequent Communion* of Arnauld he threw himself vigorously into the campaign against Jansenism. At court, in his conferences with the bishops and priests, in university circles, and in the seminaries he exposed the insidious character of its tenets. At Rome he urged the authorities to have recourse to stern measures, and in France he strove hard to procure acceptance of the Roman decisions. And yet in all his work against the Jansenists there was nothing of the bitterness of the controversialist. He could strike hard when he wished, but he never forgot that charity is a much more effective weapon than violence. In his own person he set the example of complete submission to the authority of the Pope, and enjoined such submission on his successors. St. Vincent died in 1660. His loss was mourned not merely by his own spiritual children, the Congregation of the Mission and the Sisters of Charity, but by the poor of Paris and of France to whom he was a generous benefactor, as well as by the bishops and clergy to whom he had been a friend and a guide. To his influence more than to any other cause is due the preservation of France to the Church in the seventeenth century.

But the work of the Congregation of the Mission was not confined to France. Its disciples spread into Italy, Spain, Portugal, Poland, Ireland, and England. They went as missionaries to Northern Africa to labour among the Barbary pirates by whom St. Vincent had been captured, to Madagascar, to some of the Portuguese colonies in the East, to China, and to the territories of the Sultan. At the Revolution most of their houses in France were destroyed, and many of the Vincentians suffered martyrdom. When the worst storms, however, had passed the congregation was re-established in France, and its members laboured earnestly in the spirit of its holy founder to recover much of what had been lost.

The founder of the Sulpicians was Jean Jacques Olier* (1608-57) the friend and disciple of St. Vincent de Paul. Impressed with the importance of securing a good education and training for the clergy, he and a couple of companions retired to a house in Vaugirard (1641), where they were joined by a few seminarists, who desired to place themselves under his direction. Later on he was offered the parish of St. Sulpice, then one of the worst parishes in Paris from the point of view of religion and morality. The little community of priests working under the rules compiled by Olier for their guidance soon changed completely the face of the entire district. House to house visitations were introduced; sermons suitable to the needs of the people were given; catechism classes were established, and in a very short time St. Sulpice became the model parish of the capital.

In 1642 a little seminary was opened and rules were drawn up for the direction of the students, most of whom attended the theological lectures at the Sorbonne. Priests and students formed one community, and as far as possible followed the same daily routine. During their free time the students assisted in the work of the parish by visiting the sick and taking charge of classes for catechism. At first Olier had no intention of founding seminaries throughout France. His aim was rather to make St. Sulpice a national seminary, from which young priests might go forth properly equipped, and qualified to found diocesan institutions on similar lines if their superiors favoured such an undertaking. But

---

* Faillon, *Vie de M. Olier*, 3 vols., 1873. Thompson, *Life of Jean Jacques Olier*.

THE COUNTER-REFORMATION 233

yielding to the earnest solicitations of several of the bishops he opened seminaries in several parts of France, and entrusted their administration to members of his own community. The first of these was founded at Nantes in 1648. During the lifetime of the founder a few of the Sulpicians were despatched to Canada, where they established themselves at Montreal, and laboured zealously for the conversion of the natives. Like St. Vincent, the founder of the Sulpicians worked incessantly against Jansenism, and impressed upon his followers the duty of prompt obedience to the bishops and to the Pope, lessons which they seem never to have forgotten. The Sulpicians according to their constitution are a community of secular priests bound by no special religious vows.

The religious order, however, that did most to stem the advancing tide of heresy and to raise the drooping spirits of the Catholic body during the saddest days of the sixteenth century was undoubtedly the Society of Jesus, founded by St. Ignatius of Loyola.[*] By birth St. Ignatius was a Spaniard, and by profession he was a soldier. Having been wounded at the siege of Pampeluna in 1521 he turned his mind during the period of his convalescence to the study of spiritual books, more particularly the Lives of the Saints. As he read of the struggles some of these men had sustained and of the victories they had achieved he realised that martial fame was but a shadow in comparison with the glory of the saints, and he determined to desert the army of Spain to enrol himself amongst the servants of Christ. With the overthrow of the Moorish kingdom of Granada fresh in his mind, it is not strange that he should have dreamt of the still greater triumph that might be secured by attacking the Mahomedans in the very seat of their power, and by inducing them to abandon the law of the Prophet for the Gospel of the Christians. With the intention of preparing himself

[*] Thompson, *Life of St. Ignatius*, 1910. Clair, *La vie de S. Ignace*, 1894.

for this work he bade good-bye to his friends and the associations of his youth, and betook himself to a lonely retreat at Manresa near Montserrat, where he gave himself up to meditation and prayer under the direction of a Benedictine monk. The result of his stay at Manresa and of his communings with God are to be seen in the *Spiritual Exercises of St. Ignatius,* a work which in the hands of his disciples has done wonders for the conversion and perfection of souls, and which in the opinion of those competent to judge has no serious rivals except the Bible and the Imitation of Christ. From Manresa he journeyed to the Holy Land to visit its sacred shrines, and to labour for the conversion of its infidel conquerors, but having found it impossible to undertake this work at the time he returned to Europe.

Realising that his defective education was a serious obstacle to the establishment of the religious order that he contemplated, he went to work with a will to acquire the rudiments of grammar. When this had been accomplished successfully he pursued his higher studies at Alcalá, Salamanca, and Paris, where he graduated as doctor in 1534. But while earnest in the pursuit of knowledge he never forgot that knowledge was but a means of preparing himself for the accomplishment of the mission to which God had called him. While at Paris he gathered around him a group of students, Francis Xavier, Lainez, Salmerón, Bobadilla, Rodríguez and Faber, with which body Lejay, Codure and Broët were associated at a later period. On the feast of the Assumption (1534) Ignatius and his companions wended their way to the summit of Montmartre overlooking the city of Paris, where having received Holy Communion they pledged themselves to labour in the Holy Land. Having discovered that this project was almost impossible they determined to place themselves at the disposal of the Pope. In Rome Ignatius explained the objects and rules of the proposed society to Paul III. and his advisers. In September 1540 the approval of the Pope

THE COUNTER-REFORMATION 235

was obtained though with certain restrictions, which were abolished in 1543, and in the following year Ignatius was elected first general of the Society of Jesus.

St. Ignatius had the greatest respect for the older religious orders, the Benedictines, the Dominicans, and the Franciscans, to all of which he was deeply indebted; but he believed that the new conditions under which his followers would be called upon to do battle for Christ necessitated new rules and a new constitution. The Society of Jesus was not to be a contemplative order seeking only the salvation of its own members. Its energies were not to be confined to any particular channel. No extraordinary fasts or austerities were imposed, nor was the solemn chanting of the office or the use of a particular dress insisted upon. The society was to work "for the greater glory of God" in whatever way the circumstances demanded. On one thing only did St. Ignatius lay peculiar emphasis, and that was the absolute necessity of obedience to superiors in all things lawful, and above all of obedience to the Pope. The wisdom of this injunction is evident enough at all times, but particularly in an age when religious authority, even that of the successor of St. Peter, was being called in question by so many. Members of the society were forbidden to seek or accept any ecclesiastical dignities or preferments.

The constitution* of the Society of Jesus was not drawn up with undue haste. St. Ignatius laid down rules for his followers, but it was only when the value of these regulations had been tested by practice that he embodied them in the constitution, endorsed by the first general congregation held in 1558. According to the constitution complete administrative authority is vested in the general, who is elected by a general congregation, and holds office for life. He is assisted by a council consisting of a representative from each province. The provincials, rectors of colleges, heads of professed

* *Constitutiones Societatis Jesu Latine et Hispanice*, 1892.

houses, and masters of novices are appointed by the general, usually, however, only for a definite number of years, while all minor officials are appointed by the provincial. The novitiate lasts two years during which time candidates for admission to the order are engaged almost entirely in prayer, meditation, and spiritual reading. When the novitiate has been completed the scholasticate begins. Students are obliged to read a course in arts and philosophy and to teach in some of the colleges of the society, after which they proceed to the study of theology. When the theological course has been ended they are admitted as coadjutors or professed members according to their ability and conduct. Between these two bodies, the coadjutors and the professed, there is very little difference, except that the professed in addition to the ordinary vows pledge themselves to go wherever the Pope may send them, and besides, it is from this body as a rule that the higher officials of the society are selected. Lay brothers are also attached to the society.

When the Society of Jesus was founded, Protestantism had already made great strides in Northern Europe, and though the Latin countries were not then affected no man could foresee what change a decade of years might bring. St. Ignatius adopted the best precautions against the spread of heresy. While he himself remained in Rome engaged in organising the members of his society and in establishing colleges and charitable institutions, he sent his followers to all parts of Italy. Bishops availed themselves freely of their services as preachers and teachers. Colleges were opened in Venice, Naples, Bologna, Florence, and in many other leading cities. St. Charles Borromeo became the patron and defender of the society in Milan. Everywhere the labours of the Jesuits led to a great religious revival, while by means of their colleges they strengthened the faith of the rising generation. In Spain, too, the home of St. Ignatius the Jesuits received a friendly welcome.

THE COUNTER-REFORMATION 237

Their colleges were crowded with students, as were their churches with the faithful. Difficulties, indeed, arose owing to the tendency of some of the Spanish Jesuits to have none but Spanish superiors, but with a little prudence these difficulties were overcome in 1593. Most of the best known writers on ecclesiastical subjects, Vasquez, Suarez, De Lugo, and Ripalda on Dogmatic Theology, Sanchez on Moral Theology, and Maldonatus and Pereira on Scripture belonged to the Spanish province.

In France the society met with serious difficulties at first. Hatred of Spain and of everything that savoured of Spanish origin, dislike of what was considered the excessive loyalty of the society to the Pope, and jealousy on the part of the University of Paris were the principal obstacles that were to be overcome. But notwithstanding these the Jesuits found a home in Paris, where they opened the Collège de Clermont (Louis-le-Grand), and they founded similar colleges in several of the leading cities of France. In the struggle against the Calvinists they were of great assistance to the Catholic body. The progress of their numerous colleges and the influence which they acquired over the young men roused the fierce opposition of the University, but being befriended by the court, where they were retained as royal confessors, the Jesuits were enabled to hold their ground. During the wars of the League against Henry III. and Henry of Navarre, though their position was one of extreme delicacy, the prudent action of their general, Aquaviva, in recommending his subjects to respect the consciences of both parties saved the situation. They were, however, expelled from Paris in 1594, but Henry IV. allowed them to return in 1603.

In the German States, Hungary, and Poland, where the fate of Catholicity seemed trembling in the balance, the Jesuit Fathers stayed what threatened to be a triumphal progress for Protestantism. St. Ignatius soon despatched some of his disciples to the scene of conflict under the leadership of the Blessed Peter Canisius.* By his sermons, his lectures as professor, his prudent suggestions to those in authority, as well as by his controversial writings, and more particularly his celebrated Catechism, Canisius did more to stay the advance of Protestantism in Germany than any single individual of his age. Colleges were founded in Vienna, Ingoldstadt, Treves, Mainz, and in most of the cities of Germany that were not subject to the Protestant princes. From these colleges went forth young men who were determined to resist the further encroachments of heresy. Maximilian of Bavaria and the Emperor Ferdinand II., both of whom took such a prominent part in the Catholic Counter-Reformation, were pupils of the Jesuits, and were but types of the men who left their colleges. In Hungary, too, and in Poland the tide was turned in favour of the Catholic Church mainly by the exertions of the Jesuits. In Ireland, England and Scotland, in the Netherlands, and Sweden, in a word wherever Catholic interests were endangered, the Jesuits risked their lives in defence of the Catholic religion. It is on account of the defeats that they inflicted on heresy at this period that the hatred of the Jesuits is so deep-rooted and so universal amongst Protestants even to the present day.

The Ursulines, so called from their patron St. Ursula, began as a religious association of pious ladies formed by Angela de' Merici† (Angela of Brescia) in 1537. At first the aim of the association was to reclaim fallen women, to visit the sick, and to educate the young. The members lived in their own homes according to a scheme of life drawn up for their guidance, meeting only for certain spiritual exercises. In 1535 the foundress succeeded in bringing a few of them together into a small community. After her death in 1540 the com-

* Duhr, *Geschichte der Jesuiten in den Ländern Deutscher Zunge*, Bd. i., 1907.

† O'Reilly, *Life of St. Angela*, 1880. Meer, *Die ersten Schwestern des Ursulinenordens*, 1897.

THE COUNTER-REFORMATION

munity increased in numbers, and was approved by Paul III., who allowed the Ursulines to change their rules according to circumstances. For a long time the Ursulines did not spread outside Brescia, but as their work became known, particularly their work as educationalists, they were invited to other parts of Italy. In Milan they had a warm friend in the person of its Cardinal Archbishop, St. Charles Borromeo. The first community of the Ursulines was formed in France by Madame de Beuve. A rule was drawn up by Father Gonterey, S.J., and others of his society, and approved by Paul V. (1612). In a comparatively short time the Ursulines spread over most of the Catholic countries of Europe, so that nearly all the most modern and best equipped schools for Catholic girls were in their hands. In 1639 they went to Canada where they opened the convent known as the Hôtel-Dieu at Quebec, and in 1727 they settled in New Orleans.

St. Teresa* (1515-82) is the reformer rather than the foundress of the Carmelite nuns. Being anxious from an early age to follow her religious vocation, much against the wishes of her father she entered the convent of the Carmelite nuns at Avila (1535). After her profession she fell ill, and for years was subject to excruciating torture. During this period she turned her mind completely to spiritual subjects, and was visited by God with most extraordinary marks of divine favour, an account of which is to be found in her life written by herself, in her *Relations,* and in many other of her works. She determined to return to the primitive austerity of the Carmelite rule, and in 1562 she founded the first convent of Discalced Carmelite nuns at Avila. Through her exertions other convents of the order adopted the reform, and in 1580 the existence of the Discalced Carmelites as a separate order was approved. She died in 1582, and forty years later she was canonised by Gregory XV.

* *Autobiography of St. Teresa,* tr. from the French by B. Zimmerman, 1904.

The Sisters of the Visitation were established by St. Francis de Sales* and St. Frances de Chantal.† St. Francis de Sales (1567-1622), so called from the castle of Sales in Savoy at which he was born, made his rhetoric and philosophical studies at Paris under the Jesuits. From Paris he went to Padua for law, and having received his diploma he returned to his native country, where his father had secured for him a place as senator and had arranged a very desirable marriage. But St. Francis, feeling that he had been called by God to another sphere of life, threw up his position at the bar, accepted the office of provost of the chapter of Geneva, and received Holy Orders (1593). A great part of the diocese of Geneva was at this time overrun by the heretics. St. Francis threw himself with ardour into the work of converting those who had fallen away especially in the district of Le Chablais, where he won over thousands to the faith. He became coadjutor-bishop of Geneva, and on the death of his friend Claude de Granier he was appointed to the See (1602). In conjunction with Madam de Chantal he established a community of women at Annecy in 1610. His idea at first was that the little community should not be bound by the enclosure, but should devote themselves to their own sanctification and to the visitation of the sick and the poor. Objections, however, having been raised against such an innovation, he drew up for the community a rule based mainly on the rule of St. Augustine. In 1618 the society received recognition as a religious order under the title of the Order of the Visitation of the Blessed Virgin. The order undertook the work of educating young girls as well as of visiting the sick. It spread rapidly in Italy, France, Germany, Poland, and later on in the United States.

* Hamon, *Vie de St. François de Sales*, 2 vols., 1875.

† Bougaud, *Histoire de Ste. J. F. Chantal et des origines de la Visitation*, 1899.

THE COUNTER-REFORMATION 241

The Sisters of Charity,* or the Grey Sisters as they were called, were founded by St. Vincent de Paul. While St. Vincent was curé of Châtillon-les-Dombes he established in the parish a confraternity of charitable ladies for the care of the sick, the poor, and the orphans. The experiment was so successful that he founded similar confraternities in Paris, and wherever he gave missions throughout the country. Having found, however, that in Paris the ladies of charity were accustomed to entrust the work to their servants he brought a number of young girls from the country, who could be relied upon to carry out his wishes. These he looked after with a special solicitude, and in 1633 Madam Le Gras took a house in Paris, where she brought together a few of the most promising of them to form a little community. In 1642 after the community had moved into a house opposite St. Lazare, some of the sisters were allowed to take vows. The Sisters of Charity have been at all times exceedingly popular in France. By their schools, their orphanages, their hospitals, and by their kindness to the poor and the suffering they won for themselves a place in the hearts of the French people. For a while during the worst days of the Revolution their work was suspended, and their communities were disbanded; but their suppression was deplored so generally that in 1801 the Superioress was commanded to re-organise the society. Outside France the Sisters of Charity had several houses in Poland, Switzerland, Spain, and Germany.

Mary Ward † (1585-1645) was born of a good Catholic family in England. She joined the Poor Clares at St. Omer in 1600, but, preferring an active to a contemplative life, she gathered around her a few companions, and formed a little community at St. Omer mainly for the work of education. According to her plan, which was derived in great measure from the constitution of the Society of Jesus (hence the name

---

* Marcel, *Les Soeurs de Charité*, 1888.
† Salome, *Mother Mary Ward, a Foundress of the 17th Century*, 1901.

Jesuitesses given to her followers by opponents), her sisters were not bound by the enclosure, were not to wear any distinctive dress, and were to be subject directly only to Rome. Serious objections were raised immediately against such an institute, particularly as Pius V. had declared expressly that the enclosure and solemn vows were essential conditions for the recognition of religious communities of women. Branches were opened in the Netherlands, Austria, and Italy under the patronage of the highest civil authorities. As the opponents of the community continued their attacks the foundress was summoned to Rome to make her defence (1629), but in the following year the decree of suppression was issued. The house in Munich was allowed to continue, and at the advice of the Pope she opened a house in Rome. The principal change introduced was that the houses should be subject to the bishops of the dioceses in which they were situated. At last in 1703, on the petition of Maximilian Emanuel of Bavaria and of Mary the wife of James II., the rule was approved formally by Clement XI. The society continued to spread especially in Bavaria. The followers of Mary Ward are designated variously, the Institute of Mary, Englische Fräulein, and Loreto Nuns from the name given to Rathfarnham, the mother-house of the Irish branch, founded by Frances Ball in 1821.

(d) The Thirty Years' War

See bibliography, chap. ii. (a). Klopp, *Der Dreissigjährige Krieg bis Zum Tode Gustav. Adolfs u.s.w.*, 3 Bde, 1891-6. Bougeant, *Histoire des guerres et des négociations qui précédèrent le traité de Westphalie*, 3 vols., 1751. Ritter, *Deutsche Geschichte im Zeitalter der Gegenreformation und des Dreissigjährigen Krieges*, 1889. Huber, *Geschichte Österreichs*, Bd. v., 1896. *Nunziaturberichte aus Deutschland*, 1892. De Meaux, *La réforme et la politique Française en Europe jusqu' à la paix de Westphalie*, 1889. *Cambridge Modern History*, vol. iii. (chap. iii.).

The Religious Peace of Augsburg (1555) did not put an end to the struggle between the Catholics and Protestants in Germany. Feeling on both sides was too intense to permit either party to be satisfied with the arrangement or to accept it as a permanent definition of their respective rights. The German Catholics were indignant that a party that had sprung up so recently and that had done such injury to their Church and country, should be rewarded for heresy and disloyalty to the Emperor by such concessions. Nor was their indignation likely to be appeased by the manner in which Lutheran and Calvinist preachers caricatured and denounced the doctrines and practices of the Catholic world. Possibly it was, however, the clause of the Augsburg Peace known as the *Ecclesiasticum Reservatum,* that gave rise to the most heated controversies, and played the greatest part in bringing about civil war. By this clause it was provided that in case any of the bishops and abbots passed over to the reformed religion they could not bring with them the ecclesiastical property attached to their office. The Lutherans, who had benefited so largely by such secessions from the Church in the past, objected to this clause at the Diet, and protested against the decision when their objections were overruled.

Having realised that the Emperor was unable or unwilling to prevent them they continued to act in open defiance of the *Ecclesiasticum Reservatum.* Where the territories of a Catholic bishop were situated in close proximity to the states of Protestant princes recourse was had to various devices to acquire the lands of the Church. Sometimes the bishop was induced to surrender them in return for a fixed grant or pension, sometimes the chapter was persuaded to elect as bishop some scion of a princely family, who was well-known to have leanings towards Protestantism, and in a few cases the bishops themselves solved the problem by seceding from the Catholic Church while continuing to administer the territories to which their episcopal office was their only title. In this way two archbishoprics and fourteen bishoprics, amongst them being such wealthy Sees as Magdeburg, Bremen, Brandenburg, and Osnabrück had passed into the hands of the Lutherans, and it required a very special effort to prevent two such important centres as Cologne and Aachen from meeting with a similar fate. Gebhard, Archbishop of Cologne, a man of scandalously immoral life, completed his infamous career by taking as his wife one who had been his concubine, announcing at the same time that he had gone over to Calvinism. The chapter of Cologne Cathedral backed by the people took steps to rid themselves of such a superior, and the chapter was supported warmly by both Pope and Emperor. Gebhard was obliged to escape to Strassburg in the cathedral of which he held a canonry, and where he succeeded in creating confusion. Two archbishops claimed the See of Strassburg, one loyal to the Catholic Church and one favouring Protestantism. This disgraceful contention went on for years, till at last the Protestant champion was induced to surrender on the payment of a large composition. The See of Aachen was seized by force in 1581, and was held for fifteen years, at the end of which the Protestants were obliged to abandon their claims.

Unfortunately for the Catholics the Emperors who succeeded Charles V. were not strong enough to deal with such a dangerous situation. Ferdinand I., sincere Catholic though he was, mindful of the terrible disasters brought upon his country by the religious wars, strove with all his might against their renewal. His successor Maximilian II. (1564-76) was so strongly inclined towards Protestantism that he made many concessions to the Protestants even in his own hereditary dominions. He invited distinguished Lutheran preachers to Vienna, conferred on Protestants influential positions at court, and gave permission for Protestant religious services at least to the nobles of Bohemia, Silesia, and Hungary. Several of the prince-bishops anxious to stand well with the Emperor attempted to introduce reforms in Catholic liturgy and Catholic

THE COUNTER-REFORMATION 245

practices without any reference to the Holy See. The alarming spread of Protestantism in Austria, Hungary, Bohemia, and Silesia, fostered as it was by the general policy of the Emperor, tended to make the position of the Catholic Church extremely insecure.*

But fortunately at the time a strong Catholic reaction began to make itself felt. The reforming decrees of the Council of Trent did not fail to produce a decided improvement in the condition of the bishops and clergy. The new religious orders, particularly the Jesuits, had thrown themselves into the work of defending the Catholic position, and the colleges established by the Jesuits were turning out the younger generation of Catholics well-equipped for the struggle that lay before them. The catechisms which the Jesuit preachers scattered broadcast through the country, and the attention paid by them to the proper religious instruction of the people helped to remove the bad impressions produced by the misrepresentations of the Lutherans, and tended to arouse a strong, healthy, educated Catholic opinion in public life. Fortunately, too, at the time when the Emperors were a danger rather than a protection to the Church, the rulers of Bavaria undertook boldly the defence of the old religion, and placed themselves at the head of the Catholic forces.† Albert V. (1550-79) insisted on the promulgation of the decrees of the Council of Trent, and made an oath of loyalty to the Catholic Church an indispensable condition for office in his kingdom. He favoured the Jesuits, encouraged their schools, and did everything in his power to strengthen Catholicism amongst his subjects. His policy was continued by Maximilian I. (1598-1651), who became the recognised leader of the advanced Catholic party in Germany.

This general unexpected revival, the success of which was shown by the fervour of the people, the unwilling-

* Lösche, *Geschichte des Protestantismus in Österreich*, 1902.
† Hartmann, *Der Prozess gegen die Protestantischen Landstände in Bayern unter Albrecht V.*, 1904.

ness of the authorities to make any further concessions, and the determination of all parties to insist on the strict observance of the *Ecclesiasticum Reservatum* filled the Protestants with such alarm that their princes began to insist on new guarantees. The Emperor, Rudolph II. (1576-1612), though, unlike his predecessor, a good Catholic, was a most incompetent ruler, devoting most of his time to alchemy and other such studies rather than to the work of government. He endeavoured to solve the religious difficulties in Silesia and Bohemia by yielding to the Protestant demands (1609), but the interference of his brother Matthias led to new complications, and finally to Rudolph's abdication of the sovereignty of Bohemia (1611). Frederick IV. of the Palatinate was a strong Protestant, and was closely connected with the reforming party in England, Holland, and France. He thought he saw in the strife between the members of the House of Habsburg an opportunity of improving the position of Protestantism in the empire, of weakening the claims of the House of Habsburg to the imperial dignity, and possibly also of establishing himself as ruler of a united Germany.

An incident that took place at Donauwörth,* a city near the Rhine, helped him to realise his scheme of a great Protestant federation. This city was almost exclusively Catholic in 1555, but in one way or another the Protestants had succeeded in improving their position till at last only the abbey church remained to the Catholics. Here on the Feast of Corpus Christi in the year 1606 the customary procession of the Blessed Sacrament was attacked and dispersed, and the Catholics were treated with the greatest cruelty. When the matter was brought before the Emperor the city was placed under the ban of the empire, and Maximilian I. of Bavaria was entrusted with the task of carrying out the decree. He advanced with a strong army, and captured the city. As the war indemnity could not be raised he retained

* Stieve, *Der Kampf um Donauwörth*, 1875.

THE COUNTER-REFORMATION 247

possession of it, restoring to the Catholics everything they had lost. Frederick IV. made a strong appeal to the Protestant princes to show their resentment at such an act of aggression, pointing out to them that the fate of Donauwörth would be the fate of all their territories unless they took united action. As a consequence when both parties met at the Diet of Regensburg (1608) the excitement was intense, and when the Emperor appealed to his princes for support against the Turks, the Protestants refused to lend their aid unless they received satisfactory explanations. The Catholics, encouraged by Maximilian, were equally unconciliatory, with the result that the Diet disbanded without having been able to arrive at an agreement.

A short time after the Diet most of the Protestant princes met at Ahausen and formed a confederation known as the *Union* (1608) at the head of which stood Frederick IV. of the Palatinate, while a little later a large number of the Catholic princes bound themselves together in the *League* and accepted Maximilian of Bavaria as their leader (1609). Thus Germany was divided once again into two hostile camps, and only a very trifling incident was required to plunge the country into another civil war. For a time it seemed as if the succession to the Duchy of Cleves was to be the issue that would lead to the catastrophe. Duke John William of Cleves had died without any direct heir, and as the religious issue was still undecided in his territory, the appointment of a successor was a matter of the greatest importance to both parties. The Emperor with the approval of the *League* nominated his brother Leopold as administrator, while the *Union*, having strengthened itself by an alliance with France, was prepared to take the field in favour of a Protestant. Henry IV. of France, anxious to turn the disputes that had broken out between the different members of the imperial family to the advantage of himself and his country, was actually on his way to take part in the campaign when he was assassinated. On his death both parties agreed to a temporary truce (1610), and thus the outbreak of the war was delayed for some time.

This delay was very fortunate for the Catholics in Germany. With such an Emperor as Rudolph pitted against a man like Henry IV. there could have been very little doubt about the issue. Even in his own territories Rudolph could not maintain his authority against his brother Matthias, in whose interest he was obliged to abdicate the throne of Bohemia (1611). On the death of Rudolph (1612) Matthias succeeded though not without considerable difficulty. As Emperor he showed himself much less favourable to the Protestants than he had been during the years when he was disputing with his brother, but, however well inclined, he was powerless to put an end to the division that existed or to control the policy of the *League* or the *Union*. The Duchy of Cleves was still an object of dispute. While the German Protestants invoked the aid of William of Orange and the Dutch Calvinists, the Catholics called in the forces of Spain. The Emperor could merely look on while his subjects allied themselves with foreigners to settle their own domestic troubles.

Meanwhile far more serious trouble was brewing in Bohemia, where the followers of Hus had blended with the disciples of Luther, and where in many centres there was a strong feeling against the Catholic Church. According to the concessions granted by Rudolph (1609), knights and free cities were at liberty to build Protestant churches, but a similar concession was not made to the subjects of Catholic lords. Regardless of or misinterpreting the terms of the concession, however, the Protestant tenants of the Archbishop of Prague and of the Abbot of Braunau built churches for their own use. The archbishop and abbot, considering themselves aggrieved, appealed to the imperial court. According to the decision of this court the church built on the lands of the archbishop was to be pulled down, and the other on the lands

THE COUNTER-REFORMATION 249

of the abbot was to be closed (1618). A deputation representing the Protestant party was appointed to interview the imperial representatives at Prague, and the reply to their remonstrances being regarded as unfavourable, the mob attacked the building, and hurled the councillors who were supposed to be responsible for it through the windows.

Under the direction of Count Thurn and some other Protestant nobles a provisional government was established in Bohemia, arrangements were made to organise an army, and as a beginning in the work of reform the Jesuits were expelled. Owing to the strong anti-German feeling of the populace the rebellion spread rapidly in Bohemia, and Count Mansfeld hastened to the relief of the insurgents with an army placed at his disposal by the *Union*. Most of the cities of Bohemia were captured by the rebels, and the whole of northern Austria stood in the gravest danger. At this critical moment the Emperor Matthias passed away, and was succeeded by Ferdinand II. (1619-37). The latter was a devoted Catholic, trained by the Jesuits, and had already done immense service to the Church by wiping out almost every trace of heresy in his hereditary dominions. That such a man should succeed to the imperial dignity at such a time was highly distasteful to the Protestants of Bohemia. It was not, therefore, to be wondered at that they refused to acknowledge him as king, and elected in his stead Frederick V. of the Palatinate (1619).

The situation looked exceedingly serious for Ferdinand II. On the one side he was being pressed hard by the Turks, and on the other he was beset so closely by the Bohemian rebels that even the very city of Vienna was in danger of falling into their hands. His opponent Frederick V. could rely upon the forces of the *Union* in the campaign, and besides, as the son-in-law of James I. of England and the nephew of Maurice of Orange the successful leader of the Dutch and the sworn ally of the French Huguenots, Frederick had little difficulty in persuading himself that at last Europe was to be freed from the domination of the House of Habsburg. He marched into Bohemia, and was crowned solemnly at Prague in 1619. But if Frederick could count upon support from many quarters so, too, could Ferdinand. Maximilian II. of Bavaria was active on his side, as were indeed the whole forces of the *League*. Saxony, too, which was devoted to Lutheranism and detested the Calvinist tendencies of Frederick, fearing that a victory for him might mean a victory for Calvinism, ranged itself under the banner of the Emperor. The Pope sent generous subsidies, as did also Spain. Finally, during the course of the campaign Ferdinand was fortunate in having the services of two of the ablest generals of their time, Tilly,* who commanded the forces of the *League*, and Wallenstein† who had charge of the imperial troops. Maximilian of Bavaria marched into Austria at the head of the army of the *League* and drove the rebels back into Bohemia, whither he followed them, and inflicted upon them a severe defeat in the battle of the White Mountain (1620). Frederick was obliged to save himself by flight after a reign of a few months. The leaders of the rebellion were arrested and put to death. In return for the services he had rendered Maximilian of Bavaria became ruler of the Palatinate, from which Frederick had been deposed. But though Frederick was defeated the struggle was by no means finished. The Count of Mansfeld, acting on behalf of the *Union*, espoused the cause of the Palgrave and was supported by an army led by Christian IV. of Denmark, Frederick's brother-in-law, who marched into Germany to the aid of his friends. James I. of England, though unwilling to despatch an army, helped by grants of money. The war was renewed with great vigour, but the allies had little chance of success against two such experienced generals as Tilly and Wallenstein. Christian IV.

* Villermont, *Tilly ou la guerre de trente ans*, 1860.
† Hallwich, *Geschichte Wallensteins*, 1910.

suffered a terrible defeat at the Barenberg near Lutter (1626), and three years later he was forced to agree to the Peace of Lübeck (1629), by which he promised to withdraw from Germany and never again to mix himself up in its domestic affairs.

The forces of the Emperor and of the *League* were so victorious all along the line that the former felt himself strong enough to deal with the burning question of the ecclesiastical property that had been seized. In a short time he issued what is known as the *Edict of Restitution* (1629), by which he ordered that all property acquired by the Protestants contrary to the *Ecclesiasticum Reservatum* clause of the Peace of Augsburg (1555) should be restored. He commanded, besides, that the terms of the Peace of Passau-Augsburg should be strictly observed, allowed Catholic and Protestant princes the right of establishing their own religion in their own territories (*Cuius regio illius religio*), and permitted Protestant subjects of Catholic princes who felt their consciences aggrieved to emigrate if they wished to do so. About the justice of this decree there could be very little dispute, for it dealt only with the return of what had been acquired by open or veiled spoliation, but it may well be doubted whether it was prudent considering the circumstances of the case. In the first place, it meant the loss of enormous territories for some of the Protestant princes who had enriched themselves from the lands of the bishops and abbots. During the earlier stages of the war many of those men had stood loyally by the Emperor in his struggle against rebels and foreign invaders, but now, mindful of their own temporal interests and the future of their religion, they were prepared to range themselves on the side of their co-religionists in what had become a purely religious war. France, too, alarmed by the victory of Ferdinand II., and fearing that a victory for the House of Habsburg might lead to the establishment of a united empire and the indefinite postponement of the project of securing for France the provinces along the Rhine, was only too glad to pledge its support to the Protestant princes in the war against the Emperor. The young and valiant king of Sweden, Gustavus Adolphus,* was a keen spectator of the trend of affairs in Germany, and was anxious to secure for his country the German provinces along the shores of the Baltic. He was not without hopes also that, by putting himself forward as the champion of Protestantism and by helping the Protestant princes to overthrow the House of Habsburg, he might set up for himself on the ruins of the Holy Roman Empire a great Protestant confederacy embracing most of Northern Europe. Finally, even though Saxony had been induced by special concessions to accept the Edict of Restitution, it might have been anticipated that in a purely religious struggle between Catholics and Protestants hatred of the Roman Church would prove stronger than the prejudices against Geneva, and its ruler would be forced to join the enemies of the Emperor.

Gustavus Adolphus, having strengthened himself by a formal agreement with France, marched into Germany at the head of a body of picked troops (1630). He issued a proclamation announcing that he had come to free the Germans from slavery, and he opened negotiations with the Protestant princes, some of whom to do them justice showed themselves very reluctant to become allies of a foreign invader. Ferdinand II. was but poorly prepared to meet such an attack. The imperial troops had been disbanded, and what was much worse, Wallenstein had retired into private life. Many of the Catholic princes, notably Maximilian of Bavaria, resented his rapid promotion and the grant that had been made to him of the Duchy of Mecklenburg. They prejudiced the mind of Ferdinand against him just at the time his services were most urgently required. Nor, when the first fit of zeal had passed away, were all the Catholic princes anxious to hasten to the support of the Emperor.

* Gfrörer, *Gustav. Adolf.*, 1863.

THE COUNTER-REFORMATION 253

Tilly with the forces of the *League* advanced to bar the progress of the Swedes. He was defeated at Breitenfeld (1631) and his army was nearly destroyed. Gustavus Adolphus pushed rapidly forward towards Bavaria, captured the cities of Würzburg, Mainz, and Augsburg, and for a time it seemed as if his advance to Vienna was going to be a triumphal march. Over-joyed with the success of his campaign he began to act as if he were really emperor of Germany, thereby giving great offence to many of his German followers. His dreams of power were, however, brought to an abrupt termination. In April 1632 he fought an indecisive battle at Rain on the Lech, where Tilly was wounded mortally, but in November he was slain at Lützen though his army was victorious.

Ferdinand found himself in great danger. He appealed for aid to Urban VIII. and to Spain but at first the former, believing that the struggle was more political than religious, refused to assist him, though later on, when he realised that the very existence of the Catholic Church in the empire was endangered, he changed his mind and forwarded generous subsidies. Maximilian of Bavaria, who had held aloof for a time, espoused warmly the cause of the Emperor, and Wallenstein, who had been recalled in the hour of danger, raised an immense army in an incredibly short space of time. Oxenstierna, the chancellor of Sweden, took up the work of his master Adolphus and succeeded in bringing about an alliance with the Protestant princes (1633). So low had the national feeling sunk in the empire that the Protestant princes consented to appoint this upstart as director of the campaign and to fight under his command. France supplied the funds to enable the Swedes to carry on the war. For some time very little was done on either side. Negotiations were carried on by Wallenstein with the Swedes, with Saxony, and with France. It was represented to the Emperor that his chosen general was guilty of gross disloyalty. Though the charge of absolute disloyalty has not been proved, still certain actions of Wallenstein coupled with his inactivity gave good colour to the accusation. The Emperor dismissed him from his command, and a little later he was murdered by some of his own soldiers.

The war and the negotiations were renewed alternately, but without any result as peace was not desired by either Sweden or France. At last the forces of the Emperor gained a signal victory at Nördlingen (1634). This success had at least one good result in that it detached the Elector of Saxony from the side of Sweden. He had never thrown himself whole-heartedly into the struggle, as he disliked the idea of supporting a foreign invader against his own Emperor, and was not sorry to escape from a very awkward position. The Peace of Prague was concluded between the Emperor and Saxony (1635), according to which the Edict of Restitution was abandoned in great measure, and religious freedom was guaranteed to the Protestants of Silesia.

But to promote their own interests the Swedes and the French insisted on complete equality between the Protestants and Catholics as an indispensable condition for peace. From this time onward it was a purely political struggle, inspired solely by the desire of these two countries to weaken Germany and to break the power of the House of Habsburg. On the death of Ferdinand II. in 1637 it was thought that the war might have been ended, but these hopes were disappointed. Ferdinand III. (1637-57) who succeeded offered a general amnesty at the Diet of Regensburg (1641) without avail. French soldiers crossed the frontiers to support the Swedes and the Protestants. Finally after long negotiations the Peace of Westphalia (1648) put an end to a struggle, in which Germany had suffered enormously, and from which foreigners were to derive the greatest benefits.

The Peace of Westphalia was dictated to Germany by France and Sweden. As a reward for the injury they had inflicted on the country both received large slices of

THE COUNTER-REFORMATION 255

German territory. France insisted on getting possession of Alsace, while Sweden received large grants of territory along the Baltic together with a war indemnity of five million thalers. In order to provide compensation for the secular princes, portion of whose territories had been ceded to these two powers, and also to reward others who had suffered for their alliance with Sweden, the secularisation of a considerable amount of the ecclesiastical states was arranged. Saxony, Brandenburg, Hesse-Cassel, Brunswick, and Mecklenburg were enriched by the acquisition of lands formerly ruled over by the bishops and abbots. This step meant that the Protestant states of Germany were strengthened at the expense of the Catholic Church, and that the people of these districts being now transferred to Protestant rulers were in great danger of being drawn over to the religion of their new masters. The jurisdiction of the bishops was abolished in these territories, and even in some of the new chapters, as for example at Osnabrück, Protestant canons were installed side by side with Catholics.

Furthermore, it was arranged that the terms of the Peace of Augsburg should be observed, with this important change, that the rights guaranteed in it to the Lutherans should be extended even to those who did not accept the Augsburg Confession. This concession was intended to meet the demands of the Calvinists. Again, complete equality was established between Catholics and Protestants in the empire. To give effect to this clause it was arranged that in all imperial committees and courts both parties should be represented in equal numbers. In case religious issues were discussed at the Diet, where the Catholics still had the majority, it was agreed that the matter should not be decided by voting but by friendly compromise. The princes were permitted to determine the religion of their subjects, the principal restriction being that those subjects who were in the enjoyment of a certain form of public or private religious worship in 1624 could not be forced to change their religion. For the others nothing remained but to seek a home where their conscientious convictions might be respected. In regard to ecclesiastical property the year 1624 was taken as the normal year, the property that the Protestants held in that year being allowed to remain in their hands. The *Ecclesiasticum Reservatum* clause was retained, and made obligatory on both parties. These terms, it was provided, should not extend to the Protestants in the hereditary dominions of the Emperor.

The Peace of Westphalia by its practical recognition of state neutrality in religious matters put an end to the constitution of the Holy Roman Empire, and reduced the Emperor to the position of a mere figurehead, depending for strength entirely on his own hereditary states. Instead of preventing disunion it made national unity almost impossible, and exposed Germany to attack from any hostile neighbour who might wish to strengthen himself by encouraging strife amongst its various states. Besides, it inflicted a severe injury on the Church not merely by its recognition of the Protestant religion, but by the seizure of ecclesiastical property, the abolition of bishoprics, the interference with cathedral chapters, and the recognition of the right of the temporal sovereign to determine the religion of his subjects. It was no wonder then that the papal legate Fabio Chigi lodged a strong protest against the Peace, and that the protest was renewed in the most solemn form by Innocent X. (1648).* This action was not inspired by the Pope's opposition to peace. On the contrary, again and again during the civil war the Holy See had sought to bring about a friendly understanding, but no Pope, unless he was disloyal to the trust confided in him, could permit such interference in purely religious matters without making it clear that he was not a consenting party. Innocent X. foresaw that this was but the herald of new

* Bull, *Zelo domus Dei*.

THE COUNTER-REFORMATION

claims on the part of the civil rulers, and that in a short time even the Catholic sovereigns would endeavour to regulate the ecclesiastical affairs of their subjects without reference to the authority of the Church. Nor was it long until events showed that his suspicions were not without good foundation.

CHAPTER V

CATHOLIC MISSIONS

Henrion, *Histoire générale des missions catholiques depuis le XIIIe siècle*, 2 vols., 1841. Marshall, *The Christian Missions*, 2 vols., 2nd edition, 1863. Hahn, *Geschichte der Katholischen Missionen*, 5 Bde, 1857-65. Da Civezza, *Storia universale delle missioni francescane*, 9 vols., 1883-96. Meyer, *Die Propaganda*, 2 Bde, 1853. *Lettres édifiantes . . . des missions . . . par quelques missionaires de la Compagnie de Jésus*, 1617. Werner, *Missionsatlas*, 1885.

WHILE heresy was spreading with such alarming rapidity that it threatened to deprive the Church of her fairest provinces in Europe, new continents were being opened up in the East and the West, and Christian missionaries were being sent forth to bear an invitation to strange races and peoples to take the place of the millions who had strayed from the fold. The restless energy and activity so characteristic of the fifteenth century manifested itself strikingly in the numerous naval expeditions, planned and carried out in face of enormous difficulties, and which led to such important geographical discoveries. The Portuguese pushed forward their discoveries along the west coast of Africa till at last Bartholomew Diaz succeeded in doubling the Cape of Good Hope (1487), thereby opening the way for Vasco de Gama's voyage to the Malabar coast in 1498. Spain, jealous of the new south sea route to the East Indies discovered by her rival, availed herself of the offer of Christopher Columbus to provide a western route, and it was while engaged in this attempt that he discovered the great continent of America. The importance of these discoveries in both East and West both from the spiritual and temporal point of view was understood clearly enough by both Spain and Portugal. The rulers of these countries, while anxious for the spread of Christianity among the pagan races of Asia and America, were not unmindful also of the important service that might be rendered by religion to their work of colonisation. Fortunately these new fields for the Christian missionaries were opened up, at a time when the religious spirit of Western Europe was beginning to recover from the state of lethargy to which it had been reduced by abuses, and the cry went forth for volunteers in an age when the older religious orders had begun to feel the influence of reform, and when the new religious orders, particularly the Jesuits, were at hand to render invaluable assistance. The foundation of the Congregation *De Propaganda Fide* (1622), the establishment of the *Collegium Urbanum* (1627) for the education and training of missionary priests, and the organisation of the *Société des Missions Étrangères* * (1663) in Paris helped to unify the work and to put it upon a solid and permanent basis.

The first place in this remarkable missionary development must be assigned to St. Francis Xavier † (1506-52), the friend and disciple of St. Ignatius of Loyola, and the most successful Christian missionary since the days of St. Paul. On the invitation of John III. of Portugal, who had heard something about the contemplated new Society of Jesus, St. Francis sailed from Lisbon, and landed at Goa, the capital of the Portuguese Indian colony (1542). Franciscans and Dominicans had preceded him thither, but the scandalous example of irreligion and immorality set by the colonists had made it nearly impossible for these devoted men to win converts amongst the pagan races. St. Francis threw himself generously into the work of re-awakening the faith of the Portuguese before attempting the conversion of the natives. When the condition of affairs in Goa had undergone a complete change for the better, he set out

* Launay, *Histoire générale de la Société des Missions-Étrangères*, 1894.
† Coleridge, *Life and Letters of St. Francis Xavier*, 1902.

for West India, where he preached with wonderful effect, and succeeded in extending his efforts as far as the Island of Ceylon. He next visited Malacca, the Molucca Islands and Sumatra. Everywhere he went he won thousands to the faith. His extraordinary kindness and charity, his untiring zeal, his simple straightforward exposition of Catholic doctrine, and the numerous miracles by which God confirmed the truth of his preaching, were the principal causes of his success. In the meantime several other members of the Society of Jesus had arrived. These he despatched to different parts of India to tend the flock whom he had won for Christ, while at the same time he established a novitiate and a house of studies to prepare a native clergy for carrying on the work.

Not content with what had been accomplished in India he set out for Japan (1549) in company with a Japanese convert, who assisted him to acquire a knowledge of the language. He landed at Kagoshima, where he remained nearly a year learning the language and preparing a short treatise in Japanese on the principal articles of faith. When he had overcome these preliminary difficulties he began the work of evangelisation, and notwithstanding the energetic opposition of the bonzes or native priests he formed a flourishing community. Through central Japan he made his way preaching with success in the principal towns, but the political troubles then raging in the capital proved a serious obstacle to the success of his work. For two years and a half St. Francis continued his apostolic labours in Japan, and then returned to Goa, not indeed to rest but only to prepare for a still more hazardous mission. In Japan he discovered that one of the principal arguments used against the acceptance of the Christian faith was the fact that the Chinese, to whom the people of Japan looked with reverence, still preferred Confucius to Christ. Inspired by the hope of securing the Celestial Empire for the Church, and of ensuring thereby the conversion of the entire Eastern races, he had himself appointed ambassador to China and set off to reach the capital. On the voyage, however, he became so seriously ill that it was necessary to land him on the little island of Sancian, where in a rude hut constructed to shelter him he breathed his last. During the ten years of his mission he had won close on a million people to the faith, and he had given Christianity a hold on the people of India and Japan which no political revolutions or religious persecution could ever loosen. He was canonised in 1622.

After the death of the Apostle of India the work that he had begun was carried on by his brethren of the Society of Jesus in face of very serious difficulties. They were opposed by the Brahmins, who tried to stir up persecutions, and their progress was impeded by political disturbances. The arrival of the Jesuit, Robert de' Nobili (1577-1656), in 1605 marked a new stage in the history of the conversion of India. After a visit paid to the city of Madura,* where one of his brethren had been labouring for years without any visible fruit, de' Nobili came to the conclusion that the comparative failure of the Christian missionaries was due to the contempt of the Brahmins for them as Portuguese or friends of the Portuguese and as associates of the pariahs, who were regarded by the Brahmins as being little better than beasts. He determined to adopt new methods, to come to them not as a Portuguese but as a Roman, to avoid all contact with the pariahs or outcasts, to respect the national customs and caste divisions of the country, and to secure a sympathetic hearing from the Brahmins by his learning and specially by his intimate knowledge of the Indian literature.

His method was crowned with instant success. In a short time he had made hundreds of converts in the very city where his colleague had laboured in vain for years; and he had secured his converts, not by minimising or corrupting Catholic truth, but by a prudent regard for

* Bertrand, *La Mission du Maduré*, 1847.

the caste system and for certain rites and customs connected with it, which he tolerated as partaking of a national rather than of an essentially religious character. Objections were raised against his methods by his fellow Jesuit in Madura. He was charged with countenancing superstition by allowing the use of pagan rites, and with encouraging schism and dissension by permitting no intermingling between the Brahmins and the pariahs even in the churches. In justice to Father de' Nobili and to those who favoured his methods, it ought to be said that they did not like the system of castes. They hoped that under the influence of Christian charity such divisions might disappear, and that just as the Church undermined rather than condemned slavery in the first centuries, so too the missionaries in India might respect the prejudices of the Brahmins till these prejudices should have been extinguished by a closer acquaintance with the doctrines and spirit of Christianity. The highly coloured reports sent in against him produced an unfavourable impression on his superiors, but when his defence was received at Rome Gregory XV. refused to issue any condemnation (1623).

During the life-time of Father de' Nobili he pursued his own method with success, though at the same time he never neglected an opportunity of providing secretly for the spiritual welfare of the poorer classes. After his death in 1656 many of the Jesuits continued his policy, notwithstanding the fact that grave objections were raised by some of the other religious orders. A crisis came, however, in Pondicherry which belonged to the French. The Capuchins were in charge of the mission, and attended both to the colonists and the natives. The bishop decided to share the work between the Capuchins who were left in charge of the colonists, and the Jesuits who were entrusted with preaching to the natives (1699). The Capuchins appealed to Rome, and brought forward against the Jesuits the old charges that had been levelled against Father de' Nobili, and that had given rise to such bitter controversies. The question of the Malabar Rites was carried once more to Rome, and de Tournon, Patriarch of Antioch, was sent as legate to investigate the case (1703). After remaining eight months in the country, and before he had an opportunity of considering both sides of the question, he decided against the Jesuits (1704). This decision was confirmed by the Pope in 1706. The controversy continued, however, till 1744, when Benedict XIV. in the Bull, *Omnium sollicitudinem,* issued a final condemnation of the Malabar Rites (1744).

In deference to the prejudices of the Brahmins a scheme was then formulated with the approval of the Pope for organising two classes of missionaries, one for the Brahmins and another for the outcasts, but the suppression of the Jesuits in the Portuguese dominions (1756) put an end to this system. The Carmelites did good service by their efforts to reconcile the Nestorian Christians with the Church. The further progress of the Catholic Church in India was impeded by the suppression of the Jesuits, the invasion of India by the Dutch, the insistence of Portugal upon its rights of patronage over all the churches of India, the downfall of the religious spirit in Europe during the eighteenth century, and finally by the destruction during the French Revolution of the colleges and religious houses that supplied workers for the mission.

St. Francis Xavier had planned to introduce the Christian faith into the Celestial Empire, but he died almost in sight of the coast. The first missionary who made any progress in that country was another Jesuit, Father Matteo Ricci* (1552-1610) who arrived in China in 1582. He was a man of great ability, well versed in mathematics and in the natural sciences, and well qualified to make an excellent impression on the educated classes. He was protected by the mandarins, and respected by the Emperor, who invited him to the imperial palace at Pekin

---

* Brucker, *Le Père Matthieu Ricci* (*Études*, 1910).

(1600). Although it was his scholarly attainments that attracted the Chinese rather than his religion, Father Ricci never failed to seize every opportunity of directing the thoughts of his pupils and admirers towards Christianity. At his death in 1610 many of the mandarins had been converted, and most of the old prejudices against the new religion had disappeared. Other Jesuits equally learned and equally prudent were ready to take his place. His successor, Father Schall, was summoned by the Emperor to Pekin, and was appointed president of the mathematical society. By his influence at court he obtained permission for his fellow-workers to open Christian churches in China, and secured the publication of various Christian books in the Chinese language. The revolution that preceded the establishment of the Manchu dynasty (1644) led to some persecution, but the trouble was only of a temporary character. On the death of Father Schall in 1666, he was succeeded by Father Verbiest who was also patronised by the court on account of his scholarly attainments. Finally in 1692 an imperial rescript was issued giving the Christian missionaries full permission to preach the gospel throughout the empire. At that period the number of converts was about twenty thousand. Two bishoprics were erected, one at Pekin and one at Nankin.

In the beginning, as the Jesuits were practically speaking the only missionaries in China, it was reserved for them as their special mission-field by Gregory XIII. (1585). But later on Clement VIII. allowed the Franciscans to go to China, and finally the country was opened to all Christian missionaries by Urban VIII. The presence of the new labourers in the vineyard was not productive of so good results as might have been expected. A fierce controversy that broke out regarding the Chinese Rites * principally between the Dominicans and Jesuits, did much to retard the progress of the Catholic Church

---

* Daniel, *Histoire apologétique de la conduite des Jésuites de la Chine*, 1724. Pray, *Historia Controvers. de ritibus Sinicis*, 1724.

in the Celestial Empire for a long period. To understand the meaning of this controversy it should be remembered that the Chinese people, deeply attached to the memory of their ancestors and to their veneration for Confucius, were accustomed to perform certain rites and ceremonies at fixed periods in memory of their departed relatives and in honour of Confucius. To prohibit these was to put an end to all hope of conversion, and to tolerate them looked like tolerating Paganism. Father Ricci decided to tolerate them, mainly on the ground that they partook more of a civil than of a religious character, that in themselves they were harmless, that the Church has been always very prudent in regard to the national and civil customs of its converts, and that with the acceptance of Christianity all danger of misunderstanding would soon disappear. Furthermore, for want of better names for the Deity Father Ricci allowed the use of Tien-tschu (Lord of Heaven), Tien and Schangti (supreme emperor), words that had been used hitherto in an idolatrous sense, but which in themselves and as explained by the Jesuit missionaries were orthodox enough. Both parties in the controversy meant well, and each could adduce very convincing arguments in favour of its own views. The Dominicans commissioned one of their number to denounce these customs to Rome as idolatrous. He submitted seventeen articles dealing with the Chinese Rites to the Inquisition, and after a long discussion a provisional condemnation was issued by Innocent X. (1645). Father Martini went to Rome to defend the Chinese Rites, and to point out the serious consequences which such a sweeping condemnation might have upon the whole future of Christianity in China. In 1656 a decision more or less favourable to the Jesuits was given by Alexander VII. The decision helped to prolong rather than to settle the controversy. A crisis was reached, however, when Maigrot, vicar-apostolic of Fu-Kien, one of the priests belonging to the Society for Foreign Missions, denounced the Chinese

Rites as pure paganism, and interdicted their observance to all converts within his jurisdiction. The case was carried once more to Rome, and de Tournon was despatched as papal legate to decide the case. In 1707 he issued a decree prohibiting the Chinese Rites, incurring thereby the enmity of the Emperor, who had him thrown into prison where he died (1710). All missionaries who obeyed his orders were banished. The decision of the legate was supported by several decrees from Rome, and at last in 1742 Benedict XIV. condemned the Chinese Rites, and ordered that all missionaries to China should take an oath against further discussion of the question.

The controversy was carried on with considerable earnestness on both sides on account of the importance of the issues at stake, and was embittered considerably by political and religious disputes in Europe that had no concern either with China or the Chinese Rites. The condemnation had a disastrous effect on the missions. Nearly all the missionaries were banished from the country, and the Christians were obliged to choose between apostasy and death.

In Japan* St. Francis Xavier had begun the work of conversion. He left behind him two of his brethren who were joined soon by other members of the Society of Jesus, with the result that about the year 1582 there were between one hundred and two hundred thousand Catholics in the country. An embassy consisting of three of the native princes visited Rome in 1585. In many districts the local chiefs granted full liberty to the missionaries, and in a short time the number of Christians rose to three hundred thousand. Some of the authorities, alarmed by the rapid growth of foreign power in the country, began to whisper among the people that the Christian missionaries were only spies working in the interest of Spain and Portugal. A violent persecution broke out against the Christians in 1587, and lasted for several years. Notwithstanding the savagery of the Pagans

* Pagès, *Histoire de la religion chrétienne au Japan*, 1598-1651, 1869.

and the punishments decreed against the missionaries the Jesuits weathered the storm, and fresh labourers arrived to support them in the persons of the Dominicans, the Franciscans, and the Augustinians.

But national jealousy of the foreigners, more especially of the Spanish and Portuguese, fomented as it was by the Dutch and English, led to new troubles for the Christian communities. In 1614 a royal decree was issued against the Christians, and a determined attempt was made to destroy the work of the missionaries.

Punishments of the most awful kind were inflicted on those who would not abjure the Christian faith, and many, both priests and people, were put to death. From 1614 till 1640 the persecution was carried on in a systematic and determined manner, so that by that time all the missionaries were either dead or banished, and the whole of the young communities they had formed were scattered. For years Japan remained closed against the missionaries who made various attempts to escape the vigilance of the authorities.

Whatever may be the explanation, whether it was due to the severity of the climate or to the savage character of the inhabitants, the Christian missions in Africa were not productive of much fruit. St. Vincent de Paul sent some of his community to work in the district around Tunis and in the island of Madagascar. Missionaries from Portugal made various attempts to found Christian communities along the whole western coast of Africa. In the Congo the results at first were decidedly promising. Here the work was begun by the Dominicans, who were assisted at a later period by the Capuchins, the Augustinians, and the Jesuits. Many of the inhabitants were won over to the faith, but as years passed, and as the supply of missionaries failed, much of what had been accomplished was undone, though the Capuchins still continued their efforts. In Angola the Jesuits led the way, in Upper and Lower Guinea the Jesuits and the Carmelites, in Morocco and in Egypt the Franciscans, while various religious bodies undertook the work of evangelising the Portuguese colonies in Eastern Africa.

By far the greatest triumph of the Church during this age of missionary effort was that which was achieved by the conversion of the native races in the territories occupied by Spain and Portugal in the western continent. The hope of extending the boundaries of the Church was one of the motives that induced Columbus and his supporters to undertake their voyage of discovery, as it was also one of the motives urging the rulers of Spain to increase the sphere of their jurisdiction. Hence from the very beginning great care was taken to provide for the conversion of the natives. Priests were despatched from Spain with all the expeditions. Dominicans, Franciscans, Carmelites, Augustinians, Fathers of the Order of Our Lady of Mercy, and after the establishment of the Society of Jesus, Jesuits vied with each other in their eagerness to risk their lives in the work. Generous provision was made by the rulers of Spain for the support of the clergy and the maintenance of religion. Churches were erected, episcopal and archiepiscopal Sees were founded and endowed, colleges and monasteries were established by the various religious orders, and in the course of less than a century the Church had gained in the new world almost as much as she had lost in the old.

The Spanish rulers were not inclined to destroy or to maltreat the native races, but they were unable to supervise the greedy officials, many of whom acted savagely towards the Indians, killing hundreds of them and forcing the others to work as slaves. The hatred of the Indian races for the Spaniards made the work of the missionaries more difficult, but from the beginning the Church espoused the cause of the Indians, sought to secure protection for them against the officials, and to restrain if not to extinguish entirely the practice of enslaving the natives. Bartholomew de Las Casas* (1474-

---

* Dutto, *The Life of Bartolomé de las Casas and the First Leaves of American Ecclesiastical History*, 1902.

1566) at first a secular priest, then a Dominican, and afterwards a bishop, took a prominent part in the struggle on behalf of the natives, and though his methods were not always of the most prudent character he helped to put down some of the most glaring abuses. Charles V. was most sympathetic towards the Indians, laid down very strict rules for his subordinates, and invited the bishops to become protectors of the Indians, while Paul III. insisted strongly on the freedom of the natives and their rights as men (1537).

Some of the West Indian Islands which Columbus discovered were thickly populated. The Franciscans and Dominicans set to work at once to convert the native people of Hayti, many of whom were destroyed by the Spaniards despite the efforts of the missionaries. Cuba was taken possession of by the Spaniards in 1511, and Mexico* or New Spain was conquered by Hernando Cortes in 1519. The people that inhabited this country were much more intelligent and cultured than the other native races. They had flourishing towns, beautiful temples and public buildings, and a fairly well organised form of government. Cortes invited the Franciscans to undertake the work of conversion. They were followed by the Dominicans, by the Order of Our Lady of Mercy and by the Jesuits. Bishop Zumárraga, the first bishop in Mexican territory, opened schools for the education of the Indians, as did also the Franciscans and the other religious orders. The Jesuits established the great college of San Ildefonso, and in 1553 the royal and pontifical University of Mexico was opened for the reception of students. By the Bull, *Universalis Ecclesiae regimini,* full rights of patronage over all the churches of New Spain were conferred on the rulers of Spain, and religious affairs were placed under the control of the Council of the Indies.

From the West Indies Christianity made its way into

* De Berbourg, *Histoire des nations civilisées du Mexique et de l'Amérique centrale,* 1851.

Central America which was acquired by Spain in 1513. The Dominicans, Capuchins, and Jesuits preached the faith in Guiana. Venezuela was evangelised at first by the Franciscans (1508) and by the Dominicans (1520). Later on Capuchins, Jesuits, and Augustinians took part in the work. By the year 1600 fully two-thirds of the natives were converted. Peru was conquered for Spain by Francis Pizarro in 1532. The inhabitants of this country were highly civilised, with a regular government, and with a form of religious worship much superior to any of the Pagan systems with which the Spaniard had come into contact. For a while the conversion of the country was delayed owing to the cruelties inflicted on the natives and the conflicts between the Spanish leaders, but in a short time the Franciscans and Dominicans undertook missions to the natives with great success. In 1546 Lima was created an archbishopric, and in a few years a university was opened. St. Rose of Lima (1586-1617) was the first saint of American birth to be canonised officially (1671). By the beginning of the seventeenth century the majority of the natives were converted.

Brazil* was discovered by the Portuguese, Alvares de Cabral (1500), who named it Vera Cruz because his ship came to anchor there on Good Friday. The Franciscans were early in the field to tend to the spiritual wants of the natives, who stood in need of some defenders to protect them from the greed of the Portuguese officials. At the request of King John III. St. Ignatius despatched some of his followers to Brazil (1549). A great college was opened by the Jesuits for the education of young men. The wars with the French, the invasion of Brazil by the Dutch, and the opposition of officials who were annoyed at the protection afforded the natives by the missionaries, rendered the work of conversion exceedingly difficult. But "reductions" or settlements of Indians were formed by the Jesuits, Capuchins,

---

* Beauchamp, *Histoire du Brésil*, 3 vols., 1815.

Carmelites, and others, and episcopal Sees were established throughout the country. The expulsion of the Jesuits in 1759 was a severe blow to the missions in Brazil.

Paraguay * was taken possession of by Spain in 1536. The Franciscan Fathers who accompanied the expedition addressed themselves at once to the conversion of the natives; but the difficulty of making themselves understood, the cruelty of the first conquerors towards the natives, and the bad example of the early colonists, made their work much more difficult than it might have been.

The Dominicans, the Augustinians and the Order of Mercy came to the assistance of the first missionaries, and three episcopal sees were established. One of the bishops, a Dominican, invited the Jesuits to come to Paraguay (1586). They established colleges in several of the leading centres, and sent out their members in all directions to preach to the Indians, over whom they acquired in a short time a very salutary influence. But the harshness of the Spanish officials, and the bad example they gave to the native converts, made it necessary for the Jesuits to form "Reductions" or special settlements, where the Indians might live apart from the Spaniards, and where they might be free from oppression and the corrupting influence of their Spanish masters. Philip III. of Spain approved this plan, and ordained that the Reductions should be subject directly to the Crown. In these settlements the Jesuits trained the natives in agriculture and in trades, but the peace of the communities was disturbed frequently by the slave-hunters against whom the Spanish officials refused to take action. As a last resource the Jesuits organised an Indian force, and provided them with arms for self-protection. Close on a million converted natives were attached to the thirty-one Reductions that formed a kind of independent principality subject only to Spain. This happy condition of affairs was not destined to last for

* Demersay, *Histoire ... du Paraguay et des Établissements des Jésuites*, 1860-4.

ever. By a treaty made in 1750 Spain, in return for some territory ceded by Portugal, handed over to Portugal seven of the Reductions. The Jesuits pleaded for delay in carrying out the eviction of the Indians who were settled in this territory, and when their appeal was refused they advised the Indians to submit. Some of them followed this advice while others of them flew to arms only to be defeated (1756). The blame for the rebellion was attributed to the Jesuits by Pombal and the other enemies of the Society in Portugal. By a royal decree issued in 1767 the Jesuits were expelled from Paraguay, and in a few years the flourishing communities which they had established were completely dissolved.*

Christianity reached the territory now known as the United States from three distinct sources, namely, the Spanish colonies in the south, the French settlements in the north, and from the English Catholic colony of Maryland in the east. The sphere of influence of the Spanish missionaries was Florida, California, New Mexico and Texas. In 1526 an expedition under the command of de Narvaez and accompanied by several Franciscan Fathers was sent to explore Florida, but the expedition ended in complete failure. Several other attempts of a similar kind were made with no better results till at last, aroused by the danger of a French occupation, Menendez established a permanent settlement at Fort St. Augustine and prepared the way for Spanish occupation (1565). Menendez, zealous for the conversion of the natives, invited the Jesuits to come to his assistance. They volunteered freely to come to Florida, as did also the Franciscans. At first the work of conversion was attended with great difficulties and proceeded very slowly, but by the year 1700 many Christian villages had been established. The attacks of the English

* De Moussy, *Mémoire historique sur la décadence et la ruine des Missions de Jésuites*, 1865. Weld, *The Suppression of the Society of Jesus in the Portuguese Dominions*, 1877.

on Florida injured the missions, and the cession of Florida to England (1763) completed the work of destruction.*

Lower California was discovered by Cortez in 1533, and Upper California by Cabrillo eleven years later. In the beginning the missionaries encountered great opposition, but after 1697 the Jesuit Fathers were very successful. They formed the natives into permanent settlements or reductions, and so rapidly did the work of evangelisation proceed that in 1767, the year in which the Jesuits were expelled by Spain, nearly all the Indians were converted. The Franciscan Fathers succeeded the Jesuits, continuing their reductions in Lower California, and introducing missions of a similar kind among the Indians of Upper California. The Dominicans, also, rendered valuable assistance. In 1822 California was ceded to the United States, and the missions were broken up owing to the hostility of the civil authorities.†

The Franciscans were the first to undertake missions in New Mexico (1539). Several of the missionaries suffered martyrdom in their attempts to convert the natives, but it was only after 1597 that any considerable progress was made. In Texas the earliest real effort at introducing Christianity among the natives was made in the last quarter of the seventeenth century. The work of the Franciscans was disturbed by rebellions among the Indians and by war, but notwithstanding these obstacles several flourishing Indian settlements were established. In 1813 the Spanish Cortes issued a decree that the missions in Texas should be secularised.‡

Although others had preceded him, yet the honour of discovering Canada § is assigned generally to Jacques

* Shea, *Catholic Missions among the Indian Tribes*, 1857. Hughes, *The History of the Society of Jesus in North America*, vol. i. (Text), 1907.
† Engelhardt, *The Missions and Missionaries of California*, 1908.
‡ Shea, *op. cit.*, pp. 76-88.
§ *The Jesuit Relations*, 1896-1901. Leclerc, *Établissement de la foi dans la nouvelle France*, 1680. Campbell, *Pioneer Priests of North America*, 1908.

VOL. I. S

Cartier who made three voyages to the country (1534-42). Early in the seventeenth century the two Jesuits Biard and Massé arrived and began the conversion of the Indian tribes settled in Acadia, which embraced Nova Scotia and New Brunswick. In 1608 Samuel de Champlain, "the Father of new France" arrived and laid the foundation of Quebec. He invited the Franciscan Recollects to preach to the Indian tribes, namely, the Algonquins and the Hurons (1615). The Franciscans went to work with a will, preaching to the people and opening schools for the young, but finding their numbers too few for the mighty task, they invited the Jesuits to come to their assistance (1625). Several Jesuits including Fathers Brébeuf and Lallemant hastened to Canada and undertook missions to the Hurons. The invasion and capture of Quebec in 1629 by the English interrupted the work for a time, but on the restoration of the territory to France in 1632 the Jesuits continued their labours with renewed vigour. The fierce tribe of the Iroquois were the strongest opponents of the Christian missionaries, many of whom they put to death. Father Jogues was put to death in 1646, and a little later Fathers Daniel, Brébeuf, and Lallemant together with several of their companions met a similar fate.

But notwithstanding these reverses the work of Christianising the native races of Canada proceeded apace. In 1642 the city of Montreal was founded, and in 1657 the superior of the Sulpicians despatched several of his community to labour in the new colony. Two years later François de Montmorency-Laval arrived as first bishop and vicar-apostolic of New France. West and east the missionaries continued to win new conquests for the Church. The English, however, gave great trouble to the missionaries by stirring up the Indian tribes to make war on the Christian settlements. Nor was the French colony, practically deserted as it had been by the mother country, able to hold its own against the English colonists. In 1713 France ceded to England

Acadia, Newfoundland, and the Hudson Bay territory. In Acadia the Catholic missions had been very successful, but in 1755 the unfortunate Catholics, who refused to take the oath that was tendered to them, were seized and deported. In 1759 Quebec was taken, and by the Treaty of Paris (1763) Canada passed under the dominion of the English.

Many French missionaries from Canada worked in the district stretching from the St. Lawrence to Lake Superior, and missions were established by the Jesuits in the states of Michigan, Wisconsin, and Illinois. In 1673 Father Marquette (1636-75) undertook a journey southward to visit the great river about which he had heard from the Indians, and to open up new fields of work for himself and his associates. He succeeded in reaching the Mississippi, and sailed down the river as far as the mouth of the Arkansas. As a result of the information acquired from those who returned from this voyage of exploration, expeditions were sent out by the French to take possession of the new territories and to erect fortifications against the further advance westward of the English colonists. The city of New Orleans was founded in 1717. Missionaries—Capuchins, Jesuits, and priests of the Society for Foreign Missions—preached the gospel with great success to the natives in Louisiana, Mississippi, Iowa, Arkansas, and Ohio.

The Jesuits, under the leadership of Father White, who settled in the colony founded in Maryland (1534), devoted themselves to the conversion of the Indians, but the expulsion of Lord Baltimore in 1644 and the victory of the Puritans led to the almost complete destruction of these Indian missions.

CHAPTER VI

THEOLOGICAL CONTROVERSIES AND STUDIES

(a) BAIANISM

Schwane, *Dogmengeschichte der neuren zeit*, 1890. Turmel, *Histoire de la théologie positive du concile de Trente au concile du Vatican*, 1906. Denzinger-Bannwart, *Enchiridion Symbolorum*, 11th edition, 1911. Duchesne, *Histoire du Baianisme*, 1731. Linsenmann, *Michael Baius*, 1863.

THE Catholic doctrine on Grace, round which such fierce controversies had been waged in the fifth and sixth centuries, loomed again into special prominence during the days of the Reformation. The views of Luther and Calvin on Grace and Justification were in a sense the very foundation of their systems, and hence it was of vital importance that these questions should be submitted to a searching examination, and that the doctrine of the Catholic Church should be formulated in such a way as to make cavilling and misunderstanding impossible. This work was done with admirable lucidity and directness in the fifth and sixth sessions of the Council of Trent, but nevertheless these decrees of the Council could not prevent the theories of Luther and Calvin from being propagated vigorously, and from exercising a certain amount of influence even on some Catholic theologians who had no sympathy with the religious revolt.

Amongst these might be reckoned Michael Baius (De Bay, 1513-89) a professor at the University of Louvain and John Hessels, one of his supporters in the theological controversies of the day. They believed that

Catholic apologists were handicapped seriously by their slavish regard for the authority and the methods of the Scholastics, and that if instead of appealing to the writings of St. Thomas as the ultimate criterion of truth they were to insist more on the authority of the Bible and of the works of the Early Fathers, such as St. Cyprian, St. Jerome, and St. Augustine, they would find themselves on much safer ground, and their arguments would be more likely to command the respect of their opponents. Hence at Louvain, in their own lectures, in their pamphlets, and in private discussions, they insisted strongly that Scholasticism should make way for positive theology, and that the Scriptures and patristic literature should take the place of the *Summa*. Not content, however, with a mere change of method they began to show their contempt for traditional opinions, and in a short time alarming rumours were in circulation both inside and outside the university that their teaching on Original Sin, Grace, and Free-will, was not in harmony with the doctrine of the Church. The Franciscans submitted to the judgment of the Sorbonne a number of propositions (18) selected from writings or lectures of Baius and his friends, and the opinion of the Sorbonne was distinctly unfavourable. As the dispute grew more heated and threatened to have serious consequences for the university and the country, Cardinal Granvelle, believing that the absence of the two professors might lead to peace, induced both to proceed to the Council of Trent as the theologians of the King of Spain (1563). Though the opinions of Baius found little sympathy with the Fathers of Trent, yet since the subjects of Original Sin and Grace had been discussed and defined already, nothing was done. On his return (1564) from the Council of Trent Baius published several pamphlets in explanation and defence of his views, all of which were attacked by his opponents, so that in a short time the university was split up into two opposing camps.

To put an end to the trouble the rector determined

to seek the intervention of Rome. In October 1567 Pius V. issued the Bull, *Ex omnibus afflictionibus,* in which he condemned seventy-nine propositions selected from the writings or lectures of Baius without mentioning the author's name.* The friends of Baius raised many difficulties regarding the reception and the interpretation of the papal document, and though Baius himself professed his entire submission to the decision, the tone of his letter to the Pope was little short of offensive. The Pope replied that the case having been examined fully and adjudged acceptance of the decision was imperative. Once more Baius announced his intention of submitting (1569), and so confident were his colleagues of his orthodoxy that he was appointed dean of the theological faculty, and later on chancellor of the university. But his actions did not correspond with his professions. Various arguments were put forward to weaken the force of the papal condemnation until at last Gregory XIII. was forced to issue a new Bull, *Provisionis nostrae* (1579), and to send the learned Jesuit, Francisco Toledo, to demand that Baius should abjure his errors, and that the teaching of Pius V. should be accepted at Louvain. The papal letter was read in a formal meeting of the university, whereupon Baius signed a form of abjuration, by which he acknowledged that the condemnation of the propositions was just and reasonable, and that he would never again advocate such views. This submission relieved the tension of the situation, but it was a long time before the evil influence of Baianism disappeared, and before peace was restored finally to Louvain.

The system propounded by Baius had much in common with the teaching of Pelagius, Luther, and Calvin. His failure to recognise the clear distinction between the natural and the supernatural was the source of most of his errors. According to him the state of innocence in which our first parents were created, their

* Denzinger, *op. cit.,* nos. 1001-1080.

destination to the enjoyment of the Beatific Vision, and all the gifts bestowed upon them for the attainment of this end were due to them, so that had they persevered during life they should have merited eternal happiness as a reward for their good works. When, however, man sinned by disobedience he not merely lost gratuitous or supernatural endowments, but his whole nature was weakened and corrupted by Original Sin which, in the system of Baius, was to be identified with concupiscence, and which was transmitted from father to son according to the ordinary laws of heredity. This concupiscence, he contended, was in itself sinful, as was also every work which proceeds from it. This was true even in case of children, because that an act be meritorious or demeritorious Free-will was not required. So long as the act was done voluntarily even though necessarily, it was to be deemed worthy of reward or punishment, since freedom from external compulsion was alone required for moral responsibility.

From the miserable condition into which man had fallen he was rescued by the Redemption of Christ, on account of which much that had been forfeited was restored. These graces procured for man by Christ may be called supernatural, not because they were not due to human nature, but because human nature had been rendered positively unworthy of them by Original Sin. The justice, however, by which a man is justified, consisted not in any supernatural quality infused into the soul, by which the individual was made a participator of the divine nature, but implied merely a condition in which the moral law was observed strictly. Hence justification, according to Baius, could be separated from the forgiveness of guilt, so that though the guilt of the sinner may not have been remitted still he may be justified. In sin two things were to be distinguished, the act and the liability to punishment. The act could never be effaced, but the temporal punishment was remitted by the actual reception of the sacraments, which were introduced by Christ solely for that purpose. The Mass possessed, he held, any efficacy that it had only because it was a good moral act and helped to draw us more closely to God.

(b) THE MOLINIST CONTROVERSY

See bibliography VI. (*a*). Molina, *Liberi arbitrii cum gratiae donis . . . . concordia*, 1588. Augustin Le Blanc, *Historia congregationis de auxiliis*, etc., 1699, 1709. Elutherius, *Historia controversiarum de auxiliis*, etc., 1705-15. Schneeman, *Enstehung und Entwicklung der thomistich-molinistischen Kontroverse*, 1880. Gayraud, *Thomisme et Molinisme*, 1890. Dummermuth, *S. Thomas et doctrina praemotionis physicae*, 1886. Frins (S.J.), *S. Thomae Aquin. doctrina de cooperatione Dei*, etc., 1892. Dummermuth, *Defensio doctrinae S. Thomae*, etc, *Responsio ad P. Frins*, 1895.

The teaching of St. Thomas on Grace was the teaching followed generally, not merely by Dominicans, but by most of the theologians belonging to the secular clergy and to the other religious orders. When, however, the systems of Calvin and Luther began to take root some of those who were brought into close contact with the new doctrines arrived at the conclusion that the arguments of their opponents could be overcome more effectually by introducing some modifications of the theories of St. Thomas concerning the operation of Grace and Free-will. The Jesuits particularly were of this opinion, and in 1584 the general, Aquaviva, allowed his subjects to depart in some measure from the teaching of the *Summa*. This step was regarded with disfavour in many influential quarters, and induced scholars to be much more critical about Jesuit theology than otherwise they might have been. In their College at Louvain there were two Jesuit theologians Lessius (1584-1623) and Hamel, who both in their lectures and theses advanced certain theories on man's co-operation with Grace and on Predestination, that were deemed by many to be dangerously akin to the doctrine of the Semi-Pelagians (1587).

The fact that the Jesuits had been the consistent opponents of Baianism induced Baius and his friends to cast the whole weight of their influence against Lessius. A sharp controversy broke out once more in the Netherlands. The Universities of Louvain and Douay censured thirty-four propositions of Lessius as Semi-Pelagian, while the Universities of Ingolstadt and Mainz declared in favour of their orthodoxy. The matter having been referred to Rome, Sixtus V. imposed silence on both parties, without pronouncing any formal condemnation or approval of the propositions that had been denounced (1588).

The controversy in the Spanish Netherlands was only the prelude to a much more serious conflict in Spain itself. In 1588 the well-known Jesuit, Luis de Molina (1535-1600) published at Lisbon his celebrated work, *Concordia liberi arbitrii cum gratiae donis etc.* with the approbation of the Dominican, Bartholomew Ferreira, and the permission of the Inquisition. Hardly had the work left the printing press than it was attacked warmly by Domingo Bañez (1528-1604), the friend and spiritual director of St. Teresa, and one of the ablest Dominicans of his time. He had been engaged already in a controversy with the Jesuit, Montemaior, on the same subject of Grace, but the publication of Molina's book added new fuel to the flame, and in a short time the dispute assumed such serious proportions that bishops, theologians, universities, students, and even the leading officials of the state, were obliged to take sides. The Dominicans supported Bañez, while the Jesuits with some few exceptions rallied to the side of Molina. The latter's book was denounced to the Inquisition, but as a counterblast to this Bañez also was accused of very serious errors. If Molina was blamed for being a Semi-Pelagian, Bañez was charged with having steered too closely to Calvinism. In the hope of restoring peace to the Church in Spain Clement VIII. reserved the decision of the case to his own tribunal (1596).

To get a grasp of the meaning of the controversy, it should be borne in mind that in all theories concerning the operation of Grace three points must be safeguarded by all Catholic theologians, namely, man's dependence upon God as the First Cause of all his actions natural as well as supernatural, human liberty, and God's omniscience or foreknowledge of man's conduct. Following in the footsteps of St. Thomas, the Dominicans maintained that when God wishes man to perform a good act He not only gives assistance, but He actually moves or predetermines the will so that it must infallibly act. In this way the entire act comes from God as the First Cause, and at the same time it is the free act of the creature, because the human will though moved and predetermined by God acts according to its own nature, that is to say, it acts freely. In His eternal decrees by which God ordained to give this premotion or predetermination He sees infallibly the actions and conduct of men, and acting on this knowledge He predestines the just to glory *ante praevisa merita*. According to this system, therefore, the efficaciousness of Grace comes from the Grace itself, and is not dependent upon the co-operation of the human will.

Against this Molina maintained that the human faculties having been elevated by what might be called prevenient Grace, so as to make them capable of producing a supernatural act, the act itself is performed by the will co-operating with the impulse given by God. Man is, therefore, free, and at the same time dependent completely upon God in the performance of every good act. He is free, because the human will may or may not co-operate with the divine assistance, and he is dependent upon God, because it is only by being elevated by prevenient Grace freely given by God that the human will is capable of co-operating in the production of a supernatural act. It follows, too, that the efficaciousness of Grace arises not from the Grace itself but from the free co-operation of the will, and that a Grace in itself truly sufficient might not be efficacious through the failure of the will to co-operate with it. The omniscience of God is safeguarded, because, according to Molina, God sees infallibly man's conduct by means of the *scientia media* or knowledge of future conditional events (so called because it stands midway between the knowledge of possibles and the knowledge of actuals). That is to say He sees infallibly what man would do freely in all possible circumstances were he given this or that particular Grace, and acting upon this knowledge He predestines the just to glory *post praevisa merita*. The main difficulty urged against Molina was, that by conceding too much to human liberty he was but renewing in another form the errors of Pelagius; while the principal objection brought forward against the Dominicans was, that by conceding too much to Grace they were destroying human liberty, and approaching too closely to Calvin's teaching on Predestination. Needless to say, however much they differed on other points, both the followers of St. Thomas and the friends of Molina were at one in repudiating the doctrines of Calvin and Pelagius.

A special commission (*Congregatio de Auxiliis*), presided over by Cardinals Madrucci and Arrigone, was appointed to examine the questions at issue. The first session was held in January 1598, and in February of the same year the majority of the members reported in favour of condemning Molina's book. Clement VIII. requested the commission to consider the evidence more fully, but in a comparatively short time the majority presented a second report unfavourable to Molina. Representatives of the Dominicans and Jesuits were invited to attend in the hope that by means of friendly discussion an agreement satisfactory to both parties might be secured. In 1601 the majority were in favour of condemning twenty propositions taken from Molina's work, but the Pope refused to confirm the decision. From 1602 till 1605 the sessions were held in the presence of the Pope and of many of the cardinals. Amongst the consultors was Peter Lombard, Archbishop of Armagh. The death of Clement VIII. in March 1605 led to an adjournment. In September 1605 the sessions were resumed and continued till March 1606, when the votes of the consultors were handed in. In July 1607 these were placed before the cardinals for their opinions, but a little later it was announced that the decision of the Holy See would be made public at the proper time, and that meanwhile both parties were at liberty to teach their opinions. Neither side was, however, to accuse the other of heresy. Since that time no definite decision has been given, and, so far as the dogmas of faith are concerned, theologians are at full liberty to accept Thomism or Molinism.

(c) JANSENISM.

Rapin, *Histoire du Jansénisme depuis son origine jusqu' en* 1644, 1861. Paquier, *Le Jansénisme, étude doctrinale d'après les sources*, 1909. Dechamps, *De haeresi janseniana ab Apostolica Sede proscripta*, 1654. Du Mas, *Histoire des cinque propositions de Jansénius*, 1699. Saint-Beuve, *Port Royal*, 3rd edition, 1867-71. Séché, *Les derniers Jansénistes*, 1891. Van den Peereboom, *Cornelius Jansénsius septième évêque d'Ypres*, 1882. Schill, *Die Constitution, Unigenitus*, 1876. Fuzet, *Les Jansénistes du XVIIe siècle*, 1876.

The influence exercised by Baius, and the ideas that he implanted in the minds of his students had a very disturbing effect on the University of Louvain. Amongst those who fell under the sway of Baianism at this period the best known if not the ablest was Cornelius Jansen (1585-1638). He studied at Utrecht, Paris, and Louvain. While in this latter place he formed a resolve to join the Society of Jesus, but for some reason or another he was refused admission, a slight which accounts in some measure for the continued antipathy he displayed during his life towards the Jesuits. At Louvain, too, he was associated very closely with a brilliant young French student, John du Verger de Hauranne (1581-1643), better known as the Abbot of St. Cyran, whom he accompanied to Paris and afterwards to Bayonne, where both lived for almost twelve years. During these years of intimate friendship they had many opportunities of discussing the condition and prospects of the Catholic Church, the prevalence of what they considered Pelagian views amongst theologians, the neglect of the study of the Fathers, above all of St. Augustine, the laxity of confessors in imparting absolution and allowing their penitents to receive Holy Communion, and the absolute necessity of returning to the strict discipline of the early Church. In 1617 the two friends separated, Jansen returning to Louvain, where he was appointed to a chair of scriptural exegesis, and du Verger to Paris, where he took up his residence though he held at the same time the commendatory abbacy of St. Cyran. As professor of Scripture Jansen showed himself both industrious and orthodox, so that in 1636 on the nomination of Philip IV. of Spain he was appointed Bishop of Ypres. From that time till 1639, when he passed away, he administered the affairs of his diocese with commendable prudence and zeal.

During the greater portion of his life he had devoted all his spare moments to the study of the works of St. Augustine especially those directed against the Pelagians, and he had prepared a treatise on Grace, in which treatise he claimed to have reproduced exactly the teaching of St. Augustine. This work was finished but not published when he took seriously ill, and the manuscript was handed over by him to some of his friends for publication. Before his death, however, he declared in presence of witnesses that "if the Holy See wishes any change I am an obedient son and I submit to that Church in which I have lived to my dying hour." * Notwithstanding various efforts that were made to prevent publication Jansen's book *Augustinus* was given to the world in 1640.

* Callewaert, *Cornelius Jansénius d'Ypres, ses derniers moments, sa soumission*, 1893.

Like Baius Jansen refused to recognise that in the condition of innocence, in which man was constituted before the Fall, he was endowed with numerous gifts and graces, that were pure gifts of God in no way due to human nature. Hence he maintained that by the sin of our First Parents human nature was essentially corrupted, and man fell helplessly under the control of concupiscence, so that, do what he would, he must of necessity sin. There was therefore in man an irresistible inclination impelling him towards evil, to counteract which Grace was given as a force impelling him towards good, with the result that he was drawn necessarily towards good or evil according to the relative strength of these two conflicting delectations. It followed from this that merely sufficient grace was never given. If the Grace was stronger than the tendency towards evil it was efficacious; if it was weaker it was not sufficient. Yet, whether he acted under the impulse of Grace or of concupiscence, man acted freely, because, according to Jansen, absence of all external pressure was all that was required to make an act free and worthy of praise or blame.

The book *Augustinus* created a profound sensation among theologians. It was hailed as a marvel of learning and ability by those who were still attached secretly to the school of Baius as well as by the enemies of the Jesuits. A new edition appeared in Paris only to be condemned by the Holy Office (1641) and by Urban VIII. in the Bull, *In Eminenti* (1642). Various difficulties were raised against the acceptance of the papal decision in Louvain and in the Netherlands, and it was only after a long delay and by threats of extreme measures that the Archbishop of Mechlin and those who followed him were obliged to submit (1653).

The real struggle regarding *Augustinus* was to be waged, however, in Paris and France. There, the Abbot of St. Cyran had been busily at work preparing the way for Jansen's doctrine, by attacking the modern laxity of the Church, and advocating the necessity of a complete return to the rigorous discipline of the early centuries. He had made the acquaintance of the family of the celebrated lawyer, Antoine Arnauld, six of whose family had entered the convent of Port Royal, of which one of them Angélique* was then superioress, while his youngest son, Antoine, a pupil of St. Cyran, was destined to be the leader of the French Jansenists. St. Cyran insisted on such rigorous conditions for the worthy reception of the Eucharist, that people feared to receive Holy Communion lest they should be guilty of sacrilege, and for a similar reason many priests abstained from the celebration of Mass. He attacked the Jesuits for their laxity of doctrine and practice in regard to the Sacrament of Penance. He himself insisted on the absolute necessity of perfect contrition and complete satisfaction as an essential condition for absolution. These views were accepted by the nuns at Port Royal and by many clergy in Paris. On account of certain writings likely to lead to religious trouble St. Cyran was arrested by order of Cardinal Richelieu (1638) and died in 1643. His place was taken by his brilliant pupil, Antoine Arnauld, who had been ordained priest in 1641, and who like his master was the determined opponent of the Jesuits. In 1643 he published a book entitled *De la fréquente Communion,* in which he put forward such strict theories about the conditions required for the worthy reception of the Eucharist that many people were frightened into abstaining even from fulfilling their Easter Communion. Despite the efforts of St. Vincent de Paul and others the book was read freely and produced widespread and alarming results.

The condemnation pronounced by Urban VIII. (1642) against *Augustinus,* though accepted by the king, the Archbishop of Paris, and the Sorbonne, found many staunch opponents. It was contended that the condemnation was the work of the Jesuits rather than of the

* Montlaur, *Angélique Arnauld,* 1902.

Pope, that it was based on the groundless supposition that the system of Jansen was identical with that of Baius, and that as no individual proposition in *Augustinus* had been condemned people were perfectly free to discuss the views it contained. To put an end to all possibility of misunderstanding Cornet, syndic of Paris University, selected from *Augustinus* five propositions, which he believed contained the whole essence of Jansen's system, and submitted them to the Sorbonne for examination (1649). Owing to the intervention of the Parliament of Paris in favour of the Jansenists the propositions were referred to the Assembly of the Clergy (1650), but the vast body of the bishops considered that it was a question on which a decision should be sought from Rome. Accordingly eighty-five of the bishops addressed a petition to Innocent X. (1651) requesting him to pronounce a definitive sentence on the orthodoxy or unorthodoxy of the five propositions, while a minority of their body objected to such an appeal as an infringement of the liberties of the Gallican Church. A commission, some of the members of which were recognised supporters of the Jansenists, was appointed by the Pope to examine the question, and after prolonged discussions extending over two years Innocent X. issued the Bull, *Cum occasione* (1653), by which the five propositions were condemned. The Bull was received so favourably by the king, the bishops, and the Sorbonne that it was hoped the end of the controversy was in sight.

The Jansenists, however, soon discovered a new method of evading the condemnation and of rendering the papal letter null and void. They admitted that the five propositions were justly censured, but they denied that these propositions were to be found in *Augustinus,* or, if they were in *Augustinus,* they contended they were there in a sense quite different from that which had been condemned by the Pope. To justify this position they introduced the celebrated distinction between law and fact; that is to say, while admitting the authority of the

Church to issue definitive and binding decisions on doctrinal matters, they denied that she was infallible in regard to questions of fact, as for example, whether a certain proposition was contained in a certain book or what might be the meaning which the author intended to convey. On matters of fact such as these the Church might err, and the most that could be demanded of the faithful in case of such decisions was respectful silence. At the same time by means of sermons, pamphlets, and letters, by advice given by priests, and by the influence of several religious houses, notably Port Royal, the sect was gaining ground rapidly in Paris, and feeling began to run high against the Jesuits. The antipathy to the Jesuits was increased and became much more general after the appearance of the *Lettres Provinciales* (1656-57) written by Pascal (1623-62). The writer was an exceedingly able controversialist, and in many respects a deeply religious man. From the point of view of literature the *Provincial Letters* were in a sense a masterpiece, but they were grossly unfair to those whom they attacked.*

The Sorbonne offered a strong opposition to the Jansenists, as did also the bishops (1656). In the same year Alexander VII. issued the Bull, *Ad Sanctam Petri Sedem,* by which he condemned the distinction drawn between law and fact, and declared that the five propositions were to be found in *Augustinus* and were condemned in the sense in which they were understood by the Jansenists. The Assembly of the Clergy having accepted this Bull drew up a formulary of faith based on the teaching it contained. The greater part of the Jansenists either refused entirely to subscribe to this formulary, or else subscribed only with certain reservations and restrictions. The nuns at Port Royal were most obstinate in their refusal. As they persisted in their attitude notwithstanding the prayers and entreaties of the Archbishop of Paris he was obliged reluctantly to exclude them from the sacraments. One of the principal

* Giraud, *Pascal, l'homme, l'oeuvre, l'influence,* 1905.

objections urged against the acceptance of the formulary being that the Assembly of the Clergy had no authority to prescribe any such profession of faith, Alexander VII. at the request of many of the bishops issued a new constitution, *Regiminis Apostolici* (1664), in which he insisted that all priests secular and regular and all members of religious communities should subscribe to the anti-Jansenist formulary that he forwarded.

Most of the Jansenists refused to yield obedience even to the commands of the Pope. They were strengthened in their refusal by the fact that four of the French bishops set them a bad example by approving publicly in their pastorals the Jansenist distinction between law and fact. The Council of State promptly suppressed these pastorals (1665), and at the request of Louis XIV. Alexander VII. appointed a commission for the trial of the disobedient bishops. In the meantime, before the commission could proceed with the trial, Alexander VII. died, and was succeeded by Clement IX. (1667). Several of the French bishops addressed a joint letter to the new Pope, in which by a rather unfair use of extracts from the works of theologians they sought to excuse the attitude of their four brother bishops, and at the same time they hinted to the king that the controversy was taking a course likely to be fraught with great danger to the liberties of the Gallican Church. Louis XIV., who had been hitherto most determined in his efforts against the Jansenists, began to grow lukewarm, and the whole situation in France was fast becoming decidedly critical. Some of the French bishops offered their services as mediators. Through their intervention it was agreed that without expressly retracting their pastorals the bishops should consent to sign the formulary drawn up by the Pope, and induce the clergy to do likewise. The bishops signed the formulary, and held synods in which they secured the signatures of their clergy, but at the same time in their conversations and in their addresses they made it perfectly clear that they had done so only with the Jansenist restrictions and reservations. The announcement of their submission pure and simple was forwarded to the Pope without any reference to any conditions or qualifications, and the Pope informed the king that he was about to issue letters of reconciliation to the four bishops. Before the letters were forwarded, however, rumours began to reach Rome that all was not well, and a new investigation was ordered. Finally, in view of the very critical state of affairs it was decided that the Pope might proceed safely on the documents received from the nuncio and the mediators without reference to the information acquired from other sources. In January 1669 the letters of reconciliation were issued. The Jansenists hailed the *Clementine Peace* as a great triumph for their party, and boasted publicly that Clement IX. had receded from the position taken up by his predecessor, by accepting the Jansenist distinction between law and fact. That their boasting was without foundation is sufficiently clear from a mere cursory examination of the papal letters. The Pope makes it perfectly evident that the letters were issued on the assumption that the bishops had subscribed without any reservation or restriction. He states expressly that he was firmly resolved to uphold the constitutions of his predecessors, and that he would never admit any restriction or reservation.

(d) THE IMMACULATE CONCEPTION

Passaglia, *De Immaculat. Concept. B.V.M.*, 3 vols., 1855. Strozzi, *Controversia dell' Immacolata Concezione*, 1700. Roskovány, *De Beata Virgine in suo conceptu immaculata*, 1873-92. Le Bachelet, *L'Immac. Conc.*, 1903. Bishop, *The Origins of the Feast of the Conception of B.V.M.*, 1904. Ullathorne, *The Immaculate Conception of the Mother of God*, 1904.

From the days of Duns Scotus the doctrine of the Immaculate Conception was received very generally by the universities and the theologians. The Dominicans, feeling themselves called upon to support the views of St. Thomas, who argued against the Immaculate Conception as understood in his own time, opposed the common teaching. The question was brought before the schismatical assembly at Basle (1439), where it was defined that the Immaculate Conception of the Blessed Virgin was in harmony with reason and Scripture, and should be approved and accepted by all Christians. This teaching was confirmed by several provincial synods in France and Germany, as well as by many of the universities. Paris and Cologne, for example, obliged all their members to swear to defend the doctrine. Sixtus IV. bestowed indulgences on those who would observe the Feast of the Immaculate Conception (1476), but although favouring the doctrine he forbade the defenders or opponents to charge each other with heresy (1483). When in the discussions on Original Sin at the Council of Trent the subject was raised, no formal decision was given because the Fathers were determined to direct all their attention to the doctrines that had been rejected by the Reformers. At the same time the opinion of the Fathers was expressed clearly enough, since they declared that in their decrees regarding the universality of Original Sin they did not mean to include the Immaculate Virgin Mary (V. Sess. 1546). Pius V. condemned a proposition of Baius, in which it was laid down that Christ alone escaped the guilt of Original Sin, and that the Blessed Virgin suffered death on account of the guilt she contracted by her descent from Adam (1567). A Spanish Franciscan, Francis of Santiago, having claimed that he had a vision in support of the doctrine, a sharp controversy broke out in Spain, to end which Philip III. besought the Pope to give a definitive decision. Paul V. contented himself, however, with renewing the decrees of his predecessors Sixtus IV. and Pius V. forbidding charges of heresy to be bandied about by the disputants (1616), but in the following year he forbade any public defence of the theses directed against the doctrine of the Immaculate Conception. Gregory XV. though unwilling to yield to the request of the Spanish Court for a formal definition, prohibited either public or private opposition to the doctrine unless in case of those who had received special authorisation from the Holy See. Finally in 1661 Alexander VII. in the constitution, *Sollicitudo omnium Ecclesiarum,* explained the true meaning of the doctrine, and forbade any further opposition to what he declared to be the common and pious belief of the Church.

(e) Tyrannicide

Hergenröther, *Katholische Kirche u. Christl. Staat,* 1872. Parkinson, *Catholic Writers on Tyrannicide* (*Month,* March - April, 1873). Duhr. *Jesuiten-Fabeln,* 3 auf., pp. 659 *sqq.*

Whether Tyrannicide is lawful or unlawful was a question on which different views were held by theologians. The murder of the Duke of Orleans by orders of the Duke of Burgundy (1407) helped to stir up the controversy. Amongst the dependents of the Duke of Burgundy was a priest, John Parvus (Petit or Le Petit), who accompanied the Duke to Paris, and in a public assembly defended the Duke of Burgundy on the ground that it was lawful to murder a tyrant (1408). Nine propositions selected from this speech were condemned by the Bishop of Paris, by the Inquisition, and by the university (1414). The Duke of Burgundy appealed to Pope John XXIII., while the representatives of France at the Council of Constance were instructed to seek the opinion of the assembly. The discussion of the subject was complicated by political issues. As the Council of Constance was anxious to avoid all quarrels with the King of France, the Duke of Burgundy, or the Emperor, it contented itself with issuing a very general condemnation of Tyrannicide. Before the council closed, however, the question was raised once more in connexion with a book published by the Dominican, John of Falkenberg, who was a strong partisan of the Teutonic Knights in their struggle against the King of Poland, and who maintained that it was lawful to kill the King of Poland. He undertook the defence of Petit's work, and wrote strongly against the representatives of the University of Paris. The Poles demanded his condemnation, but though he was arrested and detained in prison his book was not condemned by the council. A Dominican chapter held in 1417 repudiated Falkenberg's teaching.

For a long time the subject was not discussed by Catholic theologians though Tyrannicide was defended by the leading Reformers, including Luther and Melanchthon, but during the religious wars in France and in Scotland it was advocated in theory by some of the French Calvinists such as Languet and Boucher as well as by the Scotch leader, John Knox, and put into practice by their followers against the Duke of Guise and Cardinal Beaton.* The Jesuits in France were accused of sympathising with this doctrine during the reign of Henry IV., but there was not sufficient evidence to support such a charge. Some of their theologians may have defended the legality of rebellion in certain circumstances, but this was a doctrine in no way peculiar to the Jesuits. The only serious argument brought forward by the opponents of the Jesuits was drawn from a work published by a Spanish Jesuit, Mariana (1536-1624). It was written for the instruction of some of the princes of Spain, and was dedicated to Philip III. In many respects it was an exceedingly praiseworthy work, but the author's reference to the murder of Henry III. of France and his defence of Tyrannicide, hedged round though it was by many restrictions and reservations, gave great offence in France, and provided the enemies of the Society with a splendid weapon for a general attack upon the entire body. As a matter of fact

* Lecky, *The History of the Rise and Influence of Rationalism in Europe*, 1913, p. 164.

Mariana's book did not represent the views of the Jesuits. In 1610 the general, Aquaviva, forbade any of his subjects to defend the teaching on Tyrannicide it contained.

(f) THE COPERNICAN SYSTEM. GALILEO GALILEI.

Müller, *Nicolaus Copernicus* (*Stimmen aus M.-Laach*, 1898, *Supp.* 72). Hipler, *Nicolaus Copernicus u. Martin Luther*, 1868. Müller, *Galileo-Galilei*, 1908. Von Gebler, *Galileo Galilei und die Römische Curie* (Eng. Trans., 1879). L'Epinois, *La question de Galilée*, 1878, *The Month* (Sept., 1867; March-April, 1868).

Nicolaus Copernicus (Koppernick or Koppernigk, 1473-1543) was born at Thorn, and was educated principally at Cracow, Bologna, Padua, and Ferrara. He was a canon of the chapter of Frauenberg, and most probably a priest. During his stay in Italy he was brought into contact with the new views put forward by Cardinal Nicholas of Cusa and others regarding the position of the earth in the system of the universe. His own studies led him to the conclusion that the sun was the centre round which the earth and all the heavenly bodies moved in their course. He communicated his conclusions to some of his special friends in 1531, but he hesitated to publish them on account of the ridicule that such a novel opinion was sure to excite. One of his pupils lectured at Rome on the subject, and explained the theories of Copernicus to Clement VII. (1533).

Yielding at last to the entreaties of Cardinal Schönberg, Archbishop of Capua, and Bishop Giese of Culm he entrusted his work for publication to one of his pupils, Rheticus, professor at Wittenberg, but the opposition of the Lutheran professors made it impossible to bring out the book in that city. It was finally published under the editorship of Osiander at Nürnberg in 1543. In the preface to the work Osiander made considerable changes out of deference to the views of Luther and Melanchthon, the most important of which was that he referred to the system of Copernicus as an hypothesis that might or might not be true. The work, *De Revolutionibus Orbium Coelestium* was dedicated to Pope Paul III. The principal opposition to the novel views of Copernicus came from the side of the Lutheran theologians, and it was only years later, when feeling was aroused by the controversy regarding Galileo, that any suspicion of unorthodoxy was directed against Copernicus by Catholic writers. Needless to say Copernicus died as he had lived, a devoted Catholic, fully convinced that he had done good service for religion as well as for science.

Galileo Galilei (1564-1642) was remarkable from a very early age for his abilities as a student of mathematics and mechanics. Indeed it was in these subjects and not in astronomy that he achieved his most brilliant and most lasting successes. He taught at Pisa and Padua, and was afterwards employed at the court of the Grand Duke of Tuscany. In 1609 he perfected the telescope by means of which he was enabled to make observations of the heavenly bodies, and from these observations and discoveries he was led to the conclusion that the heliocentric system as advocated by Copernicus was the only one scientifically tenable. He came to Rome, where he was welcomed by the Pope and the cardinals, and set up his telescope in the Vatican gardens (1611). At first Galileo's views excited no great opposition, but owing to the imprudent propaganda carried on by some of his own friends, notably by the Carmelite, Foscarini, a violent controversy broke out in which the scientific side of the theory was almost completely forgotten. Against Galileo it was contended that his system contradicted the Scripture, which spoke of the sun standing still in its course at the prayers of Josue, and that it was, therefore, inadmissible. At the time in Italy the ecclesiastical authorities were markedly conservative and hostile to innovations, particularly as there was then a strong party in Italy, of whom Paul Sarpi may be taken as a typical example, who were liberal and Lutheran in their tendencies and sympathies. Had the discussion been confined to learned circles no notice might have been taken of it, but once an appeal was made to the masses of the people it was almost inevitable that Galileo should have been denounced to the Inquisition.

In the circumstances a decision favourable to Galileo could hardly have been expected. The old Ptolemaic system was so closely bound up with the philosophic and scientific teaching of the age that its abandonment meant little less than a complete revolution in the world of learning. As yet the vast body of those who were specially versed in the subject treated the new theory with derision, while the arguments put forward by Galileo in its defence were so weak and inconclusive that most of them have been long since abandoned. The hostile attitude, too, of the Lutheran divines could hardly fail to exercise some influence on the Roman consultors. In 1615 Galileo appeared before the Inquisition to defend his views, but without any result. The heliocentric system was condemned as being opposed to Scripture and therefore heretical, and Galileo was obliged to promise never again to put it forward (1616). The work of Copernicus and those of some other writers who advocated the Copernican system were condemned *donec corrigantur*. The decision of the congregation was wrong, but in the circumstances not unintelligible. Nor can it be contended for a moment that from this mistake any solid argument can be drawn against the infallibility of the Pope. Paul V. was undoubtedly present at the session in which the condemnation was agreed upon and approved of the verdict, but still the decision remained only the decision of a congregation and not the binding *ex-cathedra* pronouncement of the Head of the Church. Indeed, it appears from a letter of Cardinal Bellarmine that the congregation regarded its teaching as only provisional, and that if it were proved beyond doubt that the sun was stationary it would be necessary to admit that the passages of Scripture urged against this view had been misunderstood.

Galileo left Rome with no intention of observing the promise he had made. After the election of Urban VIII. who, as Cardinal Barberini, had been his faithful friend and supporter, Galileo returned to Rome (1624) in the hope of procuring a revision of the verdict; but though he was received with all honour, and accorded an annual pension from the papal treasury his request was refused. He returned to Florence, where he published eight years later a new book on the subject, couched in the form of a dialogue between supporters of the rival systems, the Ptolemaic and the Copernican, in which Simplicissimus, the defender of the old view, was not only routed but covered with ridicule. Such a flagrant violation of his promise could not pass unnoticed. He was summoned to appear once more before the Inquisition, and arrived in Rome in February 1633. At first he denied that he had written in favour of his views since 1616, then he pleaded guilty, confessed that he was in error, and appealed to the court to deal gently with an old and infirm man. He was found guilty, and was condemned to recite the seven penitential psalms once a week for three years, and to be imprisoned at the pleasure of the Inquisition. It is not true to say that Galileo was shut up in the dungeons of the Inquisition. He was detained only for a few days, and even during that time he was lodged in the comfortable apartments of one of the higher officials. Neither is it correct to state that he was tortured or subjected to any bodily punishment. He was released almost immediately on parole, and lived for a time at Rome in the palace of the Grand Duke of Tuscany. Later on he retired to his villa at Arcetri, and finally he was allowed to return to Florence. In 1642, fortified by the last sacraments and comforted by the papal benediction, he passed away. His body was laid to rest within the walls of the Church of Santa Croce at Florence. Most of his misfortunes were due to his own rashness and the imprudence of his friends and supporters. His condemnation is the sole scientific blunder that can be laid to the charge of the Roman Congregation. That his condemnation was not due to any hatred of science or to any desire of the Roman ecclesiastics to oppose the progress of knowledge is evident enough from the favours and honours lavished upon his predecessors in the same field of research, Cardinal Nicholas of Cusa, Peurbach, Müller (Regiomontanus), and Copernicus.

(g) Progress of Theological Studies

Hurter, *Nomenclator Literarius Theologiae Catholicae* 3 auf., 1903. Werner, *Geschichte der apologetischen und polemischen Literatur der Christlichen Theologie,* 1865. Turmel, *Histoire de la théologie positive,* etc., 1906. Slater, *A Short History of Moral Theology,* 1909. Gigot, *General Introduction to the Sacred Scriptures,* 1900. De Smedt, *Introductio Generalis ad Historiam Ecclesiasticam,* 1876. Benigni, *Historiae Ecclesiasticae Repertorium,* 1902. Collins, *The Study of Ecclesiastical History,* 1903.

In the latter half of the fifteenth and the first quarter of the sixteenth centuries theological studies had reached a very low ebb. The great philosophico-theological movement of the thirteenth century had spent its force, and it seemed highly probable that in the struggle with Humanism theology would be obliged to abandon its position of pre-eminence in favour of the classics. Yet as events showed the results of Humanism were far from being so harmful to theology as seemed likely at first. Zeal for the pagan authors of antiquity helped to stir up zeal for the writings of the Fathers, new editions of which were published in various centres; while at the same time the value of the spirit of historical and literary criticism, so highly prized by the devotees of Humanism, was recognised by theologians, and availed of largely in defending the authority of the documents that they cited. In the controversies with the Reformers, who rejected entirely the authority and the methods of the

Scholastics, Catholic authors and controversialists were obliged to fix their attention upon the Scriptures and on the historical side of theology as evidenced in the doctrines and usages of the early centuries. The revival, too, at this period of the older religious orders, particularly the Benedictines and the Dominicans, and the establishment of new bodies such as the Jesuits and the Oratorians were in the highest degree providential. It gave to the Church the services of trained and devoted scholars, who were free to devote all their energies to the defence of Catholic interests. In the remarkable theological movement of the sixteenth century Spain and Italy held the leading place. The University of Salamanca contended with the *Collegium Romanum* for the supremacy once yielded freely to the theological faculty of Paris. The founder of the new school of theology, which had its seat in Salamanca but which exercised a very considerable influence on the Jesuit teachers in Rome, Ingolstadt, and Prague, was the Dominican, Francis of Vittoria (1480-1546). Realising the necessities of the age better than most of his contemporaries he put an end to the useless discussions and degenerate style of his immediate predecessors, re-introduced the *Summa* of St. Thomas, insisted on supplementing it by a close study of the Scriptures and the writings of the Fathers, and inaugurated a new style of theological Latinity freed both from the barbarisms of the later Scholastics and the pedantry of the classical enthusiasts.

Amongst the Catholic theologians of Germany who defended the Church against the attacks of the Reformers may be mentioned *John Eck* (1486-1543) connected for the greater part of his life with the University of Ingolstadt, who in his publications proved himself the leading champion on the Catholic side against Luther; *John Faber* (1478-1541) the friend of Erasmus and the staunch though moderate opponent of Luther and Zwingli, whose work, *Malleus Haereticorum* (1524), secured for him the title of "the hammer of heretics";

CONTROVERSIES AND STUDIES 301

John Cochlaeus (1479-1552) who published more than two hundred treatises against the Reformers, nearly all of which suffered from the haste and temper in which they were prepared; *John Gropper* (1503-59) whose early training as a lawyer led him at first to favour proposed compromises hardly compatible with Catholic doctrine, but who laboured earnestly to save Cologne for the Catholic Church; *John Nas* (1534-90) the Franciscan Bishop of Brixen, and the *Blessed Peter Canisius, S.J.* (1521-97) who did more than any other man to save the entire German nation from falling under the sway of Lutheranism, thereby meriting the title of the second apostle of Germany.

Tommaso de Vio (1469-1534), surnamed *Cajetan* * from his place of birth, Gäeta, joined the Dominicans at an early age, taught at Padua and Pavia, and was elected general of his order (1508). Seven years later he was created cardinal and was entrusted with a mission to Germany (1518), in the course of which he sought vainly to procure the submission of Luther. During the closing years of his life he acted as one of the principal advisers of Clement VII. By his example and his advice he did much to revive theological studies amongst the Dominicans and to recall them to the study of St. Thomas. As a theologian and an exegetist he showed himself to be a man of great ability and judgment sometimes slightly erratic and novel in his theories, while from the point of view of style he was vastly superior to most of his predecessors. His principal works are the Commentary on St. Thomas (1507-22) and his explanations of nearly all the books of the Old and New Testament. *Ambrosius Catharinus* † (1487-1553) was born at Siena, graduated a doctor of canon and civil law at the age of sixteen, pleaded as a lawyer in the consistorial court of Leo X., joined the Dominicans at an advanced age, took a prominent part in the discussions at the earlier sessions of

* Quétif-Echard, *Scriptores Ordinis Praedicatorum*, ii. 14.
† *Id.*, ii. 144-51.

the Council of Trent, was appointed bishop in 1546, and died in 1553 when, as it is said, he was on the point of receiving the cardinal's hat. Catharinus was a keen controversialist, but as a theologian he was brilliant rather than solid. His strong leaning towards novelties brought him into conflict with Cajetan and in fact with the whole Dominican Order, the most cherished opinions of which he loved to attack. *Dominic Soto* (1494-1560) was a student of Alcalá and Paris, joined the Dominicans in 1524, taught theology at Salamanca from 1532 till 1545, when he went to the Council of Trent, where his services were invaluable especially on the question of Grace and Justification, acted for a time as confessor to Charles V., and returned finally to his chair at Salamanca. He was the last of the great commentators on the *Sentences* of Peter Lombard. His principal works were *De Natura et Gratia,* written for the information of the Fathers of Trent and *De Justitia et Jure* (1556). Another of the distinguished Spanish Dominicans of this period was *Melchior Cano* (1509-60), who had as his professor at Salamanca Francis of Vittoria. He taught at Alcalá and Salamanca, accompanied Soto to the Council of Trent, was appointed bishop but resigned almost immediately, and served for some time as provincial of the Dominicans. His greatest work was the *De Locis Theologicis* (1563), in which as a kind of introduction to theology he endeavoured to establish scientifically the foundations of theological science. He discusses the ten *loci* or sources which he enumerates, namely, Scripture, Tradition, the Catholic Church, the Councils, the Fathers, the Roman Church, the Scholastics, Reason, the authority of philosophers, and the authority of historians. His style is simple, concise, and elegant.

Robert Bellarmine [*] (1542-1621) was born in Tuscany, joined the Society of Jesus (1560), studied at the *Collegium Romanum* and at Louvain, where he taught for some time, was recalled to Rome to assume charge of

---

[*] Couderc, *Robert Bellarmin,* 2 vols, 1893.

the new chair of controversy in the *Collegium Romanum,* took a prominent part in the preparation of the Clementine edition of the Vulgate, in the *Congregatio de Auxiliis,* and in the trial of Galileo, engaged in controversy with James I. of England in regard to the Catholic Oath, was created cardinal (1599), and appointed Archbishop of Capua (1602). Cardinal Bellarmine was a deeply religious man, severe only with himself, an indefatigable student always anxious to be just to his opponents, and specially gifted as a lecturer and writer. His greatest work was undoubtedly the *Disputationes de controversis Christianae fidei articulis,* in which he displayed a most minute and accurate knowledge of the religious tenets of all the sects of the Reformers. The book created such an enormous sensation in Europe at the time that special lecturers were employed at some of the Protestant universities to undertake its refutation. His commentary on the Psalms, and the Catechism prepared by him at the request of Clement VIII. also deserve special notice. The last complete edition of his writings was published at Paris in 1870. *Francis Suarez* * (1548-1617) was born at Granada, joined the Society of Jesus in Salamanca (1564) and taught at Valladolid, Rome, Alcalá, Salamanca, and Coimbra. Like Bellarmine Suarez was a man of great personal piety, well versed in the writings of the Fathers and in the literature of the Reformers. His works are clear and well arranged but somewhat too diffuse. The last edition (Vives) of his works was published at Paris (1856-61). *John de Lugo* (1583-1660) was born at Madrid, went to Salamanca to study law, and there joined the Jesuits. He lectured at first in Valladolid, and later on at Rome where he attracted crowds of students, and he was created cardinal in 1643. In his works he has covered practically the entire field of dogmatic and moral theology. The best known are perhaps *De Justitia et Jure* and his

* Werner, *Franz Suárez und die Scholastik der letzten jahrhunderte,* 1861.

treatises on the Incarnation, the Sacraments, the Eucharist, and the Sacrifice of the Mass. The last edition of his published works was issued at Paris (1868-9). *Dionysius Petavius* * (Petau, 1583-1652) was born at Orleans, studied arts and theology at Paris, entered the Society of Jesus (1605), and taught theology at Paris for twenty-two years. He was one of the best known and most respected scholars of his age. Quite apart from his merits as a theologian, his works on chronology, notably the *De doctrina temporum* and the *Tabulae Chronologicae* would have been sufficient to place him in the first rank of the scholars of his period. In theology he is chiefly remarkable for the introduction and application of the historical method in his discussion of dogma, and hence he is referred to rightly as the " Father of the History of Dogma." His principal theological work is the *Dogmata Theologica* (1644-50).

The splendid example of a scientific treatment of moral theology set by St. Thomas produced very little effect during the fourteenth and fifteenth centuries, for the simple reason that the *Sentences,* and not the *Summa,* was the text-book used generally in the schools. Following along the lines marked out by Raymond of Penafort in his *Summa de poenitentia et matrimonio* (1235) a large number of *Summae* or manuals for the use of confessors were published during the fourteenth and fifteenth centuries, the last of them being that of Silvester Prierias, one of the earliest opponents of Luther. One of the few writers of this period who undertook to give a scientific exposition of moral principles was St. Antoninus (1389-1459), the Dominican Archbishop of Florence, in his *Summa Theologica Moralis*.

The rejection of the *Sentences* in favour of the *Summa,* and the reform decrees of the Council of Trent gave a new impetus to the study of moral theology during the sixteenth and seventeenth centuries. Most of the great writers of this period, Gregory of Valencia (1550-1603),

* Chatellain, *Vie du Père D. Petavius*, 1884.

CONTROVERSIES AND STUDIES 305

Vasquez (1549-1604), Lessius (1554-1623), Bañez (1528-1604), Medina (1527-81), Sanchez (1550-1610), Suarez, and De Lugo devoted special attention to the underlying principles of moral theology, and in some cases to their practical application. The *De Poenitentia* and the *Responsa Moralia* of De Lugo served as models of what might be called the mixed treatment, partly scientific and partly casuistical. The *Theologia Moralis* of the Jesuit writer, Paul Laymann (1574-1635), the *Instructio Sacerdotum* of Cardinal Toledo and the *Medulla Theologiae Moralis* of Hermann Busenbaum (1600-68), which went through forty editions in his own lifetime, may be cited as examples of this method.

The controversy regarding Probabilism did not assume a serious aspect till the rise and condemnation of Jansenism. During this period the enemies of the Jesuits pointed to the approval given to Probabilism by the Fathers of the Society as a proof of the laxity of view introduced by the Jesuit theologians. Whatever may be said of the system, one thing is certain, namely, that the Jesuit theologians were not the first to put it forward. It was followed in practice long before the institution of the Society of Jesus, was enunciated clearly enough as a theory by the Spanish Dominican Bartholomew Medina (1527-81) and was adopted, at least in their solutions of particular cases, by most of the great writers during the latter half of the sixteenth and the first half of the seventeenth centuries.

Amongst the most notable writers on ascetical theology of this period were St. Ignatius of Loyola, the author of the *Spiritual Exercises,* St. Teresa (1515-82) the zealous reformer of the Carmelites, St. John of God (1495-1550) the founder of the Brothers of St. John of God, the Dominican Louis of Granada (1504-88), St. Francis de Sales (1567-1622), the two Jesuit writers Alphonsus Rodriguez (1526-1616) and Louis de Ponte (1554-1624), and Jean Jacques Olier (1608-57) the founder of the Sulpicians.

Many causes combined to bring about a great revival in Scriptural studies. The Humanist movement ensured that commentators would bring to their task a ready knowledge of Greek and a critical appreciation of the age and value of manuscripts. The study of Hebrew was taken up enthusiastically by scholars like Reuchlin, and was rendered comparatively easy by the grammars and dictionaries published by Reuchlin, Santez, Pagnino, Pelikan, and Cardinal Bellarmine. The contention of the early Reformers that the Bible was the sole source of divine revelation, though never accepted by Catholic scholars, necessitated a close study of the words and literal meaning of the sacred text. In opposition to the private interpretation of the Reformers Catholics contended that the teaching authority of the Church and the interpretation of the Fathers were the only sure guides. The distinction between deutero-canonical and proto-canonical books was ended for Catholics by the decision of the Council of Trent attributing to both equal authority. The question of the extent of inspiration was left by the Council of Trent practically in the position in which it stood when the Council of Florence defined that God was the author of the sacred books. Many writers were inclined to hold the view that the divine assistance extended to the style and the words, while others rejected verbal inspiration. A few Catholic scholars, for example Lessius and Hamel, seemed to maintain that a book composed by human industry and without the assistance of the Holy Ghost might be regarded as inspired if afterwards the Holy Ghost testified that it contained no error. Since the Vatican Council such a view is no longer tenable.

The activity in the field of Scriptural studies is witnessed to by the edition of the Greek and Latin text of the New Testament prepared by Erasmus, by the Complutensian Polyglot published under the direction of Cardinal Ximenes (1514-17) to be followed by similar publications at Antwerp (1569-72) and at Paris (1628-

45), by the edition of the Septuagint at the command of Sixtus V. and the edition of the Vulgate under Clement VIII. Amongst the great Catholic commentators of the age may be mentioned Cardinal Cajetan (+1534), the Dominican Santez Pagnino (+1541), Cornelius Jansen (1576), the Jesuit, John Maldonatus (+1583), whose commentary on the four Gospels is still unrivalled, William Estius (+1613), professor at Douay, whose views on Grace were not unaffected by the controversies then raging at Louvain, and Cornelius à Lapide, S.J. (+1673), professor at Louvain and Rome, who published an excellent commentary on the entire Scriptures.

Ecclesiastical History profited largely from the Humanist movement which brought to light many new documents, and tended to awaken a spirit of scholarly criticism. The contention put forward by the Reformers, that primitive Christianity had been completely corrupted by semi-Pagan novelties during the Middle Ages, made it imperative on Catholic scholars to direct their attention to the practices and teaching of the early centuries. New editions of the writings of the Fathers were prepared by the Dominicans, Jesuits, and by the Benedictines of St. Maur. The attempt made by the Magdeburg Centuriators to justify Lutheranism at the bar of history called forth the *Annales Ecclesiastici* of Cardinal Baronius (1538-1607). These Annals dealt with the history of the Church from the beginning till the year 1198. The work was continued by the Oratorians Raynaldus and Laderchi, by de Sponde, Bzovius and Augustine Theiner. The History of the Popes was written by the Augustinian Panvinio (+1568) and by the Dominican, Ciacconius (+1599). Hagiographical studies were pursued by Surius (+1578) and by the Jesuit Heribert Rosweyde (1569-1629). It was the latter who first conceived the plan of publishing the Lives of the Saints in one series. He died without having done much except to collect an immense mass of materials. The scheme was, however, taken up by other members of the society, notably, John Van Bolland (Bollandus, 1596-1665), Godfrey Henschen (1601-81) and Daniel von Papenbroeck (Papebroch, 1628-1714). These were the first of the Bollandists, and the first volume of the *Acta Sanctorum* appeared in 1643.

CHAPTER VII

THE AGE OF ABSOLUTISM AND UNBELIEF

New Controversies and Errors

THE centralisation movement, that began in the fifteenth century, and that tended to increase the power of the sovereign at the expense of the lesser nobles and of the people, was strengthened and developed by the religious revolt. The Protestant reformers appealed to the civil rulers for assistance against the ecclesiastical authorities, and in return for the aid given to them so generously they were willing to concede to the king all power in civil and ecclesiastical matters. Thenceforth the princes were to be so supreme in spirituals as well as in temporals that their right to determine the religion of their subjects was recognised as a first principle of government. During the days of the Counter-Reformation, when religious enthusiasm was aroused to its highest pitch, the Catholic sovereigns of Europe fought not so much for the aggrandisement of their own power as for the unity of their kingdoms and the defence of the religion of their fathers, threatened as it was with complete overthrow.

But once the first fervour had passed away, and once it was recognised that religious harmony could not be secured by the sword, Catholic sovereigns began to understand that the Protestant theory of state supremacy meant an increase of power to the crown, and might be utilised to reduce the only partially independent institution in their kingdoms to a state of slavery. Hence they increased their demands, interfered more and more in ecclesiastical matters, set themselves to diminish the jurisdiction of the Pope by means of the *Royal Placet* and other such legal contrivances, and asserted for themselves as much authority as could be reconciled with Catholic principles interpreted in their most liberal sense. They urged the bishops to assert their independence against the Holy See, and the bishops, forgetful of the fact that freedom from Rome meant enslavement by the State, co-operated willingly in carrying out the programme of their royal masters. Men like Bossuet, carried away by the new theories of the divine right of kings, aimed at reducing the power of Rome to a shadow. They were more anxious to be considered national patriots than good Catholics. They understood only when it was too late that in their close union with the Holy See lay their only hope of resisting state aggression, and that by weakening the authority of the Pope they were weakening the one power that could defend their own rights and the rights of the Church. Their whole policy tended to the realisation of the system of national churches, and were it not for the divine protection guaranteed by Christ to the society that He Himself had founded, their policy might have been crowned with success.

The principle, too, of individual judgment introduced by the Reformers was soon pushed to its logical conclusions. If by means of this principle Luther and his disciples could reject certain doctrines and practices that had been followed for centuries by the whole Catholic world, why could not others, imitating the example that had been given to them, set aside many of the dogmas retained by Luther as being only the inventions of men, and why could their successors not go farther still, and question the very foundation of Christianity itself? The results of this unbridled liberty of thought made themselves felt in religion, in philosophy, in politics, in literature, and in art. Rationalism became fashionable in educated circles, at the courts, and at the universities. Even Catholics who still remained loyal to the Church were not uninfluenced by the spirit of religious indifference. It seemed to them that many of the dogmas and devotions of the Church were too old-fashioned, and required to be modernised. The courts in many cases favoured the spread of these anti-religious views because they meant the weakening of the power of the Church. They joined with the apostles of rationalism in attacking the Society of Jesus, because the rationalists realised that the Jesuits were their strongest opponents, while the politicians believed them to be the most strenuous supporters of the jurisdiction of Rome. It was only when the storm of revolution was about to burst over Europe that the civil rulers understood fully the dangerous tendency of the movement which they had encouraged. They began to open their eyes to the fact that war against Christianity meant war against established authority, and that the unbridled liberty of thought and speech which had been tolerated was likely to prove more dangerous to the cause of monarchy than to the cause of religion.

(a) GALLICANISM

Richer, *De ecclesiastica et politica potestate*, 1611. Puyol, *Edm. Richer, Étude sur la renovation du gallicanisme au XVIIe siècle*, 2 vols., 1877. Lavisse, *Histoire de France* (vii.), 1905. Bossuet, *Defensio declarationis cleri gallicani* (ed. 1885). Gérin, *Recherches historiques sur l'assemblée de 1682*, 1878. De Maistre, *De L'Église gallicane*, 1821. Gérin, *Louis XIV. et le Saint-Siège*, 1894. Mention, *Documents relatifs au rapport du clergé avec la royauté de 1682 à 1705*, 1893. Picot, *Mémoires pour servir à l'histoire ecclésiastique pendan le XVIIIe siècle*, 7 vols., 1853-57.

For centuries France had been the zealous defender of the Church and of the Holy See. From the days of Clovis the French nation had never wavered in its allegiance to the successors of Saint Peter, many of whom had been obliged to seek refuge on the soil of France. In return for this support given ungrudgingly in many a dangerous crisis, several important privileges were conferred by the Popes on the French rulers, in which privileges moderate supporters of Gallicanism were inclined to seek the origin and best explanation of the so-called Gallican Liberties. But the extreme Gallicans, realising that such a defence could avail but little against the Pope, who could recall what his predecessors had granted, maintained that the Gallican Liberties were but the survival of the liberty possessed by individual churches in the early centuries, that these liberties had been restricted gradually by the Holy See, which succeeded in reducing the national churches to servitude, and that the French Church alone had withstood these assaults, and had maintained intact the discipline and constitution of the apostolic age. The rulers of France, well aware that every restriction upon the authority of the Church meant an increase of the power of the Crown, gladly fostered this movement, while the French bishops, unconscious of the fact that independence of Rome meant servitude to the king, allowed themselves to be used as tools in carrying out the programme of state absolutism.

The Pragmatic Sanction of Louis IX., referred to by many writers as the first indication of Gallicanism, is admitted by all scholars to be a forgery. The exorbitant demands formulated by Philip the Fair during his quarrel with Boniface VIII. are the first clear indication of the Gallican theory that confronts the historian. The principles laid down by the rulers of France during this quarrel were amplified considerably in the writings of William of Occam, Jean of Jandun, and Marsilius of Padua, and were reduced to definite form in the time of the Great Western Schism. At that time, mainly owing to the influence of Gerson, D'Ailly, and other French leaders, the doctrine of the superiority of a General Council over the Pope was accepted, and received official confirmation in the decrees of the fourth and fifth sessions of the Council of Constance (1414-17), and in the Council of Basle (1431-6). The decrees passed by the

Synod of Bourges (1438) were strongly anti-papal, and despite the efforts of Nicholas V. and his successors to procure their withdrawal most of them remained in force till the Concordat of 1516. Partly owing to this Concordat, by which the right of nomination to all bishoprics and abbacies in France was secured to the Crown, and partly to the strong feeling aroused in France during the conflict with Calvinism, little was heard of Gallicanism during the sixteenth century. It was mainly, however, as a result of the opposition of the French bishops that the decree of the Council of Florence regarding papal supremacy was not renewed at the Council of Trent, and it was in great measure due to the influence of Gallican principles that the decrees of the Council of Trent were not received in France for years.

Gallicanism was renewed in the beginning of the seventeenth century by Edmund Richer (1559-1631), syndic of the Paris University and editor of the works of Gerson. He was a man who held novel views about the constitution both of Church and State, and who professed his sincere admiration for Gerson's exposition of the relations that should exist between a General Council and the Pope. In 1610 one of the Dominican students undertook to defend publicly the supremacy and infallibility of the Pope, whereupon a violent controversy broke out, but it was settled for the time by the prudent intervention of Cardinal Du Perron. The Parliament of Paris, however, undertook the defence of Richer and of the work that he published in explanation of his theories. In this book, *De Ecclesiastica et Politica Potestate* (1611) he laid it down that the Church was a limited not an absolute monarchy; that the whole legislative power rested in the hands of the hierarchy, composed according to him of both bishops and parish priests; that this legislative power should be exercised in a General Council, which as representing the entire hierarchy was the repository of infallibility, and was not subject to the Pope; that the power of executing the decrees of General Councils and of carrying on the administration of the Church rested in the hands of the Pope, who could not act contrary to the canons; that neither Pope nor hierarchy could undertake to enforce ecclesiastical decrees by any other means except persuasion; and that if force were required it could be exercised only by the head of the State, who was the natural protector of the Church, and responsible to God for the due observance of the canons.

This book was condemned by the provincial Synod of Sens, held under the presidency of Cardinal Du Perron in 1612, by the provincial Synod of Aix, by the Bishop of Paris, and by the Pope. The Parliament of Paris, however, supported Richer, who lodged an appeal with the civil authorities against the action of the bishops, and sought to secure for his theories the support of the Sorbonne. Though forced by the king to resign his office at the University he continued to defend his views stubbornly till 1629, when for political rather than for religious reasons he was called upon by Cardinal Richelieu to sign a complete recantation. Shortly before his death in 1631 he declared in the presence of several witnesses that this submission was made freely and from conviction, but some papers written by him and discovered after his death make it very difficult to believe that these protestations were sincere.

The writings of Pithou, Richer, and Dupuy, and above all the rising influence of the Jansenist party helped to spread the Gallican teaching among the French clergy, and to make them more willing to yield obedience to the king than to the Pope. The Abbot of St. Cyran attacked the authority of the Holy See, but fortunately the extreme nature of his views, and the need felt by both the priests and the bishops of France for the interference of the Holy See against the Jansenists, served to restrain the anti-papal feeling, and to keep the leading theological writers, like Duval, Du Perron, Ysambert

ABSOLUTISM AND UNBELIEF

and Abelly, free from any Gallican bias. The accession of Louis XIV. (1661) marked a new era in the history of the Gallican Liberties. He was young, headstrong, anxious to extend the territories of France, and determined to assert his own supreme authority at all costs. With Louis XIV. firmly seated on the French throne, and with the Jansenist party intriguing in the Parliament of Paris, which had shown itself hostile to papal claims, it was not difficult to predict that the relations with the Holy See were likely to become unfriendly. The Duke of Créqui,* Louis XIV.'s ambassador at Rome, set himself deliberately to bring about a complete rupture. Owing to an attack made by some Corsicans of the papal guard on the French embassy, the ambassador refused to accept any apology and left Rome, while Louis XIV. dismissed the nuncio at Paris, occupied the papal territories of Avignon and Venaissin, and despatched an army against the Papal States. Alexander VII. was obliged to yield to force, and to accept the very humiliating terms imposed upon him by the Peace of Pisa (1664).

The Jansenist party and the enemies of the Holy See took advantage of the policy of Louis XIV. to push forward their designs. A violent clamour was raised in 1661 against a thesis defended in the Jesuit schools (*Thesis Claromontana*) in favour of papal infallibility, and a still more violent clamour ensued when it was maintained in a public defence at the Sorbonne (1663) that the Pope has supreme jurisdiction over the Church, and that General Councils, though useful for the suppression of heresy, are not necessary. The Jansenist party appealed to the Parliament of Paris, which issued a prohibition against teaching or defending the doctrine of papal infallibility, but the majority of the doctors of the Sorbonne stood by their opinion, and refused to register the decree of Parliament. The opponents of the Sorbonne, hastening to avenge this first defeat, denounced

* De Moüy, *L'ambassade du duc de Créqui*, 2 vols., 1893.

the defence of a somewhat similar thesis by a Cistercian student as a violation of the prohibition. The syndic of the university was suspended from his office for six months, and the university itself was threatened with very serious reforms unless it consented to accept the Gallican theories. As a result of the interference of intermediaries a declaration satisfactory to the Parliament was issued by the doctors of the faculty (1663). In this document they announced that it was not the teaching of the university that the Pope had any authority over the king in temporal matters, that he was superior to a General Council, or that he was infallible in matters of faith without the consent of a General Council. On the contrary, they asserted that it was the teaching of the university that in temporal affairs the king was subject only to God, that his subjects could not be dispensed from their allegiance to him by any power on earth, and that the rights and liberties of the Gallican Church must be respected. This decree was signed by seventy-seven doctors, and was published by the Parliament as the teaching of the entire theological faculty and as a guide that should be followed in all theological schools. A violent agitation was begun against all who attempted to uphold the rights of the Holy See either in public disputations or in published works, an agitation that was all the more inexplicable, owing to the fact that at this time both the king and Parliament were endeavouring to persuade the Jansenists to accept as infallible the decrees by which the Pope had condemned their teaching.

Before this agitation had died away a new cause of dissension had come to the front in the shape of the *Regalia*. By the term *Regalia* was meant the right of the King of France to hold the revenues of vacant Sees and abbacies, and to appoint to benefices during the vacancy, and until the oath of allegiance had been taken by the new bishops and had been registered. Such a privilege was undoubtedly bad for religion, and though

ABSOLUTISM AND UNBELIEF

it was tolerated for certain grave reasons by the second General Council of Lyons (1274), a decree of excommunication was levelled against anyone, prince or subject, cleric or layman, who would endeavour to introduce it or to abet its introduction into those places where it did not already exist. Many of the provinces of France had not been subject to the *Regalia* hitherto, but in defiance of the law of the Church Louis XIV. issued a royal mandate (1673-75), claiming for himself the *Regalia* in all dioceses of France, and commanding bishops who had not taken the oath of allegiance to take it immediately and to have it registered.

The bishops of France submitted to this decree with two exceptions. These were Pavillon, bishop of Alet, and Caulet, bishop of Pamiers, both of whom though attached to the Jansenist party were determined to maintain the rights of the Church. The king, regardless of their protests, proceeded to appoint to benefices in their dioceses on the ground that they had not registered their oath of allegiance. They replied by issuing excommunication against all those who accepted such appointments, and, when their censures were declared null and void by their respective metropolitans, they appealed to the Holy See. During the contest Pavillon of Alet died, and the whole brunt of the struggle fell upon his companion. The latter was encouraged by the active assistance of Innocent XI., who quashed the sentence of the metropolitans, encouraged the bishop and chapter to resist, and threatened the king with the censures of the Church unless he desisted from his campaign (1678-79). The bishop himself died, but the chapter showed its loyalty to his injunctions by appointing a vicar-capitular in opposition to the vicar-capitular nominated by the king. A most violent persecution was begun against the vicar-capitular and the clergy who remained loyal to him. Both on account of the important interests at stake and the courage displayed by the opponents of the king the contest was followed with the greatest interest not only in France itself but throughout the Catholic world. While feeling was thus running high another event happened in Paris that added fuel to the flame. The Cistercian nuns at Charonne were entitled according to their constitution to elect their own superioress, but de Harlay, Archbishop of Paris, acting in conformity with the orders of Louis XIV. endeavoured to force upon the community a superioress belonging to an entirely different order. The nuns appealed to Innocent XI., who annulled the appointment and insisted upon a free canonical election (1680). The Parliament of Paris set aside the papal sentence, and when this interference was rejected by the Pope, the papal document was suppressed.

In view of the difficulties that had arisen an extraordinary meeting of the bishops of France was summoned. Fifty-two of them met in Paris (March-May, 1681). The two leading men in favour of the king were Francis de Harlay, Archbishop of Paris, and Le Tellier, Archbishop of Rheims. Acting under the influence of these men the bishops agreed that it was their duty to submit to the claims of the crown in regard to the *Regalia;* they condemned the interference of the Pope in favour of the Paris community of Cistercian nuns as well as his action against the metropolitan of the Bishop of Pamiers; and they expressed the opinion that a general assembly of the clergy of France should be called to discuss the whole situation.

The General Assembly consisting of thirty-four bishops and thirty-seven priests elected to represent the entire body of the French clergy met at Paris (October 1681-July 1682). The most prominent men of the Assembly were Francis de Harlay of Paris, Le Tellier of Rheims, Colbert of Rouen, Choisseul of Tournay, and Bossuet, the recently appointed Bishop of Meaux. The latter, whose reputation as a preacher had already spread throughout France, delivered the opening address, which was moderate in tone, and not unfriendly to the rights of the Holy See though at the same time strongly pro-Gallican. Certain minor rights claimed by the king having been abandoned, the bishops gratefully accepted the *Regalia,* and despatched a letter to the Pope urging him to yield to the royal demands for the sake of peace. But the Pope, more concerned for the liberty of the French bishops than they were themselves, reminded them sharply of their duty to the Church, while at the same time he refused to follow their advice. In their reply to the Pope the bishops took occasion to praise the spirit of religious zeal shown by Louis XIV., who, according to them, was forced reluctantly to take up the gauge of battle that had been thrown at his feet by Rome. Meantime an attempt was made by the Assembly to formulate definitely the Gallican liberties. These were:—

(1) That Saint Peter and his successors have received jurisdiction only over spiritual things. Kings are not subject to them in temporal matters, nor can the subjects of kings be released from their oath of allegiance by the Pope.

(2) That the plenitude of power in spiritual things enjoyed by the Holy See does not contradict the decrees of the fourth and fifth sessions of the Council of Constance, which decrees, having been passed by a General Council and approved by the Pope, were observed by the Gallican Church.

(3) That the apostolic authority of the Roman Church must be exercised in accordance with the canons inspired by the Holy Ghost, and with the rules, constitutions, and customs of the Gallican Church.

(4) That though the Pope has the chief part in determining questions of faith, and though his decrees have force in the entire Church and in each particular church, yet his decisions are not irreformable, at least until they are approved by the verdict of the entire Church.

This Declaration (the Four Gallican Articles) was approved by the king, who ordered that it should be observed by all teachers and professors, and should be accepted by all candidates for theological degrees. Although the Archbishop of Paris recommended warmly the acceptance of the Gallican Articles the doctors of the Sorbonne offered strong opposition to the new royal theology, so that it was only after recourse had been had to the most violent expedients that the consent of one hundred and sixty-two doctors could be obtained, while the majority against the Gallican Articles was over five hundred. The decision of the minority was published as the decision of the faculty, and steps were taken at once to remove the opponents of the articles, and to make the Sorbonne strongly Gallican in its teaching. While protests against the articles poured in from different universities and from many of the countries of Europe the Pope kept silent; but when two priests, who took part in the Assembly of 1682, were nominated for vacant bishoprics Innocent XI. refused to appoint them until they should have expressed regret for their action. The king would not permit them to do so, nor would he allow the others who were nominated to accept their appointments from the Pope, and as a result in 1688 thirty-five of the French Sees had been left without bishops.

In this same year another incident occurred that rendered the relations between the Pope and Louis XIV. still more strained. The right of asylum possessed by various ambassadors at the papal court had become a very serious abuse. Formerly it was attached only to the residence of the ambassador, but in the course of time it was extended until it included the whole of the quarter in which the embassy was situated, with the result that it became impossible for the guardians of the peace to carry out their duties. For this reason the right of asylum was suppressed by the Pope. All the other nations submitted to such a reasonable restriction, but Louis XIV., anxious rather to provoke than to avoid a quarrel, refused to abandon the privilege. He

ABSOLUTISM AND UNBELIEF

sent as his ambassador to Rome (1687) the Marquis de Lavardin, who entered Rome at the head of a force of five hundred armed men, and whose conduct from first to last was so outrageous that Innocent XI. was obliged to excommunicate him, and to lay the Church of Saint Louis under interdict. Immediately Louis XIV. occupied Avignon and Venaissin, assembled an army in Southern France to be despatched against the Papal States, and ordered that an appeal to a future General Council should be prepared for presentation. Twenty-six of the bishops expressed their approval of this appeal, and so successful had been the dragooning of the university that nearly all the faculties adopted a similar attitude (1688).

For a time it seemed as if a schism involving the whole of the French Church was unavoidable, since neither Pope nor king seemed willing to give way. But Louis XIV. had no wish to become a second Henry VIII. The threatening condition of affairs in Europe made it impossible for him to despatch an army against Rome. At the same time the fear of civil disturbance in France in case he rejected completely the authority of the Pope, and the danger that such a step might involve for French interests abroad kept him from taking the final plunge. He recalled the obnoxious ambassador from Rome, (1689), abandoned the right of asylum as attached to the quarter of the French embassy (1690), and restored Avignon and Venaissin to the Pope. Alexander VIII. demanded the withdrawal of the royal edict of March 1683 enjoining the public acceptance of the Gallican Articles. He required also a retractation from the clergy who had taken part in the Assembly, and issued a Bull denouncing the extension of the rights of the *Regalia* and declaring the Gallican Articles null and void (1690). Louis XIV., finding that the public opinion of the Catholic world was against him, and that a reconciliation with the Papacy would be very helpful to him in carrying out his political schemes, opened friendly negotiations with Innocent XII. In the end an agreement was arrived at, whereby the clerics who had taken part in the Assembly of 1682, having expressed their regret to the Pope for their action, were appointed to the bishoprics to which they had been nominated; while the king informed the Pope (1693) that the decrees issued by him insisting on the acceptance of the Gallican Articles, would not be enforced.

But in spite of this royal assurance, Gallicanism had still a strong hold upon France. The younger men in the Sorbonne could be relied upon to support the Articles, and the influence of writers like John de Launoy (1603-1678) and of Dupin helped to spread Gallicanism among the clergy and laymen of the rising generation. Throughout the whole controversy Bossuet had shown himself too accommodating to the crown, though at the same time he was not unfriendly to the claims of the Holy See, nor inclined to favour such extreme measures as most of his episcopal colleagues. Acting on the request of the king he prepared a defence of the Gallican Articles, which was not published till long after his death. During the eighteenth century, when the crown and the Parliament of Paris interfered constantly in all religious questions, the bishops and clergy of France had good reason to regret their defence of the so-called Gallican Liberties. The Concordat concluded by Napoleon with Pius VII. and the action taken by the Pope with the approval of Napoleon for the carrying out of the Concordat dealt a staggering blow to Gallicanism, despite the attempt made to revive it by the Organic Articles. The great body of the bishops of France during the nineteenth century had little sympathy with Gallican principles, which disappeared entirely after the definition of Papal Infallibility at the Vatican Council.

(b) FEBRONIANISM AND JOSEPHISM

Febronius, *De statu ecclesiae deque legitima potestate Romani Pontificis*, etc., 1762. Idem, *Commentarius in suam retractationem*, etc., 1781. Kuentziger, *Fébronius, et le Fébronianisme*, 1890. Werner, *Geschichte der Katholischen Theologie in Deutschland*, 1866. *Codex iuris ecclesiastici Josephini*, etc., 1788. Gendry, *Les débuts de Joséphisme* (*Revue des Quest. hist.*, 1894). *Recueil des actes concernant le voyage du Pape Pie VI. à Vienne*, 1782. Stigloher, *Die errichtung der päpstlichen Nuntiatur und der Emser Kongress*, 1867. Münch, *Geschichte des Emser Kongresses*, 1840. De Potter, *Vie de Scipion de Ricci*, 1825.

The spirit of opposition to the Holy See soon spread from France to the various states of the Holy Roman Empire. The violent onslaughts of the Reformers and the imminent danger of heresy had driven the Catholics of Germany to cling more closely to the Holy See, and had helped to extinguish the anti-Roman feeling, that had been so strong in the early years of the sixteenth century. But once the religious wars had ended without a decisive victory for either party, and once the theory of imperial neutrality had been sanctioned formally by the Peace of Westphalia (1648), the Catholic rulers of Germany, not excluding even the spiritual princes, showed more anxiety to increase their own power than to safeguard the interests of their religion. The example of the Protestant states, where the rulers were supreme in religious as in temporal affairs, could not fail to encourage Catholic sovereigns to assert for themselves greater authority over the Church in their own territories, in utter disregard of the rights of the Pope and of the constitution of the Church. Frequently during the reigns of Leopold I. (1657-1705), of Joseph I. (1705-11), and of Charles VI. (1711-40) the interference of the civil power in ecclesiastical affairs had given just cause for complaint. But it was only during the reign of Francis I. (1745-65), and more especially of Joseph II.

(1765-90), that the full results of the Jansenist, Gallican, and Liberal Catholic teaching made themselves felt in the empire as a whole, and in the various states of which the empire was composed.

The most learned exponent of Gallican views on the German side of the Rhine was John Nicholas von Hontheim (1701-90), who was himself a student of Van Espen (1646-1728), the well-known Gallican and Jansenist professor of canon law in the University of Louvain. On the return of von Hontheim to his native city of Trier he was entrusted with various important offices by the Prince-bishop of Trier, by whose advice he was appointed assistant bishop of that See (1740). He was a man of great ability, well versed especially in ecclesiastical and local history, and a close student of the writings of the Gallicans (Richer, Dupin, Thomassin, and Van Espen). At the time the hope of a reunion between the Lutherans and the Catholics in Germany was not abandoned completely. It seemed to von Hontheim that by lessening the power of the Papacy, which was regarded by the Protestants as the greatest obstacle to reconciliation, Gallicanism provided the basis for a good reunion programme, that was likely to be acceptable to moderate men of both parties in Germany. With the object therefore of promoting the cause of reunion he set himself to compose his remarkable book, *De Statu Ecclesiae et de Legitima Potestate Romani Pontificis,* published in 1762 under the assumed name of Justinus Febronius.

According to Febronius Christ entrusted the power of the keys not to the Pope nor to the hierarchy, but to the whole body of the faithful, who in turn handed over the duty of administration to the Pope and the hierarchy. All bishops according to him were equal, and all were independent in the government of their own dioceses, though at the same time, for the purpose of preserving unity, a primacy of honour should be accorded to the successor of Saint Peter. But this primacy was not necessarily the special prerogative of the Roman See; it could be separated from that Church and transferred to another diocese. In the early ages of Christianity the Roman bishops never claimed the power wielded by their successors in later times. These pretentions to supreme jurisdiction were founded upon the false decretals of Isidore and other forgeries, and constituted a corruption that should not be tolerated any longer in the Church. In reality the Pope was only the first amongst equals, empowered no doubt to carry on the administration of the Church, but incapable of making laws or irreformable decrees on faith or morals. He was subject to a General Council which alone enjoyed the prerogative of infallibility. Febronius called upon the Pope to abandon his untenable demands, and to be content with the position held by his predecessors in the early centuries. If he refused to do so spontaneously he should be forced to give up his usurpations, and if necessary the bishops should call upon the civil rulers to assist them in their struggle. As a means of restoring the Papacy to its rightful position, Febronius recommended the convocation of national synods and of a General Council, the proper instruction of priests and people, the judicious use of the Royal *Placet* on papal announcements, the enforcement of the *Appelatio ab Abusu* against papal and episcopal aggression, and, as a last resort, the refusal of obedience.

The book was in such complete accord with the absolutist tendencies of the age that it was received with applause by the civil rulers, and by the court canonists, theologians, and lawyers, who saw in it the realisation of their own dreams of a state Church subservient to the civil ruler. The book was, however, condemned by Clement XIII. (1764), who exhorted the German bishops to take vigorous measures against such dangerous theories. Many of the bishops were indifferent; others of them were favourable to von Hontheim's views; but the majority suppressed the book in their dioceses. Several treatises were published in reply to Febronius, the most notable of which were those from the pen of Ballerini and Zaccaria. New editions of the work of Febronius were called for, and translations of the whole or part of it appeared in German, Italian, French, Spanish, and Portuguese. It was received with great favour in Austria, where the principles of Febronius were adopted by most of the leading court canonists. At a meeting held in Coblenz (1769) the three Prince-bishops of Mainz, Trier, and Cologne presented a catalogue of complaints (*Gravamina*) against the Roman Curia, many of which were extracted from or based upon the work of Hontheim. After repeated appeals of the Pope to the Prince-bishop of Trier to exercise his influence upon von Hontheim, the latter consented to make a retractation in 1778, but his followers alleged that the retractation having been secured by threats was valueless. This contention was supported by a commentary published by Hontheim in explanation of his retractation, in which he showed clearly enough that he had not receded an inch from his original position. Before his death in 1790 he expressed regret for the doctrines he put forward, and died in full communion with the Church.

The teaching of Febronius, paving the way as it did for the supremacy of the State in religious matters, was welcomed by the Emperor Joseph II., by the Elector of Bavaria, as well as by the spiritual princes of the Rhine provinces. In Austria, especially, violent measures were taken to assert the royal supremacy. Joseph II. was influenced largely by the Gallican and liberal tendencies of his early teachers and advisers. He dreamed of making Austria a rich, powerful, and united kingdom, and becoming himself its supreme and absolute ruler. During the reign of his mother, Maria Theresa, he was kept in check, but after her death in 1780, in conjunction with his prime minister, Kaunitz, he began to inaugurate his schemes of ecclesiastical reform. He insisted upon the Royal *Placet* on all documents issued by the Pope or by the bishops, forbade the bishops of his territories to hold any direct communication with Rome or to ask for a renewal of their faculties, which faculties he undertook to confer by his own authority. He forbade all his subjects to seek or to accept honours from the Pope, insisted upon the bishops taking the oath of allegiance to himself before their consecration, introduced a system of state-controlled education, and suppressed a number of religious houses. In order that the clergy might be instructed in the proper ecclesiastical principles, he abolished the episcopal seminaries, and established central seminaries at Vienna, Pest, Louvain, Freiburg, and Pavia for the education of the clergy in his dominions. Clerical students from Austria were forbidden to frequent the *Collegium Germanicum* at Rome lest they should be brought under the influence of ultramontane teaching. Even the smallest details of ecclesiastical worship were determined by royal decrees. In all these reforms Joseph II. was but reducing to practice the teaching of Febronius.

By personal letters and by communications through his nuncio Pius VI. sought to induce Joseph II. to abstain from such a policy of state aggression; but, as all his representations were ineffective, he determined to undertake a journey to Vienna, in the hope that his presence might bring about a change in the policy of the Emperor, or at least stir up the bishops to defend the interests of the Church (1782). He arrived at Vienna, had frequent interviews with the Emperor and with his minister Kaunitz, and was obliged to leave without any other result, except that he had assured himself of the fact that, whatever about the Emperor or the bishops, the majority of the people of Austria were still loyal to the head of the Catholic Church. The following year (1783) Joseph II. paid a return visit to Rome, when he was induced by the representations of the Spanish ambassador to desist from his plan of a complete severance of Austria from the Holy See.

Joseph II. had, however, proceeded too quickly and too violently in his measures of reform. The people and the large body of the clergy were opposed to him as were also the Cardinal-Archbishop of Vienna, the bishops of Hungary, and the bishops of Belgium under the leadership of Cardinal Frankenberg. The state of affairs in the Austrian Netherlands became so threatening that the people rose in revolt (1789), and Joseph II. found himself obliged to turn to the Pope whom he had so maltreated and despised, in the hope that he might induce the Belgian Catholics to return to their allegiance. He promised to withdraw most of the reforms that he had introduced, but his repentance came too late to save the Austrian rule in the Netherlands. He died in 1790 with the full consciousness of the failure of all his schemes.

While Joseph II. was reducing Febronianism to practice in the Austrian territories, the Prince-bishops of Mainz, Trier, and Cologne hastened to show their anxiety for the suppression of ultramontanism in the Rhinelands. The list of grievances against Rome presented to the Emperor in 1769 indicated clearly their attachment to Gallican principles, and this feeling was not likely to be weakened by the erection of an apostolic nunciature at Munich in 1785. This step was taken by the Pope at the request of Carl Theodore, Elector of Bavaria, a great part of whose territory was under the spiritual rule of the prince-bishops. The prince-bishops of the west, together with the Prince-bishop of Salzburg, all of whom were hostile already to the papal nuncio, were greatly incensed by what they considered this new derogation of their rights, and sent representatives to a congress convoked to meet at Ems (1786). The result of the congress was the celebrated document known as the *Punctuation of Ems,* in which they declared that most of the prerogatives claimed by the Pope were unknown in the early centuries, and were based entirely on the false decretals. They insisted that there should be no longer appeals to Rome, that papal ordinances should be binding in any diocese only after they had been accepted by the bishop of the diocese, that the oath of allegiance taken by all bishops before consecration should be changed, that no quinquennial faculties should be sought as bishops already had such faculties by virtue of their office, and that religious orders should not be exempt from the authority of the ordinaries, nor be placed under the jurisdiction of foreign superiors. The *Punctuation of Ems* reduced the primacy of the Pope to a mere primacy of honour, and had it been acted upon, it must have led inevitably to national schism.

The bishops forwarded the document to Joseph II., who, while approving of it, refused to interfere. The Elector of Bavaria opposed the action of the bishops as did also Pacca* (1756-1854), the papal nuncio at Cologne. The latter issued a circular to the clergy warning them that the dispensations granted by the prince-bishops without reference to Rome were worthless. This circular gave great annoyance to the prince-bishops, particularly as they found themselves deserted by most of those on whose support they had relied. Even the Protestant ruler Frederick II. of Prussia took the part of Rome against the archbishops. In face of the unfriendly attitude of the bishops and clergy nothing remained for the prince-bishops but to withdraw from an untenable position. The Archbishop of Cologne for reasons of his own made his submission, and asked for a renewal of his quinquennial faculties (1787). The Archbishop of Trier made a similar application, not indeed as Archbishop of Trier, but as Bishop of Augsburg. But their submission was meant only to gain time. They sought to have the matter brought before the Diet at Regensburg in 1788, but the action of the Elector of Bavaria prevented an unfavourable verdict. Having failed in their design, they addressed a letter to the Pope asking him to put an end to the disedifying quarrel by with-

* Pacca, *Memorie storiche della nunziatura di Colonia*.

drawing the papal nuncio from Cologne, and by sending a representative to the Diet to arrange the terms of peace. The reply of Pius VI., covering as it did the whole ground of the controversy, contained a masterly defence of the papal rights and prerogatives (1789). The Archbishop of Trier publicly withdrew his adhesion to the *Punctuation,* and advised his Gallican colleagues to do likewise, but they refused, and in the election agreement of 1790 and 1792 they sought to pledge the emperors to support their policy. At last the Archbishops of Cologne and Salzburg made their submission, but the Archbishop of Mainz clung obstinately to his views, until the storm of the French Revolution broke over his city and territory, and put an end to his rule as a temporal prince.

In Tuscany where Leopold, brother of Joseph II., reigned (1765-90), a determined attempt was made to introduce Febronian principles as understood and applied in Austrian territory. Leopold was supported strongly in this attempt by Scipio Ricci, who, though a Jansenist at heart, had been appointed to the Bishopric of Pistoia at the request of the Grand-Duke. The Bishop of Pistoia set himself deliberately to introduce Jansenism and Gallicanism amongst his clergy. For this purpose he established a seminary at Pistoia, and placed it in the hands of teachers upon whom he could rely for the carrying out of his designs. In 1786 the Grand-Duke called a meeting of the bishops of the province, and explained to them in detail his programme of ecclesiastical reforms. With the exception of the Bishop of Pistoia and two others they refused to co-operate with him in his designs. This plan having failed recourse was had to other measures. A synod was summoned at Pistoia, which was presided over by Scipio Ricci, and guided in its deliberations by Tamburini the well-known Gallican professor of Pavia (1786). It was attended by over two hundred priests, some of whom belonged to the diocese, while others were total strangers. As might be expected the decrees of the synod were strongly Gallican and Jansenist. To ensure their introduction into the province of Tuscany a provincial synod of the bishops was called, but the bishops expressed their strong disapproval, and the people attacked the palace of the bishop. He was obliged to retire from his diocese, though at the same time he remained the active adviser of Leopold until the death of Joseph II. led to Leopold's election to the imperial throne (1790), and put an end to the disturbances in Tuscany. Pius VI. appointed a commission to study the decrees of Pistoia, and in 1794 he issued the Bull, *Auctorem Fidei,* in which the principal errors were condemned. The unfortunate bishop refused for years to make his submission. It was only in 1805, on the return journey of Pius VII. from the coronation of Napoleon at Paris, that he could be induced to make his peace with the Church.*

(c) JANSENISM

See bibliography, chap. vi. (c). Barthélemy, *Le cardinal de Noailles,* 1888. Doublet, *Un prélat janséniste. F. de Caulet,* 1895. Ingold, *Rome et la France. La seconde phase du jansénisme,* etc , 1901. Le Roy, *Un janséniste en exil. Correspondance de Pasquier Quesnel,* 1900. Van Vlooten, *Esquisse historique sur l'ancienne église catholique des Pays-Bas,* 1861. De Bellegarde, *Coup d'oeil sur l'ancienne église catholique de Hollande,* etc., 1896.

The Clementine Peace,† obtained as it was by trickery and fraud, was used by the Jansenists as a means of deceiving the public and of winning new recruits. They contended that Clement IX., regardless of the action of his predecessors, had accepted the Jansenist principle of respectful silence. Several who had signed the formulary of Alexander VII. withdrew their signatures, and amongst the bishops, clergy, university graduates, and religious orders, particularly amongst

---

* Scaduto, *Stato e chiesa sotto Leopoldo I., granduca di Toscana,* 1885. Venturi, *Il vescovo de Ricci e la Corte Romana,* 1885.

† *See* p. 291.

the Oratorians and Benedictines of St. Maur, the Jansenists gained many adherents. Though outwardly peace reigned in France, yet the Jansenist spirit made great headway, as was shown by the opposition to several popular devotions and in the spread of rigorist opinions and practices in regard to confession and communion. The controversy on the Gallican Liberties complicated the issue very considerably, and made it impossible for the Pope to exercise his authority. Even bishops like Bossuet, who were strongly opposed to Jansenism, were inclined to regard papal interference with suspicion, while Louis XIV. was precluded from enforcing the decrees of the Pope as his predecessors had enforced them. The Jansenist party became much stronger, and only a slight incident was required to precipitate a new crisis.

This incident was supplied by the publication of the *Réflexions Morales sur le Nouveau Testament* by Pasquier Quesnel (1634-1719). The writer had been an Oratorian, but having been expelled from that society in 1684 he took refuge with Antoine Arnauld in Brussels. Upon the death of the latter in 1694, he became the recognised head or grand-prior of the Jansenist party. An earlier edition of this work had been published, bearing the approbation of Vialart, Bishop of Châlons, and though several additions had been made, this approbation was printed on the new edition side by side with the approbation of Louis Noailles, then Bishop of Châlons (1695). The following year Noailles having become Archbishop of Paris felt called upon by his new position to condemn a work closely akin in its ideas to those expressed in the *Réflexions Morales*. He was accused of inconsistency by the Jansenist party, one of whom published the *Problème ecclésiastique,* inquiring whether people were bound to follow the opinions of Louis Noailles, Bishop of Châlons in 1695, or of Louis Noailles, Archbishop of Paris in 1696? The controversy suddenly grew embittered. When a new edition was required in 1699, Noailles requested the judgment of Bossuet, who formulated certain changes that in his opinion should be made.* In the end the edition was published without the suggested changes and without the approbation of the archbishop.

While the controversy was raging round Quesnel's book, another incident occurred that tended to arouse all the old partisan feeling. A confessor submitted to the judgment of the Sorbonne the celebrated case of conscience. He asked whether a priest should absolve a penitent, who rejected the teaching set forth in the five propositions of Jansenius, but who maintained a respectful silence on the question whether or not they were to be found in the book *Augustinus*. In July 1701 forty doctors of the Sorbonne gave an affirmative reply to this question. The publication of this reply created such a storm in France that Clement XI. felt it necessary to condemn the decision of the Sorbonne (1703). The papal condemnation was supported by Louis XIV., as well as by the great body of the bishops. Two years later Clement XI. issued the Bull *Vineam Domini*,† confirming the constitutions of his predecessors, Innocent X. and Alexander VII., and condemned once more in an authoritative form the doctrine of respectful silence. The document was accepted by the king, by the Assembly of the Clergy, and by the majority of the bishops, though the attachment of some of the latter to Gallican principles led them to insist on certain conditions which the Pope could not accept. As the nuns of Port Royal still refused to submit, their community was broken up, the sisters being scattered through different convents in France (1709), and the following year the convent buildings were completely destroyed.

Meanwhile the controversy regarding the *Réflexions Morales* grew more bitter. Several of the bishops con-

* Ingold, *Bossuet et le jansénisme*, 1904.
† Denzinger, 11th edition, n. 1350.

demned the book as containing much in common with
the writings of Jansenius and of his followers in France.
Acting upon the demand of some of the bishops Clement
XI. issued a brief condemning Quesnel's book (1708).
The Jansenists refused to accept the papal decision and
the Parliament of Paris, then dominated to a great extent by Jansenist influence, adopted a hostile attitude.
Cardinal Noailles, considering the verdict of the Pope
as more or less a personal insult to himself, hesitated as
to what course he should take, but at last he consented to
accept the condemnation provided the Pope issued a
formal sentence. On the application of Louis XIV. the
Pope determined to put an end to all possibility of
doubt or misunderstanding by publishing the Bull,
Unigenitus[*] (1713) in which 101 propositions taken
from Quesnel's book were condemned. As is usual in
such documents the propositions were condemned *in
globo*, some as rash, some as offensive to pious ears,
and some as heretical. The Bull, *Unigenitus,* was
accepted immediately by one hundred and twelve bishops
of France, by the majority of the clergy, by the Sorbonne, and by the king and Parliament. The Jansenists refused to admit that it contained a final verdict on
the ground that, as it did not make clear which propositions were heretical and which only rash or offensive,
it was only a disciplinary enactment and not a binding
doctrinal decision. Cardinal Noailles wavered for a
time, but in the end he allied himself definitely with the
fourteen bishops who refused to accept the Bull
Unigenitus. Louis XIV., though opposed strongly to
the Jansenists, was unwilling to allow the Pope to take
serious action against the Archbishop of Paris lest the
liberties of the Gallican Church should be endangered,
while the Parliament of Paris sympathised openly with
those who refused to accept the papal decision.

The death of Louis XIV. (1714) and the accession of
the Duke of Orleans as regent led to a great reaction in

[*] Denzinger, *op. cit.*, nos. 1351-1451.

favour of Jansenism. Cardinal Noailles was honoured by a seat in the privy council, and became the principal adviser of the regent in ecclesiastical affairs. The Sorbonne withdrew its submission to the Bull *Unigenitus* (1715), and its example was followed by the Universities of Nantes and Rheims. Many of the Jansenist chapters and priests rebelled against their bishops, and were taken under the protection of the Parliament. The Archbishop of Paris was encouraged by addresses from his chapter and clergy to stand out firmly against the tyranny of Rome. More than once the Pope remonstrated with the regent, who promised much but refused to take decisive action. The Sorbonne was punished by the Pope by the withdrawal of its power to confer theological degrees (1716), while many of the bishops refused to allow their students to attend its courses. As a last desperate expedient four of the bishops of France appealed selemnly to a General Council against the Bull *Unigenitus* (1717), and their example was followed by large numbers. The *Appellants* as they were called created such a disturbance in France that they appeared to be much more numerous than they really were. Less than twenty of the bishops and not more than three thousand clerics, seven hundred of whom belonged to Paris, joined the party, while more than one hundred bishops and one hundred thousand clerics remained loyal to Rome. The fact, however, that Cardinal Noailles, Archbishop of Paris, placed himself at the head of the *Appellants* made the situation decidedly serious.

When private protests and remonstrances had failed Clement XI. issued the Bull, *Pastoralis Officii,* by which he excommunicated the *Appellants* (1718). Undaunted by this verdict a new appeal in solemn form was lodged by Cardinal Noailles, backed by his chapter and by a large number of the Paris clergy. Negotiations were opened up with Innocent XIII. and Benedict XIII. in the hope of inducing them to withdraw the

Bull *Unigenitus,* or at least to give it a milder interpretation, but the Popes refused to change the decisions that had been given by their predecessors. The Parliament of Paris espoused the cause of the *Appellants,* and refused to allow the bishops to take energetic action against them, until at last the king grew alarmed at the danger that threatened France. The energetic action taken by the provincial council of Embrun against some of the *Appellant* bishops (1727) received the approval of the court. In the following year (1728) Cardinal Noailles was induced to make his submission, and in a short time the Sorbonne doctors by a majority imitated his example. Though these submissions were not without good results, yet they served only to embitter still more the minds of a large body of the Jansenist party, and to strengthen them in their opposition to the Bull, *Unigenitus.*

The Jansenists having failed to secure the approval of Pope or king for their heretical teaching appealed to the visible judgment of God. The deacon, Francis of Paris,* who was one of the leaders of the sect, and whose sanctity was vouched for, according to his friends, by the fact that he had abstained from receiving Holy Communion for two years, died in 1727, and was buried in the cemetery of Saint Médard. Crowds flocked to pray at his tomb, and it was alleged that wonderful cures were being wrought by his intercession. One of the earliest and most striking of these alleged miracles was investigated by the Archbishop of Paris and was proved to be without foundation, but others still more remarkable were published broadcast by the party, with the result that hosts of invalids were brought from all parts of France in the hope of procuring recovery. Many, especially women, went into ecstacies and violent convulsions round the tomb, and while in this state they denounced the Pope, the bishops, and in a word all the

---

* Matthieu, *Histoire des miracles et des convulsionnaires de St. Médard,* 1864.

ABSOLUTISM AND UNBELIEF

adversaries of Jansenism. Owing to the unseemly and at times indecent scenes that took place the cemetery was closed by the civil authorities (1732), but the *Convulsionnaires,* as they were called, claimed that similar miracles were wrought in private houses, in which they assembled to pray, and to which clay taken from the tomb of the Deacon of Paris had been brought. The great body of the people ridiculed the extravagances of the sect, and many of the moderate Jansenists condemned the *Convulsionnaires* in unsparing terms. Instead of doing Jansenism any good these so-called miracles, utterly unworthy as they were of divine wisdom and holiness, served only to injure its cause, and indeed to injure the Christian religion generally, by placing a good weapon in the hands of its rationalist adversaries.

But even though heaven had not declared in favour of the Jansenists the Parliament of Paris determined to protect them. It defended bishops who refused to accept the Bull *Unigenitus* against the Pope, tried to prevent the orthodox bishops from suspending appellant priests, and forbade the exclusion of appellant laymen from the sacraments. The Parliament of Paris condemned the action of the clergy in refusing the last sacraments to the dying unless they could prove they had made their confession to an approved priest. Though the privy council annulled this condemnation Parliament stood by its decision, and challenged the authority of the Archbishop of Paris by punishing priests who refused the sacraments (1749-52). The bishops appealed to the king to defend the liberty of the Church, but the Parliament asserted its jurisdiction by depriving the Archbishop of Paris of his temporalities and by endeavouring to have him cited before the civil courts. Louis XIV. annulled the sentence of the Parliament, and banished some of the more violent of its members from the capital (1753). They were, however, soon recalled, and a royal mandate was issued enforcing silence on both parties. For infringing this order de Beaumont, Archbishop of Paris, was banished from his See, and several other bishops and priests were summoned before the legal tribunals.

The Assembly of the Clergy in 1755 petitioned the king to give more freedom to the Church, and to restore the exiled Archbishop of Paris to his See. A Commission was appointed to examine the whole question of the refusal of the sacraments, and as the Commission could not arrive at any decision, the case was submitted to Benedict XIV., who decided that those who were public and notorious opponents of the Bull, *Unigenitus,* should be treated as public sinners and should be excluded from the sacraments (1756). The Parliament of Paris and some of the provincial parliaments forbade the publication of the papal decision, but a royal order was issued commanding the universal acceptance of the Bull, *Unigenitus,* even though it might not be regarded as an irreformable rule of faith. According to this mandate the regulation for allowing or refusing the administrations of the sacraments was a matter to be determined by the bishops, though any person who considered himself aggrieved by their action might appeal against the abuse of ecclesiastical power. This decree was registered by the Parliament (1757), whereupon the Archbishop of Paris was allowed to return. From that time Jansenism declined rapidly in France, but the followers of the sect united with the Gallicans of the Parliament to enslave the Church, and with the Rationalists to procure the suppression of the Jesuits, whom they regarded as their most powerful opponents.

Many of the Jansenists fled to Holland, where the Gallicans were only too willing to welcome such rebels against Rome. The old Catholic hierarchy in Holland had been overthrown, and the Pope was obliged to appoint vicars apostolic to attend to the wants of the scattered Catholic communities. One of these appointed in 1688 was an Oratorian, and as such very partial to Quesnel and the Jansenists. Owing to his public alliance with the sect he was suspended from office in 1702 and deposed in 1704, but not before he had given Jansenism a great impetus in Holland. About seventy parishes and about eighty priests refused to recognise his successor, and went over to the Jansenist party. In 1723 a body of priests calling themselves the Chapter of Utrecht elected Steenhoven as Archbishop of Utrecht, and a suspended bishop named Varlet, belonging formerly to the Society for Foreign Missions, consecrated him against the protests of the Pope. Supported by the Calvinist government the new archbishop maintained himself at Utrecht till his death, when he was succeeded by others holding similar views. Later on the Bishoprics of Haarlem (1742) and of Deventer were established as suffragan Sees to Utrecht. The Catholics of Holland refused to recognise these bishoprics as did also the Pope, whose only reply to their overtures was a sentence of excommunication and interdict. The Jansenist body of Holland, numbering at present about six thousand, have maintained their separate ecclesiastical organisation until the present day. They resisted the establishment of the hierarchy in Holland (1853), opposed the definition of Papal Infallibility, and allied themselves definitely with the old Catholic movement in Germany.

(d) QUIETISM

Molinos, *Guida spirituale*, 1681. *Oeuvres spirituelles de Madame Guyon*, 42 vols., 1713. Guerrier, *Madame Guyon*, 1881. Fénelon, *Explication des maximes des Saints sur la vie intérieure*, 1697. Bossuet, *Sur les états d'oraison*, 1696. Crouslé, *Fénelon et Bossuet*, 1896. Delmont, *Fénelon et Bossuet d'après les derniers travaux de la critique*, 1896.

Mysticism as implying the substantive union of the soul with God was the distinguishing feature of the pantheistic religious creeds of India, as it was also of some of the Greek philosophical systems. In the Middle

Ages, while many of the ablest exponents of Scholasticism were also distinguished mystics, yet more than once Mysticism or the theology of the heart, unrestrained by the guiding influence of the theology of the intellect, fell into grievous errors akin to the Pantheism of the Buddhists and the Stoics. Many of these Middle Age mystics maintained that perfection consisted in the union of the soul with God by quiet contemplation, so that those who reached that state had no need of external aids to sanctity, such as good works, the sacraments, or prayer; that they were under no obligation to obey any law, ecclesiastical or divine, since their will was united to God's will; and that they need make no effort to resist carnal thoughts or desires, as these came from the devil and could not possibly stain the soul. Such, however, was not the teaching of the great Spanish authorities on mystical theology, Saint Teresa, Saint John of the Cross, and Louis of Granada, whose works on spiritual perfection and on the ways that lead to it have never been surpassed. But side by side with this school of thought, another and less orthodox form of mysticism manifested itself in Spain. Many of the sectaries, such as the Alumbrados or Illuminati, carried away by pantheistic principles, fell into error, and put forward under the guise of mystical theology not a few of the extravagances that had been condemned by the Council of Vienne (1311) and by the judgment of the universal Church.

Closely akin to the errors of this Spanish school was the doctrine known as Quietism taught by Michael de Molinos (1640-96), a Spanish priest, who having completed his studies at Valencia took up his residence in Rome. He published a work entitled *Guida Spirituale* in 1675, the ascetical principles of which attracted so much attention that translations of the book appeared almost immediately in nearly every country of Europe. The teaching of Molinos was denounced to the Inquisition by the Jesuits and the Dominicans, and in 1687

Innocent XI. issued the Bull *Coelestis Pastor*,* in which he condemned sixty-eight propositions put forward by Molinos. The author having been arrested was obliged to make a public recantation, and remained a prisoner until his death (1696).

According to Molinos perfection consists in a state of self-annihilation in which the soul remains entirely passive, absorbed completely in the contemplation and love of God. By means of this passivity or complete surrender of the human faculties to God the soul of man is transformed, and is in a sense deified. While in this condition there is no need to act or to desire to act, to think of rewards or punishments, of defects or virtues, of sanctification, penance, or good works, nor is there any necessity to resist carnal thoughts or motions since these are the works of the devil. Such a system, founded nominally on the pure love of God, and leading of necessity to the overthrow of law, morality, and religious authority, found great favour in Italy and Spain, where it required all the energies and powers of the Inquisition to secure its suppression. It was backed by the Oratorian, Petrucci, afterwards created a cardinal (1686), whose books on the spiritual life were attacked by the Jesuit, Paul Segneri, and condemned by the Inquisition.

Quietism found favour in France through the writings and teaching of Francis Malaval of Marseilles and of the Barnabite Père Lacombe. The individual whose name is most closely identified with Quietism in France is, however, Madame Jeanne de la Mothe Guyon, a young widow who on the death of her husband gave herself up to the practice of prayer and to the study of the principles of the spiritual life. Admitting as she did the fundamental doctrine of the system of Molinos, namely, that perfection consists in a state of self-abnegation in which the soul is wrapped up completely in pure love of God, she rejected most of the absurd and immoral conclusions that seemed to follow from it. According to her, and more especially

* Denzinger, *op. cit.*, nos. 1221-88.

according to her principal defender, Fénelon, pure love of God without any thought of self-interest or of reward or punishment, constitutes the essence of the spiritual life, and must be the principle and motive of all deliberate and meritorious acts. This teaching constitutes what is known as Semi-Quietism. Madame Guyon published several works and gave many conferences in various cities of France. The close connexion between her teaching and the mysticism of de Molinos attracted the unfriendly notice of the French authorities, particularly as Louis XIV. was a strong opponent of Quietism. As a result Madame Guyon and her spiritual director, Père Lacombe, were arrested in Paris (1688), but owing to the interference of Madame de Maintenon, Madame Guyon was released.

Fénelon, then a priest and tutor to the Duke of Burgundy, grandson of Louis XIV. and prospective heir to the throne of France, was deeply interested in the teaching of Madame Guyon whose acquaintance he had made in Paris. Fénelon, while rejecting the false mysticism of de Molinos, agreed with Madame Guyon in believing that the state of perfection in this life is that in which all righteous acts proceed from pure love without any hope of reward or fear of punishment, and that all virtuous acts to be meritorious must proceed directly or indirectly from charity. This teaching found a strenuous opponent in Bossuet, Bishop of Meaux. A commission consisting of Bossuet, de Noailles, then Bishop of Châlons, and Tronson, superior of the Sulpicians, was appointed to examine the whole question (1695). A little later Fénelon, who had just been promoted to the Archbishopric of Cambrai, was added to the list. The conference met in the Sulpician seminary at Issy, and as a result thirty-four articles were drawn up, all of which were accepted by Madame Guyon and by Père Lacombe. The former having returned to Paris was arrested, and forced to sign another recantation of her theories and to promise that she would never again

ABSOLUTISM AND UNBELIEF

attempt to spread them. From that time till her death in 1717 she took no further part in the discussion.

But the controversy regarding Semi-Quietism was to be carried on between the two greatest churchmen and literary giants of their age, namely, Bossuet, Bishop of Meaux, and Fénelon, Archbishop of Cambrai. Bossuet, not content with the partial victory that he had secured at the Issy conference, determined to expose the dangerous tendencies of Madame Guyon's teaching by a short statement of the Catholic doctrine on perfection and the spiritual life. This he did in his book *Instructions sur les états d'oraison,* which he submitted to Fénelon in the hope of obtaining his approval. This Fénelon refused to give, partly because he thought Madame Guyon had been punished severely enough and should not be attacked once she had made her submission, and partly also because he believed the views of Bossuet on charity and self-interest were unsound. Before Bossuet's book could be published Fénelon anticipated him in a work entitled *Explication des maximes des Saints sur la vie intérieure,* in which he defended many of Madame Guyon's views. This book was submitted to the Archbishop of Paris, to Tronson, and to some of the theologians of the Sorbonne, from all of whom it received the highest commendations.

The Bishop of Meaux, annoyed at the action of Fénelon, denounced the book to Louis XIV., who appointed a commission to examine it (1697). Fénelon, fearing that a commission, one of the members of which was his rival Bossuet, would not be likely to give an impartial decision, forwarded his book to Rome for judgment. While the Roman authorities were at work a violent controversy was carried on between Fénelon and Bossuet, which, however much it may have added to the literary reputation of the combatants, was neither edifying nor instructive. On the side of Bossuet especially it is clear that personalities played a much greater part than zeal for orthodoxy. In Rome opinion was very much divided about the orthodoxy of Fénelon's work. Louis XIV. left no stone unturned to secure its condemnation. In the end Innocent XII. condemned twenty propositions taken from the book (1699).* This sentence was handed to Fénelon just as he was about to mount the pulpit in his own cathedral on the Feast of the Annunciation. After mastering its contents he preached on the submission that was due to superiors, read the condemnation for the people, and announced to them that he submitted completely to the decision of the Pope, and besought his friends earnestly neither to read his book nor to defend the views that it contained.

* In the Brief, *Cum alias*, Denzinger, *op. cit.*, nos. 1327-49.

CHAPTER VIII

RATIONALISM AND ITS EFFECTS

(a) ANTI-CHRISTIAN PHILOSOPHY OF THE EIGHTEENTH CENTURY

Lecky, *History of the Rise and Influence of Rationalism in Europe*, 1913. Windleband-Tufts, *A History of Philosophy*, 1898. Uberweg-Morris, *History of Philosophy*, 2nd edition, 1876. Turner, *History of Philosophy*, 1906. Binder, *Geschichte der philosophie . . . mit Rücksicht auf den Kirchlichen Zustände*, 1844-45. Lanfrey, *L'Église et les philosophes au XVIIIe siècle*, 1879. Faguet, *Étude sur le XVIIIe siècle*, 1890. Lange, *History of Materialism*, 1877 (Tr. from German). Stephen, *History of English Thought in the XVIIIth Century*, 1881. Taine, *Les origines de la France contemporaine* (vol. ii.), 1907.

IN the Middle Ages the theory that human reason was to be placed above faith found able exponents, and more than once men arose who questioned some of the fundamental principles of Christianity, or who went farther still by rejecting entirely the Christian revelation. But such views were expounded in an age when the outlook of society was markedly religious, and they exercised no perceptible influence on contemporary thought. Between the fourteenth century and the eighteenth, however, a great change had taken place in the world. Dogmatic theology had lost its hold upon many educated men. The Renaissance movement ushering in the first beginnings of literary and historical criticism, the wonderful progress made in the natural sciences, revolutionising as it did beliefs that had been regarded hitherto as unquestionable, and the influence of the printing press and of the universities, would in themselves have created a dangerous crisis in the history of religious thought, and would have necessitated a more careful study on the part of the theologians to determine precisely the limits where dogma ended and opinion began.

But the most important factor in arousing active opposition to or studied contempt of revealed religion was undoubtedly the religious revolution of the sixteenth century, and more especially the dangerous principles formulated by Luther and his companions to justify them in their resistance to doctrines and practices that had been accepted for centuries by the whole Christian world. They were driven to reject the teaching authority of the visible Church, to maintain that Christ had given to men a body of doctrines that might be interpreted by His followers in future ages as they pleased, and to assert that Christians should follow the dictates of individual judgment instead of yielding a ready obedience to the decrees of Popes and Councils. These were dangerous principles, the full consequence of which the early Reformers did not perceive. If it was true, as they asserted, that Christ had set up no visible authority to safeguard and to expound His revelation, that for centuries Christianity had been corrupted by additions that were only the inventions of men, it might well be asked what guarantee could Luther or Calvin give that their interpretation of Christ's doctrine was correct or binding upon their followers, and what authority could they produce to warrant them in placing any dogmatic restrictions upon the freedom of human thought? The very principles put forward by the Reformers of the sixteenth century to justify their rejection of certain doctrines were used by later generations to prepare the way for still greater inroads upon the contents of Christianity, and finally to justify an attitude of doubt concerning the very foundations on which Christianity was based. Empiricism, Sensualism, Materialism, and Scepticism in philosophy, undermined dogmatic Christianity, and prepared the way for the irreligious and indifferentist

RATIONALISM AND ITS EFFECTS

opinions, that found such general favour among the educated and higher classes during the eighteenth century.

The movement, that owed so much of its widespread popularity on the Continent to the influence of the French rationalistic school, had its origin in England, where the frequent changes of religion during the reigns of Henry VIII., Edward VI., Mary, and Elizabeth, the quarrels between the Puritans and High Church party, and the spread of revolutionary principles during the reign of Charles I., had contributed not a little to unsettle the religious convictions of a large section of the community. Many individuals, influenced by pantheistic teaching, did not believe in the existence of a personal God distinct from the world; others, while holding fast to the belief in a personal supreme Being, rejected the Trinity and the Incarnation, and a still larger section insisted on the subjection of Christian revelation to the judgment of reason, and as a consequence on the rejection of everything in Christianity that flavoured of the supernatural. The works of these men were imported from the Netherlands into France in spite of all restrictions that could be imposed by the police authorities, and their views were popularised by a brilliant band of *littérateurs,* until in a short time Deism and Naturalism became quite fashionable in the higher circles of French society.

The principal writers of the English school were Lord Herbert of Cherbury (1581-1648), whose works tended to call in question the existence of a supernatural religion; John Hobbs (1588-1679) the apostle of absolute rule, who saw in religion only a means of keeping the people in subjection; John Locke (1632-1704), nominally a Christian himself, whose philosophy of Empiricism and Sensualism barred the way effectively against belief in a supernatural religion; Charles Blount (1630-93), who like Flavius Philostratus sought to discredit Christianity by setting up Apollonius of Tyana as a rival of Christ;

Collins, the patron of free-thinkers (1676-1729); John Toland (1670-1722), who although originally a believer in Christian revelation tended more and more towards Pantheism; and Tyndal (1656-1733), who changed from Protestantism to Catholicism and finally from Christianity to Rationalism. In England Deism and Naturalism secured a strong foot-hold amongst the better classes, but the deeply religious temperament of the English people and their strong conservatism saved the nation from falling under the influence of such ideas.

In France the religious wars between the Catholics and Calvinists, the controversies that were waged by the Jansenists and Gallicans, the extravagances of the *Convulsionnaires,* the flagrant immorality of the court during the rule of the Duke of Orleans and of Louis XV., and the enslavement of the Church, leading as it did to a decline of zeal and learning amongst the higher clergy, tended inevitably to foster religious indifference amongst the masses. In the higher circles of society Rationalism was looked upon as a sign of good breeding, while those who held fast by their dogmatic beliefs were regarded as vulgar and unprogressive. Leading society ladies such as Ninon de Lenclos (1615-1706) gathered around them groups of learned admirers, who under the guise of zeal for the triumph of literary and artistic ideals sought to popularise everything that was obscene and irreligious. Amongst some of the principal writers who contributed largely to the success of the anti-Christian campaign in France might be mentioned Peter Bayle (1647-1706), whose *Dictionnaire historique et critique* became the leading source of information for those who were in search of arguments against Christianity; John Baptist Rousseau (1671-1741), whose life was in complete harmony with the filthiness to which he gave expression in his works; Bernard le Bouvier de Fontenelle (1657-1757), who though never an open enemy of the Catholic Church contributed not a little by his works to prepare the way for the men of the

Encyclopædia; Montesquieu (1689-1755), whose satirical books on both Church and State were read with pleasure not only in France but in nearly every country of Europe; D'Alembert (1717-83) and Diderot (1713-84), the two men mainly responsible for the *Encyclopédie;* Helvetius (1715-1771), and the Baron d'Holbach, who sought to popularise the irreligious views then current amongst the nobility by spreading the rationalist literature throughout the mass of the poorer classes in Paris.

But the two writers whose works did most to undermine revealed religion in France were François Marie Arouet, better known as Voltaire (1694-1778), and Jean-Jacques Rousseau (1712-1778). The former of these was born at Paris, received his early education from the Jesuits, and was introduced while still a youth to the salon of Ninon de Lenclos, frequented at this time by the principal literary opponents of religion and morality His earliest excursions into literature marked him out immediately as a dangerous adversary of the Christian religion. He journeyed in England where he was in close touch with the Deist school of thought, in Germany where he was a welcome guest at the court of Frederick II. of Prussia, and settled finally at Ferney in Switzerland close to the French frontiers. Towards the end of his life (1778) he returned to Paris where he received a popular ovation. Poets, philosophers, actresses, and academicians vied with one another in doing honour to a man who had vowed to crush *L'Infâme,* as he termed Christianity, and whose writings had done so much to accomplish that result in the land of his birth. The reception given to Voltaire in Paris affords the most striking proof of the religious and moral corruption of all classes in France at this period. Jean-Jacques Rousseau was born at Geneva and reared as a Calvinist. Later on he embraced the Catholic religion, from which he relapsed once more into Calvinism, if indeed in his later years he was troubled by any dogmatic beliefs. His private life was in perfect harmony with the moral tone of most of his works. He had neither the wit nor the literary genius of Voltaire, but in many respects his works, especially *Le Contrat Social,* exercised a greater influence on the France of his own time and on Europe generally since that time than any other writings of the eighteenth century. His greatest works were *La Nouvelle Heloise* (1759), a novel depicting the most dangerous of human passions; *Émile,* a philosophical romance dealing with educational ideas and tending directly towards Deism, and *Le Contrat Social,* in which he maintained that all power comes from the people, and may be recalled if those to whom it has been entrusted abuse it. The *Confessions* which tell the story of his shameless life were not published until after his death.

To further their propaganda without at the same time attracting the notice of the civil authorities the rationalist party had recourse to various devices. Pamphlets and books were published, professedly descriptive of manners and customs in foreign countries, but directed in reality against civil and religious institutions in France. Typical examples of this class of literature were the *Persian Letters* of Montesquieu, *A Description of the Island of Borneo* by Fontenelle, *The Life of Mohammed* by Henri de Bouillon Villiers, and a *Letter on the English* from the pen of Voltaire. The greatest and most successful work undertaken by them for popularising their ideas was undoubtedly the *Encyclopédie.* The professed object of the work was to give in a concise and handy form the latest and best results of scholarship in every department of human knowledge, but the real aim of the founders was to spread their poisonous views amongst the people of France, and to win them from their allegiance to the Catholic Church. In order to escape persecution from the government and to conceal their real purposes many of the articles were written by clerics and laymen whose orthodoxy was above suspicion, and many of the articles referring to religion from the pen of the rationalistic collaborateurs were

RATIONALISM AND ITS EFFECTS

respectful in tone, though a careful reader could see that they did not represent the real views of the author. Sometimes references were given to other articles of a very different kind, where probably opposite views were established by apparently sound arguments. The originator of the project was D'Alembert, who was assisted by Diderot, Voltaire, Montesquieu, Condillac, Buffon, and D'Holbach. The work was begun in 1750, and in spite of interruptions and temporary suppressions it was brought to a successful conclusion in 1772. The reviewers and the learned world hailed it with delight as a veritable treasure-house of information. New and cheap editions of it were brought out for the general public, and in a remarkably short time the influence of the Encyclopædists had reached the lowest strata of French society. Many of those in authority in France favoured the designs of the Encyclopædists, and threw all kinds of obstacles in the way of those who sought to uphold the teaching of the Church, but soon they had reason to regret their approval of a campaign that led directly to revolution.

(b) The Aufklärung Movement in Germany

See bibliography (viii. *a*). Tholuck, *Abriss einer geschichte der Umwälzung seit 1750 auf dem Gebiete der Theologie in Deutschland*, 1839. Stäudlin, *Geschichte des Rationalismus und Supranaturalismus*, 1826. Brück, *Die rationalistischen Bestrebungen im Kath. Deutschland*, 1867. Weiner, *Geschichte der Kath. Theologie in Deutschland*, 1889. Wolfram, *Die Illuminanten in Bayern und ihre Verfolgung*, 1898-1900.

In Germany the religious formularies, composed with the object of securing even an appearance of unity or at least of preventing religious chaos, were not powerful enough to resist the anti-Christian Enlightenment that swept over Europe in the eighteenth century. At best these formularies were only the works of men who rejected the authority of the Church, and as works of men they could not be regarded as irreformable. With the progress of knowledge and the development of human society it was thought that they required revision to bring them more into harmony with the results of science and with the necessities of the age. The influence of the writings imported from England and France, backed as it was by the approval and example of Frederick II. of Prussia, could not fail to weaken dogmatic Christianity among the Lutherans of Germany. The philosophic teaching of Leibniz (1646-1710), who was himself a strong upholder of dogmatic Christianity and zealous for a reunion of Christendom, had a great effect on the whole religious thought of Germany during the eighteenth century. In his great work, *Théodicée,* written against Bayle to prove that there was no conflict between the kingdoms of nature and grace, greater stress was laid upon the natural than on the supernatural elements in Christianity. His disciples, advancing beyond the limits laid down by the master, prepared the way for the rise of theological rationalism.

One of the greatest of the disciples of Leibniz was Christian Wolf (1679-1754), who was not himself an opponent of supernatural religion. The whole trend of his arguments, however, went to show that human reason was the sole judge of the truths of revelation, and that whatever was not in harmony with the verdict of reason must be eliminated. Many of his disciples like Reimarus, Mendelssohn, and Garve developed the principles laid down by Wolf until the very mention of dogma was scouted openly, and Theism itself was put forward as only the most likely among many possible hypotheses. In the revulsion against dogmatic beliefs the party of the Pietists founded by Spener towards the end of the seventeenth century found much support, while the Conscientiarians, who maintained that man's own conscience was the sole rule of faith, and that so long as man acts in accordance with the dictates of conscience

RATIONALISM AND ITS EFFECTS

he is leading the life of the just, gained ground rapidly. Some of its principal leaders were Matthew Knutzen and Christian Edlemann who rejected the authority of the Bible. The spread of Rationalism was strengthened very much by the appearance of the *Allgemeine Deutsche Bibliothek,* founded in 1764 by Nicolai in Berlin, through the agency of which books hostile to Christianity were scattered broadcast amongst a large circle of readers.

These rationalistic principles, when applied to the Bible and the interpretation of the Bible, helped to put an end to the very rigid views regarding the inspiration of the sacred writings entertained by the early Lutherans. Everything that was supernatural or miraculous must be explained away. To do so without denying inspiration the " Accommodation " theory, namely, that Christ and His apostles accommodated themselves to the mistaken views of their contemporaries, was formulated by Semler (1725-1791). But more extreme men, as for example, Lessing (1729-1781), who published the *Wolfenbüttler Fragments* written by Reimarus in which a violent onslaught was made upon the Biblical miracles more especially on the Resurrection of Christ, attacked directly the miracles of Christianity, and wrote strongly in favour of religious indifference.

The rationalistic dogmatism of Wolf when brought face to face with the objections of Hume did not satisfy Immanuel Kant (1720-1804), who in his *Critique of Pure Reason* (1781) denied that it was possible for science or philosophy to reach a knowledge of the substance or essence of things as distinguished from the phenomena, and that consequently the arguments used generally to prove the existence of God were worthless. In his own *Critique of Practical Reason* (1788), however, he endeavoured to build up what he had pulled down, by showing that the moral law implanted in the heart of every human being necessarily implied the existence of a supreme law-giver. For Kant religion was to be identified with duty and not with dogmatic definitions. Such a line of defence, attempting as it did to remove religion from the arena of intellectual discussion, thereby evading most of the objections put forward by the rationalistic school, was a dangerous one. It led gradually to the rejection of external revelation, and to dogmatic indifference. Such a theory in the hands of Herder and above all of Schleiermacher (1768-1834) meant an end to Christian revelation as generally understood. For Schleiermacher religion was nothing more than the consciousness of dependence upon God. Given this sense of dependence, variations in creeds were of no importance. Between the religion of Luther and the religion of Schleiermacher there was an immense difference, but nevertheless it was Luther who laid down the principles that led to the disintegration of dogmatic Christianity, and in doing what he did Schleiermacher was but proving himself the worthy pupil of such a master.

The unrestrained liberty of thought, claimed by so many Protestant reformers and theologians and ending as it did in the substitution of a natural for a supernatural religion, could not fail to have an influence in Catholic circles. Many Catholic scholars were close students of the philosophical systems of Wolf and Kant in Germany, and of the writings of the Encyclopædists in France. They were convinced that Scholasticism, however valuable it might have been in the thirteenth century, was antiquated and out of harmony with modern progress, that it should be dropped entirely from the curriculum of studies, and with it should go many of the theological accretions to which it had given rise. Catholicism, it was thought, if it were to hold the field as a world-wide religion, must be remodelled so as to bring it better into line with the conclusions of modern philosophy. Less attention should be paid to dogma and to polemical discussions, and more to the ethical and natural principles contained in the Christian revelation.

The spread of Gallicanism and Febronianism and the adoption of these views by leading rulers and politicians, thereby weakening the authority of the Pope and of the bishops, helped to break down the defences of Catholicity, and to make it more easy to propagate rationalistic views especially amongst those who frequented the universities. As a rule it was only the higher and middle classes that were affected by the *Aufklärung*. Everywhere throughout Europe, in France, in Spain, in Portugal, in Germany, and in Austria this advanced liberalism made itself felt in the last half of the eighteenth century, particularly after the suppression of the Jesuits had removed the only body capable of resisting it successfully at the time, and had secured for their opponents a much stronger hold in the centres of education.

It was in Germany and Austria that the *Aufklärung* movement attracted the greatest attention. The Scholastic system of philosophy had been abandoned in favour of the teaching of the Leibniz-Wolf school and of Kant. The entire course of study for ecclesiastical students underwent a complete reorganisation. Scholasticism, casuistry, and controversy were eliminated. Their places were taken by Patrology, Church History, Pastoral Theology, and Biblical Exegesis of the kind then in vogue in Protestant schools.

The plan of studies drawn up by Abbot Rautenstrauch, rector of the University of Vienna (1774), for the theological students of that institution meant nothing less than a complete break with the whole traditional system of clerical education. In itself it had much to recommend it, but the principles that underlay its introduction, and the class of men to whom its administration was entrusted, were enough to render it suspicious. The director of studies in Austria, Baron von Swieten, himself in close contact with the Jansenists and the Encyclopædists, favoured the introduction of the new plan into all the Austrian universities and colleges, and took good care, besides, that only men of liberal views were appointed to the chairs. In the hands of professors like Jahn and Fischer, Scriptural Exegesis began to partake more and more of the rationalism of the Protestant schools; Church History as expounded by Dannenmayr, Royko, and Gmeiner, became in great part an apology for Gallicanism; the Moral Theology taught by Danzer and Reyberger was modelled largely on a purely rationalist system of ethics, and the Canon Law current in the higher schools was in complete harmony with the views of Febronius and Joseph II.

The Prince-bishops of Mainz, Trier, and Cologne spared no pains to propagate these liberal views amongst those who were to be the future priests in their territories. In the University of Mainz Isenbiehl's views on Scripture brought him into conflict with the Church; Blau, the professor of dogma, denied the infallibility of the Church and of General Councils; while Dorsch, the professor of philosophy, was an ardent disciple of Kant. A similar state of affairs prevailed at the University of Trier, at Bonn which was established for the express purpose of combating the ultramontanism and conservatism of Cologne, and to a more or less degree at Freiburg, Würzburg, Ingolstadt, and Munich. By means of the universities and by the publication of various reviews these liberal theories were spread throughout Germany. An attempt was made to reform the discipline and liturgy of the Church so as to bring them into harmony with the new theology. Many advocated the abolition of popular devotions, the substitution of German for the Latin language in the missal and in the ritual, and the abolition of clerical celibacy.

In Bavaria matters reached a crisis when Weishaupt, a professor of canon law in Ingolstadt, founded a secret society known as the *Illuminati* for the overthrow of the Church and the civil authority, to make way for a universal republic in which the only religion would be the religion of humanity. His speculative views were borrowed largely from the Encyclopædists, and his plan of organisation from the Freemasons. At first the society was confined to students, but with the accession of the Freiherr von Knigge it was determined to widen the sphere of its operations. Every effort was made to secure recruits. The Freemasons gave it strong support, and Ferdinand of Brunswick became one of its members. It had its statutes, ritual, and degrees. Fortunately the members quarrelled, and were foolish enough to carry their controversies into the public press. In this way the Bavarian government became acquainted with the dangerous character of the sect of the *Illuminati*, and a determined effort was made to secure its suppression (1784-1785).

(c) Freemasonry

Gould, *History of Freemasonry*, 3 vols., 1883-87. Findel, *Geschichte der Freimaurer*, 3 auf., 1870 (Eng. Trans.). Claudio Jannet, *Les précurseurs de la Franc-maçonnerie au XVIe et au XVIIe siècle*, 1887. Deschamps et Jannet, *Les sociétés secrètes et la société*, 1882. Kloss, *Geschichte der Freimaurer in England, Irland und Schottland*, 1847. Hughan, *Origin of the English Rite of Freemasonry*, 1884.

Whatever about the value of the fantastic legends invented to explain the origin of Freemasonry it is certain that the first grand lodge was formed in London on the Feast of St. John the Baptist (1717). That before this date there were a few scattered lodges in England, Scotland, and Ireland, and that these lodges were the sole remaining relics of a peculiar trade guild, composed of masons and of some of the higher classes as honorary members, there can be little doubt. The society spread rapidly in England, Scotland, and amongst the Protestant colony in Ireland. From Great Britain its principles were diffused throughout the rest of Europe. Freemason lodges were established in Paris (1725-1732), in Germany (1733), Portugal (1735), Holland (1735), Switzerland (1740), Denmark (1745), Italy (1763), and

Sweden (1773). The Freemasons were bound together into a secret society, the members of which were obliged by oath and by the threat of severe penalties to obey orders and to maintain silence regarding its affairs. The society had its ritual, its degrees of apprentice, fellow, and master, and its passports and signs. The particular lodges in each country were united under a national grand lodge, and though the various attempts that have been made to bring about an international organisation have failed, yet there can be little doubt that Freemasons throughout the world maintain the closest relations, and at least in general policy act usually as one man. Freemasonry was patronised by members of the royal family in England, by Frederick II. of Prussia, Francis I. of Austria, the Grand Duke Francis Stephen of Tuscany, and by Philip Duke of Orleans, who accepted the office of grand master in France. Its members were recruited principally from the higher and middle classes, as the entrance fees and expenses made it impossible for any body except the comparatively wealthy to become members. At the time when the society was formed it was the nobility and middle classes who formed public opinion in most countries, and it was thought that if these classes could be won over to support the principles of Freemasonry, they in turn could influence the mass of the people.

Freemasonry was established at a time when Deism and Naturalism were rampant in England, and it secured a foothold in most of the continental countries in an age noted for its hostility to supernatural religion. In the first article of the *Old Charges* (1723) it is laid down that, "A mason is obliged by his tenure to obey the moral law, and if he really understands the art he will never be a stupid atheist nor an irreligious libertine." The precise meaning of this injunction has been the subject of many controversies, but it is clear from the continuation of the same article that the universal religion on which all men are agreed, that is to say, a kind of natural Christianity, was to be the religion of Freemasonry. The society professed to be non-sectarian in its objects, but the whole tendency of the rules and of the organisation in its practical working has been to promote contempt for dogmatic orthodoxy and for religious authority, and to foster a kind of modified Christianity from which specifically Catholic doctrines have been eliminated.

In France and in Austria Freemasons and Rationalists worked hand in hand for the overthrow of the established Church and for the spread of atheistical views. The society professed also to forbid political discussions, but here too the articles of the constitution are intentionally vague, and it is fairly evident that in most of the revolutions that have disturbed the peace of Europe during the last hundred years Freemasons have exercised a very powerful influence. For many reasons the anti-religious and revolutionary tendencies of Freemasonry have been more striking in the Latin countries, France, Spain, Portugal, and Italy, than in England or Germany. In 1877 the Grand Orient of France abolished the portions of the constitution that seemed to admit the existence of God and the immortality of the soul, and remodelled the ritual so as to exclude all references to religious dogma. This action led to a rupture between the Grand Orient and the lodges of England, Germany, and America. Yet many of the Freemasons in these latter countries sympathised with the attitude of their French brethren, and insisted on interpreting after their own fashion the very ambiguous formula by which the existence of a grand architect is recognised. There can be no doubt that even in England a man may be a Freemason accepting loyally all its articles, and yet refuse to believe in the existence of a personal God distinct from the world. Freemasonry aims at establishing a spirit of comradeship and brotherhood among its members. They are bound to aid one another in every possible way and practically in all conceivable circumstances. However objectionable such a practice, and however dangerous to the public weal and to the interests of the state it may be, it is precisely this feature of the society that won for it its greatest number of adherents.

Freemasonry was condemned by Clement XII. in 1738. In the constitution *In eminenti,* in which this condemnation was promulgated, he explained the reasons that induced him to take this step. These were the anti-religious tendencies of the society both in its theory and practice, the oaths of secrecy and obedience to unknown superiors, and the danger to Church and State involved in such secret combinations. This condemnation has been renewed by several of his successors, as for example Benedict XIV. (1751), Pius VII. (1821), Gregory XVI. (1832), Pius IX. (1865), and Leo XIII. (1884). Since 1738 Catholics have been forbidden under penalty of excommunication to become members of the society or to promote its success. According to the constitution *Apostolicae Sedis* (1869), which is in force at the present time, excommunication is levelled against those who join the Freemasons or similar bodies that plot against the Church and established authority, as well as against those who favour such organisations and do not denounce their leaders.

(d) THE SUPPRESSION OF THE SOCIETY OF JESUS

Crétineau-Joly, *Clément XIV. et les Jésuites,* 1847. De Ravignan, *Clément XIII. et Clément XIV.,* 1856. Theiner, *Histoire du pontificat de Clément XIV. d'après des documents inédits des arch. secr. du Vatican,* 2 vols., 1852. Weld, *The Suppression of the Society of Jesus in the Portuguese Dominions,* 1877. Rosseau, *Règne de Charles III. d'Espagne,* 1907. Riffel, *Die Aufhebung des Jesuitenordens, 3 auf.,* 1855. Foley, *Records of the English Province of the Society of Jesus,* 1877. Hogan, *Hibernia Ignatiana,* 1880. Taunton, *The Jesuits in England,* 1901.

From its foundation by St. Ignatius of Loyola and its approval by Paul III. the Society of Jesus had remained true to the teaching and spirit of its holy founder and loyal to the Holy See. In the defence of the Church, especially in Germany, Austria, Poland, Hungary, and France, in the domain of education and of literature, in the work of spreading Christianity amongst the races and peoples in India, China, Japan, and America, the Jesuit Fathers took the foremost place. They laboured incessantly to stay the inroads of heresy, to instil Catholic principles into the minds of the rising generation, and to win new recruits to take the place of those who had gone over to the enemy.

But their very success was sufficient to arouse the wrath of their adversaries and the jealousy of their rivals. Lutherans and Calvinists, enraged by the success of the Counter-Reformation, denounced the Jesuits as enemies of progress and enlightenment, whose very existence was a danger to the peace and the liberty of Europe. These charges were re-echoed by Jansenists and Gallicans, by infidel philosophers and absolutist politicians, and, stranger still, by many whose orthodoxy could not be questioned, but whose judgment was warped by their annoyance at the wonderful success of a comparatively young organisation. The Jesuits were accused of favouring laxity of morals on account of the support given by some of them to Probabilism, of sympathising with Pelagianism on account of the doctrine of Molina, of supporting tyrannicide on the strength of the work of Mariana, of upholding absolutism on account of their close relations with the rulers of France, and Spain, and of seeking to undermine governments and constitutions by their secret political schemes and their excessive wealth. Garbled extracts taken from the works of individual Jesuits were published as representing the opinions of the body, and the infamous *Monita Secreta,* purporting to contain the instruction of Aquaviva to his subjects, was forged (1612) to bring discredit upon the Society.*

* On the *Monita Secreta, cf.* Bernard, *Les instructions secrètes des Jésuites,* 1903. Duhr, *Jesuitenfabeln,* 1904. Gerard, *Jesuit Bogey, etc.* (*The Month,* Aug., 1901, p. 179).

More than once the combined assaults of its enemies seemed on the point of being crowned with success. During Aquaviva's tenure of office as general (1585-1615) the society was banished from France and from Venice, while the demands of the Spanish Jesuits for a Spanish superior, backed as it was by the influence of the court, threatened to destroy the unity of the Society. Again in the time of Paul Oliva (1664-1681) and Charles Noyelle (1682-1686) controversies regarding Jansenism, Probabilism, the *Regalia*, and the Gallican Declaration of the French clergy (1682), endangered the existence of the Society in France, and threatened to lead to misunderstandings with the Holy See, but under the Providence of God these dangers were averted, and the eighteenth century found the Jesuits still vigorous in Europe and not less vigorous in their labours among the heathen nations.

But their opponents though beaten time and again were not disheartened. The infidel philosophers of the eighteenth century recognised in the Jesuits the ablest defenders of the Catholic Church. If only they could succeed in removing them, as Voltaire declared, the work of destroying the Church seemed comparatively easy. Hence they united all their forces for one grand assault upon the Society as the bulwark of Christianity. They were assisted in their schemes by the Jansenists, eager to avenge the defeat they had received at the hands of the Jesuits, and by the absolutist statesmen and rulers of Europe, who aimed at the enslavement of the Church, and who feared the Jesuits as the ablest exponents of the rights of religion and of the Holy See. The Jesuits controlled to a great extent Catholic education both lay and clerical, and it was hoped that by installing teachers devoted to state supremacy and Enlightenment in their place the future of absolutism and of rationalism might be assured.

The attack on the Jesuits was begun in Portugal during the reign of Joseph Emmanuel (1750-1777). He

was a man of liberal views, anxious to promote the
welfare of his country, as well as to strengthen the power
of the crown. In accomplishing these objects he was
guided by the advice of the prime minister, Joseph
Sebastian Carvalho, better known as the Marquis of
Pombal.* The latter had travelled much, and was
thoroughly imbued with the liberal and rationalistic
spirit of the age. He regarded the Catholic Church as
an enemy of material progress, and the Jesuits as the
worst teachers to whom the youth of any country could
be entrusted. A treaty concluded with Spain, according
to which the Spaniards were to surrender to Portugal
seven of the Reductions of Paraguay in return for San
Sacramento, afforded him the long desired opportunity
of attacking the Jesuits (1750). The Indians on the
Reductions, who had been converted by the Jesuits, were
to be banished from their lands to make way for mining
operations in search of gold, and though the Jesuits
tried hard to induce their people to submit to this decree,
the Indians, maddened by the injustice and cruelty of
the treatment of the Portuguese, rose in revolt. The
Jesuits were blamed for having fomented the rebellion.
By orders of Pombal they were arrested and brought to
Portugal, where the most extravagant charges were
published against them in order to damage them in the
eyes of the people.

The Portuguese government appealed to Benedict
XIV. to take action against the Society. The Pope
appointed Saldanha as apostolic visitor to examine into
the charges that had been made. Though the instructions laid down for the guidance of the visitor were
precise in every detail, Saldanha, unmindful of the restrictions imposed by the Pope and without hearing any
evidence that might favour the accused, decided against
the Jesuits and procured the withdrawal of their faculties
in Lisbon (1758). In September of that year a plot

* Du Breuil, *Un ministre philosophe, Carvalho, marquis de Pombal*
(*Revue historique*, 1895, pp. 1 *sqq.*).

directed against one of the royal officials, but supposed to have for its object the murder of the king, was discovered and attributed without any evidence to the Jesuits. They and many of their supposed allies amongst the nobility were arrested and thrown into prison; their schools were closed, and various fruitless attempts were made to induce the younger members to disown the Society. Finally in September 1759 a decree of banishment was issued against the Jesuits. Most of them were arrested and despatched to the Papal States, while others of them, less fortunate, were confined as prisoners in the jails of Portugal. Father Malagrida, one of the ablest and most saintly men of the Society, was put to death on a trumped-up charge of heresy (1761). Clement XIII. (1758-1769) made various attempts to save the Society, and to prevent a breach with Portugal, but Pombal determined to push matters to extremes. The Portuguese ambassador at Rome suddenly broke off negotiations with the Holy See and left the city, while the nuncio at Lisbon was escorted to the Spanish frontier (1760). For a period of ten years (1760-1770) friendly relations between Rome and Portugal were interrupted.

In France the Jesuits had many powerful friends, but they had also many able and determined enemies. The Jansenists who controlled the Parliament of Paris, the Rationalists, the Gallicans, and not a few of the doctors of the Sorbonne, though divided on nearly every other issue, made common cause against the Society. They were assisted in their campaign by Madame de Pompadour, the king's mistress, for whom the Jesuit theology was not sufficiently lax, and by the Duc de Choiseul, the king's prime minister. The well-known Jesuit leanings of Louis XV. and of the royal family generally, imposed a certain measure of restraint upon the enemies of the Society, until the famous La Valette law suit afforded its opponents an opportunity of stirring up public feeling and of overcoming the scruples of the weak-minded king. The Jesuits had a very important mission in the island of Martinique. The natives were employed on their large mission lands, the fruits of which were spent in promoting the spiritual and temporal welfare of the people. La Valette, the Jesuit superior on the island, had been very successful in his business transactions, and encouraged by his success, he borrowed money in France to develop the resources of the mission. This money he could have repaid without difficulty, had it not been that during the war between France and England some vessels bearing his merchandise were seized by the English (1755). La Valette was in consequence of this unable to pay his creditors, some of whom sought to recover their debts by instituting a civil process against the procurator of the Paris province. For several reasons the Jesuits, though not unwilling to make a reasonable settlement, refused to acknowledge any responsibility. The creditors insisted on bringing the case to trial, and the court at Marseilles decided in their favour. The Jesuit procurator then appealed to the Parliament of Paris, at that time strongly Jansenist in its tendencies. The Parliament, not content with upholding the verdict, took advantage of the popular feeling aroused against the Society to institute a criminal process against the entire body (1761).

A commission was appointed to examine the constitutions and privileges of the Jesuits. It reported that the Society was dangerous to the state, hostile to the *Gallican Liberties,* and unlawful. The writings of Bellarmine and Busenbaum were ordered to be burned, and the famous *Extrait des Assertions,* a kind of bluebook containing a selection of unpopular views defended by Jesuit writers, was published to show the dangerous tendencies of the Society and to prejudice it in the eyes of the people. The Provincial of the Jesuits offered for himself and his subjects to accept the Declaration of the French clergy and to obey the instructions of the bishops, but the offer, besides being displeasing to the Roman authorities, did not soften the wrath of the anti-Jesuit party, who sought nothing less than the total destruction of the Society.

Louis XV. endeavoured to bring about a compromise by procuring the appointment of a vicar for France. With this object he called a meeting of the French bishops (1761), the vast majority of whom had nothing but praise for the work of the Jesuits, and wished for no change in the constitution of the Society. Similar views were expressed by the assembly of the French clergy in 1762. Clement XIII. laboured energetically in defence of the Jesuits, but in open disregard of his advice and his entreaties, the decree for the suppression of the Society was passed by Parliament in 1762, though its execution was delayed by orders of the king. Meanwhile proposals were made to the Pope and to the general, Ricci,* for a change in the constitution, so as to secure the appointment of an independent superior for France, which proposal was rejected by both Pope and general. In 1763 the Jesuit colleges were closed; members of the Society were required to renounce their vows under threat of banishment, and, as hardly any members complied with this condition, the decree of banishment was promulgated in 1764. Clement XIII. published a Bull defending the constitution of the Society, and rejecting the charge against its members (1765), while the French bishops addressed an earnest appeal to the king on its behalf (1765).

The example of Portugal and France was soon followed by Spain. Charles III. (1759-1788) was an able ruler, anxious to restore the former greatness of his country by encouraging the establishment of industries and by favouring the introduction of foreign capital and foreign skill. He was by no means irreligious, but he was influenced largely by the liberal tendencies of the

* Carayon, *Le père Ricci et la suppression de la compagnie de Jésus en* 1773, 1869.

RATIONALISM AND ITS EFFECTS

age, as were also in a more marked degree his two principal ministers Aranda and de Roda. Popular feeling was aroused by the favour which the king showed towards French capitalists and artisans, and in some places ugly commotions took place. The ministers suggested to the king that the Jesuits were behind this movement, and were the authors of certain dangerous and inflammatory pamphlets. Secret councils were held, as a result of which sealed instructions were issued to the governors of all towns in which Jesuit houses were situated that on a fixed night the Jesuits should be arrested (1767). These orders were carried out to the letter. Close on six thousand Jesuits were taken and hurried to the coast, where vessels were awaiting to transport them to the Papal States. When this had been accomplished a royal decree was issued suppressing the Society in Spain owing to certain weighty reasons which the king was unwilling to divulge. Clement XIII. remonstrated vigorously against such violent measures, but the only effect of his remonstrances was that the bishops who defended the papal interference were banished, those who would seek to favour the return of the Society were declared guilty of high treason, and the punishment of death was levelled against any Jesuit who attempted to land in Spain.

In Naples, where Ferdinand, son of Charles III. of Spain then ruled, the suppression of the Jesuits was planned and carried out by the prime minister, Tanucci, a man hardly less unfriendly to the Society than Pombal. The Jesuits were arrested without any trial, and were sent across the frontier into the Papal States (Nov. 1767), Much the same fate awaited them in the territories of the Duke of Parma and Piacenza, where the minister du Tillot had pursued for years a campaign against the rights of the Catholic Church. In 1768 Clement XIII. issued a strong protest against the policy of the Parmese government. This aroused the ire of the whole Bourbon family. France, Spain, and Naples demanded the withdrawal of this *Monitorium* under threat of violence. The Papal States of Avignon and Venaissin were occupied by French troops, while Naples seized Benevento and Pontecorvo. Various attempts were made to secure the support of the Empress Maria Theresa, and to stir up opposition in the smaller kingdoms of Italy. But Clement XIII., undaunted by the threats of violence of the Bourbons, refused to yield to their demands for the suppression of a Society, against which nothing had been proved, and against which nothing could be proved except its ardent defence of the Catholic Church and its attachment to the Holy See. In January 1769 an ultimatum was presented by the ambassadors of France, Spain, and Naples demanding the suppression of the Society. The Pope refused to agree to it, but before the threats it contained could be carried into execution Clement XIII. passed away (Feb. 1769).

In the conclave that followed the Bourbon rulers made every effort to secure the election of a Pope favourable to their views. Their representatives were instructed to use the veto freely against all cardinals known to be favourable to the Jesuits. After a struggle lasting three months Cardinal Ganganelli was elected and took the title Clement XIV. (1769-1774). He restored friendly relations with Parma, opened negotiations with Portugal, created the brother of Pombal a cardinal, appointed Pereira, one of the court theologians, to a Portuguese bishopric, despatched a nuncio to Lisbon, and brought about a formal reconciliation (1770).

It is not true that before his election Clement XIV. had bound himself formally to suppress the Jesuits. Hardly, however, had he been crowned when demands were made upon him by the representatives of France and Spain similar to those presented to his predecessor. Clement XIV. promised to agree to the suppression (1769), but asked for time to consider such a momentous step. In the hope of satisfying the opponents of the Jesuits the Pope adopted an unfriendly attitude towards

RATIONALISM AND ITS EFFECTS

the Society, and appointed apostolic visitors to examine into the affairs of the seminaries and colleges under its control, from most of which, as a result of the investigation, the Jesuits were dismissed. He offered to bring about a complete change in the constitution of the Society, but this offer, too, was rejected. Charles III. of Spain forwarded an ultimatum in which he insisted upon the instant suppression of the Society under threat of recalling his ambassador from Rome. This ultimatum had the approval of all the Bourbon rulers. Faced with such a terrible danger, the courage of Clement XIV. failed him, and he determined to accept the suppression as the lesser of two evils (1772). In July 1773 the Brief *Dominus ac Redemptor noster*, decreeing the suppression of the Society in the interests of peace and religion, was signed by the Pope. The houses of the Jesuits in the Papal States were surrounded by soldiers, and the general, Ricci, was confined as a prisoner in the castle of St. Angelo. The decree was forwarded to the bishops to be communicated by them to the Jesuits resident in their dioceses. In most of the countries of Europe the decree of suppression was carried out to the letter, the Jesuits as a body submitting loyally to the decision of the Pope.

Catharine II. of Russia, however, and Frederick II. of Prussia were impressed so favourably by the work of the Jesuits as educators that they forbade the bishops to publish the decree in their territories. In 1776 an agreement was arrived at between Pius VI. and Frederick II., according to which the Jesuits in Prussian territory were to be disbanded formally and were to lay aside their dress, but they were permitted to continue under a different name to direct the colleges which they possessed. The Empress Catharine II. of Russia continued till her death to protect the Society. In 1778 she insisted upon the erection of a novitiate, for which oral permission seems to have been given by Pius VI. In the other countries many of the Jesuits laboured as secular priests, others of them united in the congregation, known as the Fathers of the Faith (1797), and others still in the congregation of the Fathers of the Sacred Heart. In 1803 the English Jesuit community at Stonyhurst was allowed to affiliate with the Russian congregation; in 1804 the Society was re-established with the permission of Pius VII. in Naples, and in 1814 the Pope issued the Bull, *Sollicitudo omnium Ecclesiarum* formally re-establishing the Society. Strange to say the very next year (1815) a persecution broke out against the Jesuits in Saint Petersburg, and in 1820 they were expelled from Russian territory.

It was fear of the Bourbon rulers that forced Clement XIV. to agree to the suppression of the Jesuits. By sacrificing a society that had been noted for its loyal defence of and submission to the Pope, he had hoped to restore peace to the Church, and to avert the many calamities that threatened its very existence in France, Spain, Portugal, and Naples. But he lived long enough to realise that his weakness led only to new and more exorbitant demands, and that the professors, who had taken the chairs vacated by the Jesuits, were only too ready to place their voices and their pens at the disposal of the civil power and against the Holy See. The suppression of the Society was hailed as a veritable triumph by the forces of irreligion and rationalism. The schemes that this party had been concocting for years were at last crowned with success; the strongest of the outposts had been captured, and it only remained to make one last desperate assault on the fortress itself. The civil rulers, who had allowed themselves to be used as tools for promoting the designs of the rationalists and the Freemasons, had soon reason to regret the cruelty and violence with which they treated the Society of Jesus. In a few years the Revolution was in full swing; the thrones of France, Spain, Portugal, and Naples were overturned, and those members of the royal families, who escaped the scaffold or the dungeon, were themselves driven to seek refuge in foreign lands, as the Jesuits had been driven in the days of Clement XIV.

(e) FAILURE OF ATTEMPTS AT RE-UNION. PROTESTANT SECTS

Bossuet, *Oeuvres complètes*, 1846 (vii.). *Oeuvres de Leibniz*, etc., 1859. Kiefl, *Der Friedensplan des Leibniz für Wiedervereinigung der getrennten Kirchen*, 1903. Lescoeur, *De Bossueti et Leibnitii epistolarum commercio circa pacem inter Christianos conciliandam*, 1852. Tabaraud, *Histoire critique des projets formés depuis trois cents ans pour la réunion des communions chrétiennes*. Kahnis, *Der innere gang des deutschen Protestantismus*, 3 Auf., 1874. Franke, *Geschichte der protestantischen Theologie*, 1865. Erbkam, *Geschichte der protestantischen Sekten im Zeitalter der Reformation*, 1848.

Whatever hopes there might have been of restoring unity to the Christian world during the early years of the Reformation movement, the prospects of a reunion became more and more remote according as the practical results of the principle of private judgment made themselves felt. It was no longer with Luther, or Calvin, or Zwingli that Catholic theologians were called upon to negotiate, nor was it sufficient for them to concentrate their attention upon the refutation of the *Confessio Augustana* or the *Confessio Tetrapolitana*. The leading followers of the early Reformers found themselves justified in questioning the teaching of their masters, for reasons exactly similar to those that had been alleged by their masters in defence of their attack on the Catholic Church. The principle of religious authority having been rejected, individuals felt free to frame their own standard of orthodoxy, and were it not for the civil rulers, who interfered to preserve their states from the temporal dangers of religious anarchy, and to supply by their own power some organisation to take the place of the Catholic hierarchy, Calvinism and Lutheranism would have assumed almost as many different forms as there were individuals who professed to accept these religious systems. As it was, despite the religious formularies, drawn up for the most part at the instigation and on the advice of the civil rulers, it proved impossible for man to replace the old bulwarks established by Christ to safeguard the deposit of faith. As a consequence new sects made their appearance in every country that accepted the reformed doctrine.

In France some attempts were made by Cardinal Richelieu to bring about a reunion between the Catholics and the Calvinists. In taking these steps he was influenced more by considerations of state than by zeal for the welfare of the Church, but the gulf separating the two parties was too wide to be bridged over even by French patriotism. In Poland, where unity was particularly required and where the disastrous consequences of religious strife were only too apparent, Ladislaus V. determined to summon a conference at Thorn in 1645 to discuss the religious differences, but though it was attended by representatives from several states of Germany it produced no good results.

In Germany the work, that had proved too great for the theologians, was undertaken by the princes in 1644, with no better results. Later on, at the instigation of the Emperor, Christopher Royas de Spinola, an Austrian bishop, spent the last twenty years of his life (1675-1695) in a vain effort to put an end to the religious dispute. Heedless of repeated rebuffs, he passed from court to court in Germany till at last at Hanover he saw some prospect of success. Duke Ernest August assembled a conference of Lutheran theologians (1679), the principal of whom was Molanus, a Protestant abbot of Loccum. The Lutheran theologians were willing to agree that all Christians should return immediately to their obedience to the Pope, on condition, however, that the decrees of the Council of Trent should be suspended, and that a new General Council composed of representatives of all parties should be assembled to discuss the principal points in dispute. On his side Royas was inclined to yield a good deal in regard to clerical celibacy and the authority of secular princes in ecclesiastical affairs. Innocent XI., while not approving of what had been done, praised the bishop for the efforts he had made to bring about a reunion.

Leibniz, the librarian and archivist of the Duke of Brunswick, having taken already some part in the work of bringing about a reconciliation, entered into a correspondence with Bossuet, the Bishop of Meaux. He favoured a compromise on the basis of acceptance of the beliefs of the first five centuries, and published his *Systema Theologicum* as a means of bringing the Catholic standpoint before the minds of his co-religionists. Bossuet and the French historian Pellisson reciprocated his efforts, but the schemes of Louis XIV. and the hopes of the English succession entertained by the House of Brunswick put an end to all chances of success.

From the beginning, though Luther and Zwingli were at one in their opposition to Rome, they were unable to agree upon a common religious platform. The Sacramentarian controversy, confined at first to Luther and Carlstadt, grew more embittered after Zwingli had espoused openly the side of the latter. Several German princes having embraced the views of Zwingli, it was felt necessary to preserve some kind of unity amongst the Reformers, especially in view of the threatening attitude assumed by Charles V. A conference was called at Marburg (1529), at which Luther, Melanchthon, Osiander, and Agricola agreed to meet Zwingli, Oecolampadius, Butzer, and the other Swiss leaders. The conference failed to arrive at a satisfactory agreement, but in 1536 the Concord of Wittenberg was concluded, whereby it was hoped that peace might be restored by the adoption of a very ambiguous formula. Luther, however, refused to allow himself to be bound by the agreement, and the controversy went on as violently as before.

In the meantime Calvin had undertaken to preach

doctrines on the Eucharist entirely different from those put forward by either Zwingli or Luther, with the result that Zurich found itself in conflict with Geneva as it had found itself previously in conflict with Wittenberg. To restore some semblance of unity among the Swiss Reformers Bullinger, the recognised head of the Zurich party, entered into communication with Calvin, and a doctrinal agreement was arrived at known as the *Consensus Tigurinus* (The Zurich Concord) in 1549. Later on this was confirmed by the *Confessio Helvetica* (1564).

After the death of Luther in 1545 Melanchthon became the acknowledged head of the Lutheran party. On many questions he was inclined to disagree with the doctrine of his master. His teaching in regard to the Eucharist began to approximate more closely to the views of Calvin, so that the Impanation and Companation theories of Luther lost favour in Germany. The Philippists or Crypto-Calvinists gained ground rapidly in the country, with the result that German Protestants were split up into hostile sections. A conference was held at Naumburg in 1561, but it broke up without having done anything to restore religious unity. At last in 1576 the Elector August of Saxony summoned an assembly of theologians to meet at Torgau, for the discussion of the differences that had arisen between the orthodox followers of Luther and the Crypto-Calvinists or followers of Melanchthon. Jacob Andreä, chancellor of the University of Tübingen, was the life and soul of the reunion movement. Taking the plan of agreement that had been formulated by him as a basis for discussion the conference drew up the *Book of Torgau*, copies of which were despatched to the Lutheran princes and theologians for an expression of their opinion. When this had been received the *Book of Torgau* was revised (1577), and a Formula of Concord (*Formula Concordiae*) was compiled, embodying the Confession of Augsburg, Melanchthon's Apology for this Confession, the Articles of Schmalkald and the two Catechisms issued by Luther

RATIONALISM AND ITS EFFECTS

(1577). But as there was no authority to enforce this Formula several of the states refused to accept it.

In Saxony under Christian I. (1586-91) the Philippists in favour at court triumphed over their adversaries, but on the death of Christian the orthodox Lutherans secured the upper hand, and Nicholas Crell, the prime minister and chancellor of Saxony during the previous reign, was thrown into prison, and later on he was put to death (1601). Calvinism continued to make steady progress in Germany. It was introduced into the Palatinate during the reign of Frederick III. (1583), and though suppressed by his son and successor, it gained the upper hand. Similarly in Hesse-Cassel, in Lippe, Brandenburg, and Anhalt, it gained many new adherents. All attempts at peace amongst the warring sects having failed, Calvinism was recognised formally at the Peace of Westphalia (1648).

Violent controversies broke out among the Lutheran party in Germany on many other matters besides the Eucharist. One of the early followers of Luther named Agricola,* afterwards a professor of Wittenberg (1539), in his efforts to emphasise the teaching of his master on good works proclaimed that the spirit of fear so characteristic of the Old Testament had given way to the mildness and love of the New, and that, therefore, Christians who had received justification were no longer under the obligations of the law. This is what was known as *Antinomism*, a form of error not unknown amongst the early Gnostics and amongst some of the heretical sects of the Middle Ages. Agricola was assailed violently by Luther (1538-40), fled to Berlin (1540), and returned at a later period to make his submission, but Luther refused all his attempts at reconciliation. Melanchthon, however, adopted a more friendly attitude. The controversy continued for years, and *Antinomism* of a much more exaggerated form spread into other countries, particularly into England, where Parliament was obliged to

* Kawerau, *J. Agricola*, 1881. Elwert, *De antinomia Agricolae*, 1837.

legislate against its supporters during the reign of Charles I.

Closely associated with the Antinomist controversy was another known as the *Osiandrist,** from the name of one of its principal participants, Andrew Osiander. The latter, a professor of Hebrew at Nürnberg, perceiving the dangerous results of Luther's teaching on good works sought to introduce some modifications that would obviate the danger involved in the latter's apparent contempt for good works. For this reason he condemned the general absolution that had been introduced to replace auricular confession, and insisted upon the elevation of the Host as a profession of belief in the doctrine of the Real Presence. Having become involved in a sharp dispute with his colleagues at Nürnberg he left the university, and accepted a professorship at Königsberg in Prussia (1549), where he was supported by the ruler Duke Albert. In regard to Justification he taught that forgiveness of sin and satisfaction should not be confounded with Justification, that the latter is effected by the indwelling of God in the person of the justified, that though the human nature of Christ is a necessary condition for redemption it is by the divine nature that the indwelling of God in man is effected, and that on account of this indwelling the holiness of God is imputed to the creature. This teaching aroused considerable opposition. Osiander was denounced by Mörlin and others as Anti-Christ. Duke Albert sought the views of leading theologians only to find that as they were divided themselves they could lay down no certain rule for his guidance. Osiander died in 1552, but the quarrel continued and for a time it seemed as if it would lead to rebellion. Finally the adversaries of Osiander triumphed, when they secured the insertion of their views in the Prussian *Corpus Doctrinae* (1567) and the execution of Funk the leading supporter of Osiandrism (1601). Another professor of Königsberg at this period,

* Möller, *Dr. Andreas Osiander*, 1870.

Stancarus, maintained that Redemption is to be attributed to the human nature rather than to the divine nature of Christ, but he was expelled from the university, and denounced on all sides as a Nestorian.

On this question of good works a violent controversy broke out after the Leipzig *Interim* (1548). Luther had depreciated entirely the value of good works as a means to salvation. On this point, however, Melanchthon was willing to make considerable concessions to the Catholics, as indeed he did in 1535 and 1548, when he admitted that good works were necessary for acquiring eternal happiness. This view was supported warmly by Major, a professor at Wittenberg, who was denounced by Amsdorf as an opponent of Luther's doctrine of Justification (1551). Amsdorf, Flacius, and others maintained that good works were a hindrance rather than an aid to salvation, while Major clung tenaciously to the position that good works were meritorious. *Majorism*, as the new heresy was called, was denounced in the most violent terms because it involved a return to the doctrine of the Papists. Major was suspended from his office as preacher (1556) and was obliged to make a recantation (1558).

The *Adiaphorist* controversy broke out in connexion with the Leipzig *Interim* (1548). In this attempt at reconciliation Melanchthon was not unwilling to yield in many points to the Catholic representatives, and to agree that several of the doctrines and practices of the Church that had been assailed by Luther were at least indifferent and might be admitted. For this he was attacked by Matthias Flacius, surnamed Illyricus[*] on account of the place of his birth, a professor of Hebrew at Wittenberg since 1544. The latter protested against the concessions made by Melanchthon, denounced as impious the union of Christ with Belial, and returned to Magdeburg, where he was joined by Amsdorf and others who supported his

[*] Preger, *M. Flacius Illyrikus und seine Zeit*, 2 Bde. 1859-61.

contention. He was driven from city to city and at last died at Frankfurt in 1575.

The question of man's co-operation in his conversion gave rise to what was known as the *Synergist* controversy. Luther had laid it down as a first principle that man contributed nothing to the work of his own conversion, but though Melanchthon agreed with this view in the beginning, he was disposed at a later period to attribute some activity to the human will, at least in the sense that it must strive against its own weakness. This view was strengthened and developed by John Pfeffinger, a professor at Leipzig, who taught publicly the necessity of man's co-operation (1550), and published a treatise in defence of this position (1555). Pfeffinger's doctrine aroused the opposition of Amsdorf, Flacius, and the other leaders of the orthodox Lutheran party. Leipzig and Wittenberg joined hands to support the doctrine of co-operation, while the majority of the professors at Jena took the opposite side. One of the latter however, Strigel, supported Pfeffinger, and a public disputation was held at Gotha under the presidency of Duke John Frederick. The Lutheran party demanded the punishment of Strigel and his supporters so vigorously that the Duke was obliged to arrest them, but, annoyed by the attempt of the Lutherans to set up a religious dictatorship to the detriment of the supremacy of the civil ruler, he established a consistory composed of lawyers and officials whose duty it was to superintend the religious teaching in his territory. The anti-Synergists, having protested against this measure as an infringement of the rights of the spiritual authority, were expelled, and Jena entered into line with Wittenberg and Leipzig for the defence of Synergism. With the change of rulers came once more a change of doctrine. The princes, alarmed by the violence of the controversy, assembled a conference at Altenburg in 1568 which lasted four months without arriving at any agreement. On the accession of the Elector August the leading opponents of the Synergists, including a large number of the superintendents and preachers, were deprived of their offices.

By his lectures and teaching at the University of Helmstädt George Calixt* gave rise to a new and prolonged discussion known as the *Syncretist* controversy. The Duke of Brunswick having refused to accept the *Formula of Concord,* the professors at the university which he had founded felt themselves much more free in their teaching than those in other centres of Lutheranism. Calixt denied the ubiquity of Christ's body and the attribution of divine qualities to Christ's human nature. Though a strong opponent of several distinctly Catholic or Calvinist beliefs he saw much that was good in both, and he longed for a reunion of Christendom on the basis of an acceptance of the beliefs and practices of the first six centuries. He was charged with aiming at a confusion of all religions, and in proof of this charge it was alleged that he rejected the Lutheran teaching on Original Sin and on man's natural powers of doing good even before justification, that he defended the meritorious character of good works, the supremacy of the Pope, at least *de jure ecclesiastico,* and the sacrifice of the Mass (1639). In 1643 a disputation was held, in which Hornejus, a colleague of Calixt, supported his doctrine especially on the meritoriousness of good works. The appearance of Calixt at the conference summoned by the King of Poland in Thorn (1645) to promote a reunion with Rome, and the friendly attitude which he had adopted towards the Catholics and the Calvinists helped to increase the suspicions of his adversaries. Calixt died in 1656, but for years after his death the spirit of toleration, that he had done so much to foster, was one of the distinguishing features of the University of Helmstädt. It was during this controversy that the Branch Theory, namely, that Catholicism, Lutheranism, and Calvinism formed three divisions of the one true Church, was formulated clearly for the first time.

* Dowling, *The Life and Correspondence of Calixt*, 1863.

Amongst the Calvinists the extremely crude doctrine on Predestination taught by Calvin soon proved too much for the faith of many of his followers. Several of them, holding fast by Calvin's teaching, contended that regardless of Original Sin God had created some for glory and others for damnation, that Christ had died only to save the elect, and that to these alone is given the grace necessary for salvation (Supralapsarians). Others, horrified by the cruelty of such a doctrine, maintained that the decree predestining some to hell followed the prevision of Original Sin (Infralapsarians). This view had been put forward by Theodore Koornhort, and had found considerable support, but it was attacked by the majority of the Calvinist ministers, and a bitter controversy ensued. The orthodox party summoned to their assistance Arminius * (Hermanzoon), a distinguished young Calvinist preacher, who had attended the lectures of Beza in Geneva, but whose strict views were modified considerably by a sojourn in Italy. Instead of supporting the Supralapsarians, his sympathies were entirely on the side of the milder doctrine, and after his appointment to a professorship at Leyden (1603) he became the recognised head of the Infralapsarians. His chief opponent was Gomar, also a professor at Leyden, who accused Arminius of Semi-Pelagianism. Arminius, while repudiating such a charge as groundless, rejoined by pointing out that according to his adversaries God was the author of sin. Both appeared before an Assembly of the States in 1608 to defend their views, and though the majority were inclined to favour Arminius, silence was imposed upon the two principals and upon their followers. In the next year Arminius himself died (1609), but his doctrines were upheld by Episcopius supported by the learned jurist, Oldenbarneveld, and the Humanist, Grotius. In replying to the charge of heresy brought against them the followers of Arminius presented

* Maronier, *Jacobus Arminius*, 1905. De Bray, *Histoire de l'église Arminienne*, 1835.

RATIONALISM AND ITS EFFECTS

to the States a Remonstrance embodying their doctrines (1610) and on this account they were styled Remonstrants. The States adopted a neutral attitude at first, but, as the Gomarists or anti-Remonstrants violated the injunction of silence by founding separate communities, the authorities were inclined not merely to tolerate but to support the Remonstrants.

Maurice, Prince of Orange, Stadtholder of Holland, anxious to strengthen his position by allying himself with the orthodox Calvinists, began a bitter campaign against the Arminians. Oldenbarneveld and Grotius were arrested and brought before the synod of Dordrecht (1617), at which the former was condemned to death, while Grotius was imprisoned for life though he succeeded in escaping after two years. Another Synod was held at Dordrecht (Nov 1618-April 1619) to which representatives came from all parts of Holland, the Palatinate, England, and Scotland. From the beginning the followers of Arminius were admitted only as accused persons, and were called upon to defend themselves against the charge of heresy. Against them the authority of Calvin was urged as if it were infallible. As the Arminians were suspected of republican principles William of Orange and his supporters were decidedly hostile. The Remonstrants, despairing of getting an impartial hearing, left the Synod. The five Articles contained in the Remonstrance were discussed, and decrees were issued regarding those portions of Calvin's doctrine that had been called in question. It was agreed that faith is the pure gift of God to be given by God to those whom He has predestined by His own mercy and without any reference to their merits for election; that Christ died only for the elect; that man's will does not co-operate in the work of his conversion; and that the elect are exempted from the dominion of sin, so that although they may be guilty of serious crimes they can never become enemies of God or forfeit the glory to which they were predestined. The decrees of the Synod of Dordrecht were received generally in Holland, Switzerland, France, in the territory of the Elector of Brandenburg, and in Hesse, but in the other portions of Calvinist Germany and in the greater part of England they met with serious opposition.

Anabaptists.*—The belief that baptism could not be conferred validly on infants who have not arrived at the use of reason was held by many of the Middle Age sectaries, and was revived at the time of the Reformation. Its supporters, claiming for themselves the liberty of interpreting the Scriptures according to their own judgment, maintained that they had divine sanction for their teaching. The leaders of the sect in Saxony and Thuringia were Thomas Münzer and Nicholas Storch. They represented the extreme left of the Lutheran party maintaining the equality of men and the community of property. In Zwickau, where the movement originated, violent disturbances broke out, and the leaders retired to Wittenberg where they were joined by Carlstadt. It required the presence of Luther himself to prevent the city from falling completely into their hands. Owing to the dangerous character of the radical principles defended by the Anabaptists several princes of Germany joined hands for their suppression. They were defeated at the battle of Frankenberg (1525) and Münzer was arrested and put to death. Before his execution he returned to the Catholic Church.

Despite this defeat the party made considerable progress in West Germany and in the Netherlands, where the people were so disgusted with their political and social conditions that they were ready to listen to semi-religious, semi-social reformers like the Anabaptists. They took possession of the city of Münster in Westphalia. The two principal leaders were John of Leyden (a tailor) and John Matthys or Matthieson (a baker), the former of whom was appointed king. The city was besieged and captured in 1535, and the principal Anabaptists were put

* Keller, *Geschichte der Wiedertäufer und ihres Reichs*, 1880.

to death. In Switzerland the movement made considerable progress. From Switzerland it spread into southern Germany, but the triumph of the princes during the Peasants' War destroyed the hopes of the extreme Anabaptists, and forced the sect to discard most of its fanatical tendencies. The leader of the more modern Anabaptist sect was Menno Simonis, a priest who joined the Society in 1535, and after whom the Anabaptists are called frequently Mennonites.* The latter rejected infant baptism and Luther's doctrine of Justification by faith alone. They protested against oaths even in courts of law and capital punishment.

Schwenkfeldians.†—This sect owes its origin to Caspar von Schwenkfeld (1489-1561), a native of Silesia, who, though attached to many of the doctrines of Luther, believed that Luther was inclined to lay too much stress on faith and external organisation to the exclusion of real religion. He thought that more attention should be paid to the mystical and devotional element, in other words to the personal union of the individual soul with God. According to him, this should be the beginning and end of all religion, and if it could be accomplished organisation and dogma were to be treated as of secondary importance. He rejected infant baptism, regarded the sacraments as mere symbols, denied the Real Presence of Christ in the Eucharist, and maintained that in the Incarnation the human nature of Christ was in a sense deified. Schwenkfeld held several interviews with Luther in the hope of winning him over to his opinions but without success. Owing to his quarrel with the master, Schwenkfeld was banished from Strassburg in 1533, and condemned by a Lutheran assembly at Schmalkald in 1540. His doctrines found considerable support in Silesia and in the states of several German princes, though it was only after Schwenkfeld's death that his followers began to organise themselves into separate

* Schyn, *Historia Christianorum qui Mennonitae appellantur*, 1723.
† Hofmann, *Caspar Schwenkfelds Leben und Lehren*, 1897.

communities. Owing to persecution many of them fled to America where they settled in Pennsylvania (1634). In 1742 the sect was tolerated in Prussia.

Socinianism.*—The doctrine of the Blessed Trinity found many opponents in the Latin countries about the time of the Reformation. Michael Servetus, Gentilis, Campanus, and Blandrata, attacked the Trinity from different points of view, but by far the most dangerous adversaries of the doctrine were Laelius Socinus (1525-1562) and his nephew Faustus Socinus (1539-1604). The former of these became a member of a secret society founded at Vicenza (1546) for the discussion and propagation of anti-Trinitarian views (1546). The principal members of this body were Gentilis, Blandrata, Alciatus, and Laelius Socinus, a priest of Siena and a man who stood in close relationship with some of the leading Lutherans and Calvinists. When the society at Vicenza was suppressed several of the prominent members fled to Poland for asylum. Laelius Socinus, though he remained at Zurich, was looked up to as the guiding spirit of the party till his death in 1562. His nephew Faustus Socinus then stepped into the place vacated by his uncle. The anti-Trinitarians in Poland, who had begun to style themselves Unitarians since 1563, had established themselves at Racow. In 1579 Faustus Socinus arrived in Poland, at a time when the anti-Trinitarians were divided into opposing factions, but in a short while he succeeded in winning most of them over to his own views. The doctrines of Socinus and of his principal disciples were explained in the *Catechism of Racow* (first published in 1605) and in the numerous theological works of Socinus. In 1638 the Socinians were banished from Poland, and violent measures were taken against them by most of the Catholic and Protestant princes of Europe.

Though Socinus professed the greatest respect for the Sacred Scriptures as the one and only source of all

* Bock, *Historia Antitrinitariorum maxime Socinianismi*, 1774-84. Lecler, *F. Socin*, 1884.

RATIONALISM AND ITS EFFECTS

religion, he claimed the right of free interpretation even to the extent of rejecting anything in them that surpassed the powers of the human understanding. In this respect he was as much a rationalist as any of the extreme rationalists who fought against Christianity in the eighteenth century. God, he maintained, was absolutely simple and therefore there could be no Trinity; He was infinite, and therefore could not unite Himself with human nature, as was assumed in the doctrine of the Incarnation; the Holy Ghost was not a person distinct from the Father, but only the energy and power of the Father as manifested in the sanctification of souls. Christ was not God; He was merely the Logos born miraculously and deputed by God to be a mediator for men. He ascended into Heaven, where He was in some sense deified and endowed with supreme dominion over the universe. Hence in opposition to the Unitarians Socinus maintained that Christ should be worshipped as God. He died on the cross according to the command of the Father, but it was by His example of obedience and by His preaching rather than by the vicarious sacrifice of His life that man's redemption was effected. The work of redemption which Christ began on earth is continued in Heaven through His intercession with the Father. From this notion of the redemption it followed as a logical consequence that the sacraments could not be regarded as channels of grace or as anything more than external signs of union with the Christian body. The Socinian doctrine was condemned by Paul IV.* (1555) and by Clement VIII. (1603).

Pietism.†—This movement among the Lutherans resembled closely some of the developments of Mysticism in the Catholic Church during the fourteenth and fifteenth centuries. Its object was to direct attention to the spiritual and ethical side of religion regardless of dogma and external organisation. One of its greatest

---

* Denzinger, *op. cit.*, no. 993.
† Ritchl, *Geschichte des Pietismus*, 1880-6.

leaders was Spener,* a student at Geneva, and later on a preacher at Frankfurt. In his endeavours to bring religion to bear on the daily lives of the people and to awaken in them a sense of their personal relations to God he founded the *Collegia Pietatis,* private assemblies for the study of the Scriptures, for the discussion of the means of redemption, and for a general revival of religious zeal. With the same object in view he wrote the *Pia Desideria* (1567), which was much prized as a spiritual reading book by the devout Lutherans of Germany. He emphasised the idea of a universal priesthood, which he thought had been somewhat neglected by the leaders of the Lutherans, advocated for those who were destined for the ministry a training in spiritual life rather than in theological lore, encouraged good works as the best means of securing eternal bliss, objected to polemical discussions, and welcomed the establishment of private societies for the promotion of Christian perfection. About the same time Franke and Anton undertook a similar work in Leipzig by founding the *Collegium Philobiblicum* principally for students and members of the university. This society was suppressed at the instigation of the Lutheran faculty of theology, and the two founders of it were dismissed. In a short time Spener was appointed to an office at Berlin and was received with great favour at the court. By his influence three of his leading disciples, Franke, Anton and Breithaupt were appointed professors in the University of Halle, which from that time became the leading centre of Pietism in Germany. Students flocked to Halle from all parts of Germany, from Denmark, and from Switzerland. An attempt was made to explain away Luther's teaching on good works, and to insist on the practical as distinct from the intellectual aspect of Christianity. This relegation of dogma to a secondary place, and the establishment of private assemblies to supplant the ecclesiastical organisation and the estab-

* Hossbach, *Ph. J. Spener und seine Zeit,* 1853.

lished liturgy, led to the development of separatist tendencies and ultimately to the promotion of dogmatic indifference. It is a noteworthy fact that Semler was one of the students most sincerely attached to Pietism at Halle.

Herrnhuters.*—This sect was only a development of the Moravian Brothers founded in 1457 by one of the Hussite leaders. It owes its development in the eighteenth century to Count Zinzendorf (1700-1760), a wealthy nobleman and a Pietist of the school of Spener. A number of the Moravian or Bohemian Brethren having appealed to him for a suitable place to establish a settlement, he offered them portion of his estate at Hutberg (1722). As they were inclined to quarrel amongst themselves he undertook in person the work of organisation. He appointed a college of elders to control the spiritual and temporal affairs of the community, together with a college of deacons to superintend specially the temporal wants of the brethren. Like the Pietists generally he paid little attention to dogmatic differences, allowing the Lutherans, Calvinists, and Moravians to have their own separate elders. As he was anxious to undertake missionary work he received Holy Orders, and wished to preach in Bohemia, but the Austrian government refused to allow him to continue his work in that province, and even secured his banishment from Saxony. He went through Europe visiting Holland and England and established some of his communities in both these countries, after which he returned to Herrnhut in 1755. During his lifetime Zinzendorf was looked upon as the head of the whole community, but after his death it was much more difficult to preserve unity. The Herrnhuters made some progress in Germany, but their greatest strength at the present day is to be found in England and the United States.

---

* Camerarius, *Historica narratio de Fratrum Orthodoxorum ecclesiis*, *etc.*, 1625. Hamilton, *A History of the Moravian Church or the Unitas Fratrum*, 1900.

Swedenborgians.*—The founder of this sect was Emanuel Swendenborg (1688-1772), who was born at Stockholm, and educated at the University of Upsala. He was a very distinguished student especially in the department of mathematics and physical science, and after an extended tour through Germany, France, Holland, and England he returned and settled down in Sweden, where he was offered and refused a chair at Upsala. From 1734 he began to turn to the study of philosophy and religion. After 1743, when he declared that Our Lord had appeared to him in a vision, had taught him the real spiritual sense of Scripture, and had commanded him to instruct others, he abandoned his mathematical pursuits and turned entirely to religion. As Judaism had been supplanted by Christianity, so too, he maintained, the revelation given by Christ was to be perfected by that granted to himself. He rejected the Justification theory of Luther, the Predestination teaching of Calvin, the doctrines of the Trinity, of Original Sin, and of the Resurrection of the body. The one God, according to him, took to Himself human flesh, and the name, Son of God, was applied properly to the humanity assumed by God the Father, while the Holy Ghost was but the energy and operation of the God Man. The new Jerusalem, that was to take the place of the Christian Church, was to be initiated on the day he completed his great work *Vera Christiana Religio* (1770). He claimed that the last Judgment took place in his presence in 1757. During his own life he did little to organise his followers except by establishing small societies for the study of the Bible, but after his death the organisation of the new Jerusalem was pushed on rapidly. From Sweden the sect spread into England, where the first community was established in Lancashire in 1787, and into America, and Germany. For a long time the Swedenborgians were persecuted as heretics in Sweden.

* Tafel, *Documents concerning the Life and Character of E. Swedenborg*, 1875-77. Görres, *Emanuel Swedenborg, seine visionen und sein verhältniss zur Kirche*, 1827.

CHAPTER IX

THE PAPACY

See bibliography, chap. iv. (*b*). Ciacconius, *Vitae et res gestae Romanorum Pontificum*, 1677. Sandini, *Vitae Rom. Pontif.*, etc., 1753. Guarnacci, *Vitae et res gestae Rom. Pontif.*, etc., 1751. Ranke, *op. cit.*, Reumont, *op. cit.* Della Gattina, *Histoire diplomatique des conclaves*, 1865. *Bullarium Romanum*.

DIFFICULT as had been the situation with which the Popes were confronted during the sixteenth century and the first half of the seventeenth century, when heresy was rampant throughout Europe, and when Catholic nations were obliged to fight for their very existence, it was not a whit more difficult or more critical than that created by the increasing and selfish demands of Catholic rulers, which confronted their successors during the age of absolute government. The Peace of Westphalia (1648), by giving official sanction to the principle of state neutrality, meant nothing less than a complete revolution in the relations that had existed hitherto between Church and State. So long as the Christian world was united in one great religious family, acknowledging the Pope as the common Father of Christendom, it was not strange that in disputes between princes and subjects or between the rulers of independent states the authority of the Pope as supreme arbitrator should have been recognised, or that his interference even in temporal matters should not have been regarded as unwarrantable.

But once the religious unity of Europe was broken by the separation of entire nations from the Church, and once the politico-religious constitution of the Holy Roman Empire was destroyed by the acceptance of the principle of religious neutrality, the Popes felt that their interference even indirectly in temporal matters, however justifiable it might be in itself, could produce no good results. Hence apart from their action as temporal sovereigns of the Papal States, a position that obliged the Popes to take part in political affairs, the whole tendency was to confine themselves strictly to spiritual matters, and to preserve harmony if possible between Church and State. This policy did not, however, satisfy the selfish designs of rulers, who had determined to crush all representative institutions and to assert for themselves complete and unlimited authority. Catholic rulers, jealous of the increased powers secured by Protestant princes through the exercise of supreme ecclesiastical jurisdiction, determined to assert for themselves a somewhat similar authority over the Catholic Church in their own territories. It was no longer the supposed inroads of the Church upon the domain of the State but the attacks of the State upon the rights of the Church, that were likely to disturb the good relations between Catholic princes and the Pope. These rulers demanded an overwhelming voice in all ecclesiastical appointments; they insisted upon exercising the *Royal Placet* upon papal documents and episcopal pronouncements; they would tolerate no longer the privileges and exemptions admitted by their predecessors in favour of clerics or of ecclesiastical property; they claimed the right of dictating to the cardinals who should be Pope and of dictating to the Pope who should be cardinals; of controlling education in their own dominions; of determining the laws and rules concerning marriages and matrimonial dispensations, and of fixing the constitutions of those religious orders the existence of which they were willing to tolerate.

Unfortunately in their designs for transferring ecclesiastical jurisdiction from the Popes to the crown the princes were favoured by many of the bishops, who were annoyed at the continual interference of Rome and

THE PAPACY

who failed to realise that the king was a much greater danger to their independence than the Pope; by a large body of clerics and laymen, who looked to the civil authority for promotion; by the Jansenists who detested Rome, because Rome had barred the way against the speculative and practical religious revolution which they contemplated; by the philosophers and rationalists, many of whom, though enemies of absolute rule, did not fail to recognise that disputes between Church and State, leading necessarily to a weakening of Church authority, meant the weakening of dogmatic Christianity; and by liberal-minded Catholics of the *Aufklärung* school, who thought that every blow dealt at Rome meant a blow struck for the policy of modernising the discipline, government, and faith of the Church. The eighteenth century was a period of transition from the politico-religious views of the Middle Ages to those of modern times. It was a period of conflict between two ideals of the relations that should exist between Church and State. The Popes were called upon to defend not indeed their right to interfere in temporal matters, for of that there was no question, but their right to exercise control in purely spiritual affairs. It is necessary to bear this in mind if one wishes to appreciate the policy of those, upon whom was placed the terrible responsibility of governing the Church during the one hundred and fifty years that elapsed between the Peace of Westphalia and the outbreak of the French Revolution.

In the conclave that followed the death of Innocent X., Cardinal Chigi, who had been nuncio at Cologne, envoy-extraordinary of the Holy See during the negotiations that ended in the Peace of Westphalia, and afterwards Secretary of State, was elected, and took the title of Alexander VII.* (1655-67). At first the people were rejoiced because the new Pope had shown himself so determined an opponent of that nepotism, which had dimmed the glory of so many of his predecessors, but

* Pallavicini, *Vita di Alessandro VII.*, 1849.

at the request of the foreign ambassadors and with the approval of the cardinals he changed his policy after some time, brought some of his relatives to Rome, and allowed them too much influence. His election had been opposed by Cardinal Mazarin in the name of France, and throughout his reign he was doomed to suffer severely from the unfriendly and high-handed action of Louis XIV., who despatched an army to the Papal States to revenge an insult to his ambassador, the Duc de Créqui, and forced the Pope to sign the disgraceful Peace of Pisa (1664). Alexander VII. condemned the Jansenistic distinction between law and fact by the Bull, *Ad Sanctam Petri Sedem* (1665), to enforce which he drew up a formulary of faith to be signed by the French clergy and religious. He observed an attitude of neutrality in the disputes between Spain and Portugal, secured the return of the Jesuits to Venice, and welcomed to Rome Queen Christina of Sweden, who abandoned Lutheranism to return to the Catholic Church.

His successor, Cardinal Rospigliosi, formerly nuncio at Madrid and Secretary of State was proclaimed Pope as Clement IX. (1667-69). He was deeply religious, generous in his donations to the poor and to hospitals, and uninfluenced by any undue attachment to his relations. He put an end to the religious disorders that had reigned in Portugal since 1648, when that country seceded from Spain to which it had been united since 1580, and proclaimed the Duke of Braganza king under the title of John IV. Matters had reached such a crisis that many of the bishoprics in Portugal and the Portuguese colonies were left vacant. In 1668 after the conclusion of the Peace of Lisbon the Pope appointed those who had been nominated to the vacant Sees. Deceived by the false representations made to him from France, he restored the French bishops who had adhered publicly to the distinction between law and fact. He offered generous assistance to Venice more especially in its defence of

Crete against the Turks. During his reign he canonised Mary Magdalen de Pazzi, and Peter of Alcantara.

On the death of Clement IX. the cardinals could not at first agree upon any candidate, but finally as a compromise they elected, much against his own will, Cardinal Altieri, then an old man eighty years of age.* He was proclaimed as Clement X. (1670-76). Unable to transact much business himself he left too much in the hands of others, especially to Cardinal Paoluzzi. He encouraged and assisted the Poles in their struggles against the Turks, and resisted the demands of Louis XIV. concerning the *Regalia*. He canonised John Cajetan, Philip Benitius, Francis Borgia, Louis Bertrand, and Rose of Lima.

In the conclave that followed the demise of Clement X. Cardinal Odescalchi, against whom France had exercised the veto on a previous occasion, was elected and took the name of Innocent XI.† (1676-1689). He was zealous for religion, charitable to the poor, economic and prudent in the administration of the Papal States, anxious for an improvement in clerical education, and a strong opponent of everything that savoured of nepotism. His whole reign was troubled by the insolent and overbearing demands of Louis XIV. in regard to the *Regalia,* the right of asylum, and the Declaration of the French Clergy (1682), but Innocent XI. maintained a firm attitude in spite of the threats of the king and the culpable weakness of the French bishops. He encouraged John Sobieski, King of Poland, to take up arms against the Turks who had laid siege to Vienna, and contributed generously to help Hungary to withstand these invaders.

After the short and by no means glorious reign of Alexander VIII. (Cardinal Ottoboni, 1689-91), the cardinals were divided into two parties, the French and the Spanish-Austrian. When the conclave had con-

---

* De Bildt, *The Conclave of Clement X.*, 1905.
† Bonamici, *De Vita Innocentii XI*, 1776.

tinued five months without any result they agreed finally to elect a compromise candidate (Cardinal Pignatelli) who took the name of Innocent XII. (1691-1700). In every respect he showed himself worthy of his holy office. Nepotism was condemned in the Bull *Romanum Decet Pontificem,* better arrangements were made for the administration of justice throughout the Papal States; the disputes with Louis XIV. regarding the Declaration of the French Clergy were settled when the bishops who signed these articles expressed their regret for their conduct (1693); and several propositions taken from the *Maximes* of Fénelon were condemned. The Pope was involved in a serious dispute with the Emperor Leopold I. concerning the right of asylum attached to the imperial embassy in Rome, and the aggressive policy of Martinitz, the imperial ambassador. As a result of this quarrel the Pope, without consulting Charles II. of Spain who had no heirs, favoured the pretensions of Philip Duke of Anjou (Philip V.) to the throne of Spain in preference to the Emperor's son the Archduke Charles.

In the conclave that assembled after the death of Innocent XII. the majority of the cardinals favoured Cardinal Mariscotti, but, as his election was vetoed by France, they concentrated their votes on Cardinal Albani. For three days he refused to accept the onerous office, but at last he gave way to the earnest entreaties of the cardinals, and allowed himself to be proclaimed as Clement XI.* (1700-21). His election was acclaimed in Rome, in Italy, and throughout the Catholic world. He was a man of great sanctity of life, devoted to prayer and labour, who set an example to others by preaching and hearing confessions regularly in St. Peter's. While he was Pope there was no danger of nepotism at the papal court, and no prospect for unworthy or greedy officials in the Papal States. During his entire reign he was involved in disputes with the Catholic powers.

* Lafiteau, *Vie de Clément XI.*, 1752

The death of Charles II. of Spain led to a conflict between Louis XIV., who claimed the crown for his grandson Philip of Anjou (Philip V.), and the Emperor Leopold I., who supported the cause of his son, the Archduke, Charles III. Clement XI. endeavoured at first to maintain an attitude of neutrality, but as Philip had been crowned and had established himself apparently on the throne of Spain the Pope was obliged to acknowledge him. This action gave great offence to Leopold I. and to his successor, Joseph I., who retaliated by interfering in ecclesiastical affairs and by despatching an army against the Papal States. Clement XI., abandoned by Louis XIV. and by Philip V. was obliged to come to terms with the Emperor, and to acknowledge Charles III. as king of Spain. Immediately Louis XIV. and Philip V. were up in arms against the Pope. The nuncio was dismissed from Madrid and relations between Spain and Rome were interrupted for a long period; the papal representatives were excluded from the negotiations preceding the Peace of Utrecht (1713); and feudal territories of the Holy See were disposed of without consulting the wishes of the Pope, Sicily being handed over to Victor Amadeus of Savoy (1675-1713) with whom Clement XI. was then in serious conflict.

To put an end to difficulties with the foreign bishops, who exercised jurisdiction in portion of his territory, the Duke of Savoy had demanded full rights of nomination to episcopal Sees. When this demand was refused he recalled his ambassador from Rome (1701), and took upon himself the regulation of ecclesiastical affairs. He appointed an administrator to take charge of the revenues of vacant Sees, enforced the *Royal Placet* on episcopal and papal documents, and forbade the publication of Roman censures (1710). A partial agreement was arrived at when the royal administrator consented to accept his appointment from the Pope, but the transference of Sicily to the Duke of Savoy led to a new and more serious quarrel. The latter attempted to revive the privileges known as the Sicilian Monarchy, accorded formerly to the ruler of Sicily. The Pope refused to recognise these claims, and as the king remained stubborn nothing was left but to place the island under interdict. To this the king replied by expelling those priests who observed the interdict. This state of affairs lasted until Sicily passed into the hands of the King of Spain (1718).

The Turks were active once more and threatened Europe by land and sea. Clement XI. sent generous supplies to Venice to equip its fleet, encouraged Stanislaus Augustus of Poland who had joined the Catholic Church, granted tithes upon ecclesiastical property to help him in the struggle, and allowed Philip V. of Spain portion of the revenues derived from benefices in Spain and in the Spanish-American colonies, on condition that the Spanish fleet should be sent into the Mediterranean to take part in the war against Turkey. The victories of Prince Eugene (1716-18) dealt a severe blow to the power of the Sultan, but the Spanish fleet instead of assisting the Christian forces was used for the capture of Sardinia from the Emperor. As evidence of the difficult position of Clement XI. in face of the powers of Europe it is sufficient to point to the fact that at one time or another during his reign, his nuncios were driven from Vienna, Turin, Madrid, and Naples.

The conclave that followed was, as might be expected, a stormy one; but in the end Cardinal Conti, who had been nuncio in Lucerne and Lisbon, was elected and took as his title Innocent XIII. (1721-24). He granted the kingdom of Naples to the Emperor, who in turn without consulting the Pope bestowed the papal fiefs of Parma and Piacenza on Prince Charles of France. Peace was restored between the Holy See and Spain (1723), and Innocent XIII., yielding very unwillingly to the importunate demands of France, conferred a cardinal's hat on Dubois, the prime minister.

His successor was Benedict XIII. (1724-30). Cardinal

Orsini, as he was known before his election, belonged to the Dominican Order, and at the time of the conclave held the Archbishopric of Benevento. As archbishop he was most zealous in the administration of his diocese, and as Pope he followed the same strict simple life to which he had been accustomed when a Dominican friar. He made peace with the Emperor by granting him practically all the rights contained in the Sicilian Monarchy, reserving to the Holy See only the final decision of important cases (1728), and with the King of Savoy by acknowledging his title over Sardinia and by granting him the right of episcopal nomination in the island. With the demand of King John of Portugal, namely, that Portugal should enjoy the privilege of presenting candidates for appointment to the college of cardinals, Benedict XIII. refused to comply, and as a consequence the Portuguese ambassador was recalled from Rome and communications with the Holy See were interrupted. The extension of the feast of Gregory VII. (Hildebrand) to the whole Church gave great offence to many rulers both Catholic and Protestant, because such a step was interpreted as a direct challenge to the new theories of secular intervention in ecclesiastical affairs. Benedict XIII. was a saintly ruler, whose only misfortune was that he relied too much on unworthy councillors like Cardinal Coscia and Cardinal Lercari, who deceived him in their negotiations with the governments of Europe and in the administration of the Papal States. A rebellion against these men broke out in Rome when the news of the Pope's death became public. Cardinal Coscia was deprived of his dignity and imprisoned, while many of his associates and subordinates were punished no less severely.

Cardinal Corsini who succeeded as Clement XII. (1730-1740) was faced with a very difficult situation in Rome and in the Papal States. The treasury was empty, the finances were in disorder, and the discontent was general. The Pope, though very old, delicate, and almost completely blind, showed wonderful energy and administrative ability. The financial affairs of the government were placed upon a proper footing. Instead of a deficit there was soon a surplus, which was expended in beautifying the city, in opening up the port of Ancona, and in the drainage and reclamation of the marshes. Like his predecessors, Clement XII. had much to suffer from the Catholic rulers of Europe. He was engaged in a quarrel with the King of Savoy because he tried to limit the privileges that had been conceded to this sovereign by his predecessor. Philip V. of Spain demanded that the Pope should confer a cardinal's hat together with the Archbishoprics of Seville and Toledo on his son, then only nine years of age. The Pope endeavoured to satisfy the king by granting the temporal administration of Toledo until the boy should reach the canonical age for the reception of Orders (1735), but owing to an attack made upon the Spanish ambassador in Rome during a popular commotion the courts of Naples and Madrid dismissed the papal ambassador and broke off relations with the Holy See. Peace, however, was restored with Spain in 1737 and with Naples in the following year. Clement XII. condemned the Freemasons (1738). He canonised Vincent de Paul, John Francis Regis, and Juliana Falconieri.

The conclave that followed lasted six months before any of the candidates could secure the required majority. At last Cardinal Lambertini was elected and proclaimed under the title of Benedict XIV.* (1740-58). In many particulars, but more especially as a scholar and a writer, he may be regarded as one of the greatest Popes of modern times. He was born in 1675, was educated at Rome and Bologna, and even as a very young man he was looked upon as a leading authority on canon law and theology. He rose steadily from position to position in Rome till at last he found himself cardinal and Arch-

* *Benedicti XIV. Opera*, 17 vols., 1839-46. Heiner, *Opera inedita*, 1904. Guarnacci, *Vie du Pape Benoît XIV.*, 1783.

bishop of Bologna. As archbishop he was most successful in the discharge of all the duties that appertained to his office. He held diocesan synods regularly, visited the most distant parishes of his diocese, superintended the education of his clerical students for whom he drew up a new plan of studies, and above all he strove to maintain most friendly relations with both priests and people. But notwithstanding his cares of office he found time to continue his studies, and to prepare learned volumes on Canon Law, Theology, and History, that placed him amongst the leading scholars of his time.

Nor did he change his policy or his course of life after his election to the papal throne. Benedict XIV. was convinced that a better training would help to strengthen the influence of the clergy, and would enable them to combat more successfully the rising spirit of unbelief. Hence he was anxious to introduce into the colleges more modern educational methods. He founded four academies, one for Christian Archæology, one for Canon Law, one for Church History, and one for the special study of the history of the Councils. He gave every encouragement to priests who wished to devote themselves to literary pursuits, and in his own person he showed how much could be done in this direction without any neglect of duty. His instructions and encyclicals were learned treatises, in which no aspect of the subject he handled was neglected. His decrees on marriage, especially on mixed marriages (*Magnæ Nobis admirationis*, 1748), on Penance, and on the Oriental Rites were of vital importance. Both before and after his elevation to the papacy he published many learned works, the most important of which were the *Institutiones Ecclesiasticae, De Synodo Diocesana, De Servorum Dei Beatificatione et de Beatorum canonizatione, Thesaurus Resolutionum Sacrae Congregationis Concilii,* and the *Casus Conscientiae.*

In his administration of the Papal States Benedict XIV. was no less successful. The enormous expenses incurred by his predecessor had depleted the papal treasury, but the schemes of retrenchment enforced by Benedict XIV. produced such good results that in a few years money was available for the development of agriculture, industries, and commerce. With the civil rulers of Europe he had a difficult part to play. Convinced that disputes between the civil and ecclesiastical authority resulted only in promoting the schemes of the enemies of religion, he was determined to go to the very limits of concession for the sake of peace and harmony. For a time at least he was able to secure a partial reconciliation, and had his overtures been met in the proper spirit a working arrangement might have been established, that would have enabled both powers to combine against the forces at work for the overthrow of Church and State.

The title of King of Prussia assumed by the Elector of Brandenburg was recognised by the Pope; peace was made with Portugal by granting to the crown rights of patronage over bishoprics and abbeys (1740), and to set the seal on this reconciliation the title of *Rex Fidelissimus* was bestowed on the King of Portugal. With the court of Turin the Pope had still greater difficulties, but an agreement was arrived at, whereby the king was to have the right of nomination to ecclesiastical benefices; the foreign bishops having jurisdiction in the territory of Savoy were to appoint vicars-general for the administration of these portions of their dioceses, and the administrator of vacant benefices appointed by the king was to act as the deputy of the Pope (1741). With Spain a formal concordat was concluded in 1753. The dispute in Naples regarding the Sicilian Monarchy was settled by the appointment of a mixed tribunal composed of laymen and clerics, presided over by a cleric for the settlement of ecclesiastical affairs. The Pope's decision that only those who refused publicly to accept the papal condemnation of Jansenism were to be excluded from the sacraments helped to ease considerably the situation in France. He condemned the Freemasons (1751), and reduced the number of holidays for Spain in 1742 and for Austria, Tuscany, and Naples in 1748.

His successor Clement XIII. (1758-69) found himself in a peculiarly unhappy position. Despite the friendly policy adopted by Benedict XIV. towards the civil rulers, or, as some would say, as a result of the concessions that he made, their demands became still more exorbitant. The Rationalists, liberal Catholics, Jansenists, and Freemasons united their forces for a grand attack upon the Society of Jesus, the suppression of which they were determined to secure. Already rumblings of the storm had been heard before the death of Benedict XIV. His successor, who had the highest admiration for the Jesuits, stood manfully by the Society, and refused to yield to the threats of the Bourbon rulers thirsting for its destruction. His sudden death was attributed not without good reason to the ultimatum, demanding the immediate suppression of the Jesuits, addressed to him by the ambassadors of France, Spain, and Naples.

In the conclave the cardinals were divided into two parties, the *Zelanti* who stood for resistance to the demands of the civil rulers, and the moderate men who supported the policy of conciliation. The representatives of France, Spain, Portugal, and Naples, left no stone unturned to prevent the election of a *Zelanti,* and the veto was used with such effect that the choice of the cardinals was at last limited to only three or four. Threats were made that, if a candidate was elected against the wishes of the Bourbons, Rome might be occupied by foreign troops, and obedience might be refused to the new Pope. In the end a Franciscan friar, Cardinal Ganganelli, who was not an extreme partisan of either party among the cardinals, received the required majority of votes, and was proclaimed as Clement XIV. (1769-74).* The new Pope was not unfriendly to the

* *See* chap. viii. (*d*).

Jesuits, nor had he any evidence that could induce him to reverse the very favourable judgment delivered in their favour by his immediate predecessor. He endeavoured to avert the storm by making generous concessions to the Bourbons and to Portugal, by adopting an unfriendly attitude towards the Society, and by offering to effect serious changes in its constitution. But these half-way measures failed to put an end to the agitation, and at last Clement XIV. found himself obliged to make his choice between suppression and schism. In the circumstances he thought it best for the sake of peace to sacrifice the Society (1773) but he was soon to realise that peace could not be procured even by such a sacrifice. His weakness led only to more intolerable demands from France, Spain and Naples.

The cardinals assembled in conclave after his death found it difficult to agree upon any candidate, but finally after a conclave lasting more than four months they elected Cardinal Braschi, who took the title of Pius VI.* (1775-99). The new Pope was a zealous ecclesiastic, anxious to promote a policy of conciliation, but immovable as a rock when there was question of the essential rights of the Church. He withstood manfully the Febronian policy of Joseph II. and of the prince-bishops of Germany, and condemned the decrees of the Synod of Pistoia (1794). He endeavoured to maintain friendly relations with Portugal, Spain, Naples, and Sardinia, though the old policy of state supremacy was still the guiding principle of the rulers and politicians. The storm that had been gathering for years broke over Europe during the latter years of his reign; the Bourbon throne in France was overturned, and no man could foretell when a similar fate awaited the other royal families of Europe. Pius VI., though not unwilling to recognise the new order, was stern in his refusal to permit the constitution of the Church to be changed.

* Ferrari, *Vita Pii VI.*, 1802. Bourgoing, *Mémoires historiques et philosophiques sur Pie VI. et son pontificat*, 1800.

For this reason his capital was occupied; his cardinals were dispersed, and he himself was brought as a prisoner to Valence, where he died in exile (1799). The enemies of religion could not conceal their delight. They declared triumphantly that with him the long line of Peter had ceased to exist, but the conclave at Venice and the election of Pius VII. (1800) soon showed the world that though kingdoms and dynasties might disappear the Papacy still survived, as Christ had foretold it should survive.

CHAPTER X

THEOLOGICAL STUDIES. RELIGIOUS LIFE

See bibliography, chap. vi. (*g*). Aubry, *La Méthode des études ecclésiastiques dans nos séminaires depuis le concile de Trente*, 1900. Picot, *Essai historique sur l'influence de la religion en France*, 1824. Joly, *Les moralistes français du XVIIe, XVIIIe, et XIXe siècles*, 1900. Andres, *Dell'origine, progressi, e stato attuale di ogni letteratura*, 1843. Backer-Sommervogel, *Bibliothèque des écrivains de la compagnie de Jésus*, 1890-98. Féret, *La faculté de théologie de Paris. Époque moderne* (vii.), 1910. Quétif-Echard, *Scriptores Ord. Praedicatorum*.

THE great theological revival that began with the Council of Trent, and that made itself felt in the Latin countries, died away gradually, to be followed in the eighteenth century by a period of decline. Scholars like Bellarmine, De Lugo, and Suarez had passed away without leaving anybody behind them worthy to take their places. Except in the field of ecclesiastical history and of historical theology the whole tendency was downwards.

The principal causes that paved the way for this universal decline were the spread of Gallicanism and Jansenism with the consequent waste of energy to which these controversies led, the state of lethargy produced by the enslavement of the Church, the withdrawal of ecclesiastical students from the universities, the suppression of the Society of Jesus, and the rejection of the Scholastic system of philosophy in favour of the vagaries of Descartes or of the Leibniz-Wolf school in Germany.

The rise of the Rationalist school in France, threatening as it did the very foundations of Christianity, called for the activity of a new group of apologists, who would do for Christianity in the eighteenth century what had been done for it against the pagan philosophers of old by men like Justin Martyr and Lactantius. Unfortunately, however, though many able works were produced at the time, few if any of them could lay claim to the literary charms or vigour of expression that characterised the works of the enemies of religion. The principal apologists in France at this period were *Huet* (d. 1721), *Sommier* (d. 1737), the Oratorian *Houteville* (d. 1742), *Baltius, S.J.* (d. 1743), *Bullet,* professor in the University of Besançon (d. 1775), *Bergier,* one of the most distinguished of Bullet's pupils (d. 1790), *Guénée* (d. 1803), the able opponent of Voltaire, and *Feller, S.J.* (d. 1802), whose *Catéchisme philosophique* and *Dictionnaire Historique* enjoyed a widespread popularity long after the writer had passed away.

In dogmatic theology the leading representatives of the Thomistic school were without doubt *Vincent Louis Gotti* (1664-1742) and *Charles René Billuart* (1685-1757). The former of these was born at Bologna, entered the Dominican novitiate at an early age, was the author of several polemical works directed against the Lutherans and Calvinists, and was created cardinal (1728). On account of his ability, prudence, and sanctity of life he exercised a wonderful influence both within and without his order in France, so much so that in the conclave of 1740 his election to the papacy was favoured by a large body of his colleagues. Cardinal Gotti's greatest work was his commentary on St. Thomas, entitled *Theologia Scholastico-Dogmatica iuxta mentem D. Thomae* (1727-1735). *Billuart* was born at Ardennes in Belgium, and on the completion of his classical studies he became a novice in the Dominican convent at Lille. For the years during which he held several positions in Dominican houses in Belgium his abilities as a writer, professor, and preacher, attracted so much attention that on the petition of Billuart's colleagues at Douay, the general of the order decided to entrust him with the work of preparing an exhaustive and authoritative commentary on the *Summa* of Saint Thomas. After five years hard work the edition was completed and was published at Liège in nineteen volumes * (1746-51). A compendium was issued in 1754.

The best known and ablest exponent of the theological system of Duns Scotus was *Claude Frassen* (1621-1711). He was born at Péronne, joined the Franciscans, and was sent to Paris, where he taught theology for years. His great work is his *Scotus Academicus*, a commentary or explanation of the theological system of Duns Scotus. Both on account of its faithful exposition of the views of Scotus and of the excellent method and style in which it is composed this work enjoyed and enjoys a considerable reputation.† Of the theologians of the Augustinian school the two best known were *Lorenzo Berti* (1696-1766) whose *De Theologicis Disciplinis* (1739-45) led to an imputation of Jansenism, from which the author was cleared by the verdict of Benedict XIV., and *Cardinal Norris* (1631-1704) for a long time professor of ecclesiastical history at the University of Padua, against whose books, *Historia Pelagiana* and *Vindiciae Augustanae,* a prohibition was levelled by the Spanish Inquisition, but reversed on appeal to Benedict XIV.

The endless controversies to which Jansenism gave rise had lowered the reputation of the Sorbonne. The greatest representative of this centre of theological learning at this period was *Honoré Tournély*, the steadfast opponent of Jansenism, whose *Praelectiones Theologicae* (1738-40) was regarded as one of the most important works of the time. In the defence of the Holy See against the attacks of Febronius the greatest writers were *Zaccaria* (1714-95) who wrote voluminously on theology, ecclesiastical history and canon law; *Alfonso Muzzarelli* (1749-1813), the Dominican, *Cardinal Orsi* (1693-1761), and *Cardinal Gerdil* (1718-1802), whose election to the papacy on the death of Pius VI. was vetoed by the

* *Summa S. Thomae hodiernis Academiarum moribus accomodata.*
† New edition, 10 vols., 1902-5.

Emperor. The *Theologia Wirceburgenis* published by
the Jesuits of Würzburg (1766-71) contained a complete
and masterly summary of the entire theological course.

Though Billuart and many of his contemporaries,
following in the footsteps of St. Thomas, dealt with both
dogmatic and moral theology, the tendency to treat the
latter as a distinct department and to give more attention
to what may be termed the casuistical side of moral
theology became more marked. To a certain extent, at
least in manuals intended for the use of the clergy, such
a method was rendered necessary by the frequent and
more comprehensive character of the confessions. Yet it
furnished some apparent justification for the onslaughts
of the Jansenists, who thought that they detected in
the new method a degradation of theology, a divorce
between religion and casuistry, and a return to the
unholy hair-splitting of the Pharisees.

Closely allied with the opposition to the new method
adopted by the moral theologians was the controversy
on Probabilism, that divided the schools during the
greater part of the seventeenth and eighteenth centuries.
In the practical solution of doubtful obligations Probabilism had been applied for centuries, but it was only
towards the end of the sixteenth century that the principle was formulated definitely by the Dominican, De
Medina. It was accepted immediately by a great body
of the Jesuits, as well as by nearly all writers on moral
theology. The Jansenists, however, in their eagerness
to damage the reputation of their Jesuit opponents
charged them with having introduced this novel and lax
system of morals with the object of catering for the
depraved tastes of their degenerate clients, and this
charge when presented in a popular and telling style by
their opponents created a distinctly unfavourable impression against the Society. The condemnation of
Probabilism by the University of Louvain (1655) and the
outcry raised against it by the Rigorist party led most
of the religious orders and the secular clergy to abandon

the system. Two incidents that took place shortly afterwards helped to strengthen the anti-Probabilist party. One of these was the condemnation by the Holy See of certain very lax principles put forward by some theologians who labelled themselves Probabilists (1679), and the other was the decision given by Innocent XI.* in the case of the defence of Probabiliorism written by Thyrsus Gonzalez (1624-1705) afterwards general of the Jesuits. His superiors refused him permission to publish his work, and on appeal to the Pope this prohibition was removed (1680). But though the Pope certainly favoured Probabiliorism it is not clear that his decision gave any practical sanction to this opinion. Rigorism was dealt a severe blow by the condemnation issued by Alexander VIII. (1690), and in the end the influence and writings of St. Alphonsus put an end to both extremes.

Amongst some of the great theologians of the time were the Jesuit *Lacroix* (1652-1714), *Paul Gabriel Antoine, S.J.* (1679-1743) professor at the Jesuit College of Pont-à-Mousson, *Billuart* (1685-1757), *Eusebius Amort* (1692-1775), and the *Salmanticenses,* the Jesuit authors of the series on moral theology begun in Salamanca in 1665. But by far the most remarkable writer on moral theology during the eighteenth century was *Saint Alphonsus de' Liguori* † (1697-1787), the founder of the Redemptorists. A saint, a scholar, and a practical missionary, with a long and varied experience in the care of souls, he understood better than most of his contemporaries how to hold the scales fairly between laxity and rigorism. Though his views were attacked severely enough in his own time they found favour with the great body of theologians, and the approbation given to them by the Church helped to put an end to the rigorist opinions, that remained even after their Jansenistic origin had been forgotten.

The spread of indifferentist or rationalist theories could

* Denzinger, *op. cit.*, no. 1219.
† Berthe-Castle, *Life of St. Alphonsus de' Liguori,* 1905.

not fail to weaken the reverence that had been inculcated by the early Reformers for the Bible as the sole source of God's revelation to men. Acting upon Luther's principle of private judgment others, regardless of their inspiration and infallibility, undertook to subject the authority of the Scriptures to the authority of human reason. Faustus Socinus (1539-1604), one of the founders of the Socinian sect, insisted that everything in the Scriptures that seems opposed to reason could not have come from God and should be eliminated. For some time while religious fervour was at its height both Lutherans and Calvinists held fast by their religious formularies and refused to accept the scriptural views of Socinus. But once dogmatic religion had been assailed by the new philosophico-rationalist school in England, Germany, and France the way was prepared for the acceptance of more liberal views. On the one hand, many of the extreme opponents of Christianity set themselves to point out the errors of the Bible as a proof that it could not have come from God, while, on the other, many of the Protestant scholars, who still held by a divine Christian revelation, endeavoured to eliminate from it the supernatural without rejecting openly the authority of the Scriptures.

It was with this design that Jacob Semler (1725-91) formulated the Accommodation Theory, according to which Christ and His Apostles accommodated their actions and their language to the erroneous notions prevalent amongst the Jews in their time, and for this reason all that bordered upon the mysterious should be regarded merely as a surrender to contemporary superstition. Another method of arriving at a similar conclusion was adopted by Kant, who maintained that the Bible was written only to inculcate morality and to strengthen man's moral sense, and that all that is recorded in it must be interpreted by reason in the light of the object which its authors had in view.

With such liberal theories about the authority and

inspiration of the Scriptures in the air it was almost impossible that Catholic exegetists could escape the contagion. One of the ablest Catholic writers at the time, the French Oratorian *Richard Simon* (1638-1712), was accused by his contemporaries of having approached too closely to the rationalist system in his scriptural theories. He was a man well-versed in the Oriental languages and well able to appreciate the literary and historical difficulties that might be urged against the inspiration and inerrancy of the Old Testament. He maintained that the Bible was a literary production, and that, as such it should be interpreted according to the ideas and methods of composition prevalent in the country or at the time in which the various books were written. His views were contained in his *Histoire Critique du Vieux Testament* (1678) and his *Histoire Critique de Texte du Nouveau Testament* (1689), both of which, though undoubtedly able works that have considerably influenced scriptural study amongst Catholics since that time, were severely criticised, and were condemned by the Congregation of the Index.

Another French Oratorian of the period, *Bernard Lamy* (1640-1715), dealt with the introduction to the Scriptures in his two books *Apparatus ad Biblia Sacra* (1687) and *Apparatus Biblicus* (1696). As a professor of philosophy Lamy had stirred up already a strong opposition owing to his evident leanings towards Cartesianism, nor was he less unhappy in his scriptural studies. He questioned the historical character of the narrations contained in the books of Tobias and Judith, and contended that notwithstanding the decrees of the Council of Trent less authority should be attributed to the Deutero-Canonical than to the Proto-Canonical books of the Bible.

Amongst the leading scriptural commentators were *Le Maistre de Saci* (d. 1684), a Jansenist, who published translations of the Old and the New Testament, the latter of which was put upon the Index; *Piconio* (Henri

Bernardine de Picquigny, 1633-1709) a Capuchin whose *Triplex Expositio in Sacrosancta D.N. Jesu Christi Evangelia* (1726), has not been surpassed till the present day; Louis de Carrières (1622-1717), whose *La Sainte Bible en Français avec un commentaire littéral* founded on De Saci's translation was recognised as one of the simplest and best commentaries on the Scriptures; Charles François Houbigant (1686-1783), also an Oratorian, who published an edition of the Hebrew Bible and the Greek text of the Deutero-Canonical books together with a Prolegomena, and Dom Calmet (1672-1757), a Benedictine, who published in twenty-three volumes a commentary on the Old and New Testament accompanied by an introduction to the various books (1707-1716).

In no department of theological science were greater advances made during the seventeenth and eighteenth centuries that in that of ecclesiastical history and historical theology. This was due largely to the labours and example of the Benedictines of St. Maur. Men like Luc d'Achéry (1609-1685), *Stephen Baluze* (1630-1718), Jean Mabillon (1632-1704), *Edmond Martène* (1654-1739), Ruinart (1657-1709), *Muratori* (1672-1750), Bouquet (1685-1754), *Jean Hardouin, S.J.* (1646-1729), Domenico Mansi (1692-1769), and the Orientalists Joseph Simeon Assemani (1687-1768) and his brother *Joseph Aloysius* (1710-82) laid the foundations of modern historical research, by their publication of correct editions of the Early and Middle Age writers and of the decrees of the various general, national, and provincial councils, as well as by the example which they set in their own scholarly dissertations of how historical materials should be used. In addition to the publication of collections of original sources, works like the *Gallia Christiana*, begun in 1715 by the Benedictines of St. Maur and continued by them till the Revolution, *España Sagrada* begun by the Augustinian Enrique Florez in 1747, and the *Italia Sacra* (1643-1662) of Ferdinand

Ughelli contained a veritable mine of information for future historians. Of the historical writers of this period the ablest were *Louis Sebastien Le Nain de Tillemont* (1637-1689), the author of the *Histoire des Empereurs pendant les six premiers Siècles* and *Mémoires pour servir a l'histoire eccl. des six premiers siècles* (1693); *Claude Fleury* (1640-1725) whose great work, *Histoire Ecclésiastique* (dealing with the period from the Ascension till the Council of Constance, 1414) is marred only by the Gallican tendencies of its author, and *Natalis Alexander* (Noël Alexandre, 1639-1724), a French Dominican who published an exceedingly valuable Church History under the title *Selecta Historiae Eccl. Capita, etc.*, but which was condemned by Innocent XI. (1684) on account of the markedly Gallican bias under which it was composed.

Amongst some of the most noted authorities on Canon Law during the seventeenth and eighteenth centuries were *Benedict XIV.* (1675-1758) many of whose treatises are regarded as standard works till the present day; *Pirhing* (1606-1679), a Jesuit, professor at Dillingen and Ingolstadt and well known as a theologian and canonist; *Reiffenstuel* (1641-1703), a Bavarian Franciscan for some time professor at Freising, the author of several theological works, and unequalled as a Canonist in his own day; *Van Espen* (1649-1728) professor at Louvain, a strong supporter of Gallicanism and Jansenism, whose great work *Jus Canonicum Universum* is marred by the pro-Gallican proclivities of its author; *Schmalzgrueber* (1663-1735), a Bavarian Jesuit, professor of Canon Law at Dillingen and Ingolstadt, who in addition to treatises on such subjects as Trials, Espousals, Matrimony, and the Regular and Secular Clergy, published a work covering the entire Canon Law (*Jus Eccl. Universum*), and the Italian *Lucius Ferraris* (d. 1763), whose *Prompta Bibliotheca Canonica* went through several editions in the author's own lifetime and has been republished more than once since his death (latest edition 1899).

In the department of sacred oratory the palm must undoubtedly be awarded to the French Church. *Jacques-Bénigne Bossuet** (1627-1704), in many senses the greatest of the French preachers, was the son of a lawyer at Dijon. Even in his early youth he was remarkable for his mastery of the Bible and classical authors. He studied at the University of Paris, and after remaining two years under the spiritual direction of St. Vincent de Paul was ordained a priest in 1662. He returned to Metz, in the cathedral of which he held a canonry, and where his abilities as a preacher and a controversialist soon attracted attention. He was appointed preceptor to the Dauphin of France, an office which he held from 1670 till 1681, when he was consecrated Bishop of Meaux. As bishop he took part in the Assembly of the French Clergy (1681-82) and, though himself not such an extreme defender of Gallicanism as many of his contemporaries, he is credited generally with having been the author of the famous Declaration of the Clergy, known as the Articles of the Gallican Church. At the invitation of Louis XIV. he composed a treatise in defence of these articles, *Defensio Declarationis, etc.*, published after his death (1730). As an orator Bossuet was far ahead of the preachers of his time, and as a writer and controversialist he had few equals. His untiring energy and ability are vouched for by the number of able works that proceeded from his pen. Of these the most instructive and best known are the *Discours sur l'histoire Universelle* (1681), and the *Histoire des Variations des Églises Protestantes* (1688-89). His want of firmness, however, in his relations with the court, leading him as it did to show a sympathy which he could not have felt in his heart towards Gallicanism, his failure to move a finger to stay the ravages of Jansenism, his want of zeal for the spiritual care of his diocese, in marked contrast with the energy which he displayed when seeking to score a personal

---

* Bausset, *Histoire de Bossuet*, 4 vols., 1814. Jovy, *Études et recherches sur Jacques-Bénigne Bossuet*, etc., 1903.

triumph over Fénelon and other less known adversaries, cannot be forgotten by any one who wishes to arrive at an impartial estimate of Bossuet's character.

*Fénelon** (1651-1715), the great contemporary and rival of Bossuet, was sent as a youth for his education to the Universities of Cahors and Paris. Later on he returned to the seminary of Saint Sulpice then presided over by M. Tronson the superior of the Sulpicians, to whose wise and prudent counsels the future Archbishop of Cambrai was deeply indebted. After the revocation of the Edict of Nantes he was sent to preach to the Huguenots, upon whom his kindness and humility made a much more lasting impression than the violence resorted to by some of the officials of Louis XIV. Later on he was appointed preceptor to the Duke of Burgundy, grandson of Louis XIV., for whose education he composed the *Fables, Télémaque, etc.,* and on the completion of his work as tutor he was nominated Archbishop of Cambrai (1695). Hardly had he received this honour than he was involved in a controversy on Quietism, which controversy cost him the friendship of Bossuet and the patronage of Louis XIV., by whom he was banished from the French court. But Fénelon found much at Cambrai to console him for what he had lost in Paris. In every sense of the word he proved himself a model bishop, visiting his parishes regularly, preaching in his cathedral and throughout his diocese, and always affable to those who came in contact with him whether they were rich or poor. Unlike Bossuet he never feared to speak out boldly against Jansenism and Gallicanism. As a preacher and a master of French literary style he was inferior to Bossuet, but as a man and as a bishop he was incomparably his superior. In addition to his works on literary and political questions he wrote voluminously on theology, philosophy, and the spiritual life.

* Bausset, *Histoire de Fénelon,* 1809. De Broglie, *Épiscopat de Fénelon,* 1884

The opposition to Scholasticism, that manifested itself in the writings and teaching of so many Humanists, grew more accentuated in the universities, especially after the establishment of ecclesiastical seminaries had led to the withdrawal from the universities of a great body of the clerical students. For centuries philosophy and theology had gone hand in hand, the former supplying the rational basis for the acceptance of revelation, the latter providing the necessary restraint upon the vagaries of human thought. The principle of individual judgment, proclaimed by the early Reformers and received so enthusiastically by their followers, had as its logical consequence an exaggeration of the powers of the human mind at the expense of authority, with the result that scepticism, atheism, and materialism, found favour in learned circles.

In face of such evident proofs of the limitations of the human mind, and with the object of preserving in one way or another the Christian Revelation, a reaction against the supposed infallibility of reason set in both amongst Protestant and Catholic scholars. Catholic philosophers were inclined to distrust reason entirely, and to rely solely on divine authority as a guarantee of truth. In other words they accepted Traditionalism, while Protestants, equally suspicious of reason, proclaimed that in judging the value of revelation the human will and sentiment must be heeded as well as the intellect, that is to say they accepted Sentimentalism.

The attempt to replace Scholasticism by some new philosophic system gave rise to various schools of thought, most of which can be traced back ultimately to Bacon and Descartes, the former a partisan of the inductive, the latter of the deductive method. *René Descartes*[*] (1596-1649) was born at Touraine, and received his early education with the Jesuits. In his desire to see the world for himself he took service as a soldier in

---

[*] Bouillier, *Histoire de la philosophie cartésienne*, 2 vols., 1868. Haldane, *Descartes, His Life and Times*, 1906.

the army of Prince Maurice of Nassau, and later on in that of the Elector of Bavaria. He retired from active life to give himself up to the study of mathematics and philosophy. At first he found a quiet retreat in Holland, from which he migrated to Stockholm on the invitation of Queen Christina. Here after a few months' residence he died. Throughout his life Descartes remained a sincere and practical Catholic. Putting aside Revelation, with which he did not profess to deal, Descartes, by an application of his principle of methodic doubt, arrived at the conclusion that the foundation of all certainty lay in the proposition *Cogito ergo sum* (I think, therefore I exist). From an examination of his own ideas of a most perfect being he arrived at the conclusion that God exists, and from the existence of a good and wise supreme Being who has given men reason, sense, and perception in order to acquire knowledge, he argued that these faculties cannot lead men into error, and that consequently the veracity of God was the ultimate basis of certitude.

The theories of Descartes were pushed to their logical conclusion by those who succeeded him. *Blaise Pascal** (1623-1662) was influenced largely by the false mysticism of the Middle Ages. He distrusted reason and exalted faith, as the only means of answering the difficulties that pure intellectualism could not solve. *Arnold Geulincx* (1625-1669) at first a Catholic and afterwards a Calvinist, arguing from the antithesis supposed by Descartes to exist between mind and matter, maintained that since matter was inert it could not produce the sensations and volitions which men experienced, and that therefore these must be caused by God. In other words he propounded the theory of Occasionalism. This doctrine of Occasionalism as furnishing an explanation of sensations was extended by Malebranche † (1638-1715), a

* Giraud, *Pascal, l'homme, l'oeuvre, l'influence*, 1905. Janssens, *La philosophie et l'apologétique de Pascal*, 1896.

† André, *Vie du R. P. Malebranche*, 1886. Ollé-Laprune, *La philosophie de Malebranche*, 2 vols., 1870.

student of the Sorbonne, so as to explain the origin of human ideas. These he maintained could not come from outside, because there can be no contact between mind and matter; they could not come from the mind itself, because creation is an attribute only of the infinite being, and therefore they must come from God. Hence, according to him, it is in God or in the divine essence that we see all things (Ontologism). If all activity and all knowledge come directly from God and if the external world and the senses are only the occasions of effects attributable to God, it was only natural to conclude, as did *Spinoza* (1632-77), that there exists only one substance endowed with the two attributes of thought and extension (Monism, Pantheism).*

From this brief sketch it will be seen that the rejection of the Scholastic System and the divorce between theology and philosophy led to dogmatic chaos, and ultimately to the rejection of divine revelation. By his attacks on the old proofs given for the existence of God and the motives of credibility, by the emphasis which he placed upon methodic doubt as the only safe way to certainty, and by the suspicions raised by him against the reliability of human reason, Descartes unwittingly paved the way for scepticism and atheism. Though his system was condemned by Rome and forbidden more than once by Louis XIV. it was taken up by the Oratorians and by most of the leading scholars in France.

The spirit of the eighteenth century was distinctly unfavourable to the religious orders. The Rationalists, the Freemasons, and the friends of absolutism joined hands in opposing the foundation of new establishments and in securing the suppression of the houses that had already been founded. In Austria, in Naples, in Spain, and in France a violent campaign was carried on to bring about the dissolution of several of the religious orders and congregations, or at least to so alter their rules and constitutions that they should be cut adrift

* Ferrière, *La doctrine de Spinoza exposée et commentée*, 1899.

from Rome and subject to the authority of the secular rulers. During the campaign many houses were suppressed in Austria and in the other territories of the empire, but by far the greatest victory of which its authors could boast was the suppression of the Society of Jesus.

Yet in spite of the enemies of the Church the religious orders held their ground, and apostolic men arose to lay the foundations of new bodies, that were destined to take a glorious part in the religious revival of the nineteenth century. One of the most remarkable of these was St. Alphonsus Maria de' Liguori* (1696-1787). He was born near Naples, adopted at first the profession of a lawyer, but he soon forsook the bar to give himself entirely to God, and was ordained a priest in 1726. In 1732 he laid the foundation of a new religious society, the Congregation of the Most Holy Redeemer, which was approved by Benedict XIV. in 1749. After having refused various honours he was compelled to accept the Bishopric of St. Agatha (1762) from which he retired in 1775 to devote himself to prayer, and to the composition of those spiritual treatises that have given him such a leading place not merely as a moral theologian but as a master in the ascetic life. In 1744 he issued his Notes on Busenbaum's Moral Theology, which notes formed the basis of his *Theologia Moralis* published in 1753-55, and which went through nine editions during his own life-time. He was declared Venerable (1796), canonised (1839), and recognised as a Doctor of the Church (1871).

The Congregation of the Most Holy Redeemer (The Redemptorists) was founded by St. Alphonsus at Scala, near Amalfi, in the kingdom of Naples (1732), and was approved in 1749. The aim of its members was to imitate the virtues and example of Jesus Christ, our Redeemer, by consecrating themselves especially to preaching the word of God to the poor. The opposition of the Neapolitan prime minister, Tanucci, was a source of great trouble to the holy founder. On the fall of

---

* Berthe-Castle, *Life of St. Alphonsus de' Liguori*, 2 vols., 1905.

Tanucci St. Alphonsus thought that a favourable opportunity had come for securing the approval of the government, but he was betrayed by his friends into accepting a modification of the constitution, the *Regolamento* (1779-80), which led to a separation between the Redemptorist houses in Naples and those situated in the Papal States. The dispute was, however, healed in 1793. The Society spread rapidly in Italy, in Germany, where its interest were safeguarded by Father Hofbauer, and during the nineteenth century houses were established in every country in Europe, in America and in Australia.

The Passionists* (The Congregation of Discalced Clerics of the Most Holy Cross and Passion of Our Lord Jesus Christ) were founded by St. Paul of the Cross (1694-1775). The latter was born at Ovada near Genoa, was ordained by Pope Benedict XIII. (1727) who at the same time gave his approval of the rules drawn up for the new society, founded his first house at Argentaro, and thereby laid the foundation of the Congregation of the Passionists. The new society received the formal sanction and approval of Clement XIV. (1769) and of Pius VI. (1775). Before the death of the founder several houses had been established in Italy, all of which were suppressed during the disturbances that followed in the wake of the French Revolution. The congregation was, however, re-constituted by Pius VII. (1814), and spread rapidly in Europe, in the United States, and in South America. The first house of the Passionists in England was established by the celebrated Father Dominic at Aston Hall in Staffordshire (1842), and the first house in Ireland was opened at Mount Argus in 1856.

* Pius a Spiritu Sancto, *The Life of St. Paul of the Cross*, 1868.

END OF VOLUME I.